THE DIRECTORY OF POSSIBILITIES

THE DIRECTORY OF POSSIBILITIES

Edited by
Colin Wilson
and
John Grant

The Rutledge Press
New York, New York

A *Webb&Bower* Book

Edited, designed and produced by
Webb & Bower (Publishers) Limited

Designed by Peter Wrigley

Copyright © Colin Wilson and John Grant/Webb & Bower (Publishers) Ltd 1981
Directory-Index Copyright © Paul Barnett (Editorial) 1981

All rights reserved. No part of this book may be reproduced or
transmitted in any form or by any means, electronic or mechanical,
including photocopying, recording or by any information retrieval system,
without permission in writing from the Publisher.

Published by The Rutledge Press, 112 Madison Avenue,
New York, New York 10016

Distributed by W. H. Smith Publishers Inc., 112 Madison Avenue,
New York, New York 10016

First Printing 1981

Library of Congress Cataloging in Publication Data
81-50171

Typesetting and monochrome origination by
Filmtype Services Limited, Scarborough, England

Printed and bound in The United States of America

ISBN 0-8317-2382-3 Hardback
ISBN 0-8317-2383-1 Paperback

CONTENTS

ABOUT THE CONTRIBUTORS / 8
INTRODUCTION:
THE NEW SCIENCE
by Colin Wilson / 11
NOTES FOR THE WARY
by John Grant / 23
PART ONE
MYTHOLOGY AND THE ANCIENT WORLD / 27
Introductory 28; Ancient Astronauts 29; Ancient Man 30; Arthur 31; Atlantis 32; Book of the Dead 33; Dinosaurs, Extinction of the 34; Elements, Aristotelian 34; Fertility Religion 35; Glastonbury 36; Gog and Magog 37; Grail 37; Humours 38; Ley Lines 38; Megalithic Monuments 39; Mythical Monsters 39; Pyramids 41; Rennes-le-Château, Mystery of 43; Vitalism 44; Evolution 45

PART TWO
THE OCCULT AND MIRACULOUS / 46
Introductory 47; Action at a Distance 48; Alchemy 48; Amulets 49; Blavatsky, Helena Petrovna 49; Crowley, Aleister 50; Demons 50; Devil 51; Doppelgängers 51; Ghosts 53; Healing 54; Jinxes and Curses 55; *Necronomicon* 57; Possession 57; Primitive Magic 58; Pyramid Power 60; Ritual Magic 61; Sai Baba 64; Voodoo 64; Witchcraft 64; Evolution 82

PART THREE
STRANGE CREATURES AND
UNUSUAL EVENTS / 83
Introductory 84; Abominable Snowmen 85; Appearing People 86; Bermuda Triangle 86; Elementals 88; Giants 89; Hauser, Kaspar 90; Lycanthropy 90; Sea Monsters 91; Spring-Heeled Jack 93; Tunguska Event 93; Vampires 95; Vanishing People 97; Zombies 98; Evolution 99

PART FOUR
TIME IN DISARRAY / 100

Introductory 101; Astrology 102; Card Prediction 104; Causality 104; Clairvoyance 105; Coincidence 106; *I Ching* 107; Numerology 108; Palmistry 108; Precognition 109; Prediction 111; Scrying 112; Seers and Prophets 112; Time 115; Time Reversal 116; Time Slip 116; Time Travel 118; Evolution 119

PART FIVE
INNER SPACE:
MIND AND BODY / 120

Introductory 121; Acquired Characteristics 122; Acupuncture 123; Aura 123; Automatic Writing 125; Biofeedback 126; Dianetics 126; Dowsing 126; Dreams and Visions 127; ESP 129; Games Theory 131; Gurdjieff, Georgei Ivanovitch 132; Homoeopathy 134; Hypnosis 134; Jung, Jungianism 136; Kirlian Photography 137; Levitation 138; Life After Death 138; Mediums 140; Multiple Personality 140; Out-of-the-Body Experiences 142; Paranormal Photography 143; Peak Experience 143; Pineal Eye 144; Plant Communication 145; Poltergeists 146; Reich, Wilhelm 148; Reincarnation 149; Revelations, Mystical 150; Rosicrucians 152; Spiritualism 152; Steiner, Rudolph 154; Stigmata 154; Tantrism 155; Transcendental Meditation 155; Yoga 156; Zen 157; Evolution 158

PART SIX
OUTER SPACE:
THE UNIVERSE AT LARGE / 159

Introductory 160; Alternate Universes 161; Antigravity 162; Antimatter 162; Ball Lightning 163; Big Bang 163; Black Holes 163; Continuous Creation 167; Cosmologies, Unorthodox 167; Extraterrestrial Intelligence 170; Flat Earth 173; Fundamental Particles 173; Galactic Club 175; Hyperspace 175; Mars 175; Neutron Soup 176; Oscillating Universe 176; Ozma, Project 176; Panspermia 193; Parallel Worlds 194; Pulsars 194; Quasars 195; Relativity 196; SETI 197; Tachyons 198; Time-Symmetric Universe 198; UFOs 198; Universe, Theories of the 201; White Holes 202; Evolution 203

PART SEVEN
THE WORLD OF TOMORROW / 204

Introductory 205; Bionics 206; CETI 206; Cybernetics 208;
Dyson Sphere 209; Fusion Power 209; Genetic Engineering 211;
Heat Death of the Universe 212; Immortality 213; Interstellar
Travel 214; Invisibility 217; Laser Science 217; Space Colonies 219;
Utopia 220; Von Neumann Probes 221; Evolution 222

FURTHER READING / 223
ACKNOWLEDGEMENTS / 226
DIRECTORY-INDEX / 227

ABOUT THE CONTRIBUTORS

PB PAUL BEGG has worked both in television and as an advertising copywriter; he has recently become a full-time writer. For several years he has been researching Fortean phenomena, and has published a book, *Into Thin Air* (1979), on the subject of vanishing people. He is currently working on a companion volume treating appearing people.

DF DANIEL FARSON is a writer and television interviewer. He is the son of the US foreign correspondent, Negley Farson, and the great-nephew of Bram Stoker. After a distinguished career as a journalist and photographer, he had a spell in the Merchant Navy. His books include *Out of Step* (1974), *The Man Who Wrote Dracula* (1975), *Jack the Ripper* (1972), *A Window on the Sea* (1977), *Vampires, Zombies and Monster Men* (1976) and two horror novels, *Curse* (1980) and *Transplant* (1981).

JG JOHN GRANT is the regular pseudonym of Paul Barnett, a books editor and writer. Under his own name he has translated from the French and substantially revised Jacques Vassal's *Electric Children* (1976); edited, with Professor Anthony Hallam and Dr Peter Hutchinson, *Planet Earth: An Encyclopedia of Geology* (1977); and been a major contributor to *The Phaidon Concise Encyclopedia of Science and Technology* (1978). As John Grant, he has edited *Aries 1* (1979) and, with Colin Wilson, *The Book of Time* (1980). He is an Associate Fellow of the British Interplanetary Society.

RH ROBERT HOLDSTOCK graduated in medical zoology from the London School of Hygiene and Tropical Medicine. He is now a full-time writer, and is recognized as one of the bright new stars of modern science fiction: his novels include *Eye Among the Blind* (1976), *Earthwind* (1977), *Necromancer* (1978) and *Where Time Winds Blow* (1981).

SH STUART HOLROYD has written extensively on the occult, the paranormal, and frontier psychology. His many books include *Emergence from Chaos* (1957), *Flight and Pursuit* (1959), *Contraries: A Personal Progression* (1975), *Prelude to the Landing on Planet Earth* (1978) and *Alien Intelligence* (1979).

DRL DAVID LANGFORD is a physicist with a special interest in nuclear fusion research who has recently become a full-time writer. He has written *War in 2080: The Future of Military Technology* (1979), edited William R. Looseley's *An Account of a Meeting with Denizens of Another World, 1871* (1980), and collaborated with Chris Morgan on *Facts and Fallacies: A Book of Definitive Mistakes and Misguided Predictions* (1981). He has received three Hugo nominations for his fan writings.

ATL A.T. LAWTON is an authority on advanced electronics and communications systems. In addition, he has played a major role in the British Interplanetary Society's study for an unmanned interstellar probe, Project Daedalus; and has found time to write numerous scientific articles and papers as well as, with Jack Stoneley, two popular books on extraterrestrial communication, *Is Anyone Out There?* (1975) and *CETI* (1976), and, on the Tunguska event, *Tunguska: Cauldron of Hell* (1977); on his own he has written *A Window in the Sky: Astronomy From Beyond the Earth's Atmosphere* (1979). He is an Associate Member of the Institute of Electrical Engineers, a Fellow of the Royal Astronomical Society, Vice-President of the British Interplanetary Society, and an Academician of the International Academy of Astronautics.

ABOUT THE CONTRIBUTORS

BM BRIAN MARRINER gained an extensive education in prison. Following his discharge in 1965 after serving a five-year sentence for robbery with violence, he devoted himself to the study of the psychology of violence. His first novel, *A Splinter of Ice*, was published in 1975. Apart from many press articles, he has recently completed two non-fiction books, his prison autobiography, *Five Years Hard*, and a study of violence, *Reactive Man*.

KMN IAIN NICOLSON lectures on astronomy at the Hatfield Polytechnic, and is well known as a writer on astronomy and space science; his books include *Astronomy: A Dictionary of Space and the Universe* (1977), *The Road to the Stars* (1978), *Gravity, Black Holes and the Universe* (1981) and, with Patrick Moore, *Black Holes in Space* (1974). He has broadcast many times on both radio and television on subjects related to astronomy, cosmology and spaceflight.

JBP J.B. PICK has worked as a hospital orderly, coalminer, social worker, movie scriptwriter and sales manager. He has published five books on sports and games including *The Phoenix Dictionary of Games* (1952); four novels; a book of personal experience; a book of criticism, *The Strange Genius of David Lindsay* (with Colin Wilson; 1970); and a philosophical work, *Freedom Itself* (1979). His historical novel *The Last Valley* was filmed in 1970.

RT ROBERT TURNER has, over the past twenty years, been engaged in an intensive study of ceremonial magic. In 1964 he founded the Order of the Cubic Stone, a group of occultists dedicated to Qabalistic research and the investigation of sixteenth-century Renaissance magic. He is co-author of *The Necronomicon* (1978), editor of *The Monolith*, and occult consultant to *Strange Phenomena*. He is currently engaged in research into the unpublished writings of John Dee.

MW MICHAEL WENYON is the author of *Understanding Holography* (1978), a standard work for the layman, and European correspondent of *Laser Focus*. In addition, he is currently engaged in research into holography at Goldsmith's College, London.

CW COLIN WILSON became internationally celebrated overnight with the publication of his first book, *The Outsider*, in 1956. His many novels include *Ritual in the Dark* (1960), *Adrift in Soho* (1961), *The World of Violence* (1963), *Man Without a Shadow* (1963), *The Glass Cage* (1967), *The Mind Parasites* (1967), *The God of the Labyrinth* (1970), *The Philosopher's Stone* (1971), *The Schoolgirl Murder Case* (1974) and *The Space Vampires* (1975). His plays are *Viennese Interlude* (1960), *Strindberg* (1970) and *Mysteries* (1979). His works of non-fiction include *Encyclopedia of Murder* (with Pat Pitman; 1961), *Origins of the Sexual Impulse* (1963), *Beyond the Outsider: The Philosophy of the Future* (1965), *Sex and the Intelligent Teenager* (1966), *Introduction to the New Existentialism* (1967), *A Casebook of Murder* (1969), *Poetry and Mysticism* (1970), *The Occult* (1971), *Order of Assassins* (1972), *Mysteries* (1978) and *Starseekers* (1980).

*I do not know what I may appear to the world;
but to myself I seem to have been only like a boy playing on the seashore,
and diverting myself in now and then finding a smoother pebble
or a prettier shell than ordinary, whilst the great ocean
of truth lay all undiscovered before me.*

SIR ISAAC NEWTON

*The full area of ignorance is not mapped: we are at present
only exploring its fringes.*

J.D. BERNAL

INTRODUCTION
THE 'NEW SCIENCE'
by Colin Wilson

In his autobiography *Free Associations* Freud's biographer Ernest Jones makes the following typical and aggressive comment: 'I would say that in the realms of both thought and action the distinction between men who believe that mental processes, or beings, can exist independently of the physical world and those who reject this belief is to me the most significant of all human classifications; and I should measure any hope of further evolutionary progress by the passage of men from one class to the other ...'

More than a century earlier, Auguste Comte had said much the same in his *Positive Philosophy*. Societies, he said, go through three basic stages. First, the theological, ruled by priests and dominated by superstition; next, the metaphysical, where men reject religion, but set up strange idealist philosophies in its place; third, the positive stage, where men realize that the material Universe is the only reality, and that progress can be achieved only through science. This third stage, according to Comte, will finally lead to the perfect society.

Intelligent men everywhere were revolted by this crude dogmatism; but their revolt usually made things worse. Kierkegaard sneered at the new religion of reason, but seemed to want to replace it with old-fashioned religious evangelism. Dostoevsky makes one of his heroes say that he rejects the 'truth' that two plus two equals four, because it strangles the human spirit. Nietzsche glorified conflict and said that a good war justifies any cause. D.H. Lawrence agreed, and wrote a story in which a woman achieves ultimate peace by allowing herself to be slaughtered as a human sacrifice. And in New York during the 1920s an eccentric genius named Charles Fort spent his days in the New York public libraries, searching periodicals for accounts of strange, unexplained events — like showers of frogs and fish falling from the sky — and published his extraordinary findings in books with titles like *Lo!* and *Wild Talents*. He hoped to convince scientists that 'there are more things in heaven and Earth ...', but there is no evidence that contemporary science was aware of his existence. From Kierkegaard to Fort, the advocates of 'unreason' have succeeded only in giving intuition a bad name.

Open any book by Fort, at any page, and you will see what is wrong. He jumbles up all kinds of weird occurrences — talking dogs, *poltergeists, wolf-children, Kaspar *Hauser — as if all were on the same level, and he fails to make the slightest attempt to explain them. But science is not just the collection of observations; it is the attempt to explain them. Early astronomers noticed that the planets sometimes temporarily reverse the direction of their progress across the sky, and they invented strange and complex theories to account for this. Their theories were nonsense, but they finally enabled Copernicus to stumble on the correct explanation. Ptolemy was wrong, but without him Copernicus could never have been right. Fort was so suspicious of the scientific habit of theorizing that he deliberately refrained from offering any kind of explanation; so his immense labours remain as unconvincing as

Dostoevsky's denial of the proposition that two plus two equals four.

But is there any alternative? The movement of the planets is a relatively straightforward problem — once you have stumbled upon the simplifying notion that they all move around the Sun. But how do you start looking for a common explanation for *ghosts, poltergeists, 'phantasms of the living', talking dogs and showers of live fish?

Well, to begin with, you can try to eliminate the lies, or the obvious inventions. They can usually be spotted by a certain quality of 'development' that belongs to fiction rather than reality. Take the widely accepted story of the sudden disappearance of David Lang (see *vanishing people). The story relates that Lang, a Gallatin farmer, was crossing a field in full sight of his whole family when he suddenly vanished. Assuming he had fallen down a hole, the family rushed to the spot; there was no hole, only hard ground. Neighbours joined in a search of the area — all to no purpose. But in the following year his two children walked across the patch of ground and noticed that the grass was dying. They began shouting 'Father, are you there?', and a man's voice shouted 'Help'. They fetched their mother, and Lang's voice again answered the shouts — but sounding now very distant. On subsequent occasions, the shouts grew fainter and fainter, until they ceased altogether.

An oddly circumstantial story, which has been repeated many times. But a telephone call to the local newspaper revealed that it has no foundation in fact; a bored commercial traveller, writing to his wife from a hotel room in Gallatin, seems to have made it up on the spur of the moment.

Compare it with the following, from a book of apparitions:[1] 'When I was ten I was walking across country to a hamlet where my grandmother lived... As I walked by the woodside, half a mile or so from the hamlet, I heard my grandmother distinctly say, "I shalln't be long". I looked all round, but nothing was to be seen, and arriving at the cottage, found it locked up, and no one about. I went down the lane... and met my grandmother, who had just got off the carrier's cart. Over tea, I told her about hearing her say "I shalln't be long", and she told me she had suddenly said this (but couldn't think why she did) when about a mile from home.'

Like the Lang story, this is circumstantial; unlike it, it seems quite pointless; it lacks 'development'. It is difficult to see why anyone should bother to invent anything so pointless. Which is, of course, no guarantee of its truth; it could be an exaggeration of something that actually happened, and which was rather less mysterious. Still, I have to admit that I am inclined to accept it.

Why? Because, unlike the Lang story, it makes sense in a wider context. To begin with, auditory hallucinations are remarkably commonplace. Julian Jaynes has described how, after a period of hard study, he was alone in his room in Boston when he heard a voice say clearly: 'Include the knower in the known.' He made a careful search of the room before he concluded that it was an auditory hallucination. He then made a study of the subject, and discovered that among the Anglo–Saxon races one man in twelve has had hallucinations, while among women the figure is higher — one in eight. In Russia the figure was twice as high, and in Brazil even higher — bringing it close to twenty-five per cent. These figures applied to normal healthy people, not those under mental stress.

---

[1] By Celia Green and Charles McCreery (London, 1975).

Now Jaynes allowed these astonishing results to lead him towards some extremely controversial conclusions, which are highly relevant to the theme of this book. His own 'voice' had apparently come from the air on his upper right-hand side. (He says he was in 'a state of intellectual despair'.) And in the past few decades a relatively new field of science known as split-brain research has explored some astonishing differences between the right and left hemispheres of the brain. The left cerebral hemisphere is our analytical side: it deals with language and logic. The right is intuitive: it deals with insight and recognition. But the most surprising discovery of all came when Roger Sperry of Caltech was experimenting with split-brain patients — patients whose two hemispheres have been sundered to cure epilepsy — and realized that, by severing the 'bridge' between the two halves (the *corpus callosum*), he was in many ways turning the patient into two people. For some odd reason — so far unfathomed — the right side of the brain controls the left side of the body, and vice versa; so the right cerebral hemisphere controls the left visual field. (For practical purposes, you could say it controls the left eye, although this is not quite accurate. But note that the right *ear* corresponds to the right hemisphere, the left to the left.) If a patient were shown an apple with the left eye and an orange with the right, and were asked what he had just seen, he would reply, 'Orange.' But asked to write with his left hand what he had seen, he would write, 'Apple.' If he were not allowed to see what he had written, and were asked what it was, he would reply, 'Orange.' Patients shown an indecent picture with the left eye (right brain) would blush; asked why they were blushing, they would reply truthfully, 'I don't know.' That is to say, the person you call 'you' — your conscious identity — lives in the left half of the brain. The right is *another person*.

Jaynes concluded that auditory hallucinations originate in the right brain — that 'other person' — and make themselves heard in the left. We could interpret his own hallucination as a comment from that other person, the instinctive self, as it were, who could see that he was placing himself under strain by trying to solve problems in purely intellectual — left-brain — terms, and who tried to tell him, 'Stop dividing reality into "you" and "it". Relax and try to *intuit* your way into things.'

Jaynes went further, and advanced the theory that our remote ancestors lacked our own sharp sense of personal identity and, consequently, our ability to hold internal debates. When I ask myself 'What do I feel about so and so?', I am, in effect, peering into the darkness of my intuitions and trying to turn them into words. According to Jaynes, the men of the Old Testament or the Homeric poems had no such ability, they reacted directly to stimuli, and when their intuitions wished to communicate they did so by means of 'voices', auditory hallucinations, which the ancients took to be the voice of God, or the gods.

In one important respect, this theory seems dubious, simply because 'self-consciousness' does not necessarily involve intuition; in fact, it is when I am feeling least intuitive that I ask myself such questions as 'Who am I?'. I suspect Jaynes is simply holding the matter upside down. The title of his book is *The Origin of Consciousness in the Breakdown of the Bicameral Mind*, which implies that the 'dividing wall' between the right and left gradually became eroded until Man gained his present self-awareness. Yet this contradicts our experience of 'expanded consciousness'; when I relax and enjoy music, my sharp sense of identity blurs, and yet the 'I' seems to become bigger rather than smaller; my 'identity' has *expanded* to include 'intuitive consciousness'. Which suggests that, far from being bicameral —

with two compartments — ancient Man was unicameral, intuitive, in some kind of direct contact with the forces of nature, while it is modern Man whose consciousness is divided.

In a remarkable book called *The Aquarian Conspiracy* Marilyn Ferguson compares the two halves of the brain to twin sailors on a long voyage: 'One is a verbal, analytical fellow, the other mute and sometimes dreamy. The verbal partner earnestly calculates with the aid of his charts and instruments. His brother, however, has an uncanny ability to predict storms, changing currents, and other navigational conditions, which he communicates by signs, symbols, drawings. [NB: The right brain appears to have little ability to understand language.] The analytical sailor is afraid to trust his brother's advice because he can't imagine its source. Actually, the silent sailor has wireless, instantaneous access to a rich data bank that gives him a satellite perspective on the weather. But he cannot explain this complex system with his limited ability to communicate details. And his talkative, "rational" brother usually ignores him anyway. Frustrated, he often stands by helplessly while their craft sails head-on into disaster. Whenever their convictions are in conflict, the analytical sailor stubbornly follows his own calculations, until the day he stumbles onto the schematics for his brother's data bank. He is overwhelmed. He realizes that by ignoring his twin's input, he has been travelling through life half-informed.'

This is an admirable summary of the position with regard to the two halves. And it emphasizes that what has actually happened over the course of history is that Man — originally a kind of Siamese twin in which the brothers were constantly aware of one another — has slowly moved into the left brain, until his sense of identity has become restricted to the logical half of the 'computer'.

Ferguson goes straight to the heart of the matter when she says the silent brother has an uncanny ability to predict storms, and that he has access to a radio and an enormous data bank. The left brain is the logical half, yet the right undoubtedly *knows* more.

Another interesting point emerged in an experiment performed by Sperry. He tried flashing red and green lights at random into the left visual field of a split-brain patient, and asking him to guess what colour he had just seen. Since the patient could not 'see' anything that entered the left eye, his score should have been fifty/fifty. In fact, the patient might incorrectly guess 'red', and would then start as if someone had nudged him and say, 'No, green.' The right hemisphere had overheard the left brain's wrong guess and communicated by making his muscles 'jerk'. Which may remind us that, when a water-diviner detects an underground stream, the dowsing rod jerks upwards *because his muscles contract involuntarily*. It seems as if the right brain picks up the 'vibrations' of underground water, and communicates by means of the rod. (The 'communication' is probably not deliberate, but more of a reflex action, an involuntary 'shiver' due to the water.)

But then, dowsers are not split-brain patients — except insofar as we are *all* split-brain patients. The point is reinforced by the problem of *poltergeist activity. It has been established for well over half a century that 'poltergeists' seem to originate in the unconscious minds of 'disturbed' children or adolescents (or, far more rarely, adults). It seems incredible that the 'unconscious mind' can cause objects to fly through the air — even cause fires to break out. But what is equally baffling is that the person responsible is usually totally unaware that he or she is causing the phenomena. The first rule of an investigator is not to tell the child that he or she is responsible — it causes bewilderment and panic. Again, it seems that the 'other person' in the right brain is probably the culprit. But these poltergeist-children are not split-brain patients either.

And *how* does the inhabitant of the right brain cause a bell to ring at a distance, or a picture to jump off the wall? No one has ever succeeded in devising an experiment to find out. But it may be worth bearing in mind that many dowsers respond so powerfully to the 'force' that flows through their muscles that they go into convulsions, as if the brain were *channelling* a force from the Earth. It seems a reasonable guess that the same force is employed by the right brain to cause objects to fly around.

So, returning to the girl who heard her grandmother's voice say 'I shan't be long', we find it rather less baffling than it at first appeared. We know the afternoon was still and warm, so the girl was presumably relaxed, thinking of nothing in particular. Her grandmother had been to do the shopping or whatever and was returning slightly late; she knew that her grand-daughter would probably be on her way, and would wonder why the house was locked. She noted that she was fairly close to home and murmured involuntarily 'I shan't be long' — a semi-conscious response to anxiety which originated in her right brain (so that she was telling the truth when she told her grand-daughter that she didn't know why she said it). And the right brain of her grand-daughter picked it up, and transferred it to the left brain as an auditory hallucination . . .

This explanation makes it seem obvious. But, without the knowledge of the peculiar powers of the right brain, it remains incomprehensible.

But perhaps the most important point here is that we find it very difficult to accept that 'we' are only half a person. It seems so *self-evident* that 'I' am this conscious being who answers to my name. We can perfectly well understand why Comte or Jones should react with angry derision to such an idea and why a group of modern sceptics, including Carl Sagan, Martin Gardner and James Randi have actually formed a society to combat belief in all forms of 'occultism'. Yet it is worth bearing in mind that Jones was Freud's foremost UK disciple, and that it was Freud who first gave definite form to the notion of the unconscious. The whole tone of Jones' autobiography — rational, dogmatic and combative — reveals that it never entered his head to say to himself, 'The person called Ernest Jones is not really "me" at all; "I" am a far larger being, the totality of my conscious and unconscious minds, and my everyday self is thus a kind of delusion . . .' He accepted the notion of the unconscious on an intellectual level, while totally failing to grasp its alarming 'antirationalist' implications.

The importance of Jaynes' book lies in its recognition that the mode of consciousness we take so much for granted — the sense of self-questioning identity — is, in evolutionary terms, a fairly recent acquisition. Jaynes surmises, and I tend to agree with him, that the change may have begun as recently as 2500 BC, when the bicameral mind 'was weakened by writing' (clearly the date differs for different cultures). It seems significant to me that the Great *Pyramid was built at about this date. There is now considerable evidence to support the view that the Pyramid was constructed as an astronomical computer — that is, a kind of gigantic sundial, whose purpose was to establish with unprecedented accuracy the movements of the stars and planets and the times of their rising. The Egyptians had always been interested in astronomy; and as long ago as the 1890s Lockyer wrote a book arguing that the temples were so aligned that the light of a certain star would shine straight down the central aisle and strike the altar at some time of ritual significance. The zodiac in the temple at Dendera suggests that they had been making astronomical observations since at least 4000 BC. But it seems that it was about 1,500 years later that some influential priest-astronomer suggested to Cheops that it was time to attempt a synthesis of all they knew about the heavens, and for this purpose to build an observatory to enable them to eliminate the old inaccuracies once and for all.

It is important to try to grasp the implications of such a decision for a people who were, by our standards, little better than primitives. My own sense of what is involved is derived from a similar kind of personal watershed at the age of thirteen. I had always loved chemistry, astronomy and — to a lesser extent — physics, in an amateur and haphazard way. During the long summer holiday of 1943 I decided to begin a notebook in which I would try to summarize the basic laws and formulae associated with heat, light, electricity and mechanics. I managed this in some fifty or so pages, and decided to go on to chemistry and astronomy. But the section about the planets led me on to geology and Lyell's *Principles*, which in turn led me into biology and the Darwinian controversy. None of these were taught at school, so I borrowed books from the library, and made considerable use of a six-volume work called *Practical Knowledge for All*. At some point I decided that my book ought to include zoology, mathematics and philosophy. The original idea went on expanding until it filled seven notebooks; what began as a scheme for occupying the summer holiday turned into a task that was still unfinished eighteen months later. If schoolmasters had tried to force that much work on me, I would have regarded it as impossible; but a dogged instinct for thoroughness led me to spend freezing winter evenings in my bedroom trying to summarize Plato, Kepler and Einstein. My *Manual of General Science* was never finished; but the attempt turned me into a writer.

What I discovered is that, once we are committed to thoroughness, we are pushed — whether we like it or not — to a higher level of discipline and organization. I felt a new 'me' taking shape, and for the next five years or so the conflict between this left-brain 'identity' and the developing adolescent was a constant source of misery. What T.E. Lawrence called 'the thought-riddled nature' and 'my gaoler' constantly interfered with normal relaxation and response, and produced explosions of rage and frustration. A similar conflict made Nietzsche a lifelong invalid; fortunately, a strong constitution and basic optimism kept me sane and reasonably healthy.

When Man began to live in cities and build civilization, he did so purely for convenience and comfort — not from any desire to become disciplined and organized. His chief need was to protect himself from other men, for human beings have always had a tendency to regard other people's property as rightly belonging to themselves (a philosophy now known as socialism). While he built magnificent temples to the gods, he lived in crude huts that could be blown away in a storm. Then why *did* he build the temples, the step pyramids, the *megalithic monuments and mounds? We do not know the answer but, as we uncover increasing evidence that *ancient Man was obsessively interested in the heavens, it seems clear that he had some instinctive rather than intellectual (i.e., 'superstitious') sense of their importance.

The clue seems to be provided by recent studies in Earth magnetism, which reveal that animals possess inbuilt magnetic detectors — these explain to a great extent the mystery of the homing instinct. (Certain areas of the Earth contain magnetic anomalies — a kind of whirlpool — and homing pigeons released in these areas fly around helplessly in circles.) Man must once have been able to make use of the same detectors, and it seems probable that this explains the ability of dowsers. In that case, ancient Man must have felt rather like a fish, constantly *aware* of the pressures of the currents around him. The rising of the Moon — even though the Moon's magnetic field is weak — must have produced an almost vertiginous sensation. (Even now, it has a medically observable effect on many people — hence 'lunacy'.) He would also have noted less powerful 'currents' as the planets changed their relative positions in the sky. He must have felt surrounded by mysterious forces which he believed, rightly or wrongly, governed his destiny. Practically speaking, it was obviously rightly — ancient Man was a hunter and the movements of animals were controlled by the magnetic forces; Man could make use of his own 'magnetic sensor' to intercept them. Later, when Man became an agriculturalist, he came to believe that these same forces influenced the Earth's fertility; this may be true or false, but the widespread association of the Moon with *fertility religions leaves no doubt that our ancestors took it for granted.

Presumably, then, Man's observation of the heavens was an attempt to pin down this important relationship between the planets and the 'magical' forces of the Earth. But until the building of monuments like Stonehenge and the Great Pyramid it probably remained a kind of 'rule of thumb' — a form of knowledge best understood by priests and shamans, but also shared by most intelligent adults. The creation of the 'great stone computers' meant that the new knowledge required specialization; it was now beyond the grasp of the average man. Yet it would be the most 'intuitive' men — those with the strongest instinctive knowledge of Earth forces — who would have to be trained for the priesthood, producing, I assume, the typical conflicts we have seen in Nietzsche and T.E. Lawrence.

Man is dragged out of the realm of intuition and into the realm of abstraction and logic by problems and complications. Jaynes produces some interesting historical evidence that seems to show that the European mind became decisively non-bicameral about 1200 BC. He points out, for example, that in early altar carvings of Babylon and Assyria the king is shown standing and listening to the god; but in 1230 BC Tukulti-Ninurti, King of Assyria, had a stone altar carved which showed him kneeling in front of the *empty* throne of the god. The old sense of oneness with the Earth — and the gods — has vanished; isolated in the left brain, Man has become 'inferior' to himself and to the god. 'Hallucinated guidance' (or direct consciousness of the Earth forces) has disappeared. Jaynes quotes from a cuneiform tablet of this period the curious lines: 'One who has no god, as he walks along the street,/Headache envelops him like a garment.'

Man becomes the victim of mental stress; as a result, he becomes cruel and violent. Jaynes argues that sadism, once almost non-existent, suddenly becomes commonplace; suddenly, tyrants begin to boast of the number of enemies they have impaled alive, the number of women and children murdered. (It seems arguable that this sudden change — from the intuitive to the abstract mind — came about as a result of the tremendous upheavals that occurred in the Mediterranean around 1200 BC from the invasions of the 'Sea Peoples'.)

What is being suggested, then, is that at a certain point in his evolution Man crossed a 'great divide' to become, in effect, a different kind of creature. He crossed the divide unwillingly, and hankered after the old simplicity, the old gods. (I have suggested elsewhere[2] that it was this craving that explains why it took so long for Man to realize that the Earth revolves around the Sun; Aristarchus, for example, suggested in the third century BC that the Sun is the centre of the Solar System, yet his idea was ignored for nearly 2,000 years; the human mind was simply not ready for such an unsettling notion.) Little by little, Man learned to trust his reason; finally, he reached a point where reason provided the sense of security that was once provided by 'the gods'. Man sees himself as a 'thinking reed', a reasoning worm. (All this is described with remarkable insight in the prophetic books of William Blake.) To ancient Man religion and science were the same thing; to the 'thinking reed' they are irreconcilable opposites. Yet the way forward does *not* lie through religion and irrationalism. It lies through a science that is finally broad enough to recognize that the split is an illusion. In that sense, Sperry's discovery of the differing functions of the right and left brains *could* be the most important single insight in the history of human knowledge. It could lead to the foundation of a 'new science' in which both forms of knowledge are recognized as equally important.

Perhaps the most exciting development in recent years is the rate at which orthodox science is providing insights into this new realm; that is, overcoming its own left-brain limitations. A single example illustrates the point. A London psychologist, Evelyn Golding, has made an intriguing discovery about the reactions of people to a simple test known as the four-card problem. It is childishly straightforward. The subject was shown four cards; then one end of each card was covered with a black strip (see Figure 1). The subject was shown the sentence 'When there is a circle on the card, the other half is red', and was asked how many cards he would have to 'unmask' to decide whether this was true or false. The startling discovery was that so many people got it wrong. Among undergraduates, only four per cent gave the correct answer. One distinguished mathematician became so frustrated that he swept the cards on to the floor. Yet brain-damaged people did far better — sixty per cent of them succeeded.

Why, wondered Golding, should intelligent people be so bad at solving a simple logical problem? The answer, apparently, is that the normal intelligent person *over-exerts*. The right brain hurls itself into a fury of perception which drowns the calm, logical voice of the left. Patients with right-hemisphere brain damage, or with the right anaesthetized, approached the problem simply and logically and solved it.[3]

Now we are all familiar with the converse phenomenon, when the over-exertion of the left damages the performance of the right — for example, in stage fright. We all know that it is often easier to solve a complex problem without thinking too much about it. So we are inclined to swallow the arguments of people like D.H. Lawrence who mistrust 'head consciousness'. Yet here, in the card test, is proof that we can overdo the intuition just as much. It is, again, an almost staggering

---

[2]*Starseekers*, Chapter 3.

[3]Obviously, the correct answer is two cards. The subject has to unmask a card that is red at one end and a card with a circle; the other two are irrelevant. If, of course, he unmasks the red card with a diamond first, he has proved it false using only one card.

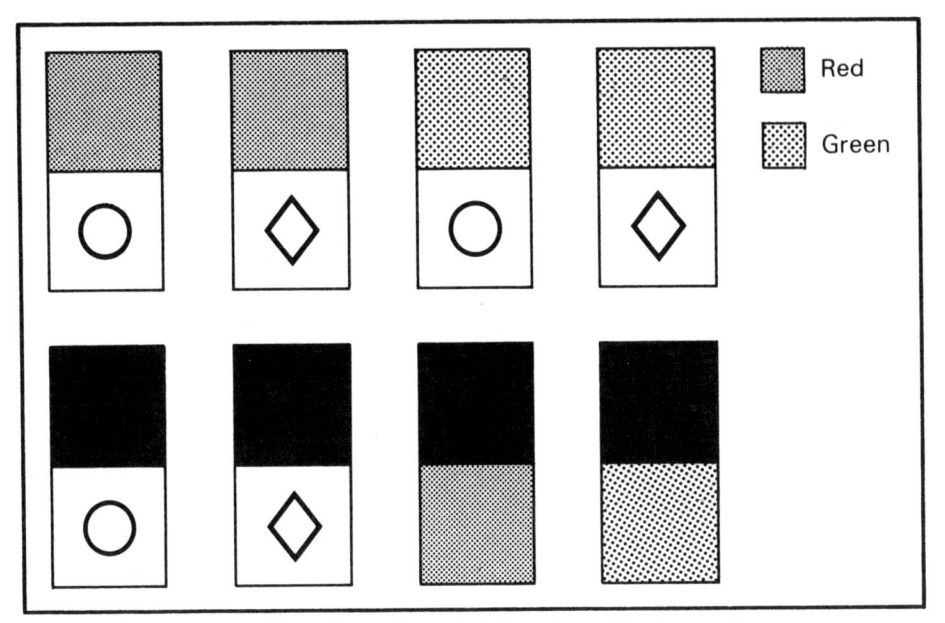

Figure 1 *The four-card problem:* above, *the cards;* below, *the problem (see text).*

recognition for modern Man, who deprecates reason as much as his nineteenth-century forefathers exalted it.

Yet the same lesson emerges again and again from this new science of the divided brain. Consider the problem of hypnosis, the nature of which is still regarded as an unsolved problem. Freud studied hypnosis under Charcot in Paris, and it was through these studies that he stumbled upon the idea of the unconscious. A hysterical woman could believe that her arm was paralysed — and, in fact, the arm became paralysed. She could believe she was pregnant, and the stomach would swell with a 'phantom pregnancy'. But strikingly similar results could be obtained through hypnosis. What was the connection between hysteria and hypnosis? Surely it lay in the fact that there is an area of the human mind which is far more powerful than normal consciousness? But if this 'unconscious' mind can overrule normal consciousness — for, surely, no one *wants* to be paralysed — then our belief that we are rational beings, *Homo sapiens*, must be false? The unconscious is the puppet-master, consciousness merely the puppet . . .

But split-brain physiology suggests a simpler explanation for hypnosis: that it puts the left brain to sleep while the right remains wide awake. The right brain seems to be far more powerful than the left. So when the hypnotist says, 'You will lie between two chairs, and become as stiff as a board', the right brain responds instantly to the authoritative voice and carries out the order. Then why will the right not obey the same order when it comes from the left? Because the left 'lacks authority'. It lacks self-confidence and self-belief; so when it says, 'You will lie between two chairs and become as stiff as a board', the right *doesn't believe it.* Clearly, then, Lawrence was wrong: it is not true that 'head consciousness' is too dominant; *it is not dominant enough.*

This also clearly implies that Freud was wrong. The 'unconscious' may be more powerful than the conscious, but it is not therefore the master — any more than the elephant is the master of the driver who sits on its head. The conscious is the master, despite its weakness; and it could be far more 'masterful' if it chose to develop its authority.

The same point has been made by a remarkable psychologist, Howard Miller. He points out that the brain is basically a vast computer, and that we often mistake the activity of the computer for 'our own' mental activity. He cites, for example, the experiment of Penfield in which an area of the temporal cortex is stimulated by an electric current, with the result that the patient 'relives' whole earlier epochs of his life in the most precise detail. Such brain activity is not really comparable to 'thinking'; it is purely mechanical, like having a tune stuck in your head. Hume used similar arguments to argue that all our mental processes are 'mechanical', mere 'association of ideas'; he said that, when he looked inside himself, he failed to find the essential David Hume — only many ideas and impressions. Miller flatly denies this; he says that, in spite of all the 'mechanical' activity of the brain, we only have to observe ourselves while thinking — or engaged in any other form of *purposeful* mental activity — to observe that there *is* a 'you' presiding over consciousness. This 'you' he calls 'the unit of pure thought'. Husserl called it 'the transcendental ego'. What we call it is unimportant; what matters is the recognition that there *is* a presiding and controlling ego in charge of consciousness. (William James once described how he managed to drag himself back from the edge of total mental breakdown by clinging to Renouvier's definition of free will — that I can choose to continue or break off a thought because *I* want to. James had recognized the existence of the 'presiding ego'.)

Lawrence and his school argue that 'head consciousness' is inferior to instinctive consciousness because it cannot induce those moods of oneness with nature, poetic insight, mystical perception. These seem to come when they feel inclined, mostly when the logical ego is off-duty. But is this really true? When I am galvanized by a sense of emergency, my vital energies respond magnificently. Graham Greene has described how he used to induce an overwhelming sense of sheer joy by playing Russian roulette; when there was just a click the sense of relief would launch him into the *'peak experience'. But what happens when we respond to emergencies? The *presiding ego* shouts 'Attention!', and the vital energies respond like a squad of well drilled soldiers. So, again, it seems that the trouble lies with the sergeant major, who simply fails to get the best out of his recruits. He lacks authority. He is too lazy to drill the squad.

There is, as Miller points out, another problem. *The sergeant major does not know that he is the sergeant major.* Because the brain hums with activity in which he seems to have no part, he mistakenly assumes that he is merely a detached observer. Recognizing that he cannot even get a persistent tune out of his head, he concludes that he is a nobody. So instead of making his wishes known he tends to intervene feebly and spasmodically, *in response* to the purely mechanical reactions of the brain and body.

Yet emergency teaches us that he *can* give orders and have them obeyed. Hemingway speaks in one of his stories about the times during the war when a soldier does 'the one thing, the only thing for a man to do, easily and naturally', and it always comes out right. These are the times when, under emergency, the presiding ego snaps out orders, and that other self provides instantly the energy and co-ordination to carry them out perfectly. But under normal conditions — what

Heidegger calls 'the triviality of everydayness' — our sense of purpose goes off duty, and the presiding ego simply forgets that it is supposed to preside.

By way of a slightly dubious analogy, you could compare him to a railway engine that mistakes itself for one of the carriages, and places itself in the middle of the train — then wonders why it is such hard work pushing the train up hills or around hairpin bends. Once a sense of purpose or crisis causes the engine to take its proper place, at the front, it finds it can negotiate the steepest hills and sharpest bends without the least difficulty.

All this amounts to the staggering, the almost unbelievable, assertion that this much maligned left-brain ego *is* the presiding ego. It is intended to give the orders. But the strange division of the brain into two watertight compartments has caused a temporary traffic-jam in human evolution; and the left brain is not only unaware of its true role, it is even unaware that it has a partner. As a result, it is crippled by self-mistrust and a sense of its own inadequacy.

In a sense, therefore, Lawrence, Whitman and the rest *were* correct. They understood that our most important revelations occur in those curious moments of intensity or serenity when the left glances sideways, recognizes its partner, and says, 'My God, where did *you* come from?' In order to evolve, to make the best possible use of his powers, Man must be aware of the existence of this tremendously powerful ally.

Let me dot the 'i's and cross the 't's. We are all accustomed to the phenomenon of feeling separated from our real powers by self-doubt and self-awareness; so we know intuitively that our trouble lies in a failure of co-operation between two halves of our being. We all know about 'the divided self'. We all know about those strange, superb moments of reconciliation when, as Hesse's Steppenwolf says, we become aware of the reality of 'Mozart and the stars'. (I have been writing about the subject for the past quarter of a century.) What we have not known, until split-brain research, is that this is not just a simple matter of conflict between instinct and reason, two *aspects* of ourselves, but a problem of two different persons, living inside the same brain, *one of whom you call 'you'*.

Why is this so important? Because while we think in terms of instinct and reason we underestimate the size of the problem, *and the importance of its solution*. We think we 'know' all about the instinctive partner. The truth is we do not even begin to know. And if, as I firmly believe, this partner is responsible for most so-called paranormal phenomena, from telepathy to poltergeists, then his powers are very unusual indeed. The correct word would be 'miraculous'.

At present, the main thing we know about the partners is that they spend most of their time getting in one another's way and reducing one another's efficiency — even the right is guilty, as the four-card problem demonstrates. (The tendency to get in one another's way is called neurosis.) All so-called mystical insights are merely glimpses of the possibilities of their co-operation. Certain men — like Jesus — seem to have been born with a naturally higher level of co-operation between the two selves; the result was the ability to work miracles.

Clearly, the implications are staggering, although this is no place to develop them. A man who fully understood these possibilities — and was thus able to turn them to practical purposes — would be, by present standards, a god. Yet there seem to be perfectly sober and down-to-earth reasons for believing that Man now at least has the power to investigate these possibilities, just as, in the nineteenth century, he investigated the mechanical possibilities of his power over nature. And if we recall the swiftness with which the scientific revolution took place, so that Man changed more in a century than in the past million years, then it seems perfectly feasible that the human race could now be on the brink of its most important evolutionary development.

It sounds, I agree, quite preposterous. But then the development of modern science would have sounded just as preposterous, even to the most intelligent layman, in the year 1750. And a writer who happened to foresee those possibilities would have had an enormous task in trying to make them sound plausible and logical. He would, to begin with, have had to trace all the major intellectual and technical developments of the past half century, and to try to show that the rate of change was accelerating steadily but predictably. In fact, such a writer did exist: Diderot, whose *Encyclopedia* began to appear in 1751 and was possibly a main cause of the French Revolution. But then Diderot and his colleagues were basically 'positivists' (although the word had not then been invented). His aim was to overthrow the superstitions of religion and establish all knowledge securely on the principles of natural science. He was firmly convinced that Man is basically a machine who responds automatically to external stimuli, and has no free will. Yet, in retrospect, Diderot was not a bad fellow, and the *Encyclopedia* can still be read with excitement by anyone who takes the trouble to try to enter into that priest-ridden period.

Since its basic position is a rejection of positivism, the present book could be called an *Anti-Encyclopedia*. Yet I think it should already be clear that its aim is far from antiscientific. It is not a collection of wonders and improbabilities; it is not devoted to the proposition that there are more things in heaven and Earth... It is, quite simply, an attempt to do what Diderot set out to do more than two centuries ago: to trace the basic development of ideas in the past decade or so, and to indicate the direction in which things seem to be moving. The core of the book is contained, I think, in the section called 'Inner Space: Mind and Body'. It is preceded by sections dealing with human history and the paranormal, and followed by sections dealing with the developments of modern science and the world of tomorrow. It aims, as it were, to be no more than a sketch map of an enormous territory in which large spaces are still labelled *'terra incognita'*.

At the risk of 'lowering the tone' and inviting ridicule, the editors have decided to include a section on 'Strange Creatures and Unusual Events'. It is arguable that they have no place in a serious work. But it is harder still to find a good reason for excluding such interesting oddities as the Tunguska explosion and vanishing people from a book called *The Directory of Possibilities*. At worst, they can be regarded as light relief; at best, they may help to complete the picture of a period in which there is more stimulating intellectual ferment than at any time since Voltaire, Diderot and d'Alembert set out to create 'a new spirit of the age'. CW

NOTES FOR THE WARY
by John Grant

This book could be described as an exploration of the fringes of knowledge, a guide to those areas of understanding where we know just enough to know that we do not know enough. Clearly, there is a great deal of variation from topic to topic in the degree of our uncertainty: in some instances we may feel that the case has been more-or-less proved, while in others we are virtually convinced that the events or phenomena described are products of the gifted or gullible imagination (which, of course, does not mean that they are not still interesting). That is, some of the topics discussed in this book would be more accurately described as 'probabilities', others as 'remote possibilities', while yet others are almost certainly fallacious yet provide valuable insights into one or more of the main themes of this book.

Colin Wilson has already stated the primary theme of this work in his Introduction. Here I would like to outline some of the other themes which seem important. I should add that these themes are not mutually distinct: like the colossal variety of subjects discussed in these pages, they are complementary, they cohere, they can all be regarded as facets of a single theme. Thus, where on page 22 Colin Wilson says that the 'core of this book is contained, I think, in the section called "Inner Space: Mind and Body"', my own feeling is that the core of this book is contained in the sections called 'Outer Space: The Universe at Large' and 'The World of Tomorrow', *and that there is no contradiction between Wilson's statement and mine*, a view which he shares. This is because I feel that the interaction between the human mind and what it discovers (or creates, or conceives) is a two-way process — that, just as an increase in the brain's ability enables the discovery or, more accurately, conceptualization of new phenomena, so the very act of understanding these phenomena has a direct effect on increasing the mind's abilities: education improves the mind, and this permits the further education of the mind. Thus, while the subject matter of Part Five is superficially quite different from those of Parts Six and Seven, it is in real terms almost identical: the two areas of interest are so interdependent that they should be considered as one. There are two simple analogies: light and dark, and the yin and the yang. In both partnerships neither component has any meaning without the existence of the other. This argument can be extended to cover Parts One to Four of this work.

This line of reasoning leads also to another primary theme of *The Directory of Possibilities*: uncertainty. The characteristic human aspiration towards definiteness has a bad track record: 'facts' regularly and, in modern times, frequently tumble by the wayside as further 'facts' appear. This realization lies at the heart of, for example, twentieth-century physics, based upon such fundamental assumptions as Heisenberg's Uncertainty Principle, Gödel's Theorem, and the 'laws' of quantum mechanics. Einstein, usually regarded as the father of modern physics, is often quoted as having said, 'I cannot believe that God plays dice with the cosmos'; the brilliant Cambridge theoretical cosmologist, Stephen Hawking, has more recently retorted: 'On the contrary, it appears that not only does God play dice, but also that he sometimes throws the dice where they cannot be seen.' Einstein himself, of course, had earlier shown that the certainty which arises from the application of common sense is unfounded.

This does not mean that it is wise or sensible to ignore or discard all the derived laws of nature. Laws, in the scientific sense, are descriptions which fit observations; and from them can be constructed models from which in turn can be derived likely explanations of the observations. The idea that scientific laws are prescriptive is, in theory, a dead one, although in practice scientists still often fall into the trap of treating them as if they were (a failing we all share). Nevertheless, although laws are only descriptions of currently accepted belief, they have generally withstood a great number of tests; we have little option but to let them stand until better laws are derived to take their place — one ignores existing laws at one's very great peril. This is not to say that many of the 'established' laws will not be challenged in the following pages; however, the challenges will be born from observation, deduction or reasoned speculation rather than from ignorance.

Which brings us to the conflict between gullibility and scepticism. Let us take the latter first. In the eyes of orthodoxy, the person who reads this book and automatically rejects its more speculative propositions will be regarded as a sceptic. Alternatively, that person may be described as someone with a closed mind, for it is the role of the true sceptic to be sceptical about his fellow-sceptics — indeed, about his own scepticism. The open-minded reader will, of course, read this book sceptically, doubting, criticizing; but he will have the same attitude also to his own previous understanding.

At the other end of the scale from the person with the closed mind is the reader whose mind is closely analogous to a black hole: gobbling up everything, sorting nothing, and reducing all to a state of ultimate entropy. Such gullibility is both dangerous and exceedingly common (many books of 'strange events' are, alas, written by the gullible for the gullible). Where the person with a closed mind attempts to order everything to the extent that observations not in accord with his preconceptions are ignored or distorted, and false order is thrust upon the Universe, the gullible thinker conversely *removes* order from those events which are in fact structured, which conform to a pattern. The gullible will gain little from this book except a string of wonders; he will find more things in heaven and Earth than are actually there.

Does this mean that we are asking you to maintain a balance between gullibility and scepticism? Almost. In more precise terms, we are asking you to be both gullible and sceptical at the same time, to both accept and reject every idea contained within this book. By this apparently dichotomous process you will be able to construct as complete as possible a model of the single coherent truth expressed in these pages. The model will owe its near completeness to a component part which we cannot put into it: you.

At an early stage in our discussions of the planning of this book, Wilson described it as being made up of pieces of a jig-saw which the reader himself could put together. I demurred, saying that, yes, it was a jig-saw, but that it differed from others in that there were at least several if not many different solutions. Here we hit upon what was apparently a point of disagreement, until further discussion showed that we were approaching the same conclusion from slightly different directions.

Let me expand upon this slightly. The Universe has laws which are everywhere obeyed. These laws are not governed by Man, and indeed it is quite possible that he will never understand them. Here is a scientific heresy: these laws are independent of there being any observer. Nevertheless, Man creates models of these laws. Some of the models are trivial. But consider the others: these are *all valid*, even if they apparently disagree with each other — for example, Newton's Laws of Motion are true even though they apparently disagree with those of Einstein, since in everyday use (that is, in their own terms) the discrepancy between the model and observation is below the theoretical limit of detectability. Thus, it is not quite true to say, as is often said, that Relativity is a more accurate model of reality than are Newton's Laws; it is, rather, a model which is 'more correct' *under certain circumstances.*

Therefore, we can suggest that the jig-saw (that is, this book) has indeed several solutions — where a solution is equivalent to a model of reality. *Of course* there is only one reality, only one set of laws which the Universe obeys, but of that reality there are numerous models, which are valid in their own terms. Moreover, they are all equivalent. Thus, the model of the Universe created by the yogi is equivalent to the model created by the cosmologist.

A few paragraphs ago I mentioned the idea of pattern. Perhaps it can be used gainfully here. Consider, for the purposes of analogy, a large array of dots, such as the intersections on a sheet of graph paper. Take any two dots. In terms of Euclidean logic the connection between these two dots takes the form of a straight line; moreover, assuming the separation between adjacent dots to be small, only adjacent dots can affect each other — for example, you get from dot 1,2 (1 along, 2 up) to dot 5,6 by passing through the sequence of adjacent dots 2,3, 3,4, 4,5. In what I would rather uneasily describe as relativistic logic (where one plus one doesn't exactly equal two) the connection between the two dots is not necessarily a straight line, although the straight line between the two dots is one of a set of patterns *of which they are both a part.* Extending this further, there is an almost infinite number of patterns to which the two dots belong. I suggest that this almost infinite number corresponds to the number of valid models of the laws of the Universe.

This theme is omnipresent in this book: to any given question there is a plurality, almost an infinitude, of answers. I would suggest that these very large numbers are possibly born from a fundamental duality in all things — that to each question there are two answers, each of which implies two further answers, and so forth. The observant reader will have noticed that this 'Principle of Duality' has been implied throughout the preceding discussion ... and so we return to the arguments expressed by Colin Wilson in his Introduction.

The main body of this book is divided into seven 'natural' sections. The reader who wishes to follow one idea through to its 'logical' conclusion can find the section in which his 'basic' idea is expressed and read it. He will find himself referred into other sections by the elements of the cross-reference system — cross-references are indicated by an asterisk preceding the keyword, *thus. In addition, he will find ideas related in the Directory-Index, within which there are again cross-references.

We would suggest, then, that the reader in search of knowledge first read the main body of the text from start to finish, and then make use of the Directory-Index, where he may find linkages that had not previously occurred to him. In addition, he will find there brief descriptions of a number of ideas which do not occur in the text; thus, the Directory-Index serves not only as an index to the body of ideas expressed in the main text but also as a linking device and as a sort of concise dictionary of the possible.

As with all worthwhile reference books, the editors of this one would be glad to receive suggestions for improvements to be incorporated in future editions, although, for obvious practical reasons, they cannot reply to every letter. Communications should be addressed to the editors, care of the publishers. JG

PART ONE
MYTHOLOGY AND THE ANCIENT WORLD

Introductory: 1

The aim of this first part of the book is to bring together all those elements in the 'jig-saw' that relate to mythology and ancient Man. So, for example, the articles on ancient astronauts, ancient Man, Arthur, Glastonbury and ley lines could be read consecutively as an extension of the Introduction to this book (all are explored in my *Mysteries*). The common 'key' to all these entries is the notion of Earth magnetism, and the fact that Man can respond to it by means of a dowsing rod while animals undoubtedly use it for homing. Robert Ardrey pointed out that every European and American eel (there are two different species) is born in the Sargasso Sea, and finds its way across thousands of miles of Atlantic to its 'home' river; how, he asks, do American elvers know that they should go to America and European ones to Europe? In *The Territorial Imperative* he discussed animal homing at length — he was the first modern writer to bring the problem to general notice — and stated that it is an unsolved mystery. But subsequent discoveries about Earth magnetism mean that this statement is no longer true.

It was Guy Underwood (see *ley lines) who first clearly recognized that these magnetic forces, particularly when they form spirals, are closely connected with the religion of our ancestors. John Michell has even suggested that there was, at some remote period, a kind of 'golden age' when Man lived in intimate contact with the forces of the Earth and knew how to utilize them — perhaps just as modern Man uses electricity. In which case, Julian Jaynes' theory of the coming of the 'non-bicameral mind' should be regarded as the next instalment in the story. Under increasing pressure from the 'complexification' of his own society, Man was forced to develop a dominant 'critical' function, the left cerebral hemisphere, which finally assumed a kind of autonomy. Blake told this story in detail in such 'prophetic books' as *The Four Zoas* and *Jerusalem*. Modern science has only confirmed Blake's intuitions. In *The White Goddess* Robert Graves argues the same case: that our remote ancestors possessed their own complex knowledge system, which was, in its way, as complete as the system developed by modern science. It differed in being 'lunar' rather than 'solar'; it was intuitive rather than intellectual; magical rather than scientific.

This is easy to grasp if we think in terms of a man driving along country lanes at night. His headlights slice ahead into the darkness, and he can safely drive at 50mph. Yet he is trapped, enclosed in the dark world of his car and its lights. If he lowers the window and leaves only the sidelights switched on, he ceases to be 'enclosed'. He can see hedges and trees and moonlit fields; he becomes *aware* of more. *But he is forced to slow down to 5mph.* Man developed the intellect — solar knowledge — for speed and efficiency. Ancient Man was not concerned with speed. And we are now beginning to recover the lost world of this older knowledge system through the use of scientific method. The dream expressed by pioneers like Graves, Underwood, Michell and Jaynes is that the two systems will one day unite to form something more powerful than either.

CW

Ancient Astronauts

The theory that our Earth has been visited, perhaps even colonized, by superbeings from outer space has been in the air a long time — ever since Kenneth Arnold, piloting his own 'plane near Mount Rainier on 24 June 1947, reported seeing nine shining airborne discs travelling at great speed. When the incident was reported in *Fate*, thousands of similar reports of 'flying saucers' poured in from all over the world.

But perhaps the most convincing single 'UFO' sighting is one described by a Russian painter in *Altai-Himalaya* (1930). Crossing the Himalayas en route to India, Roerich and his party observed a big, shining oval moving at great speed; as they watched, it changed direction at a right angle — a movement typical of *UFOs — and disappeared behind a mountain peak. This occurred on 5 August 1926 — twenty-one years *before* Arnold's sighting.

George Hunt Williamson became convinced that spacemen were contacting him through automatic writing, and in *Secret Places of the Lion* explained that visitors from space landed on Earth 18 million years ago, and have since been devoting themselves to the evolution of mankind.

Two years later, in 1960, the best-selling *Le Matin des Magiciens (The Morning of the Magicians)* by Pauwels and Bergier gave the 'ancient-astronaut' theory worldwide circulation. It was this book that probably inspired Arthur C. Clarke's script for the film *2001: A Space Odyssey* (1968), in which benevolent aliens help apemen over the 'barrier' towards becoming intelligent human beings. (In *African Genesis* Robert Ardrey had suggested the rather more plausible theory that it was the use of simple weapons — and the consequent need to develop co-ordination between hand and eye — which caused the development of the human brain.)

Erich von Däniken's *Chariots of the Gods?* was, relatively speaking, a latecomer; but newspaper serializations of his book gave the theory a wider currency than ever before. What excited the reading public was the enormous mass of evidence, which made the theory seem almost unassailable. Unfortunately, even a brief examination reveals that von Däniken is incredibly careless, and that much of his evidence is so full of mistakes as to be virtually valueless. He insists that the Easter Island statues must have been erected by spacemen because men would have been unable to do it — yet modern Easter Island natives, using the equipment that would have been available to their ancestors, have carved and erected such a statue in a short time. He argues that the pyramids were built by spacemen on much the same grounds, but asserts, mistakenly, that the ancient Egyptians had no rope; he also multiplies the weight of the Great Pyramid by five. He asserts that the Nazca lines, which run for miles across the desert in the Peruvian Andes, are giant runways for spaceships, without reflecting that spaceships would probably land vertically, or that the blast from one of them would scatter the small stones of which the lines are made.

In a later book, *Gold of the Gods*, he describes visiting a vast underground cave system in Ecuador and seeing a marvellous library of metal leaves covered with unknown characters. The companion with whom he claimed to have visited the caves flatly denied that von Däniken went beyond the entrance; faced with this, von Däniken back-pedalled, admitted he had not been in the cave, and said that he allowed himself the latitude of a creative writer. A UK expedition to the caves concerned found them to be natural, with signs of the habitation of primitive Man, but without the 'library' or elaborately engineered walls described by von Däniken.

Must the ancient-astronaut theory, then, be dismissed as wishful thinking? Certainly, most of the evidence collapses on close examination; moreover, our ancestors were certainly more intelligent and sophisticated than von Däniken gives them credit for (see *ancient Man). Yet certain puzzles remain. The giant creatures drawn on the desert's surface at Nazca — birds, spiders, even monkeys — can be seen only from the air, which has led one investigator to suggest that the Nazca Indians of AD 500 (the approximate date of the lines) constructed hot-air balloons. Maria Reiche, who has spent her life studying the lines, is convinced that they are of astronomical and religious significance.

Perhaps the most convincing evidence so far is to be found in Robert Temple's *The Sirius Mystery*, which points out that an African tribe, the Dogon, know that Sirius is actually a double star; that the companion, invisible to the naked eye and discovered only in 1862, is 'the heaviest of all stars' (it is, in fact, a white dwarf); and that it revolves around Sirius every fifty years. Sirius was the sacred star of the Egyptians, and Temple argues that the Dogon tradition could have originated in Egypt; but this still leaves such precise astronomical knowledge unexplained. A suggestion by Sagan that the Dogon obtained their knowledge of Sirius B from missionaries around the turn of the century is unsupported by the slightest evidence.

The late T.C. Lethbridge arrived at the astronaut theory independently, through study of alignments of *megalithic monuments and stories of intercourse between human beings and angels in the Old Testament; but he takes the precaution of subtitling his *Legend of the Sons of God* 'A Fantasy?'. And until more convincing evidence appears this is probably a valid assessment of the status of the ancient-astronaut theory.   CW

Ancient Man

The *ancient-astronaut theory depends heavily upon the assumption that our distant ancestors were primitive and unsophisticated creatures, only one degree more intelligent than gorillas. An increasing body of evidence throws doubts on this, and suggests that ancient Man was far more intelligent than we have given him credit for. It seems quite unnecessary to introduce 'astronauts' to aid his cultural evolution.

Earth is about 4.6 billion years old; it had been in existence for perhaps as much as 1.5 billion years when life first appeared, possibly from outer space (see *panspermia). Evolution as we know it began over half a billion years ago, when life invented reproduction, and death. About 400 million years ago, in the early Devonian, a few fishes crawled on to the land. The reptiles evolved in the early Carboniferous, some 360 million years ago, and their age lasted nearly another 300 million years; then the mammals took over. Over 100 million years ago, evolution invented the technique of allowing the embryo to develop in the mother's body.

Among Man's earliest mammalian ancestors was a small, ratlike creature that took to the trees; these tree shrews became apes and monkeys. Between 10 and 20 million years ago, an upright ape called *Ramapithecus* appeared in Africa and India; then, a mere 5 million years ago at most, the 'missing link' appeared. By 2 million years ago he was using bones as clubs, and fashioning primitive tools. In *African Genesis*, Ardrey argues that it was the development of weapons that required a new co-ordination, and led to the development of the brain and nervous system that produced modern Man. Around 700,000 years ago, *Homo erectus* learned the use of fire and, 400,000 years ago, he made the first 'houses' of branches.

Sometime around 100,000 years ago, Neanderthal Man began to colonize Europe. He was short and apelike, walked with a stooping posture, lived in caves, and was a cannibal. Some 70,000 years later, he vanished abruptly, and the evidence suggests that he was wiped out by a newcomer on the scene, Cro-Magnon Man, the probable direct ancestor of modern Man. It was Cro-Magnon Man who produced the first cave paintings.

Science has been inclined to take the view that the extinction of Neanderthal Man was brutal but necessary to the development of *Homo sapiens*. Modern discoveries throw doubt on this view. Neanderthal Man had a brain as large as or larger than that of modern Man; he wove coloured flowers into screens; he carved stones into spheres and discs, which suggests Sun worship; and he buried his dead with care and with some form of religious ritual. Stan Gooch has even suggested that Cro-Magnon males mated with Neanderthal females, producing an offspring who was more intuitive and 'mystical' than Cro-Magnon; these, Gooch suggested, could be the ancestors of the Jewish race.

The cave paintings of Cro-Magnon Man led the Victorians to assume that he was artistically inclined; but in this century it has become increasingly clear that the purpose of the paintings was basically 'magical'. The shamans sketched bison and other animals as part of some ritual to influence them, or to guide the hunters towards them. Nor would it be wise to dismiss such rituals as an expression of ignorance and superstition. Dozens of examples could be cited, from students of modern primitives, to indicate that they often *do* work (see *primitive magic).

One of the most interesting developments is described in *The Roots of Civilization* by Alexander Marshack. He examined dozens of pieces of marked bone from the Stone Age. It had been previously assumed that the 'scratches' were some form of decoration, further proof of the 'artistic' tendency of Cro-Magnon Man. Examining an 8,000-year-old reindeer bone through a microscope, Marshack established that its 167 marks were made with different tools at different times. He argues convincingly that the 'snakey' path of the dots is an attempt to record the times of the Moon's rising and setting over many months. But why should Cro-Magnon Man have been interested in the Moon? The answer is suggested on page 17 — that the Moon causes changes in the Earth's magnetic field, to which ancient Man was sensitive. In all cultures, the Moon is the goddess of magic. Marshack examined dozens of bones, some dating as far back as 34,000 BC, and concluded that the marks are all concerned with the Moon and the seasons. So Cro-Magnon Man had evolved his own form of notation thousands of years before the Sumerians invented writing (*c* 3500 BC).

We must conclude, then, that both Neanderthal and Cro-Magnon Man were more 'civilized' and inventive than we earlier assumed. This, of course, neither proves nor disproves the *ancient-astronaut theory; but it certainly undermines the assertions of writers like von Däniken that prehistoric Man could never have invented the wheel or built the great *megalithic monuments without 'help' from more advanced intelligences.   CW

Arthur

This legendary British warrior king was probably a Roman general. Evidence for his existence is so scanty that some historians are convinced he is mythical.

His real fame began with the publication of Geoffrey of Monmouth's *History of the Kings of Britain*, *c* 1145; this recounted the now familiar legend of the birth of Arthur at Tintagel Castle, Cornwall, sired by King Uther Pendragon on the wife of Duke Gorlois after the magician Merlin had 'changed' Uther to look like Gorlois. Geoffrey goes on to describe how Arthur conquered Ireland, Scandinavia and France, and was about to march on Rome when news of rebellion forced him back to England. All this, like most of Geoffrey's history, is invention. Tintagel Castle was not built until 1141. By then the real Arthur had been dead 600 years.

The true story seems to be as follows. Around 410 the Romans began pulling out of Britain to defend Rome against the barbarians. A chieftain named Vortigern set himself up as King of Britain, but soon found himself in trouble with the wild Picts who poured over his northern borders; he invited Saxon mercenaries from the European continent to come and fight for him. They did; then decided to stay on and colonize England by the sword. Slowly the original Britons were driven back into Cornwall and Wales, until, after about 200 years, Britain had become England, the land of the Anglo-Saxons.

The reason it took the Saxons so long to conquer was that the Britons rallied. An ex-Roman warrior, Ambrosius Aurelianus, inflicted many defeats on them. When he died, he was succeeded by Uther Pendragon. A young commander named Artorius (later Arthur) succeeded Uther, and defeated the Saxons in twelve major battles. The last, the battle of 'Mount Badonicus', lasted three days; the decimated Saxons withdrew and made no further attempts to advance for another fifty years.

The Battle of Badon took place about 515, and established Arthur as the Dark-Age equivalent of Montgomery. He was then about forty-five, and lived on for another twenty years. Unfortunately, his allies bickered among themselves; he was wounded fatally at the Battle of Camlan, probably on Hadrian's Wall. Legend has it that he was taken to *Glastonbury to die, and secretly buried there in the Abbey grounds, so that the Saxons could not desecrate his grave. The legend may well be true — in 1190, monks located a stone slab with a leaden cross inscribed: 'Here lies buried the renowned King Arthur in the Isle of Avalon.' Underneath was an enormous coffin containing a huge male skeleton, the head smashed with a heavy blow, and a female skeleton, assumed to be that of Guinevere. The Saxons reached Glastonbury about 568, by which time Arthur had been dead for three decades.

Within a century of his death, Welsh poems were describing his exploits. The popularity of the legends among the Celts was undoubtedly due to the belief that Arthur would rise again and drive all foreigners out of Britain. (In 1155 Hugh of Laon described how he came to Bodmin, and how his servant came to blows with a Cornishman who assured them that Arthur was still alive.) The *Grail legends again added mystical and religious overtones to the story. The sword Excalibur may well also have existed; it would have been a short Roman sword. The later legends of Arthur, like Malory's *Le Morte Darthur*, must be regarded as entirely fictional. CW

Atlantis

The story of the 'lost continent of Atlantis' is told in two of Plato's dialogues, the *Timaeus* and *Critias*. Critias — a real person — claims the story of Atlantis was told to Solon by Egyptian priests. The tale describes how there had been a great continent in the Atlantic, 'beyond the Pillars of Hercules', containing a remarkable civilization which had flourished some 9,000 years earlier. Their armies conquered North Africa, including Egypt, and much of Europe. The Atlanteans accomplished great feats of engineering and architecture, and their major city was built in concentric rings around a temple of the sea-god Poseidon. It was destroyed by earthquakes and floods in a single day and night.

In both dialogues, it seems that Plato believes the story. There is a wealth of precise detail that would be unnecessary were it intended as a parable; besides which the tale cannot be regarded in any way as an illustration of Plato's philosophical arguments.

In 1882 Ignatius Donnelly inaugurated the modern interest in Atlantis with *Atlantis, the Antediluvian World*, in which he examines flood legends and archaeological evidence. *Blavatsky insisted that the Atlantean civilization had really existed.

The modern theory that has captured most attention is that of A.G. Galanopoulos, who excavated on the island of Santorini (Thera), north of Crete. Around 1500 BC Santorini was destroyed by a tremendous volcanic explosion, followed by a tidal wave, which must have depopulated the northern coast of Crete and many of the smaller Mediterranean islands. Galanopoulos points out that, if all Plato's figures are divided by ten — including the 9,000 years — then they fit the island of Santorini and the city it once contained. He believes the error arose from the mistake of an Egyptian copyist who confused the symbol for 100 with the symbol for 1,000. His theory has been welcomed with joy by the tourist board of Santorini.

Yet another recent discovery suggests that Plato may have been correct after all. In the 1960s Charles Hapgood became interested in medieval navigation charts. In the Library of Congress he found a map dated 1531 which showed the Antarctic coast free of ice. Samples from the sea bottom had revealed that Antarctica had been frozen solid since about 6,000 years ago, so it seemed possible that the original of the map had been made before then. But long-distance seafaring did not begin until 2,000 years later. Hapgood asked his students to undertake an extended 'project', studying the medieval maps known as portolans. His conclusion, announced in *Maps of the Ancient Sea Kings*, was that there is abundant evidence for the existence of a worldwide maritime civilization thousands of years before the Egyptians or the Babylonians. He never suggests, at any point, that this civilization is the lost Atlantis; yet he is inclined to believe that it was destroyed so completely that few traces remain. One map studied by Hapgood's pupils shows a landbridge across the Bering Straits — a bridge that has not existed for some 30,000 years.

Some of his evidence comes from China. A map dated 1137 shows the same techniques as the portolans and the famous Piri Re'is map (discovered in 1929 in the Topkapi Palace, Constantinople). But even Plato had not suggested that the Atlanteans had reached China.

On the other hand, the Maya of South America have their own legends of a continent, Mu, which disappeared beneath the waves of the Pacific. The name seems to have been invented by a French scholar, the Abbé Brasseur, who believed he had succeeded in translating ancient Mayan books in the 1860s (it is now generally accepted that his translations were largely wishful thinking). In the 1920s James Churchward began writing a series of books purporting to reveal secret evidence (from ancient Indian documents) about Mu, but internal evidence suggests that most of his facts were invented.

In the mid-nineteenth century scientists trying to account for the resemblance between fossils found in India and South Africa suggested that there had once been a great continent, called Lemuria (after the lemur, a squirrel-like mammal found in both countries), linking the two. Modern explanations rely upon the process of continental drift: the two landmasses were adjacent some 180 million years ago.

Again, Blavatsky took over the idea, as did *Steiner. Hapgood's 'worldwide maritime civilization' sounds as much like Mu or Lemuria as Atlantis.

The latest instalment of the saga moves the scene back to the Atlantic. In 1968 airline pilots photographed what appeared to be underwater buildings off the coast of Bimini. (Edgar Cayce had prophesied that Atlantis would begin to rise again in 1968 or '69.) Undersea exploration in the area seemed to reveal the remains of ancient roads on the ocean floor. Other 'sightings' include great walls, pyramids, and even circles of standing stones like Stonehenge. Yet none of these sightings has been positively confirmed; and sceptics insist that the 'Bimini roads' and walls are natural features (they say the same of the 100-mile 'wall' that runs under the sea off the coast of Venezuela). In 1975 a team of oceanographers announced that they were now convinced that there is a sunken block of continent in the mid-Atlantic. The enormous depths involved make confirmation difficult, and the arguments continue.

Yet modern evidence that *ancient Man was rather more sophisticated than we once believed seems to make Plato's myths and Hapgood's theories altogether more plausible. CW

Book of the Dead

Both the Egyptian and Tibetan Books of the Dead are intended as 'instruction manuals' to guide the soul through the perils that it encounters immediately after death. The Egyptian Book consists of scrolls found in tombs dating from *c* 1600–1300 BC, and of texts found on tomb walls of earlier date. It assumes the *ka* (or spirit body) will spend the whole of the night after death on its way to the underworld, and will encounter en route various perils: *demons in the form of crocodiles, beetles, serpents, etc. The deceased identifies with many gods: 'I am the Fire-god, the divine brother of the Fire-god, I am Osiris the brother of Isis ...' The actual title is *The Book of Coming Forth by Day* — an allusion to the safe emergence of the spirit into the underworld the next morning.

The Tibetan Book, the *Bardo Thodol*, is

a series of Buddhist texts which a priest is intended to read to the dying; it aims to allow the spirit to become liberated from the snares of this world, and to achieve *reincarnation. Huxley took it sufficiently seriously to make its descriptions the basis of the after-death experience of a character in *Time Must Have a Stop*.

From the viewpoint of speculative parapsychology, the most interesting thing about both Books is that their descriptions of 'entities' encountered 'outside the body' sound remarkably like those of similar entities encountered in *out-of-the-body experiences.   CW

Dinosaurs, Extinction of the

About 65 million years ago, at the end of the Cretaceous, the dinosaurs rather suddenly died out. For many million years they had ruled the Earth, and they were still evolving new forms rapidly; so it seems unlikely that they were merely an evolutionary dead end. Similarly, it seems improbable that they died out owing to competition from their successors, the mammals: these had emerged from reptilian stock at about the same time as the dinosaurs, and so would presumably have ousted their reptilian rivals some considerable time earlier.

Moreover, at the time of their extinction the dinosaurs seem to have been a flourishing, evolutionarily active group — for example, during the Cretaceous new herbivorous species had evolved to take advantage of the vegetational changes then taking place.

Why, then, did they become extinct? One generally accepted explanation is that the world became too cold for them: there is evidence that there was an overall cooling in the late-Cretaceous climate.

Very recent researches seem to indicate that about 65 million years ago the Earth was hit by an extremely large meteorite. Every 150–200 million years, the Earth (and, of course, the rest of the Solar System) passes through one of the Galaxy's spiral arms; in these regions there is a very much higher concentration of cosmic debris than between the arms. That the Earth should suffer extensive meteoritic bombardment at such times is to be expected. And if a very large body hit the Earth then the impact could be expected to throw up a column of debris which would stay in the upper atmosphere for a considerable length of time — the same sort of thing happened after Krakatoa and the *Tunguska event — and this layer of drifting debris, by blocking off much of the Sun's light, would cool surface temperatures. No suitable crater has been found — but this might be because the meteorite landed in the ocean. One should remember that the end of the Cretaceous saw the extinction of other creatures — ammonoids, ichthyosaurs, pterosaurs, and various bivalves and gastropods. So it would seem likely that whatever caused the extinction of the dinosaurs was responsible also for these other extinctions. This would suggest that we must look for a cause whose effect was worldwide, experienced by both marine and terrestrial organisms — yet which was survived by most!

Solving this mystery must be important. The dinosaurs dominated the Earth for over 100 million years, yet their demise was rapid; Man has existed, so far, for less than 4 million years. We cannot yet be said to be a well established creature.   JG

Elements, Aristotelian

To us, the concepts of atoms and of elements are inseparable — carbon is different from nitrogen because carbon atoms are different from nitrogen atoms, and so on. That matter was made up of atoms (*a-tomos*, cannot be cut), ultimate and undividable particles, is an idea generally attributed to Leucippus and Democritus (both fifth century BC): atoms could combine in different ways to produce the diversity of materials we observe. Nearly 2,500 years later, Dalton was to show that the principle was correct.

Aristotle rejected atomism for the idea that matter consisted essentially of four qualities: dry, cold, wet and hot. These combined to give the four elements: earth (dry and cold), water (cold and wet), air (wet and hot) and fire (hot and dry). As could be seen, earth was the heaviest, above it lying water, then air, and finally fire, whose natural tendency was to rise towards the heavens, which were formed of a fifth element, the incorruptible aether.

The theory lay at the heart of Aristotelian cosmology (see *unorthodox cosmologies). For example, the Earth lay at the centre of the cosmos because it was formed of the heaviest element; if not at the centre it would be falling towards it because it was so heavy, leaving surface objects behind! (See also *humours.) JG

Fertility Religion

When European travellers of the seventeenth and eighteenth centuries visited India and other Far East countries, they were often startled and embarrassed to see temples adorned with phalluses, breasts, and gods proudly displaying their sexual characteristics; they no doubt felt that these non-Christian foreigners 'knew no better'. Yet if they had chosen to look in the right places they would have found just as much immodesty in Europe. Many old churches display carvings showing a crouching naked woman with outsize genitals (Sheila-na-gigs); even the maypole symbolizes an erect penis.

As anthropology developed into a science in the course of the late nineteenth century, it became clear that sexual imagery plays an important part in all ancient religion. The book that made this clear was Frazer's *The Golden Bough*. He wanted to know why, in Roman times, a man with a sword — a priest of Diana — guarded a tree in a sacred grove at Nemi; if a runaway slave could kill him, he himself became the priest of the Moon goddess. To explain this curious rite, Frazer made a wide study of primitive religion. He recognized the widespread importance of the priest who ensures the fertility of the Earth; and he pointed out also the universality of myths about the god who is slain, buried, and rises again in the spring. In that age such an observation was regarded as almost blasphemous, since it appeared to bracket Jesus with Attis, Adonis, Osiris, etc.

In spite of his immense erudition, Frazer regarded all magic as superstition; but in criticizing *The Golden Bough* Andrew Lang made the important point that there are many people in the Scottish Highlands who possess 'second sight' and can cure warts, etc. But at least Frazer recognized the importance of the Moon goddess to magic.

In 1921, Margaret Murray's *The Witch Cult in Western Europe* took the thinking a startling stage further. Studying famous witchcraft trials, she concluded that witchcraft was, in fact, the ancient fertility religion, which had been forced by Christianity to 'go underground', but which persisted in rural areas. In fact, she must have known of a remarkable work called *Aradia, or the Gospel of the Witches*, translated by an anthropologist, Charles Leland, and published in 1899: in Italy, the country in which *Aradia* originated, witchcraft is still called *la vecchia religione*, 'the old religion'.

According to *Aradia*, Diana had an incestuous affair with her brother Lucifer and gave birth to Aradia (or Herodias); when the people were heavily oppressed, Diana sent Aradia down to Earth to teach the oppressed the secrets of magic to strike back at the aristocracy and the priests. According to Murray, the witches worshipped the horned god Pan, who became the Christian *Devil. In recent years the notion of witchcraft as worship of the Earthmother was popularized by Gerald Gardner in *Witchcraft Today*, the book most responsible for the modern 'witchcraft revival'.

What now seems clear is that *ancient Man worshipped the Moon; he undoubtedly believed that the Moon could influence the Earth's fertility. The earliest evidence of primitive religion consists of 'Venus figurines', statuettes of women with enlarged thighs, breasts and buttocks; many of these fertility symbols date back more than 20,000 years.

The fertility of the Earth and human fertility are inextricably intermingled. For example, the mistletoe, whose berries the slave at Nemi had to pluck, represents human semen, and was the sacred plant of the Celtic druids. The custom of kissing under the mistletoe at Christmas is an example of the 'Christianization' of a pagan ceremony, as is the dance around the maypole at the beginning of spring.

In pre-Christian times, the chief representatives of the 'old religion' were the Celts, a people as remarkable as the Greeks or Romans. They swept across Europe in the sixth and fifth centuries BC, and inaugurated the Iron Age. Their priests were druids who worshipped in sacred groves and performed sacrifices by burning (the flames symbolized the Sun). The Celts chose hilltop sites for their forts and some of their places of worship. Oddly enough, as T.C. Lethbridge pointed out, the Christians took over many of these sites for their churches, usually named after St Michael, the traditional enemy of Lucifer (the Sun god). It is, as he added, as if the ground had some traditional sacred power — a power that can be detected still by the *dowsing rod.

Murray's theories about witchcraft and the old religion are now widely discredited — indeed, even her admirers will admit that in books like *The Divine King in England* (which insists that half the kings of England were really priests of the old religion) she went too far.

Yet it is impossible to study such popular customs as floral dances and harvest festivals without realizing that they represent a survival of the pre-Christian religion of Diana. In *The Roots of Witchcraft* Michael Harrison mentions that when Professor Geoffrey Webb was Secretary of the Royal Commission on Historical Monuments he discovered that many altars in ancient churches contained stone phalluses. Webb estimated that such fertility symbols could be found in 90 per cent of churches built before the Black Death, which was also the beginning of the witch craze (see *witchcraft). Harrison also quotes the Bishop's Register of Exeter, which tells how, in the fourteenth century, the Bishop of Exeter caught the monks of Frithelstock Priory worshipping a statue of 'the unchaste Diana' in the woods — the term 'unchaste' clearly indicating the connection between Moon-worship and sex. The monks were made to destroy it.

It seems clear that the full significance of the old fertility religion is still not understood. If Jaynes is correct in his belief that the brain of ancient Man differed from that of modern Man (see page 17), it seems conceivable that our 'left-brain' approach makes it almost impossible for us to understand the relation between our ancestors and the Earth. But Robert Graves' remarkable *The White Goddess* offers some fascinating hints. (See also *primitive magic.)

CW

Glastonbury

With the publication of John Michell's *The View Over Atlantis* in 1969 (see *ley lines), Glastonbury suddenly became a modern 'cult' centre; throughout the 1970s it was invaded regularly every summer by crowds of enthusiastic hippies and ley-hunters. Michell had pointed out that Glastonbury is one of the most important junctions of 'ley lines' in the UK.

Glastonbury Tor, with its ruined church tower of St Michael on top, is certainly a striking landmark rising 500ft above sea-level. 'Glastonbury' means Isle of Glass — it was once surrounded by water. Remains of a Celtic settlement have been found nearby. In *King Arthur's Avalon*, Geoffrey Ashe (who himself lives in Glastonbury) points out that Glastonbury's alternative name, Avalon, means a Celtic rendezvous of the dead — evidence that the Tor was probably a Celtic religious site before it became the Christian centre of England. A spiral path winds round the Tor, and a spiral is a familiar Celtic symbol which seems to be associated with the forces of the Earth.

Legend asserts that St Joseph of Arimathea brought the *Grail to Glastonbury, and also planted a thorn tree (which can still be seen in the Abbey grounds). It asserts also that Queen Guinevere was kidnapped by Melwas, King of Somerset, and King Arthur freed her by besieging Glastonbury — later, he was buried there. There was a monastery on the site of the present Abbey at this period. When the

Saxons overran Glastonbury (about 568), they had been converted to Christianity, so it continued as a major Christian site. Under St Dunstan, who became Abbot in the tenth century, it became a centre of the revival of learning after the Dark Ages.

In about 1180 Henry II was told by a Welsh bard that *Arthur was buried at Glastonbury; he passed on this information to the Abbot, specifying the site. As a result, the 'grave of Arthur' was found, and Glastonbury thereafter became a centre of pilgrimage for all Europe — and, incidentally, its Abbey one of the richest in Europe. (Some historians regard the finding of the grave as a publicity stunt engineered by the monks, but it seems that it really happened.) The Abbey succumbed to Henry VIII's dissolution of the monasteries in 1539.

From 1914 until the mid-1920s, the composer Rutland Boughton tried to turn Glastonbury into a British Bayreuth, with an annual festival; the most successful composition to emerge was *The Immortal Hour*. The 'occultist' Dion Fortune made Glastonbury her home for many years — her house is now occupied by Ashe. In *The Ancient Wisdom* Ashe speculates at length on the problem of the location of Shambala, the 'spiritual navel' of the world according to Tibetan mythology; but he omits to mention an extraordinary comment contained in Stephen Jenkins' important 'geomantic' study *The Undiscovered Country*. Jenkins, who studied in Tibet, says that high-ranking lamas told him that Shambala was located in England at a site called Glastonbury. CW

Gog and Magog

Statues of these two mythical giants stand outside the Guildhall in London. According to Geoffrey of Monmouth (see *Arthur), a Trojan warrior named Brutus came to the shores of England after the fall of Troy and found the country peopled by 18ft giants, including Goemagot or Gogmagog, who was slain by a hero named Corineus, the 'founder' of Cornwall. Gogmagog later became two giants.

The hills behind Cambridge are called the Gogmagog Hills, and include an important Celtic fort at Wandlebury which is connected with a legend of a giant. Lethbridge heard that the figure of a giant had once been cut into the hillside below Wandlebury Camp, and in autumn 1954 he tried to locate the figure by driving a long metal rod into the turf and noting where it was less deep than elsewhere. He ended by re-creating three hillside figures — a woman on horseback with a chariot, a giant warrior with a sword, and a man. The woman, he came to believe, was the Celtic Earth goddess (Magog, or Ma-god, mother-god). His theory, advanced in *Gogmagog*, caused much controversy; it also led him to begin a series of investigations into 'ancient religion' and Earth forces that is expounded in eight remarkable books, beginning with *Witches* and ending with the posthumous *The Power of the Pendulum*. CW

Grail

It may come as a surprise that originally the Grail was by no means 'holy' in the Christian sense. Long before Christ the idea of the Grail existed, although of course the object itself did not take the form of the chalice used by Christ at the Last Supper and later used to catch his blood as he hung from the cross. Indeed, it was originally a *fertility symbol, and as such took several forms — for example, a lance (male principle), a dish (female principle), or even the two together.

It seems that the Grail was adopted like many other pagan ideas (although not officially) by the early Christian Church; it was said to have been brought to Britain by Joseph of Arimathea. It became widely regarded as a symbol of an unattainable ideal, of purity and virtue, an object that could be gazed upon only by the pure-hearted. This was especially the case after it had been incorporated into the Arthurian cycle of legends — it has even been identified with a (hypothetical) ritual drinking-vessel belonging to *Arthur but stolen by his foes. The quality of chivalrousness was added to the catalogue of virtues required by anyone seeking to find the Grail; of the Round Table knights, only the unwordly Percival was successful in the quest.

That the Grail is a powerful symbol is evidenced by its numerous appearances in literature — Chrétien de Troyes's *Conte del Graal*, Wolfram von Eschenbach's *Parzival, Titurel* (partly written by von Eschenbach) and Thomas Malory's *Le Morte Darthur* from the Middle Ages, and T.H. White's *The Once and Future King* from this century are a few of many, many examples. But I would suggest that it is more than a mere symbol. Voltaire said: 'If God did not exist one would need to invent him.' This is often (deliberately) revised to: 'If God had not existed, Man would have created him.' And the same can be said of the Grail. There is a very powerful, creative, constructive force in Man's mental make-up: it is compounded of such characteristics as curiosity, the urge to see what is on the other side of the next hill, and charity (in its purest sense). In short, the Grail symbolizes a complex of Man's positive attributes — even Hitler recognized this, although his list of 'positive attributes' might differ from ours.

This complex exists; there can be no question of that. And so — in a much more real sense than if it were merely a mystical object — the Grail, too, exists. JG

Humours

The four humours were a concept of ancient and medieval medicine. The humours were bodily fluids corresponding to the Aristotelian *elements — earth = melancholy (or black bile); water = phlegm; air = choler (or yellow bile), and fire = blood — and it was thought necessary to maintain a balance between these in order to ensure a person's health. If one displayed symptoms of an imbalance in favour of one humour one would be treated to its opposite (this kind of medicine is known as enantiopathy); for example, if you suffered a fever you would be placed in a cold, draughty room, and this killed you or cured you.

Enantiopathy, in modified form, is still in use today. JG

Ley Lines

On 30 June 1921 a brewer named Alfred Watkins was travelling on horseback near Bredwardine, on the Welsh border, when he observed that footpaths and farm tracks appeared to form an interesting network, connecting old churches, ancient mounds, standing stones, and other 'sacred' sites. He was familiar with *The Green Roads of England* (1914) by R. Hippesley Cox, which had argued that the pre-Christian Celts had a highly developed system of travel ways. Cox had also suggested that *megalithic monuments like Stonehenge were astronomical observatories, a view now widely accepted.

Watkins believed that the ancient trackways can be easily located — even when they have vanished — by studying maps and connecting up known pathways with sacred sites; he argued that it was astonishing how often such 'connections' formed straight lines across a map. He called them 'ley lines', arguing that a ley (or lea) was a grassy track across country. He believed that they were ancient trade routes, and expounded his view in *The Old Straight Track*. Antiquarians indignantly rejected him as a crank; but his work gained so many adherents that a Straight Track Postal Club was founded to report on newly discovered leys. Towards the end of his life (he died in 1935), he was beginning to find his own trade-route theory inadequate, and speculated that leys could have some religious significance.

After World War II, by which time leys had been more than half forgotten, a retired solicitor named Guy Underwood decided to test a theory that barrows and other prehistoric sites were crossed by underground streams (see *dowsing). His researches led him to conclude that his theory was correct. But he also found that his dowsing rod responded to another force, which seemed to be some kind of magnetic force within the Earth. In sacred sites like Stonehenge it formed a kind of whirlpool or spiral; and it often ran across country in straight tracks. These tracks also seemed to be used by animals for homing. In his important *Pattern of the*

Past he suggested there is a close connection between these underground 'magnetic' forces and the religion of *ancient Man (see *fertility religion). Examination of the White Horse of Uffington, a Celtic hill figure, convinced him that its strange outline is defined almost exactly by 'geodetic lines'.

A younger student of ley lines, John Michell, suggested that the leys are purely 'magnetic' in character, and also pointed out that their nodes, or crossing points, are often associated with *UFO sightings. His *The View Over Atlantis* quickly gained an immense cult following, and renewed interest in leys. He also pointed out that the Chinese have their own equivalent of ley lines (with which the science of *feng-shui* (wind and water) is concerned), which they regard as sacred. 'Atlantis' is Michell's own term for the ancient knowledge system concerning these forces. His theories link closely with those of Underwood and Jaynes (see page 28). CW

Megalithic Monuments

The term 'megalithic monuments' must be stretched to include not only 'temples' like Stonehenge, Avebury and Carnac, but also mounds and barrows like Silbury Hill, Castle Dor and the Ohio Snake mound — as well as thousands of 'standing stones' in fields all over the world. In the 1890s, Norman Lockyer suggested that the purpose of great circles like Stonehenge was astronomical; the stones were intended as 'markers' to predict the movements of the Sun and Moon. In the early 1960s Gerald Hawkins, a professor of astronomy at Boston, fed the complex data about Stonehenge into a computer and was surprised to find the result unambiguous: Stonehenge was a solar *and* lunar calendar. Most circles of standing stones contain 19 stones; there is an eclipse of the Moon or Sun every 19 years. The exact figure is 18.61 years, so a more accurate calendar would cover a treble period, nearly 56 years; and the outer ditch of Stonehenge contains 56 'Aubrey Holes'. Alexander Thom has devoted many years to demonstrating how the megalithic circles were used as calendars, and works like his *Megalithic Lunar Observatories*, at first largely dismissed, are now widely accepted.

But what is the purpose of the thousands of single standing stones? Both Underwood and Michell (see *ley lines) advanced the view that they are intended as markers for places of exceptional 'magnetic force' — Underwood believed that *ancient Man regarded such places as sacred. These single stones are often associated with *healing. Like healing wells, they derive their power from the Earth (Amerindians also have healing stones, against which patients rub themselves). It has even been suggested, on an analogy with *acupuncture, that the standing stones may be intended to somehow stimulate or tap the force at these points. All these theories depend, of course, upon the notion that the Earth's magnetic field has a direct influence on health and vitality.

The 'mounds' seem rather more mysterious. For example, the purpose of Silbury Hill, the largest man-made mound in Europe, has been a matter of debate for centuries. But a solution put forward by Michael Dames in *The Silbury Treasure: The Great Goddess Rediscovered* sounds highly convincing. Dames believes that the hill, with its oddly shaped moat, resembles a woman about to give birth in a squatting position (the position of Sheila-na-gigs). He argues that, at harvest time, the reflection of the rising Moon in the moat would give the impression of the baby's head emerging from between her legs — a theory that is certainly in line with the views on the 'ancient religion' held by Lethbridge, Margaret Murray and others. (See *fertility religion.) CW

Mythical Monsters

Although stories of mythological monsters seem grotesque to us now, they had roots in political, historical and religious analogies. The Furies, for example, can be interpreted as pangs of conscience. And the Chimaera may have symbolized the seasons of a sacred year: the head of the lion representing spring; the body of a goat, summer; and the tail of a serpent, winter.

Mount Chimaera was a volcanic mountain in Lycia, which explains the fire-breathing power of the monster slain by Bellerophon. The constant reference to animal heads may reflect the masks worn by kings, or their combatants, in contests fought at their election.

Envy and jealousy are further ingredients. Falling in love with the sea nymph Scylla, Glaucus appealed to Circe for help, but she used her powers instead to eliminate her rival, pouring the juice of poisoned herbs into the waters where Scylla swam. The result was an appalling combination of a beautiful girl's face with a body composed of the heads of six wild dogs which grabbed at passing seamen and ate them. Even so, Odysseus found her preferable to the dangerous whirlpool of Charybdis, daughter of Poseidon and Gaea, who had been cast into the sea by Zeus.

The Gorgons were similar sea monsters: they had snakes for hair and teeth like tusks. Medusa, the only one of the three sisters who was mortal, had a look so terrible it could turn a man to stone — Perseus, who decapitated her, was able to use the severed head to literally petrify his foes. He had, on his quest to slay Medusa, forced the assistance of another trio of ugly women, the Graeae, who shared but one eye and one tooth between them.

The Cyclopes of the *Odyssey*, giant sons of Poseidon with a single eye in the middle of the forehead, dwelt near Mount Etna and were thus said to be the craftsmen who made Zeus' thunderbolts. Odysseus killed one by thrusting a red-hot olive pole into the eye, twisting it 'till the blood boiled up round the burning wood'.

Among the constant symbols are snakes for fertility and the bull for strength. The Minotaur, half-man, half-bull, is one of the most fascinating and significant of all mythological monsters. One story has it that Minos, son of Zeus and King of Crete, boasted that the gods would answer his prayer that a bull might emerge from the sea. This happened, but the white bull that swam ashore was so beautiful that Minos spared it the intended sacrifice. Poseidon, insulted, took his revenge by encouraging Pasiphae, the wife of Minos, to fall in love with the bull. The proud animal took little notice of her until the resident engineer at the palace, Daedalus, designed a dummy cow into which Pasiphae slipped. The result was the Minotaur, with the body of a man but the head of a bull, confined in a labyrinth below the palace of Knossos.

After Minos conquered Athens to avenge his son, he demanded the annual sacrifice of seven young men and seven virgin girls to placate the monster. One of these was Theseus, with whom Minos' daughter, Ariadne, fell in love, promising, 'I will help you to kill my half-brother the Minotaur, if I may return to Athens with you as your wife.' She gave him a ball of twine, which he rolled down the corridors of the labyrinth until he reached the sleeping monster. Having slain it in the name of Poseidon, he was able to make his way out by following the string.

There are other myths with the same elements of revenge and unfaithfulness: Demeter was turned into a mare but failed to deceive Poseidon, who transformed himself into a stallion and covered her, fathering the nymph Despoena and the wild horse Arion — little wonder that she was known afterwards as 'Demeter the Fury'. Minos' father, Zeus, seduced his mother Europa in the guise of a beautiful white bull, and adopted other animal disguises for similar seductions.

There are plausible 'explanations' of the myths. The 'consummation' between the bull and Pasiphae could be a ritual marriage between a Moon-priestess wearing cow's horns and the king with the mask of a bull — the union of Moon and Sun. Also, the search for the Minotaur might have been an Athenian raid led by Theseus to kill the king, pursuing him down the corridors of Knossos. There was also at Knossos a courtyard with a maze set in the mosaic which was used for ritual dancing. To begin with, the dancers evoked the love-play of the partridge, but this was replaced by the cult of the bull. The mythical ball of twine could represent the string that kept the dancers apart (as still practised today, although sometimes with a handkerchief).

Certainly the bull was celebrated in the frescoes found by Sir Arthur Evans at Knossos. One depicts a Cretan bullring in which brave and certainly acrobatic young men seize the bull by the horns and somersault over him. Robert Graves has suggested, 'This was evidently a religious rite: perhaps here also the performers represented the planets.' As he writes elsewhere: 'Four thousand years ago the Chimaera can have seemed no more bizarre than any religious, heraldic or commercial emblem does today.'

Clearly other mythologies, too, possess tales of monsters — often to the same purpose.

In addition, there are the remarkably widespread tales of unicorns, mermaids and dragons. The unicorn, which took the form of a pure white horse with a straight horn growing from its head, was in medieval Europe closely linked to virginity (it would obey a virgin's call: the symbolism of the horn seems clear) and to Christ; it is found also in Indian, Islamic and Chinese art and literature. Mermaids were like beautiful women but with the tails of fishes, and like the Sirens lured men to their deaths — although there are some stories of their mating with men. One theory suggests that the mermaid myth is based on the sea cow (the order named, significantly, Sirenia). But most 'popular' of these are dragons: in Europe, terrifying, fire-breathing, bat-winged scaly creatures such as the one St George had to cope with; in the Far East, smaller, wingless and benevolent creatures. That the image of the dragon is still a powerful one is evidenced by recent bestselling books about them, including a series of novels by Anne McCaffrey. DF

Pyramids

The pyramids of Egypt are the tombs of kings — with one possible but notable exception, the Great Pyramid of Cheops at Gizeh (Giza).

The ancient Egyptians seem to have believed that a man's spirit would continue living after death only as long as his body was preserved — hence the practice of embalming. The earliest tombs were simply underground vaults, carved out of rock, and reached by a shaft. This was in the 'prehistoric' period in Egypt, beginning c 4500 BC. Then, during the first and second dynasties (3188–2515), kings began to build over the entrance to the shaft large rectangular buildings, mastabas, which might be regarded as the ancient equivalent of chapels in which relatives could pray for the dead. Around 2800, Zoser (or Djoser) had his builders construct another, smaller mastaba on top of the first, then another on top of that, then still another ... finally forming a six-step pyramid; this was at Saqqura. Other kings of the third dynasty built pyramids, but many never got beyond the substructure stage. Huni, last king of the dynasty, began a step pyramid at Medun, and seems to have decided to fill in the sides to make it a true pyramid; but the sides were too steep and it collapsed — the rubble still lies around its base. The completion of the pyramid is sometimes attributed to his successor, Snefru, who also built the so-called 'bent pyramid', whose angle changes half-way up the sides. Kurt Mendelssohn concluded in the 1960s that the two pyramids were under construction at the same time, and that the collapse of the Medun pyramid led the builders to make the angle of the bent pyramid less steep. But if so, they could not both have been intended as tombs for the same man, particularly as he built yet a third further north. Mendelssohn has suggested that the real purpose was to unite many tribes into a nation by involving them in some great common labour.

The Great Pyramid of Cheops (or Khufu) has always been something of a mystery. When Herodotus visited Egypt around 440 BC (by which time the pyramid was already more than 2,000 years old), he was told that it had been built on the orders of a wicked pharaoh called Cheops who closed all the temples; Herodotus adds that it was constructed on an underground island. In the ninth century AD, Al Mamun, son of Haroun al Raschid (of *Arabian*

Nights fame), heard a legend that the Great Pyramid contained a secret chamber full of ancient maps; so he ordered his men to tunnel into the masonry. After hacking their way in for 100ft, they found a tunnel which led up to a forgotten entrance in the north side of the pyramid, and which led down to a tiny room full of debris. In the ceiling of the passage was a hole which had contained a prism-shaped stone; it looked like the entrance to another rising passage, so the Arabs hacked their way around the granite plug that sealed it. They did find a passage, blocked at intervals by two more granite plugs and one made of limestone. Beyond these they found a horizontal passage leading to a small, empty room. Retracing their steps, they found yet another passage, rising upward. When they scrambled up into this, they found themselves in the most impressive part so far, a vast gallery that stretched 28ft above them. At the top they found an antechamber, then a huge chamber of polished granite blocks. It contained nothing but an empty sarcophagus. This room became known as the King's Chamber, and the smaller room below as the Queen's Chamber. This, it seemed, was all the Great Pyramid contained, an empty sarcophagus — a sarcophagus that must always have been empty, since it was obvious that they were the first to break through the various granite plugs.

Then what was its purpose? Arabs of later generations stripped the pyramid of its shining casing of limestone. In 1638, John Greaves discovered a kind of well or shaft leading down from the passage near the Queen's Chamber, but it had been blocked with rubble from above. Two centuries later, it was discovered that this shaft led back into the original descending passage.

Eventually, two tiny 'attics' were discovered above the King's Chamber — apparently intended simply to reduce the immense pressure of stone on its ceiling — and also two air vents leading into the Chamber.

In 1798, Napoleon arrived in Egypt, and French scholars began to study the mystery of the pyramid. Edmé-François Jomard measured it accurately, and also noted that its four sides point to the four points of the compass; diagonals drawn from north-east and north-west of the pyramid neatly enclosed the Nile Delta. But why all this fanatical accuracy? In the 1830s John Taylor realized that the length of the whole base, divided by twice the height, equalled π, which suggested to him that the ancient Egyptians had chosen these measurements to represent half a globe. This led him to assume that the pyramid had been built to incorporate various divine revelations, the architect having been guided by God. This has given rise to a whole crank literature on the pyramid, measuring its various passages in inches, and finding in these lengths representations of various important dates in world history. Piazzi Smyth, Astronomer Royal of Scotland, even worked out that the Second Coming would occur in 1911.

The man who, it is now widely believed, solved the problem of the pyramid was R.A. Proctor, who noted an observation by Proclus that the pyramid had been used as an astronomical observatory *before* its completion. Several Arab historians had stated that it was designed as an 'observatory'. But how? An observatory — like Stonehenge (see *megalithic monuments) — needs 'markers', and the Great Pyramid is smooth. But *before its completion* it could have made the perfect observatory, if the Grand Gallery were used as a 'telescope', with its top left open to observe the stars above.

The first step in building such an observatory would be to align the building on true North; in fact, the original descending passage *is* aligned on true North — it points at the pole star. But in the days when the Pyramid was built, about 2500 BC, our pole star, Polaris, did not occupy its present position in the sky, due to the 'wobble' of the Earth's axis; the Egyptians would have had to use Thuban, which would have led them to slope the tunnel at an angle of 26° 17′ up from the horizon — which happens to be precisely the angle it *is* sloped at.

So, according to Proctor, the Egyptians

completed the pyramid as far as the Grand Gallery, and then used the pyramid to construct, with unparalleled accuracy, a map of the heavens and a calendar telling them the precise times of rising and the positions of various stars.

Of course, the observatory would have become useless once the builders had got beyond the top of the Grand Gallery (which is now in the heart of the Pyramid). But this would have taken ten years or so — ample time for the astronomers to make their star tables and maps.

This also solves the other mystery of why no skeletons were found inside. For the granite plugs that blocked the ascending passage were slid into place *from above*, sealing the chambers off from the entrance passage. So how did the workmen escape? The 'well' was also filled with rubble from above, so this was not the 'escape hatch'. But, if we assume that the plugs were slid into place after the priests had achieved their purpose, the problem vanishes: the passage was sealed while the 'telescope' was still open; then the remainder of the Pyramid was constructed — which would imply also that, in spite of the empty sarcophagus, it was never intended to be used as a tomb.

And *why* should they have gone to so much trouble to map the sky? The only star that mattered to them was Sirius, which rose behind the Sun when the Nile itself began to rise, and thus became the basis of the calendar. But then we also have to take into account the evidence that Norman Lockyer offered in *The Dawn of Astronomy*, that the temples themselves — long before the Great Pyramid was built — were 'star clocks'. If the Egyptians were observing the stars for 1,000 years before the Great Pyramid, they would have noted the odd fact that the Earth's axis 'wobbles', causing the 'precession of the equinoxes'. The stars rise about twenty minutes later each year, so that a temple built in 4000 BC would be hopelessly inaccurate as a star clock a century later. But since the Egyptians did not know that the Earth rotates on its axis — they thought it was the centre of the Universe, and that the Sun revolved around it — it must have struck them as a sacred mystery that the stars were inconstant in such a regular manner.

They were a fanatically religious people. If the priests were to understand the mind of God, they had to understand the mechanism of the sky. And, if our basic premise about *ancient Man is correct, this was because they were also deeply concerned with the 'dark gods' of the Earth beneath their feet, and its strange influences.

Yet, if this view *is* correct, the building of the Great Pyramid also marks the beginning of a new epoch in human history — the rise of the 'bicameral mind', and the beginning of the self-division that now forms such an obstacle to human evolution. (See also *pyramid power.)   CW

Rennes-le-Château, Mystery of

Rennes-le-Château is a tiny village on the French side of the Pyrenees. In early centuries it was a prosperous town, known to the Phoenicians and the Romans, who called it Reddae. In the fourteenth century half the town was destroyed in a siege, and the plague carried off most of the rest of the inhabitants. Since then, Rennes-le-Château has been a mere village.

In 1885, the new priest there was a man of thirty-three called Bèrenger Saunière. He was something of a rebel, and had been sent to Rennes-le-Château — pretty well the end of the world — as a kind of punishment.

For the next three years, as his account books show, he was very poor indeed. Then, in 1888, he started to do some repairs to the church. Workmen lifted the top of the high altar, and discovered that one of the two pillars on which it rested was hollow, and that hidden inside were three wooden tubes containing rolls of parchment. The parchment seemed to be in some kind of code. Saunière tried to decode it, and showed them to the Bishop of Carcassonne, who sent him to Paris to consult experts at St Sulpice.

When Sauniére returned to Rennes-le-Château he was a rich man. No one knows where his wealth came from, and for years many people have investigated the mystery. He built the villagers a mountain road and a water tower, and had the church elaborately but strangely decorated with such oddities as an enormous lame demon carrying the font of holy water. Over the door he had the words 'dreadful is this place' inscribed.

The only clue is that, while in Paris, he had bought reproductions of two pictures — 'St Antony the Hermit' by Teniers and Poussin's 'Les Bergères d'Arcadie' ('The Shepherdesses of Arcadia').

The lame demon has been identified with Asmodeus, the guardian of King Solomon's legendary treasure. It has been speculated that the coded manuscript led Sauniére to a treasure — possibly the treasure of the Cathars, a heretical sect associated with this region, whose last adherents were burned alive in 1243 after being besieged at Montséguar. It is said that three men escaped carrying the 'treasure of the Cathars'. However, others believe this treasure was the holy books.

In recent years, Henry Lincoln, an English scholar, has thrown an interesting new light on the mystery. He has succeeded in decoding Sauniére's manuscript (or, rather, claims that it has been decoded for him by a computer), and also in discovering the hidden secrets of the two paintings by Teniers and Poussin — particularly the latter, which pictures a tomb close to the village of Rennes-le-Château. Lincoln is convinced that Sauniére's secret was a simple one. Rennes-le-Château was once called Aereda, and was an important centre of the Knights Templar, the order dedicated to guarding the Temple of Jerusalem. Lincoln has uncovered evidence that shows that the Templars were connected with an even more ancient secret order known as The Priory of Sion, also connected with the Temple at Jerusalem. There seems to be strong evidence that this secret society continued down the ages, and that the Rosicrucians, launched in the seventeenth century, were the Priory of Sion under another name. Sir Isaac Newton was one of the Grand Masters of the Rosicrucians, and the last Grand Master was the poet Jean Cocteau. In short, Sauniére discovered some secrets of the order of Rosicrucians, and the money he received came from them.

There is still a great deal of mystery involved. When Sauniére died, he made a confession that deeply shocked the priest who heard it. In 1910, his Bishop suspended him from his duties as a priest, but he continued to say Mass in a chapel he built himself. Was Sauniére, in fact, some kind of a devil-worshipper or, at least, a member of a secret magical order? Lincoln has left many questions unanswered, but has thrown an interesting new light on the secret order of *Rosicrucians. CW

Vitalism

This theory asserts that living material is somehow different from inorganic material, that the former possesses a vital principle or 'life force'. The idea dates back to Aristotle. Its first major setback came in 1828 when Wöhler showed that the organic compound urea, a main waste product of the body, could be synthesized using entirely inorganic chemicals. A further major blow came in the 1840s when Du Bois-Reymond showed that nerve impulses were akin to electric currents. The discoveries by Rubner in 1894 that the amount of energy extracted from food by the body obeyed the laws of thermodynamics, and by Buchner in 1896 that fermentation did not require the presence of living yeast cells dealt final death-blows to the traditional concept of vitalism.

More recently, however, it has been shown that living organisms *do* possess some kind of a 'life field' that dead ones do not. The nature of this field is not understood, but it seems that it can be observed by means of *Kirlian photography. This cannot be seen as a renaissance of vitalist ideas, however, since it seems certain that the life field results from the life of the organism, rather than being a necessary quality without which the organism would be dead. That said, there is considerable and occasionally persuasive evidence that the life field may survive the death of the organism, even if only for a short period; moreover, it has been claimed that before conception a potential life field, as it were, can be detected during ovulation. Nevertheless, it is easier to explain these phenomena in terms of the field being a property of living material rather than a motive force.

JG

Evolution: 1

In the Ancient World there was little real conception of the past, and even less of the future. This was probably because the rate of change was slow: one could (in theory) leave one's village and return a century later to find that, fundamentally, nothing had changed. There was a recognition that in the very remote past Man had not existed; but, since the instant of his creation, things had carried on very much as they were now. Some ideas of flux were to be found in the lives of the gods, but most of those changes had happened a long time ago. There was no conception that things evolve, a state of affairs that was to last for millennia — as late as the nineteenth century we have the suggestion that when God created the Earth he made it complete with fossils, in order to fool palaeontologists into believing in evolution.

From here on, in this book, we shall find evolutionary ideas appearing increasingly frequently, reaching their apotheosis in the final section, where we view some aspects of the astonishingly diverse forms our future physical, cultural and technological evolution may take.

JG

PART TWO

THE OCCULT AND MIRACULOUS

Introductory: 2

This and the following part of the book are concerned with the curious hinterland that lies between the subjective and the objective. *Alchemy is a case in point: it seems merely a primitive science based on superstition and ignorance; closer examination reveals that it is altogether more complex and interesting. The same thing applies to *witchcraft, *possession, *jinxes and curses, *ghosts, and magic. In every case, there proves to be 'more there than meets the eye'. The real problem is that it is extremely difficult to find some simple common denominator that enables us to explain them. The recognition that our right cerebral hemisphere is 'another person', and the suspicion that this person controls so-called paranormal experience, certainly goes a long way towards it. But then how do we explain the ability of wart charmers to perform their cures at a distance, without even meeting the person whose warts they intend to cure? How do we explain the fact that most wart charmers are not 'healers', in the sense of possessing thaumaturgic gifts, but have simply memorized a 'charm' — usually a passage from the Bible — which seems to work?

The one thing that seems clear is that there is something wrong with our paradigm — the basic picture of reality into which we try to fit these matters. And what is wrong with it is, oddly enough, the same thing that was wrong with that of the ancient alchemists and astrologers: we are too *literal-minded*. The alchemist believed certain chemical processes could turn lead into gold, or produce the elixir of life. Perhaps the greatest single step in the history of paranormal research was taken by those scientists who, in the late nineteenth century, realized that *poltergeists are not genuine 'ghosts' but emanate from the unconscious minds of disturbed adolescents. This also removed such matters as magic, witchcraft and possession from the realm of crude literalism, and made them more comprehensible to the scientific intellect. Yet we still lack a paradigm that could explain, for example, the mechanism of 'psychic projection' that enables *doppelgängers to be seen far from the physical body of the 'projector'. In *The Occult* I suggested that perhaps one of the most important underlying assumptions of 'occultism' is the notion of a 'psychic ether', rather like the luminiferous aether of nineteenth-century physics, but able to conduct psychic energies and impressions. This would certainly go a long way towards explaining doppelgängers and poltergeists; but it hardly seems to explain why some 'ghosts' are seen hanging around the scenes of their past lives, as if unaware that they are dead.

But the success of the split-brain theory and Lethbridge's 'field theory' of ghosts suggests that the 'new paradigm' could be closer than we think; one simple piece of information — about space or *time or the structure of matter — might provide the key that would make every psychical researcher clutch his forehead and say, 'Of *course*!' CW

Action at a Distance

Man has ever dreamt of being able to affect things or people at a distance. This is still evident among both primitive and sophisticated cultures today. For example, the Australian Aborigines have a number of devices for smiting enemies, one being the *munguni*, which comprises a bone, a string, and a sealed receptacle. Pointing the *munguni* at the victim, who may be many miles away, not only smites him with a deadly force but also draws some of his blood into the receptacle. Burning the *munguni* kills him; or you can torment him by simply warming it up from time to time.

The lure of action at a distance has given the fighters arrows, guns and ICBMs; it has encouraged research into psychokinesis (see *ESP); it has given rise to much effort to master magic; and it is one of the cluster of urges that may one day take us to the stars. JG

Alchemy

Of all the ancient 'occult' sciences, alchemy seems by far the most irrelevant, since it is based upon a proposition now known to be false — that 'base elements' can be changed into gold by purely chemical reactions.

It is true that various mystics, like Jacob Boehme, have seen alchemy as a symbol of a spiritual transformation in Man, and that this view became popular with 'occultists' at the end of the nineteenth century (for example, members of the Golden Dawn). Jung also came to believe that the alchemical texts are concerned with psychic transformations and symbols rather than with chemistry; the soul, he said, has become 'fragmented' — partly the fault of the Church — and Man longs for wholeness, of which the Philosophers' Stone is the symbol.

The Great Work, as the alchemists call it, begins with the selection of the *prima materia*. The nature of this material is unknown — one modern alchemist thinks it is earth. The work must be begun in spring, preferably under Aries (the most forceful sign). It contains two elements, one male and one female — sol and luna, or sulphur and mercury. These have to be mixed with 'secret fire' and heated in a sealed vessel; if the operation is successful the two elements are 'married', and then blacken and putrefy, a stage known as the *nigredo*. Further heating should drive off the 'soul' of the black mess, which slowly turns white — the *albedo*. After a dozen further obscure processes, the substance turns green (the Green Lion) then red (the Philosophers' Stone). For Jung, the various processes are symbolic — for example, the heating that produces the nigredo is a kind of 'dark night of the soul' produced by inner conflict — he himself went through a similar process that came close to destroying him — which ends with the first stage of self-transformation. But then, although Jung's interpretations are convincing, it is clear that he regards the whole *chemical* process as a 'hair-raising fantasy'.

The alchemists themselves had no doubt that they were involved in a scientific, not a spiritual, quest. And at least two modern practitioners have claimed that alchemy is 'practical', not symbolic. In *Gold of a Thousand Mornings* Armand Barbault claims to have manufactured 'oil of gold', and to have captured the vital essence of plants by collecting them at dawn and distilling them with dew — he offers signed medical testimonies to the efficacy of his products. And Albert Riedel also claims to have manufactured various plant 'essences' — a process known as the Lesser Work; his *Alchemist's Handbook* is an interesting if obscure treatise. (The alchemists made a virtue of obscurity, possibly because they were afraid of being burnt for heresy, possibly because they felt that their secrets could be used for evil purposes.) It should be mentioned that the history of alchemy is full of circumstantial stories of the discovery of the Philosophers' Stone by men like Nicholas Flamel, van Helmont, Helvetius, Alexander Seton and James Price — the last of whom is said to have transmuted mercury into gold in front of a select audience from the Royal Society.

*Gurdjieff also laid enormous emphasis on the alchemical processes; he saw the human body as the 'vessel' that transmutes

lower into higher energies; we already possess, he says, higher 'centres', but lack the energy to 'drive' them.

But the likeliest explanation of the 'secret of alchemy' is that it was both a spiritual and a chemical process — a chemical process in which the 'spirit' had to intervene decisively at a certain point. This may be the explanation of the 'secret fire' and of a mysterious 'double mercury' referred to by many alchemists.

Knowledge concerning the two cerebral hemispheres throws an interesting new light on the problem. If the basic argument of this book is correct, then Man originally possessed the same kind of simple mental unity as the animals. He learned to achieve power over nature, and himself, by becoming self-divided. *The Secret of the Golden Flower*, a Chinese alchemical treatise that influenced Jung, speaks of the necessity to 'heat the roots of consciousness and life' and to 'kindle light in the blessed country close at hand'. States of ecstasy and insight, states in which we feel that 'all is well', momentarily unite the two halves of our being, and make us aware that *our powers are far greater than we had realized*.

Now such matters as *poltergeist phenomena also seem to originate in the right brain, and to contradict our left-brain, scientific view of the world. *Ancient Man may have known how to utilize the forces of the Earth. And alchemy — at least, the Lesser Work — is undoubtedly concerned with such forces.

What seems to be implied is that a man who had achieved what Jung calls 'individuation' — a new unity of the right and left hemispheres — would be able to produce *controlled* poltergeist effects and other forms of 'magic'. And it seems perfectly conceivable that such powers could influence the structure of matter, and cause chemical transformations. In which case, the alchemist's real task would be to establish contact with 'the blessed country close at hand', the 'source of power, meaning and purpose' inside us — to become a 'magician'.

The argument is that most of the 'occult sciences' can be understood in the light of modern discoveries about the brain and Earth magnetism — *astrology, for example, is developing into the science of astrobiology, whose advocates include Professor H.J. Eysenck. But it seems clear that *if* alchemy is ever to be justified in this way it will require a far wider knowledge of 'science' than anything yet envisaged.

Alchemy seems to be the most complex and profound of all the 'occult sciences'; the alchemists themselves claimed that it is the science of sciences. This is certainly the secret of its fascination for some of the most powerful minds of our century.   CW

Amulets

Amulets or charms are devices intended either to bring their owner good luck (in which case they may be called talismans) or to shelter him from evil. They may either be worn or placed in some suitable position — for example, over the hearth. In modern Western society the commonest amulets are the horseshoe (iron combats demons) and the rabbit's foot; the lump of coal carried at Hogmanay by the Scots 'first-footer' is another survival.

The supposed power of amulets is thought to reside not in the object itself but in the owner, who uses the amulet as a focus for his psychic protective energies.

JG

Blavatsky, Helena Petrovna

Medium, occultist, founder of the Theosophical Society, Blavatsky was born Helena von Hahn in Russia, 1831. She worked as a bareback rider in a circus, a piano-teacher in Paris and London, and significantly, perhaps, as assistant to Daniel Dunglas Home for a time. She travelled widely: Mexico, Texas, India, Canada and Tibet.

It was not until she was forty-two that she found her vocation. In 1873 she went to the USA, finding *Spiritualism all the rage. A meeting with H.S. Olcott proved to be a turning-point in her career. He became her devoted backer and publicist.

She began demonstrating her mediumistic powers for wealthy socialites, becoming known as HPB to her devotees, and earning a comfortable living. When the Spiritualist boom slumped, she had to rely mainly on the financial support of Olcott.

In 1875, she founded the Theosophical Society for the study of psychic phenomena. This lent a kind of spurious scientific validity to what might have seemed pure chicanery. HPB wrote its bible, *Isis Unveiled*, a two-volume work published in 1877, which sold well. She claimed it had been dictated to her by spirits, and it was certainly an erudite blend of Cabalistic and Taoist scripture.

HPB insisted that the inexplicable phenomena she produced were performed *through* her by certain yogis or adepts from caves in Tibet, whose *chela* (disciple) she was. Like a telephone exchange, she simply passed on messages from other intelligences unbounded by space or time.

The Theosophical Society flourished, but in 1879 HPB decided to go to India. There her powers increased vastly. At a party, she materialized a cup and saucer. Outraged by suggestions that she might have planted them, she asked her hostess if there were anything she particularly wanted. The hostess mentioned a brooch she had lost some years before. After communing with her 'masters', HPB announced that it was buried in a flower-bed. The company trooped outside, dug among the flowers, and promptly found the brooch.

In 1884, she visited London, where she agreed to allow the SPR to investigate her powers. Unfortunately, back in India a jealous housekeeper, Emma Coulomb, chose this moment to confess all to the press. She produced letters from HPB making it plain that some of her psychic effects had been a fraud. Accordingly, the SPR produced a sceptical report.

It was the end. Dying slowly of Bright's Disease, she spent her last years writing *The Secret Doctrine* (published 1888), in which she stressed that miracles do not defy the laws of nature, but obey deeper laws of a harmonic Universe as yet not comprehended by science.

She died in 1891. To the end she never lost her intense vitality. Part-charlatan, part self-deceiver, there can be little doubt that she did indeed possess some genuine psychic powers.   BM

Crowley, Aleister

Born 12 October 1875, Crowley is the joker in the pack. A thoroughly unpleasant character, it would be too easy to dismiss him as an egotistical, ruthless exhibitionist.

While at Oxford, he was initiated into the Order of the Golden Dawn, on the lowest of the society's ten grades. He later effectively brought about the dissolution of the society because of their refusal to grant him a higher grade. He travelled extensively, undergoing yogic training in Ceylon. The rites he was later to practise were based on a form of Tantric sex-magic.

His prodigious writing included *The Book of the Law*, which he claimed was dictated to him by a spirit. Its message was essentially 'Do What Thou Wilt', borrowed from Rabelais, as was the title of the abbey, Thelema, which he founded in Sicily. Here he practised sex-magic rituals, including animal sacrifice. The unsavoury goings-on at the abbey were exposed in the UK press, earning him the title of 'the wickedest man in the world' and expulsion from Sicily.

A flamboyant character, revelling in the name 'The Great Beast 666' (from *Revelation*), he possessed one crucial insight: a recognition that occult feats are procured by the exercise of pure will, rather than any mystic props.

His magnetic personality — or power of psychic-hypnotism — was demonstrated at a dinner-party when he called on a fellow guest to go down on all fours and bark like a dog. He also claimed to use astral projection to commit psychic rape on women.

Sadist, drug-addict, completely self-centred, he took the 'left-hand path', misusing his powers. He died in 1947, a penniless, pitiful wreck.   BM

Demons

Demons are believed to be intermediate between men and gods. The word 'demon' derives from a Greek word that originally meant divinity or genius; it was in the

Hebrew tradition that demons developed their reputation as malevolent spirits or supernatural creatures. According to the Talmud there are 7,405,926 of them.

The idea that they can be called up and made to do the will of a human has been attributed to Solomon, and the seminal works of demonology are the *Testament of Solomon* and the *Lemegoton*. These ancient grimoires set out for the benefit of aspiring magicians precise descriptions of the powers and functions of scores of demons, and also prescribe rituals to enable humans to evoke and control them.

There is, for example, Amon, with a wolf's body and a serpent's head, who vomits flame but, despite his formidable appearance, can be prevailed upon to procure love, reconcile enemies or divine the future. Then there is Glasyalabolas, who incites to bloodshed and murder, and makes people invisible, but also has the power to teach all the arts and sciences instantaneously. He has the form of a winged dog. Shax appears as a wild dove with a hoarse voice, and a magician may employ him to destroy a victim's sight, hearing or understanding, to transport anything or to discover anything hidden. Astaroth appears as a beautiful angel riding a dragon and carrying a viper in his right hand, and although his breath stinks infernally he will teach great truths about science and the cosmos to whoever summons him, and will answer any question about the past, present or future truthfully.

Although these beings may seem extravagantly fanciful creations, level-headed people today with experience of the occult are convinced of the reality of demons and warn about the folly and danger of consorting with them. For instance, David Conway, a high-ranking UK civil servant, in his *Magic, An Occult Primer* cautions that, for the novice practitioner of *ritual magic, 'a time may come when his experiments may introduce him to the delinquents of the astral dark, those devils and demons so beloved of story-tellers the whole world over'. He also writes: 'Physical assaults by demonic agents are comparatively rare, *though by no means unknown*.' SH

Devil

All systems of religion and metaphysics must deal with the problem of the manifest existence of evil and destructive forces in the world and in Man, and reconcile this with the existence of an omnipotent God worthy of worship and respect. Many do so by postulating a supernatural adversary or enemy of the deity. The Jewish and Christian religions, inheriting a dramatic dualist theology from Persian Zoroastrianism, made it very much their own and developed a rich mythology of the nature and doings of Satan. In the Bible there are represented quite different views of the Devil, from the tempter and accuser of humans who consorts with God in *Job* to the 'prince of demons' and of a rival kingdom of evil that Jesus pits himself against, according to *Matthew*. For most of the great theologians of the Christian centuries the Devil was a terrible reality, stalking the world in various guises trying to subvert the good offices of God and His Faithful. For Martin Luther it appears that familiarity bred contempt: 'Another time in the night I heard him above my cell walking in the cloister, but as I knew it was the Devil I paid no attention to him and went to sleep.' SH

Doppelgängers

Doppelgängers, 'phantasms of the living', are among the commonest but also the most puzzling forms of 'apparition' (see *ghosts). Lewis Spence has described the doppelgänger (or 'double') as 'the etheric counterpart of the physical body, which ... may temporarily move about in space ...'. In his autobiography, Yeats writes: 'One afternoon ... I was thinking very intently of a fellow student for whom I had a message ... In a couple of days I got a letter from a place some hundreds of miles away where the student was. On the afternoon when I had been thinking so intently I had suddenly appeared there amid a crowd of people in a hotel and seeming as solid as if in the flesh. My fellow student had seen me, but no one else, and had asked me to come again when the people had gone. I had vanished, but had come again in the middle of the night and given him the message. I myself had no knowledge of either apparition.'

This at first sounds as if Yeats' desire to pass on the message could have produced telepathic contact with the student; but since he returned — on request — to deliver the message, this seems unlikely. The 'doppelgänger' behaved like a person with a will of his own. And this raises one of the oddest problems encountered in such cases. It seems as if the 'double' is quite unconnected with the conscious ego. It may even cause it distress and embarrassment. Emilie Sagée, an attractive French schoolmistress, lost eighteen jobs in sixteen years between 1829 and 1845 because her 'astral double' had a habit of appearing beside her, terrifying her pupils. On a typical occasion, Emilie was picking flowers in the garden in full view of a class of girls whose teacher had gone off to consult the headmistress. Suddenly, Emilie's form appeared in the teacher's chair. Two girls tried to touch her and said she felt like muslin. Emilie later said she had looked into the room, noticed the teacher was away, and had felt worried about discipline; so the 'double' was apparently a spontaneous 'projection', unwilled and unintended. One girl remarked that the 'real Emilie' in the garden became very pale when her double appeared in the classroom.

In the case of the Glastonbury scripts (see *automatic writing), the 'communicator', who claimed to be a monk called Johannes, made the interesting remark: 'Why cling I to that which is not? It is I, and it is not I, but part of me which dwelleth in the past and is bound to that which my carnal soul loved and called "home" these many years. Yet I, Johannes, am of many parts, and ye better part doeth other things.' And, certainly, the study of cases of doppelgängers and vardøgers, as well as of *multiple personality, suggests that our minds — even our personalities — may be 'of many parts'.

This is again illustrated by another celebrated case. S.G. Soal had been at school with a boy named Gordon Davis; in 1920 he heard that Davis had been killed in the war. In 1921, Soal was at a séance at which his brother Frank, also killed in the war, was apparently communicating. Frank then 'introduced' Davis, who gave many factual details about himself. Davis returned at a later séance, and spoke about the house he used to live in. He explained that it was not in a street, 'more like half a street', and that there was something like a veranda in front of the house. The name of the 'street', he said, contained Es. He described the interior of the house in some detail, including a mirror, pictures and 'two funny brass candlesticks'. In due course, Soal located the house, in Eastern Esplanade (two Es), Southend; an esplanade, facing the sea, could be described as 'half a street'. There was a bus shelter opposite the house. The description of the inside proved to be remarkably accurate. But — Davis was still alive and living there. And he had no knowledge whatever of his appearance at the séances.

Aldous Huxley used a similar situation in his play *The World of Light*.

Yet it *does* seem to be possible for people to 'project' themselves consciously. A well known case — cited by Myers in *Human Personality and Its Survival of Bodily Death* — concerned a young man named S.H. Beard, who told his fiancée, L.S. Verity, that he would attempt to 'project' himself to her house. He made a powerful effort of concentration, and was seen not only by Verity but by her eleven-year-old sister. Similarly, John Cowper Powys projected himself into the sitting-room of his friend Theodore Dreiser. Powys had dined with Dreiser in his New York apartment, and left hurriedly to catch his train back to a town on the Hudson. As he left, he told Dreiser that he would 'appear' to him later. Dreiser assumed he was joking. Two hours later, Dreiser looked up from his book to see Powys standing in the doorway. Dreiser stood up, saying: 'Well, you've kept your word — now tell me how you did it.' As he moved towards his friend, Powys vanished. He immediately rang Powys at home, but Powys refused, then or later, to say how he 'did it'.

On the 'left and right' hypothesis already discussed, we may theorize that 'doppelgängers' are basically telepathic images, projected by the right cerebral hemisphere or the unconscious — this certainly fits the majority of cases, as it also fits Andrew Green's story of the woman in the telephone kiosk (see *ghosts). Yet it is hard to see how such a telepathic image could be seen by a whole class, as in the Sagée case. Here we are forced to give serious consideration to Spence's suggestion that the doppelgänger is 'the astral double'. CW

Ghosts

All civilizations have believed in ghosts — there is even a Buddhist text describing how the Buddha trained himself to overcome fear by sitting in a haunted graveyard. The usual assumption has been that they are spirits of the dead. In the twentieth century it has become increasingly clear that at least one type of ghost, the *poltergeist, emanates from the unconscious minds of living human beings. In recent years, there has also been an increasing tendency to accept a theory put forward by Sir Oliver Lodge, that some ghosts may be a kind of 'recording' in rooms in which some tragedy has taken place (see *jinxes and curses). An interesting experiment was carried out by Robert Morris of the Psychical Research Foundation of Durham, North Carolina, in which a rat, a cat, a dog and a rattlesnake were taken to a reputedly haunted house in Kentucky; violent deaths had occurred in two of the rooms. In one of the rooms, the dog snarled and backed out; the cat leapt onto its owner's shoulders, digging in its claws; and the rattlesnake assumed an attack posture towards an empty chair. Only the rat showed no kind of reaction. It is interesting to wonder why the rat should have been indifferent.

T.C. Lethbridge arrived at the 'tape-recording theory' as a result of his own experiences, described in such books as *Ghost and Ghoul* and *Ghost and Divining Rod*. When he was eighteen, for example, he was walking with his mother in the Great Wood near Wokingham; at a particular spot, both felt deeply depressed. A few days later the body of a suicide was found close to the spot. This, and other similar experiences, led him to believe that water, woodland, deserts and mountains each have their own individual kind of electrical field, and that emotions can be 'imprinted' on this field; dowsers and other 'sensitives' are more likely to notice them than the average non-sensitive person. (Robert Graves is of the opinion that one person in twenty possesses natural psychic sensitivity.) Lethbridge also believed that some 'ghosts' may be 'psychic projections'.

A modern ghost-hunter, Andrew Green, has cited a typical case. In September 1975 a young priest was standing outside a telephone booth in Birmingham; the box was occupied by a young woman in a dark blue costume. Suddenly, she vanished. This, Green believes, was not a ghost but a 'phantasm of the living' (see *doppelgängers), caused by someone deeply anxious to make a phonecall, and imagining being in the box.

This form of 'telepathy' also seems to account for another commonly reported experience: apparitions of people on the point of death or (less often) in danger. In such cases, a close relative might look up and see someone enter the room, then vanish; in most cases, the appearance corresponds with the death of the person who is seen. It should be noted that most 'apparitions' look quite solid and normal.

Certain cases are difficult to explain by any of the usual hypotheses — telepathy, 'recordings', etc. Louisa Rhine has cited a case in which a woman was watching her husband repair a second-hand motorcycle when a young man walked into the yard and also stood watching. She asked her husband to introduce her and the man vanished. The woman's description was precise, and enabled her husband to state that he was the previous owner of the motorcycle, who had been killed two years ago. Had it been the husband who saw the apparition, then hallucination might be suspected; but it is difficult to explain why the *wife* should have seen the man. In another case cited by Mrs Rhine, a young woman in a queue in the bank noticed in another queue a man she knew well; he looked ill. As she was about to speak to him, he walked out. When she mentioned this later to an acquaintance she learned that the man had died some time before.

*Spiritualism takes the view that there are many Earthbound spirits who are not aware that they have died, and who therefore continue to visit scenes of their past lives in a state analogous to delirium.

There are a number of well authenticated accounts of apparent return from the dead. A typical example is cited in Sir Ernest Bennett's *Apparitions and Haunted Houses*, one of the most reliable of its kind. A chimney sweep named Samuel Bull had died of cancer, leaving his family in a small cottage in overcrowded conditions. His wife was bed-ridden and everyone was under a great deal of strain. Nine months after his death, Bull was seen to walk through the room in which he had died, and in which his widow lay, and to place his hand on her forehead. She said that it felt cold, but otherwise normal. This happened repeatedly over two months, witnessed by the whole family, who were at first terrified, then gradually became accustomed to it. On one occasion the apparition stood there for over an hour. The SPR took signed statements from the family. When they were rehoused, the apparitions ceased.

Under the circumstances, it would be rash to rule out the hypothesis that at least some ghosts are genuine 'revenants' — spirits who have returned from the dead. Nevertheless, it seems clear that in the majority of cases apparitions can be explained in terms of such powers as *ESP.

CW

Healing

The notion that healing is a magical process is older than civilization, and in primitive tribes the healer and the magician (witchdoctor) are still the same person. 'Magical' (or miraculous) healing is also a powerful part of the Christian tradition; it began to be weakened only in the Middle Ages, when the great plagues made it clear that death struck the faithful and the unfaithful impartially.

Mesmer (see *hypnosis) believed that he had discovered that illness can be cured by magnets, which stimulate some unknown vital 'fluid'; he later called this fluid 'animal magnetism'. His disciple, the Marquis de Puységur, stumbled upon the phenomenon of hypnotism. Its nature was not understood, but it was clear that the 'everyday self' of the patient could be put to sleep, while some 'deeper' aspect of his mind could continue to obey orders. Most surprising was that this deeper mind could let the subject perform tasks impossible were he in his waking state — for example, lying rigid between two chairs while a heavy man stood on his stomach. Charcot was fascinated by the power of hypnosis to cure hysterical patients. Émile Coué and Johannes Schultz both realized that hypnosis was a matter of the will not so much of the hypnotist as of the hypnotized subject, which produced its effects by autosuggestion. Coué's patients were told to repeat: 'Every day in every way I am becoming better and better.'

But what was important was that both Coué and Schultz recognized that healing is a matter of activating the body's 'homoeostatic' mechanism, its natural tendency to counteract disease. Freud's disciple Rank even posited a basic 'will to health' in people — and, as a consequence, ceased to be a member of the psychoanalytic movement.

And so, oddly enough, the Spiritualist movement — with its belief in 'faith healing' — and orthodox psychological medicine began to draw closer together. In the 1930s Selye made the important discovery that many illnesses are caused, quite simply, by 'stress'. Stress, which can be regarded as a mild hysteria, prevents the homoeostatic mechanism from working, and the result is illness.

One modern exponent of the theory, Ian Pearce, has even gone so far as to state that 75 per cent of the illness he has ever treated has been basically psychological in nature, and that the other 25 per cent is due to gross abuses of the body. He observed that patients with an inherited disposition to some illness (say, diabetes) would not become ill until problems had produced in them a state of depression or defeat.

In the same way, Selye was intrigued to note how illness can be cured by sudden shock, just as a child can be 'snapped' out of a tantrum by having a glass of water thrown in its face. Ronald Duncan has given an interesting example in his autobiography. About to leave India, he found himself suffering from an unusually heavy cold that made breathing difficult. Gandhi recommended him to go and see a certain doctor. The doctor strapped him to an upright iron bed-frame, pulled a lever, and released the frame, which hit the floor with a crash. Duncan staggered to his feet shaken and furious — then discovered that his cold had gone.

The recognition of the 'two selves' in the brain's two cerebral hemispheres seems to provide the key to the healing mechanisms. Oddly enough, this duality was recognized as long ago as the 1890s by a remarkable US physician, Thomson Jay Hudson; in *The Law of Psychic Phenomena* he suggests that there is evidence that 'man possesses two minds, each endowed with separate and distinct attributes and powers'. There is the 'objective mind', which deals with the outside world, and whose task is to aid Man in his struggle with the material environment, and the subjective mind, the seat of intuitions and emotions — 'the intelligence which makes itself manifest in a hypnotic subject'. In short, the objective mind is the left hemisphere, the subjective mind the right.

Medically speaking, our problem is twofold: first, the objective mind (the 'coper') gets overanxious, and tends to interfere with the smooth working of the subjective mind, producing the effect of 'too many cooks'; and, second, the objective mind is unaware that it has a powerful helper, and so is prone to exaggerate every problem. It is like an exhausted man who insists on remaining at the wheel of an automobile, and driving badly and dangerously, because he is unaware that he has a partner who can take over. This produces the stress and exhaustion that paralyse the body's homoeostatic mechanism, causing illness.

The development of *biofeedback has been one of the most important advances in medicine in recent years. Biofeedback machines enable the patient to see his own 'brain waves' on a screen. Alpha rhythms are associated with relaxation and 'idling', as are theta rhythms; when we 'pay attention' alpha changes to beta. It might be said, then, that alpha and theta rhythms are the 'voice' of the right hemisphere, the 'subjective mind', while beta rhythms are the 'voice' of the left. When we are in a state of tension, it is practically impossible to 'switch off' voluntarily, because a kind of alarm mechanism keeps switching on the beta rhythms again. But patients who can watch their alpha rhythms on a screen can quickly learn to induce relaxation states (*transcendental meditation aims at precisely the same effect). One US subject described in *Beyond Biofeedback* by Elmer and Alyce Green is able not only to withstand all kinds of torment that would normally cause pain — burning, battering, etc. — but can do so without sustaining injury — the effect demonstrated by fakirs.

Here, then, is an area in which the teachings of Christian Scientists and faith healers are merging with the latest scientific discoveries to create an interesting new synthesis. CW

Jinxes and Curses

Teen-idol James Dean was killed when his Porsche collided head-on with another vehicle in 1955. From then on, the car seemed to be 'jinxed'. Bought by garage-owner George Barris, it slipped while being unloaded from the breakdown truck and broke a mechanic's leg. The engine was sold to a doctor, who was killed when the car it was transferred to went out of control during a race. Another car in the race contained the drive-shaft from the Porsche; it also went out of control and the driver was injured. The battered shell of the car was used in a road-safety campaign; in Sacramento it fell off the mounting and broke a teenager's hip. Later, en route to another display, the truck carrying it was involved in an accident; the driver was thrown out and killed by Dean's car as it rolled off the back. A racing driver who bought tyres from the Porsche was almost killed when both tyres exploded simultaneously. In Oregon, the truck carrying the car slipped its handbrake and crashed into a store. In New Orleans the car broke into eleven pieces when on supports. Finally, it vanished in transit by train back to Los Angeles.

Dozens of similar stores about 'jinxes' could be told of other cars (like the one that was carrying Franz Ferdinand when he was assassinated at Sarajevo), ships, even aircraft. In many cases, it is significant that the jinxed object has been associated with some accident or violence. (For example, in *Together We Wandered*, C.J. Lambert describes how he and his wife began suffering agonizing toothaches after they had bought a statuette of the Chinese god of luck, Hotei, in a Kote junkshop. It was made from an elephant's tusk, and there was a tiny hole in the bottom where the elephant's nerve had ended. The toothaches continued until they got rid of the statuette. Obviously, the elephant had died violently.)

At the turn of the century, Lodge suggested that *ghosts might be a kind of 'photograph' of some tragedy that had occurred in the same room — a photograph of the *emotions* involved. Lethbridge developed a similar theory of 'ghosts and ghouls' after he had noted that a certain spot on Ladram Beach seemed to be associated with an acute feeling of misery, and that he could step in or out of this area as if crossing over a dividing line. His wife felt that someone was urging her to jump over the cliff at a certain point; he later found that a man had committed suicide by jumping from this spot. He concluded that powerful emotions, tragic or otherwise, can be 'imprinted' on electrical 'fields' — he believed the 'field' of water is probably the most common. These unpleasant 'feelings' Lethbridge called 'ghouls'.

This is, in fact, a revival of a theory developed in the mid-nineteenth century by Joseph Rodes Buchanan and William Denton — the notion that events leave their imprints on objects, and that a 'sensitive' can pick up these 'vibrations'; they called this ability psychometry.

This theory certainly goes far towards suggesting an explanation of 'jinxes'. Arthur Guirdham has spoken of a house where a succession of suicides has taken place, because, he is convinced, the depression of previous tenants hangs over the place. (It is built, significantly, above an underground stream, providing a 'water field'.) But it clearly leaves unexplained the actual physical 'bad luck' associated with an object like Dean's car, or the massive ship the *Great Eastern*, whose career was one continuous disaster, and in whose double-hull the skeletons of a missing riveter and his assistant were eventually found. We can, of course, assume that the 'thought field', the 'recording', associated with such an object causes depression, which leads to carelessness, which leads to accidents. But in many cases the bad luck goes far beyond carelessness — as in the disastrous career of the *Scharnhorst*, which went from misfortune to misfortune from the moment it rolled over when half-completed, crushing sixty men to death. Here we seem to need a new concept, something like a 'bad synchronicity', to borrow *Jung's term for meaningful coincidences.

The notion that objects, or persons, can be 'cursed' belongs to all nations and all ages. The *Observer* journalist Colin Cross had an unpleasant experience of this when he went to interview a well known witch, and wrote slightingly about her sale of 'love philtres'. He was told he had been cursed, and admits that, in fact, for the next six months of his life he suffered a series of absurd disasters. The occult tradition insists that 'cursing' is highly dangerous for the curser as well as the potential victim; it can easily 'rebound'. Lethbridge was convinced that his neighbour in Devon, a 'white witch', died as a result of a curse she had put on a local farmer which 'rebounded'. (M.R. James' short story 'Casting the Runes' deals with the same subject, and is a basically accurate account of 'ritual cursing'.)

Clearly, then, the idea of the 'curse'

suggests that the human will can interact with nature in a 'magical' manner, often unconsciously. Robert Graves remarked to me that many young men use an unconscious form of sorcery in seducing women; that once the unconscious, as well as the conscious, mind is focused on an object of desire it can produce magical effects. We might say, then, that the question of 'cursing' (or blessing) should be regarded as an extension of the problem of *poltergeist activity and its relation to the 'occluded' part of the human mind.   CW

Necronomicon

The earliest reference to the infamous *Necronomicon* of the mad Arab Abdul Alhazred is to be found in Lovecraft's 'The Nameless City' (1921). It is alleged that the book first appeared in Arabic as *Al Azif* (c AD 730, Damascus), re-emerging over the centuries in Greek, Latin, Spanish and, finally, English translations. The last is attributed to John Dee.

The work is held to be the ultimate repository of forbidden lore, containing formulae designed to summon forth the Great Old Ones — dark and terrible entities from dimensions outside space and time, the archetypal enemies of mankind; sworn to take possession of the Earth in revenge against the Elder Gods, ancient guardians of humanity.

During the past decade, *The Necronomicon* and its associated *Cthulhu Mythos* (the name used by Lovecraft to represent his anticosmology) have attracted the interest of occultists worldwide. Cults have emerged — some showing striking similarities to the sinister Thule Group of the Nazis — their devotees dedicated to the establishment of chaos in a desperate attempt to gain ultimate power.

Several editions have been published in recent years, each claiming to be the authentic text. The truth depends on viewpoint. Perhaps we should reflect upon the words of Fort, who wrote of his *Book of the Damned*: 'This book is fiction, like *Gulliver's Travels*, *The Origin of Species*, Newton's *Principia*, and every history of the United States.'   RT

Possession

'The Demoniac possession of the Middle Ages . . . was largely hysterical in character, and generally occurred in epidemics,' says a typical article in the *Journal of Abnormal Psychology*. And when the encyclopedic *Man, Myth and Magic* wanted an article on possession, the editor chose William Sargant, a psychiatrist, whose view is that 'possession' is, quite simply, a clinical problem. In an enormous number of cases this is undoubtedly true, as Huxley demonstrated very clearly in *The Devils of Loudon*: the nuns who writhed and blasphemed on the floors of their convent were undoubtedly 'possessed' only by an unconscious sexual desire directed towards their amorous confessor, Father Urbain Grandier — their behaviour resembling that of modern teenagers at a rock concert.

But not all possession can be explained quite so simply. There is, to begin with, some interesting evidence for what might be called 'the transference of personality'. In 1877 thirteen-year-old Lurancy Vennum began having trances and convulsions. Under hypnosis, she told the doctor that she was having problems with evil spirits, but that an 'angel' named Mary Roff had offered to protect her. Soon Lurancy began having detailed memories of the life of Mary Roff, a girl who had died in the same town, Watseka, a year after Lurancy was born. Mary Roff's family were so convinced by these 'memories' that they allowed Lurancy to move in and live with them for three months, after which time the 'possession' ceased, and Lurancy moved back to her own family. The case is exceptionally well documented, as is the similar case of Jasbir Lal Jat (see *reincarnation). In both, it is worth noting that the 'possessing' personality died *after* the 'possessed' person was born.

Cases of *multiple personality often pose the same interesting problem, in that one of the 'personalities' is often far more mature than the patient has had a chance to become. *Jung closely observed the case of a teenaged female cousin who would sink into a trance and then speak with various different voices, some of them male. But one personality, a woman called Ivenes, claimed to be 'the real S.W.' (the initials under which Jung concealed his cousin's name), and was obviously far more 'grown up' than the fifteen-year-old girl. In fact, the girl died in her twenties, leading Jung to speculate whether she anticipated her own death and was somehow compensating for it by allowing her 'future self' an opportunity to live.

Many cases of apparent possession are undoubtedly a kind of 'poltergeist phenomenon'. The novel *The Exorcist* was based on the case of Douglass Deen, a fourteen-year-old Washington boy. All kinds of *poltergeist phenomena occurred in the house — smashing crockery, furniture moving of its own accord, and so on. His bed would tremble violently while he was asleep. When attempts at exorcism were made the boy began to curse and blaspheme; the priest who conducted the exorcism alleges that often Douglass spoke in Latin, a language he had never been taught. Yet apart from this one aspect — which could be due to unconscious memory of Latin he had heard — the case sounds typical of poltergeist phenomena, which almost certainly originate in that 'other self' in the right cerebral hemisphere (see page 13).

If we can accept the possibility of *life after death, then many cases certainly become easier to explain. Alan Vaughan has described (in *Patterns of Prophecy*) how he became 'possessed' by the 'spirit' of a Nantucket housewife after several sessions with an ouija board, and was finally 'un-possessed' with the help of another 'spirit' summoned up by a friend. He claims, interestingly enough, that in the moment of 'dispossession' he was suddenly able to see into the future (see *precognition).

It is necessary also to consider the possibility that there *is* such a thing as possession by 'alien entities'. Many who have had *out-of-the-body experiences have spoken about encountering unpleasant or mischievous entities in the 'bodiless' state.

But, in most cases of possession, the verdict must remain open. The case of Michael Taylor, of Barnsley, Yorkshire, is typical. In September 1974, Taylor and his wife Catherine joined a Christian Fellowship group. At a meeting of this group, a twenty-two-year-old schoolteacher, Marie Robinson, began 'speaking in tongues', then performed a group exorcism, during which Taylor also began 'speaking in tongues' (a phenomenon known as glossolalia). A few days later, Taylor (who was depressed about being unable to get a job) announced that he was possessed by the *Devil, and became noisy and violent. Eventually, the local vicar decided he needed exorcism, and six exorcists spent six hours carrying out the ceremonies in the vestry of the church. They claimed they had rid Taylor of at least forty devils. But, when Taylor returned home with his wife, he attacked her violently, tearing out her eyes and tongue; he was later found lying, naked and unconscious, in the street. Tried for murdering his wife, he was found not guilty and sent to Broadmoor. But apparently the 'demons' had left him; and he was later released and allowed to take charge of his children.

A case like this strongly suggests hysteria, and seems to support Sargant's view. But others are more complex. In Chicago recently a Filipino woman, a doctor's wife, began speaking in the voice of a Filipino nurse, Teresita Basa, who had been murdered by an unknown assailant in her apartment, and named the murderer. The man — Allen Showery, a colleague of the murdered woman at the Edgewater Hospital — was arrested, confessed, and was brought to trial, where the evidence of the doctor's wife was allowed in court. Cases like this make it difficult to accept that the 'hysteria' hypothesis is always adequate.

CW

Primitive Magic

One day in 1869 a dog belonging to Don Marcelino de Sautuola fell down a crack in the ground; the huntsmen who followed it found themselves in a spacious cave, the cave of Altamira. Incredibly, Don Marcelino had it sealed up and forgot about it. Nine years later, he visited the Paris

Exhibition of 1878, saw some Ice Age tools and artefacts, and decided to look in his own cave. At first he found little; then one day his five-year-old daughter noticed drawings on the walls and ceiling of a small cave — bison, wild boars, horses. The 'pigment' still seemed sticky.

The discovery brought him nothing but misfortune. A congress of European scholars decided it was all a fake, that the pictures had been made by an artist who had stayed with Don Marcelino. He died an embittered man. But he was rehabilitated, posthumously, when similar cave paintings were found in caves in the Dordogne in France.

At first it was assumed that Ice Age art proved only that our Cro-Magnon ancestors were more civilized than anyone had supposed — and more talented (see *ancient Man). But gradually anthropologists recognized that the basic purpose of these paintings was not artistic but magical. The Stone Age shaman (or magician) dressed himself in a bison skin to draw herds of bison within the territory of the hunters. The paintings were an extension of this custom.

In a remarkable passage in his *Pattern of Islands*, Sir Arthur Grimble, land commissioner in the Gilbert Islands, describes witnessing the ceremony of the 'calling of the porpoises', a typical piece of primitive magic. He was told that an hereditary porpoise-caller in Kuma village could summon the porpoises by entering a trance. After a feast, the porpoise-caller retired to his hut, and there was silence. Hours later, he staggered out, clawing at the air and crying, 'They come, they come!' The villagers all rushed into the water and stood breast high; the porpoises began to swim in to the shore in an orderly manner, slowly, as if in a trance, and beached themselves. The villagers dragged them ashore and slaughtered and ate them.

A more recent example of primitive magic was vividly described by Ross Salmon in a television programme, complete with film of the occurrence. He was visiting the Calawayas, descendants of the original Incas, who live north of Lake Titicaca. The medicine man had gone to the city to earn money for the tribe, and his wife, Wakchu, was suspected of being unfaithful to him. A council of local women and a council of elders was undecided about her guilt, so the priests announced that they would 'call the condor' to resolve their doubts. The Calawayas believe that human beings are reincarnated as condors, and that a particular 'great condor' is a reincarnation of a great Inca leader who conquered that part of the world.

Salmon was convinced that nothing would happen; he had never seen a condor at close quarters. He watched the priests throwing coca leaves in the air and chanting. The next day, Wakchu was taken to the ceremonial site, stripped to her loincloth, and tied to a post. For half an hour, the elders waited. Then, to Salmon's amazement, the condor appeared, flew around overhead, and landed on a rock facing Wakchu. It sat there for a time, then stepped right in front of the girl, and pointed its beak up at her. The elders cried, 'Guilty — she must take her own life!' If Salmon had any doubts about the genuineness of the ceremony, they vanished ten days later when the girl threw herself from a high clifftop. In writing of the incident later, he admits that he 'watered it down', having been persuaded by scientists that he had been 'conned' for money. But his film of the whole incident is extraordinarily convincing.

Mircea Eliade's *Shamanism* makes it clear that there is a remarkable similarity in the selection and training of shamans throughout the world, from Africa to the Arctic Circle. A man usually realizes that he is destined to become a shaman because he has dreams and visions. He gains his supernatural powers by ordeal — starvation, exposure to the elements, chastity, self-flagellation. An Eskimo shaman told Knud Rasmussen that he often fell to weeping without understanding why, then would be overwhelmed with ecstasy. 'I could see and hear in a totally different way ... The same bright light also shone out from me, imperceptible to human beings but visible to all spirits of Earth and sky and sea, and these now came to me to become my helping spirits.' When his powers have crystallized through ordeal, the shaman can enter a trance state, visit the realm of the gods, or of the dead, and bring messages back to his tribesmen.

To the modern reader, who begins with the patronizing assumption that such ceremonies are merely evidence of superstition, the astonishing thing that emerges from so many accounts, like those of Grimble, is that the 'magic' *works*. Bruce Lamb's *Wizard of the Upper Amazon*, describing the experiences of a Peruvian youth, Manuel Cordoba, who was captured by the Amahuaca Indians of Brazil, contains some interesting examples. After drinking *hini xuma*, a 'vision extract', the natives experienced shared visions of snakes, birds and animals; Cordoba recalled a black jaguar, which instantly appeared among them, causing a shudder. He also describes how the hunters try to kill the leader of a herd of wild pigs in order to bury its head with certain rituals; if this is done correctly, the herd of pigs will always return that way, and can be killed for meat. The method sounds absurd; but for the Amahuaca Indians it works.

Dr Charlotte Bach is convinced that the explanation of the powers of the shaman is basically sexual. She believes that all human beings contain basic polarities of male and female, and that there is a perpetual urge — in 'normal' people — for the male to become female and vice versa. All creativity, she believes, springs from this inner tension. The transvestite has resolved the conflict in a crude and simplistic manner and so has lost this inner tension. The 'normal' person has also acquired a low-level equilibrium. Various types of sexual perverts attempt a more active balance of the forces. A creative artist balances them on a higher level still. But the 'asexual' shaman brings them to equilibrium on a level that involves such tension that the result is a glowing discharge of nervous energy which produces an ecstasy which can last for hours. The ecstasy enables the shaman to make use of his innate paranormal powers, suppressed in most of us by the need for social and personal equilibrium.

Whether or not Charlotte Bach's 'sexual theory' is wholly correct, her insight into the shamanistic ecstasy certainly rings true, and may be supported by passage after passage in Eliade's book. The powers of the shaman are undoubtedly due to some form of internal tension whose precise psychological nature is at present a mystery.

CW

Pyramid Power

The man chiefly responsible for the 'pyramid boom' in the 1970s was Lyall Watson, who in *Supernature* cited this story: Monsieur Bovis went into the Great *Pyramid to shelter from the sun and noticed that litter in the garbage cans, including a dead cat, had mummified rather than decayed; he wondered if the actual proportions of the pyramid contained the secret and, constructing a scale model, found that, indeed, a dead cat placed inside it did not decay... Then a Czech engineer, Karel Drbal, discovered that if razor blades were placed in pyramids between shaves they seemed never to grow blunt. Watson said that he himself had been able to use the same blade dozens of times by keeping it in a pyramid. Pyramids, it seemed, could trap some mysterious force.

Watson's 'facts' are taken from *Pyramid Power* by G. Pat Flanagan, published privately in Glendale, California. All books that discuss 'pyramid power' refer simply (as he does) to 'M. Bovis' without a Christian name, revealing that all have simply borrowed from Flanagan, who runs a flourishing business selling miniature pyramids and pendants. The 'report by Bovis' that he claims to have read is not cited in the bibliography.

Tests on seeds carried out by Art Rosenblum of the Aquarian Research Foundation in Philadelphia indicated that seeds grown under pyramids took just as long to germinate as other seeds, and that none of the claims made for pyramids seemed to have any basis in fact.

CW

Ritual Magic

Ritual magic is an elaborate use of ceremony to contact the supernatural world, to summon up spirits or *demons in order to obtain knowledge from them or enlist their help. Such use of ceremony is of great antiquity and is found in virtually all cultures, although generally proscribed in theocratic societies. Its ill-repute in our culture is partly because the Church proscribed it and persecuted its practitioners. But the fact that it survived at all through a long period when its devotees risked terrifying punishments is surely evidence that it must have been found effective.

Testimonies abound. One of the best known is in the autobiography of Cellini. He tells how he and his twelve-year-old apprentice, Cenci, went one night to the empty Coliseum in Rome with two friends and a Sicilian sorcerer. The sorcerer drew circles on the ground and had the group step inside one for protection. He instructed Cellini's friends Romoli and Gaddi to tend a fire and put perfumes on it. Cellini himself was given a pentacle and told to point it in whichever direction the sorcerer indicated.

When the elaborate ceremonial preparations had been completed, the sorcerer began calling on a vast multitude of demons in Hebrew, Greek and Latin. Almost at once the amphitheatre was filled with them. Cellini, encouraged to put a request, asked to be reunited with his Sicilian mistress. 'Do you hear what they have told you?' the sorcerer said. 'Within a month you will be where she is.'

Soon the magician began to get worried because there were a thousand times more fiends than summoned, and they were dangerous. He asked Cellini to be brave and give support while he tried to dismiss them civilly and gently, as required by the ritual. Meanwhile, young Cenci cowered with terror, declaring that he saw a million fierce men menacing them, and four armed giants trying to force a way into the circle. The sorcerer, quaking with fear, tried all the soft words he could think of to persuade them to go. Cellini attempted to encourage the others but Cenci, head between his knees, began to moan that they were doomed. Cellini tried to convince him the demons were all under control, and assured him that he would see only smoke and shadows if he looked up. Cenci looked up, and cried out in terror. He said the whole Coliseum was on fire, and the flames were coming towards them.

The sorcerer tried one last remedy. He burned some asafetida, a stinking substance from the root of a certain plant. This, and perhaps Gaddi's involuntary contribution to the foul smell, broke the spell. Soon Cenci reported the demons had started to withdraw in fury. The group stayed in the safety of the circle until dawn, and the magician meantime repeated ceremonial exorcisms. Even when they had packed up and were returning home, Cenci insisted that two fiends were still with them, gambolling along the roofs and the road.

Whatever may actually have happened at the Coliseum, it is clear that the men were convinced they were surrounded by demons, and were scared out of their wits. Today psychologists might say they were all hallucinating, the boy most vividly. This may be true, but we must ask: what degree of reality do hallucinations have?

Are the subjective and objective worlds as separate as we think? Drawing on the insights gained by *Relativity and quantum theory, Lawrence Leshan has recently proposed that two kinds of reality exist, sensory reality and clairvoyant reality. He suggests both are equally real, and complement and shade into each other like the colours of the spectrum. We conduct our normal lives at one end of the spectrum, sensory reality, but gifted mystics and poets move easily to the other. Controlled experiments have shown that subjects under hallucinogenic drugs can also make the transition. Traditional ritual magic may be regarded as another technique for making this shift to levels of the mind where individuality can become merged in totality, and where the concepts of subjective and objective no longer apply. The powers of the mind at these levels are not fully understood; they *might* include the power of materialization, or of summoning fiends from hell.

Eliphas Lévi was perplexed by the problem of the reality of the phenomena produced in ritual magic. Although he wrote volumes on magic and taught the subject, he did not practise it much. But on one occasion, he could not resist the temptation to take a stab at it.

Lévi was staying in London. One day he returned to his hotel to find an envelope addressed to him. It contained half a card cut diagonally, with the Seal of Solomon, a six-sided figure, drawn on it. A note with it read, 'Tomorrow, at three o'clock, in front of Westminster Abbey, the second half of this card will be given to you.'

Of course he felt compelled to keep the assignation. He was met by a footman and ushered into a carriage in which a veiled woman in black showed him the other half of the card. She knew of him through a friend, she said, and wanted to offer him facilities for the practice of a ritual of spirit evocation. They drove to her house where she showed him a complete magical cabinet and a collection of vestments, instruments, and rare books on magic.

He decided to try to call up the spirit of one of the great legendary magicians of antiquity, Apollonius of Tyana. For this the prescribed ritual required a month of continued meditation on the dead person's life, work and personality. The preparation also included a three-week vegetarian diet and a week of severe fasting. This was no small sacrifice for Lévi who, like most Frenchmen, was fond of his food.

The night chosen for the attempted evocation duly arrived. He tells how he prepared the ritual, uttered the invocations, and then — as smoke floated around the altar — felt the Earth shake. A huge figure of a man appeared. But, before Lévi could put the two questions he had wanted to ask, he fell into a dream-filled swoon. When he came to, it seemed the questions were answered in his mind.

'Am I to conclude from all this that I really evoked, saw and touched the great Apollonius of Tyana?' Lévi asks. He realized the circumstances he had created had put him in what psychologists today would call an 'altered state of consciousness'.

'The effect of the preparations, the perfumes, the mirrors, the pentacles, is an actual drunkenness of the imagination, which must act powerfully upon a person otherwise nervous and impressionable,' he writes. But he did not believe the apparition had been only an insubstantial figment of his imagination. 'I do not explain the physical laws by which I saw and touched; I affirm solely that I did see and I did touch, apart from dreaming, and this is sufficient to establish the real efficacy of magical ceremonies.'

If this sounds incredible, consider some of the accounts of Tibetan ritual magic given by Alexandra David-Neel in her *Magic and Mystery in Tibet*. She was one of those extraordinary British women of the late nineteenth and early twentieth centuries who travelled alone in the East. She was honoured as a lady lama. Tough-minded and with a sharp eye for charlatanism, she was not so conditioned by the Western way of thinking as to dismiss anything that did not fit into its idea of reality. Living among one of the most mysterious and religious races in the world, she remained open-minded, observant, and ready to test for herself the rituals and disciplines by which the Tibetan lamas and magicians acquired and exercised their strange powers.

One was the ability to create a phantom being, a *tulpa*, from their own mind. Despite a lama's warning that these 'children of our mind' can get out of their maker's control and become mischievous or even dangerous, she decided to try creating a *tulpa*. She chose for her experiment a harmless character, a short fat monk 'of an innocent and jolly type'.

She had to shut herelf away for several months, concentrate her thoughts and practise certain prescribed rituals; then she succeeded in creating the phantom monk, and came to regard him as a guest in her apartment.

She decided to go on a journey on horseback, taking her servants, tents and the monk. During the journey she would sometimes turn and see him performing 'various actions of the kind that are natural to travellers, and that I had not commanded'. Once a herdsman brought a present of butter to her tent, saw the monk, and took him for a live lama.

Then, as she had been warned, her creation began to escape her control. He grew leaner and his face developed a mocking, malignant look. She decided to get rid of the phantom, but it took her six months' hard struggle. Afterwards she said: 'There is nothing strange in the fact that I may have created my own hallucination. The interesting point is that in these cases of materialization, others see the thought-forms that have been created.'

Magic originates in Man's desire for power. On the one hand, this desire may manifest as an aspiration to work in harmony with great cosmic and natural forces, and on this level magic is a noble art, requiring of its practitioners great self-discipline and dedication. But on the other hand the desire for power may manifest as an aspiration to subject another person to one's will or to do him injury. As may be expected, the rituals prescribed in the grimoires for such purposes do not involve the degree of patience, discipline and dedication that the practice of 'white' magic demands, and very often are little more than verbal rituals, spells or incantations.

The ancient Greeks believed the power of a spell was limitless. When, in the *Odyssey*, Ulysses is wounded in the thigh the bleeding is stopped by a magic spell. Circe could change men into beasts with her incantations. According to Pliny, the belief that the women of Thessaly could enchant the Moon out of the sky was so strong that during an eclipse the people set up a din with brass trumpets to prevent the Moon hearing the spells. Fire could be controlled, rivers made to change their course or flow backward, crops blighted or enticed from one field to another, men rendered impotent or women submissive — all by the power of incantation or the magic spell.

Spells are often associated with plants or herbs. (It was believed that the reason the Thessalian witches wished to bring the Moon down to Earth was to concentrate its influence on the plants they used for magical purposes.) Best known is the mandrake. It has a similar reputation and use in many cultures, probably because its root resembles a human figure.

As magic originates in the will it is not surprising that one aspect should be concerned with sexual conquest. But sexual magic concerns sex in quite a different way: in it the sexual act itself is an integral part of the ritual.

The fundamental idea behind it is that at the moment of orgasm a tremendous force is released. The practice demands the same training in visualization as is involved in rituals based on the Cabala or the grimoires. The participants must be able to prolong intercourse and defer orgasm until a subjective reality of such intensity has been built up that at the moment of orgasm it is projected as an objective reality and produces a magical effect in the real world. Alcohol or drugs may assist the process, and, if the invocation of a *demon or a planetary spirit is intended, the appropriate defensive symbols, incenses, and other essentials to the ritual are usually employed as well.

Lévi said of ritual magic, 'I regard the practice as destructive and dangerous.' A.E. Waite makes it clear in the opening pages of his *Book of Ceremonial Magic* that he too deplores it as the 'hunger and thirst of the soul seeking to satisfy its cravings in the ashpits of uncleanness, greed, hatred, and malice'. He calls the grimoires 'little books of wicked and ultra-foolish secrets'. He justifies the publication of his own *Complete Grimoire* only as a definitive act of scholarship and 'a contribution of some value to certain side issues of historical research'.

The examples we have given seem to illustrate his objection to ritual magic as normally practised for trivial or ignoble purposes. Yet even if all the 'ultra-foolish secrets' of the grimoires are dismissed as charlatanism or superstition, and their elaborate rites as so much mumbo-jumbo, there remains a fascination about ritual magic — a fascination with the strange powers and hidden potentials of our own minds. SH

Sai Baba

Born 1926 in Puttaparti, a remote Indian village where he still presides over his ashram, Sai Baba is the most impressive of all modern Indian yogis.

He was a normal child, but at the age of fourteen, following a strange seizure which left him ill for a long time — during which he would burst into song or poetry, reciting long passages of Vedanta philosophy — he suddenly announced to his astonished parents that he was Sai Baba; that is, an avatar, or divine reincarnation of India's most powerful mystic, Sai Baba of Shirdi, who died in 1918. Baba's mission then began in earnest.

What distinguishes him from India's long tradition of miracle-working gurus is the extraordinary range of his paranormal abilities. Levitation, transportation, PK, ESP, the ability to produce objects from thin air, transmutation, healing powers (including a successful operation on a terminal cancer patient), making food for 100 miraculously expand to feed 1,000, and even — on at least one occasion — raising the dead. All these manifestations, or *siddhis*, have been demonstrated frequently in the presence of highly respected professional people.

His teachings are basically those of the *Bhakti marga* — the *yoga of divine love which preaches self-surrender and control over the bodily appetites — and are given usually in the form of simple parables. His message contains an almost Nietzschean note in that he preaches that all men possess godlike potential. We are at present the link between animal and god; but given spiritual evolution we can become a race of supermen. BM

Voodoo

Voodoo is a religion, practised primarily in Haiti. In it *ritual magic plays a prominent part. The religion is a bizarre amalgam of tribal African and Catholic Christian traditions and practices. Its ceremonies involve a good deal of vigorous dancing and loud chanting, the purpose of which is not worship but to enable the voodoo gods to possess the physical bodies of the devotees. *Possession is an experience eagerly sought by the devotee because it is seen as the means by which the gods manifest themselves and interact with humans.

There are sinister aspects, however. The supernatural world its rituals invoke is inhabited not only by gods but also by hosts of evil spirits, *baka*; these are believed to be able to transform themselves into certain kinds of animal — for example, the wild grey pig found in Haiti, and the *loup-garou*, or werewolf.

Some of its magical practices are very unpleasant, such as the ritual injuring of some representation of a person — for example, a doll — with the object of inflicting injury or death upon that person. There are many testimonies as to the effectiveness of such rituals, although a psychologist would attribute the effects to suggestion rather than magic. The believer in voodoo also has to fear the *Zombie.

From all these supernatural horrors the only reliable protection, voodoo teaches, is regular attendance at the voodoo church and sacrifice to the gods. Although it affords us convincing evidence of the powers of ritual to alter human perceptions of reality, voodoo can hardly be regarded otherwise than as a debased religion founded on the craven human characteristics of fear and the urge to seek security through propitiation. SH

Witchcraft

Despite the image of ugly old women flying about on broomsticks and casting malevolent spells, witchcraft is remarkably widespread, and usually harmless. Most rural areas have their wart-charmers, for example, and most country doctors will admit that this method of getting rid of warts is quicker and less painful than burning them off. The charmers are usually able also to cure ringworm, snakebite and bleeding. Doctors are inclined to believe that some

Continued on page 81

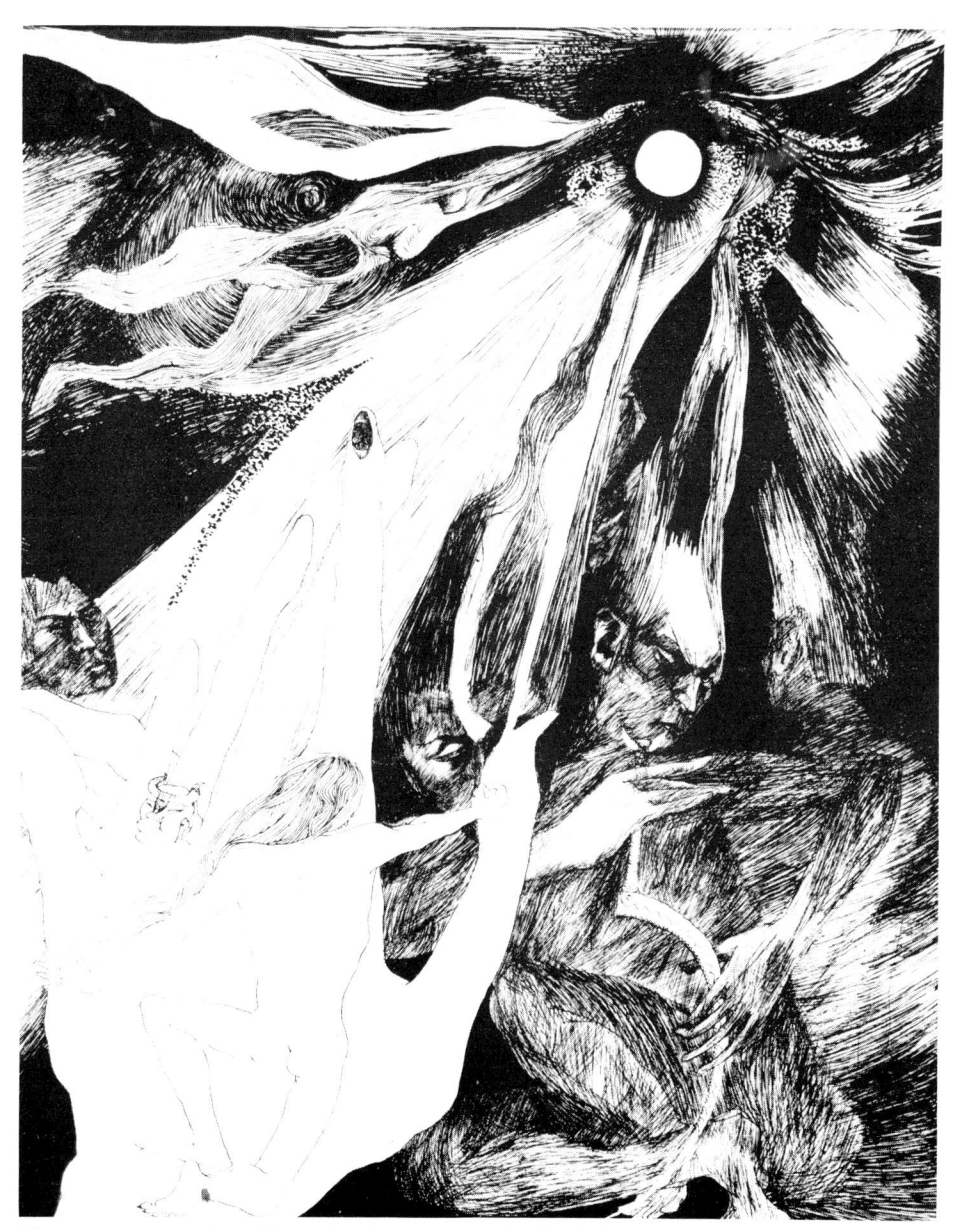

There now seems to be evidence that the Moon has a greater influence on us than common sense would suggest — on all of us, not just 'lunatics'. It is possible that our distant ancestors may have been very strongly influenced by the interaction between the Moon's magnetic field and that of the Earth (see page 17). This picture by Steffi Grant, 'Full Moon', portrays the intuitive suggestion of certain occultists that the Moon can be thought of as a hole in the sky, through which shines light from the astral plane beyond: to this astral plane our minds may fly.

Above: The Great Pyramid at Giza has been the focus of more unorthodox speculation than any other single monument. However, it does seem possible that, like Stonehenge, it was originally designed as an astronomical observatory. (See page 41.)

Below: Stonehenge was probably designed to facilitate astronomical observations. The astonishing number of apparently meaningful alignments of its constituent members was revealed in 1963 when Professor Gerald Hawkins analysed the arrangement of the monument using a computer. (See page 39.)

Sighthenge is a megalithic observatory with a difference: it was built in 1978/9, to the design of Duncan Lunan. In the background the skyscrapers of modern Glasgow eerily echo the standing stones. The monument was designed according to the principles thought to have been followed by the builders of ancient monuments such as Stonehenge and Carnac, and allows the making of a number of astronomical measurements.

Glastonbury Tor, centre of numerous legends and theories concerning ancient knowledge. Even today, thousands arrive every year in quest of the spiritual meaning behind the mythologies concerning Arthur and the Grail. (See page 36.)

Above: The Holy Thorn at Glastonbury Abbey. (See page 36.)

Below: 'Sir Percival and the King', an illustration from a manuscript account of the quest for the Holy Grail. According to some versions of the legend, Percival was one of the three knights whose purity allowed them success in their quest (the other two were Galahad and Bors). (See page 38.)

Aleister Crowley, the 'Great Beast 666', as he was in 1910, drawn from memory in 1953 by the prominent artist of the occult, Austin Osman Spare. (See page 50.)

Above: 'The Demon Feast', a grotesque painting by Margaret Cook, leaves little doubt as to the malevolence of such entities. (See page 50.)

Right: Some of the best evidence for the existence of ghosts takes the form of photographs which show ghostly figures, although the photographer believed when he took the picture that there was no such figure to be seen. In 1956 a certain Mr Bootman, a bank manager, took this photograph of what he thought was the empty church at Eastry (See page 53.)

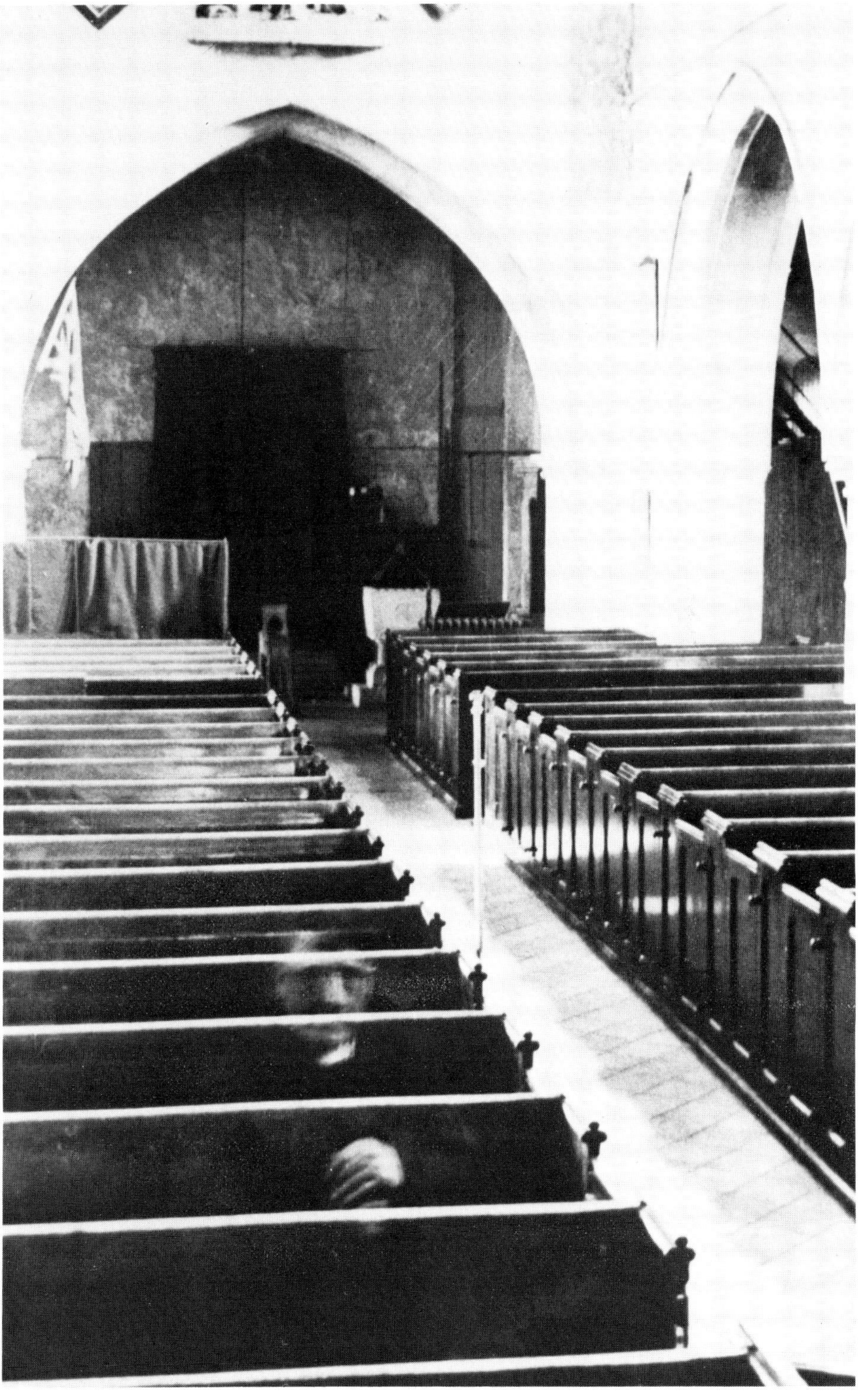

Above: A recurring theme throughout all the literature of ritual magic is that the unwary magician may suffer drastically for his actions or draw upon himself exactly the dire punishment which he wished to inflict upon others (see page 61). This illustration, 'The Pylon of the Pit' by Steffi Grant, symbolizes these dangers to the ritual magician. Any failure of concentration on the part of the incautious practitioner, or his affection by any untoward influence, can cause him to topple into an infernal pit of demons.

Right: One of the photographs taken on the Menlung Glacier by Eric Shipton of footprints thought possibly to be those of a Yeti. The prints were about $12\frac{1}{2}$in long by $6\frac{1}{2}$in wide, and have yet to be satisfactorily explained. It should be borne in mind that sunlight upon snow can cause recognizable markings to adopt bizarre new configurations. (See page 85.)

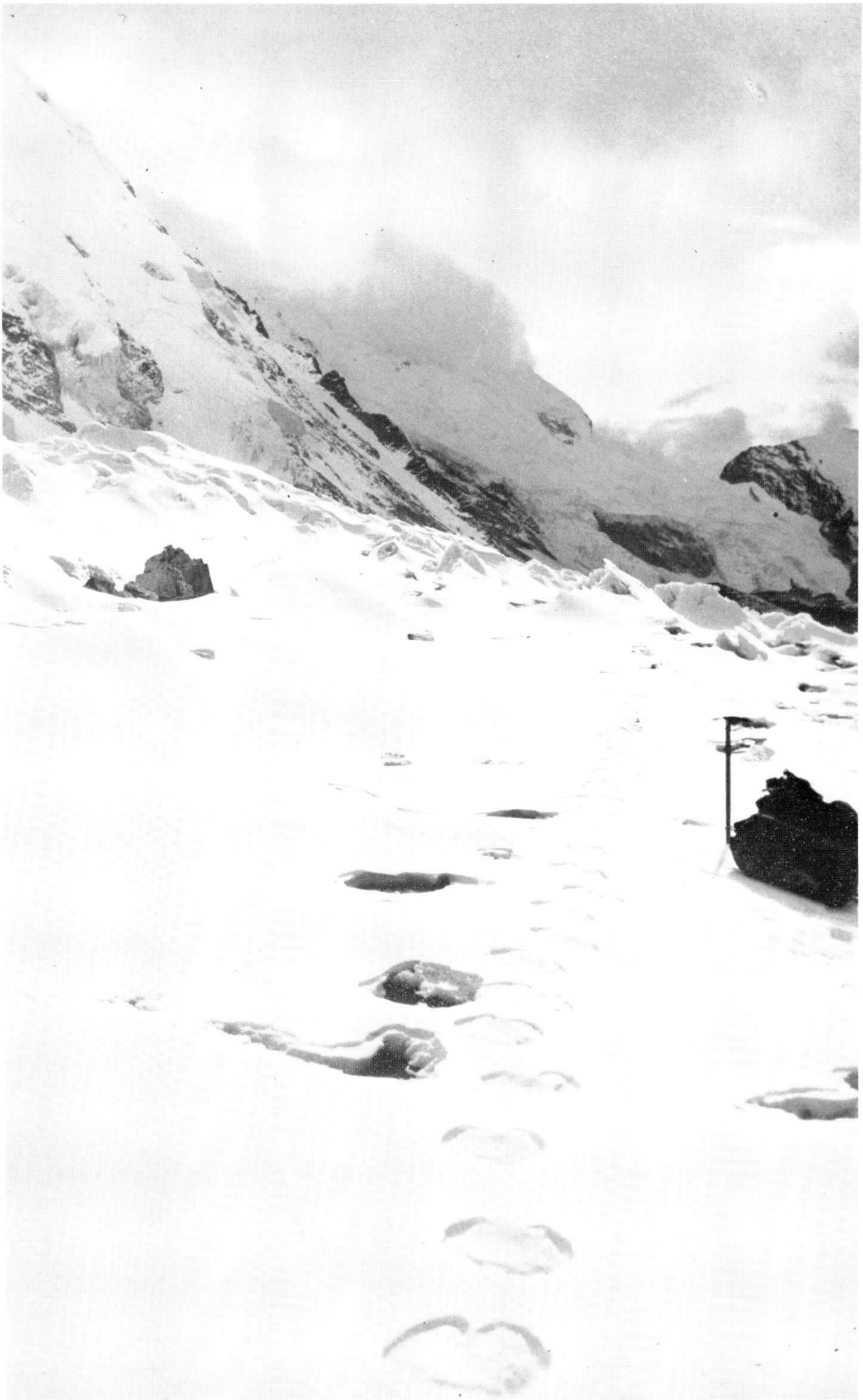

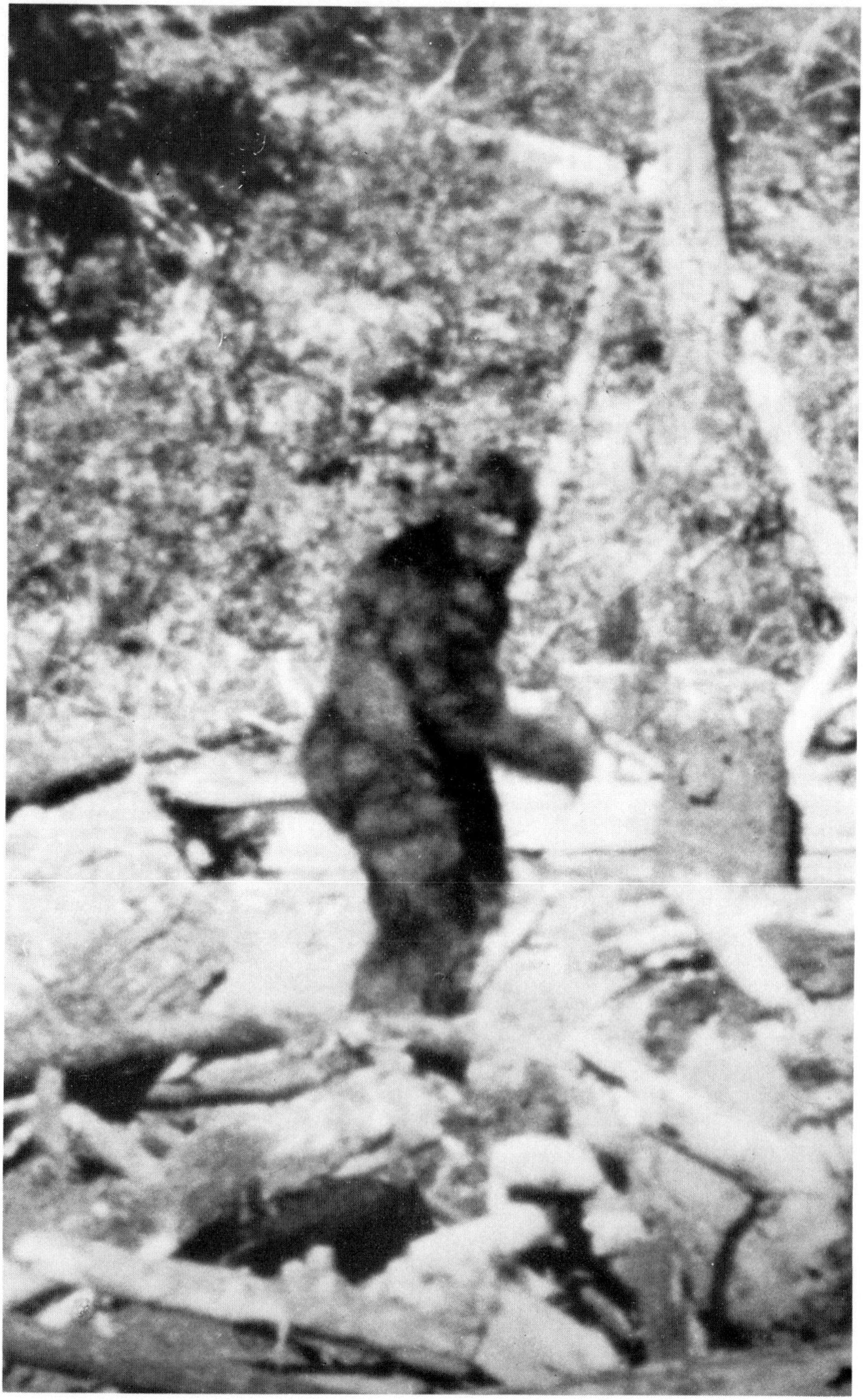

Left: Part of a frame from the famous film shot by Roger Patterson in late 1967 at Bluff Creek, Northern California, which appears to show Bigfoot. Scientists who have viewed the film have been able to tell a great deal about the nature of its 'star' — in particular, that there are considerable inconsistencies. For example, the film shows an artificiality of gait which can best be explained by imagining a man attempting to extend his stride, in order to make his footprints more convincing. (See page 85.)

Above: One of the famous series of photographs taken between 1917 and 1920 by two young girls, Elsie Wright and Frances Griffiths, in Cottingley, Yorkshire. According to 'believers' no scientific test has yet shown how these photographs could have been faked. However, there are various internal inconsistencies which are hard to explain; moreover, it is strange that these fairies should so closely resemble those in Victorian picture books, and not at all the 'little people' of more traditional legend. (See page 88.)

Above: A photograph taken in 1977 by Anthony Shiels of what appears at first sight to be the Loch Ness Monster. The nature of the patterns of ripples on the surface suggest that it must be a very small monster, but it seems more likely to be a photograph of a water-bird whose body is temporarily submerged. (See page 92.)

75

Above: A great Norwegian sea serpent, from Olaus Magnus's *Historia de Gentibus Septentrionalibus* (1567). (See page 91.)

Below: An artist's impression based upon the descriptions given by six twelve-year-old girls of a sea monster which they claimed to have seen at Barmouth, Gwynedd, Wales. There are those who detect an uncanny resemblance to a drawing that an artist might make of a turtle from memory, especially if he had not seen a turtle before. (See page 91.)

Spontaneous combustion, if it occurs (and there is almost compelling evidence that it does), is one of the most bizarre and inexplicable of 'Fortean' phenomena. This illustration, 'The Appointed Time' by Phiz, is for the most famous fictional account of the phenomenon, that in Dickens's *Bleak House*. Guppy and Weevle have just arrived to discover that the remarkably unpleasant Krook has received his just deserts.

No. 1.]
Nos. 2, 3 and 4 are Presented, Gratis, with this No.
[Price 1d.
VARNEY
THE
VAMPIRE.
OR THE
FEAST OF BLOOD
A ROMANCE OF EXCITING INTEREST.
BY THE AUTHOR OF
"GRACE RIVERS; OR, THE MERCHANT'S DAUGHTER."
LONDON: E. LLOYD, SALISBURY-SQUARE, AND ALL BOOKSELLERS.

Left: The vampire has featured in many phenomenally popular works of fiction, of which Bram Stoker's *Dracula* is only one. This illustration shows the title-page to the first part of the partwork edition of one of the most successful Victorian vampire fictions, Thomas Prescott-Prest's *Varney the Vampire, or The Feast of Blood*, first published in 1847. (See page 95.)

Above: Mir Bashir, possibly the world's leading palmist. When in the 1960s Dr J. Barker was writing his *Scared to Death* he conducted a survey of clairvoyants and other predictors, asking them about his own life expectations. Mir Bashir was the only interviewee who refused to make such a prediction; the rest told Barker that he had a long and happy life ahead of him. Barker died while *Scared to Death* was still in proof. This minor but interesting example is only one from an illustrious career. (See page 108.)

An illustration by an unknown artist showing the great Elizabethan mystic John Dee engaged in scrying; in the background is his colleague Edward Kelley. In fact, in most accounts their roles were reversed: Kelley was by far the better scryer of the two. (See pages 112 and 57.)

form of *hypnosis is involved (deep hypnosis can be used to cure warts) but this seems to leave out of account the fact that it works as well over the telephone as in personal contact.

In most primitive or rural communities, witches were tolerated and respected until the thirteenth century; then the 'witch craze' began, and during the next 400 years hundreds of thousands of women were tortured and burnt all over Europe. And the change in attitude was basically due to misunderstanding. It began in the eleventh century with the rise of the Cathars who, like the earlier Gnostics and Manichees, believed that everything to do with the world and the flesh was evil, and everything to do with the spirit was good. This meant they believed the world was created by the *Devil. The Catholic Church condemned this attitude because the Bible states that God created the world 'and saw that it was good'. But, because of the corruption of the Church, the Cathar heresy spread fast, from northern France to Constantinople. In the thirteenth century the Church called for a crusade against the heresy, and thousands of Cathars died for their faith in the Toulouse area, a Cathar centre. The survivors fled, often taking refuge in remote Swiss valleys. Their belief that 'this world' and its pleasures are evil led easily to the misunderstanding that they worshipped the Devil. Witchcraft trials began in the Pyrenees and the Alps, and in 1390 the first witch trial took place in Paris. Dominican inquisitors descended on the areas where 'Dualism' was still accepted, and the witch craze spread like any other mass psychosis.

This is not to say that the whole idea of witchcraft was a delusion. There is abundant evidence that magic *can* work (see *primitive magic), and the simple magic of country people may have often been connected with the ancient nature religion based on the worship of Diana. Margaret Murray became convinced that 'witches' Sabbaths' were pre-Christian ceremonies of nature worship. *Aradia, or the Gospel of the Witches* (see *fertility religion) indicates that, in Italy at least, witches may have regarded themselves as 'freedom fighters' against the Church and the aristocracy. And, while it is impossible to accept accounts of witches' intercourse with the *Devil and assorted demons and incubi, there can be no doubt that witches often attempted to apply their powers to malevolent purposes.

The North Berwick witch trial is a case in point. Gilly Duncan, a servant girl with a gift for *healing, was tortured by her master, the deputy bailiff of Tranent, until she confessed to intercourse with the Devil, and implicated many other people, including a schoolmaster, John Fian, an elderly gentlewoman, Agnes Sampson, and two other women of good reputation. Under torture, they also confessed. James VI of Scotland (later James I of England) was present at the 'questioning', because Sampson admitted she had raised the storm that had almost wrecked the King's ship when he returned from Denmark with his bride. All were tortured and burnt, as was Richard Graham, an associate of the Earl of Bothwell. Bothwell was accused of conspiring with the witches to kill the King and imprisoned, but was later released.

In his *Encyclopedia of Witchcraft and Demonology*, Russell Hope Robbins expressed the view that this was basically a case of hysteria and stupidity. Yet it is worth bearing in mind that Bothwell had a sinister reputation in later life as a dabbler in black magic, and that Fian had at one time been his secretary. Bothwell had every reason to want to kill the King. And, if we also make the plausible assumption that some witches may have the same kind of power as African witch-doctors use to summon rain, then it is no longer possible to take it for granted that the witches concerned were totally innocent, and that James — who wrote his *Demonologie* as a result of the experience — was a dupe of the inquisitors.

In the UK the death penalty for witchcraft was repealed in 1736, although the practice of throwing suspected witches into ponds to see if they would float continued for another fifty years. In fact, witchcraft was forbidden by law until 1951.

The repeal of the Witchcraft Act in this year was a signal for the modern 'witchcraft revival'. Gerald Gardner achieved fame in 1954 with his *Witchcraft Today*, in which he declared that witchcraft was still alive and well, and that there were dozens of 'covens' throughout the UK, practising their rites and worshipping Diana and Mother Earth. Whether or not his assertion was true at the time, it soon became true as bored householders on housing estates formed covens.

We should be cautious about assuming that the whole thing was pure imagination. *Crowley was in many ways a thoroughly unadmirable character, yet he undoubtedly possessed genuine 'magical powers'. And those who have studied the modern witch cults in the UK have no doubt that witchcraft *can* work. But the fact that Gardner's book contained an approving introduction by Margaret Murray indicates that witchcraft has ceased to carry sinister overtones, and can once again be studied with detachment. CW

Evolution: 2

Evolutionary scientists know a great deal about the way that physical evolution has taken place over the last few billion years; for example, they can tell us the details of the way in which the bones of the joint of a reptilian jaw adapted and were incorporated into the mammalian middle ear. For details like this they rely upon good fossil evidence.

Such evidence, for obvious reasons, is not available when one tries to trace the evolution of intelligence: while we can guess at the mental powers of our fossil ancestors by examining the insides of skulls, we can do little else until we reach the comparatively recent stage where cultural relics can be found, where archaeology takes over from palaeontology.

Occultists, whether they realize it or not, believe in a dynamic evolution in which their minds may play a role; in this they are at one with modern technologists. The miraculous, too, may be considered in evolutionary terms; as Arthur C. Clarke has pointed out, any technology sufficiently advanced upon one's own is indistinguishable from magic.

In the next section we consider what could — just possibly — be sports of evolution. JG

PART THREE
STRANGE CREATURES AND UNUSUAL EVENTS

Introductory: 3

In May 1932 there died in a New York hospital a man who had devoted his life to trying to convince people that the Universe is an odder place than we realize.

Haldane once made the same comment — that the Universe is not only queerer than we imagine, but queerer than we *can* imagine.

Charles Hoy Fort was not a scientist like Haldane. He was just an amateur writer who believed quite literally that Man needs to be shaken awake to the wildly improbable world he inhabits. His first (unpublished) book, called simply *X*, argued that Earth is controlled from Mars. His next (also unpublished) book, *Y*, supported the theory that Earth is hollow — a view that still has many supporters. But he was by no means a member of the 'lunatic fringe'. He defended his strange theories in a state of humorous cussedness. And when, at forty-two, a small legacy enabled him to become a man of leisure, he spent his days in the New York public libraries, searching old newspapers for accounts of strange happenings. His first collection, *The Book of the Damned*, achieved far less impact than it should have done because he made no attempt to argue any new and exciting theory: he simply dumped a great load of weird 'facts' in front of the reader and left him to make up his own mind. He liked to point out that when, in 1768, French peasants in the fields near Luce saw a great stone object hurtling out of the sky and the French Academy of Sciences asked Lavoisier to investigate, Lavoisier reported that the witnesses must be mistaken or lying, because everyone knows that stones do not fall out of the sky. Another three decades passed by before science accepted the existence of meteorites...

Of course, Fort's attempt was doomed to failure, for a perfectly straightforward reason. Science *will* do its best to take account of 'oddities'; but before it can even begin the oddities need to be explainable with some kind of theory. Showers of live fish and frogs may be well authenticated, but it seems impossible to understand *how* they could happen. So science has decided, for the moment, that they do not.

Fort's name and ideas lived on — Tiffany Thayer founded a Fortean Society, and there is in the UK at the moment an excellent magazine, *The Fortean Times*. More important, other determined spirits have done their best to present 'strange happenings' in a more readable form — Vincent Gaddis (*Mysterious Fires and Lights*), Ivan T. Sanderson (*Things*) and, more recently, John Michell, whose *Phenomena* (with R.J.M. Rickard) is in the truly Fortean tradition. After the 'coming of the UFOs' in 1947, books with titles like *Strange World* became commonplace, and something of a joke, for the authors were concerned only to amaze and astound, and seldom bothered to check their facts (Michael Harrison's *Fire From Heaven*, about the mystery of spontaneous combustion, is an honourable exception). And meanwhile the most remarkable of all modern Forteans, William F. Corliss, collects strange happenings more deliberately and scientifically than Fort; he runs his 'Sourcebook Project' from Glen Arm, Maryland, and brings out immense volumes containing original reports from newspapers and scientific periodicals. (Interested readers should contact him direct at The Sourcebook Project, Glen Arm, Md 21057, USA.)

And why bother about weird phenomena and unusual events? Not, certainly, because they may one day provide us with a new type of science; I, for one, am perfectly contented with the kind we already have. The reason can be found at the beginning of my *The Occult*, in which I quote Ouspensky's *A New Model of the Universe*: his description of how, when he was working as a journalist reporting the Hague conference, his desk drawer was full of books with titles like *The Occult World, Atlantis and Lemuria, Ritual Magic* and *The Temple of Satan*. No doubt all were basically nonsense — as we now know, for example, that the incredible 'Cosmic Ice Theory' of Hörbiger is nonsense. But what *is* important is the hunger that such works were intended to satisfy: that imaginative craving for a more interesting and complex reality than the one that seems to surround us. Ouspensky's interest in the Great *Pyramid and *Atlantis led him to seek out *Gurdjieff, through whom he received genuine 'esoteric knowledge'. And Gurdjieff himself had been led to seek out such knowledge because of a childhood interest in occultism and the 'supernatural'.

It is in this spirit, then, that we offer the following section. Treat it, by all means, as something of a joke. But bear in mind Shaw's comment that every jest is in earnest in the womb of time.　　　　　　　　　　　　　　　　　　　　　　　　CW

Abominable Snowmen

Does the 'Abominable Snowman' exist? Many 'witnesses' say so; but although footprints have been photographed no such creature has been caught, and much of the 'evidence' has been exposed as fake. This does not deny the possibility, of course. Obviously, he would be hard to trace, lurking in remote areas, quick to disappear at the first hint of danger. The Yeti of the Himalayas deserves his privacy: existence cannot be easy in such extreme cold, 20,000ft above sea-level, needing sufficient food to sustain a man of reputed strength and maybe exceptional size (5–15ft tall).

Perhaps the most authoritative report is of the giant, fresh footprints, 13 by 18in, seen by two UK mountaineers crossing the Menlung Glacier in 1951. Eric Shipton's photograph, revealing a print the length of his ice axe, with definite toe formation, caused controversy. Ten years later, he reaffirmed his belief: 'There could be no doubt whatever that a large creature had passed that way a very short time before, and that whatever it was it was not a human being, not a bear, not any species of monkey known to exist in Asia.' Sceptics suggested that such footprints *were* those of a langur monkey or red bear, and of course they might have expanded as they melted at the edges — make a footprint in fresh snow on a sunny winter's day and watch the results: they can be dramatic. The *Lancet*, however, left the possibility open: 'Even in the twentieth century there are many thinly populated and almost unexplored regions of the world, and in several of these there have arisen rumours of the existence of large animals still awaiting scientific discovery.'

The first Western report of a Yeti dates from 1832, when the UK Resident Officer in Nepal wrote that some of his porters had fled from a hairy beast they called the *rakshas*, 'demon', and told him that similar wild men had been seen there for centuries. This suggests that such creatures have become part of folklore as if people *wanted* to believe in them. Significantly, Tibetan children were threatened with warnings of the wild men if they were naughty (see *lycanthropy). This could also explain reports of similar wild men in North America: the Bigfoot first reported by the Indians, and the Sasquatch ('hairy giant') in Canada.

John Napier, however, has written of Bigfoot: 'Too many people claim to have seen it, or at least to have seen footprints, to dismiss its reality out of hand.' Equally, the huge popularity of *King Kong* confirms the appeal that such a creature has to the imagination.　　　　　　　　　　　DF

Appearing People

Only a handful of people are known to have appeared as if from nowhere — best known are Kaspar *Hauser and *Spring-Heeled Jack. This is probably because such people would go unnoticed if attention were not for some reason focused on them. On the other hand, every mortuary has its share of John Does, some of whom prove impossible to identify: it is as if they had appeared from nowhere.

The legends, myths and folklore of every nation contain accounts of a spectacular assortment of weird apparitions. It is particularly interesting to note the way in which the phenomenon, which has not changed throughout history, has modified itself to what is familiar at the time. In the ninth century the Archbishop of Lyon, St Agobard, wrote of the peasants' belief in people who flew in cloud-ships and came from a land called Magonia. Agobard was involved with four people who claimed to have been kidnapped by Magonians, but he disbelieved their story and, apparently, concluded that Magonia was a manifestation of paganism.

The Magonians did not go away. Three hundred years later, the chronicler Gervaise of Tilbury told how a cloud-sailor left a cloud-ship to untangle an anchor from a tomb. He died in the act, we are told, 'stifled by the breath of our gross air'.

Fairy-lore (see *elementals) is a fund of remarkable stories about appearing people. Fairies were often depicted as no different in appearance and stature from humans, but they were believed to belong to a distinct species evolved separately from Man. A particularly haunting story was told in the twelfth century by William of Newburgh, a reliable chronicler of the period. Two green children were found. They spoke an unknown language and refused all food except broad beans. One died, but the other gradually lost her green hue and was eventually able to tell her story, explaining that she came from an underground world of perpetual twilight where everybody was coloured green.

Other people have claimed to come from lands not known to exist. In 1851 a certain Joseph Vorin came to the attention of the German authorities; he said that he was from Laxaria, in a country called Sakria. In 1905 a young man was arrested in Paris; he spoke an unknown language but managed to convey that he was a citizen of Lisbian — *not*, it should be stressed, Lisbon. And in 1954 a passport check in Japan is alleged to have produced a man with papers issued by the nation of Taured. Between 1904 and 1905, ten 'wild men' were found in different parts of England. One spoke a language nobody had heard before and carried a book full of unknown writing.

But do people actually appear out of thin air? It *could* be happening all the time, spectators simply disbelieving their senses and assuming that they just had not noticed the person there before. In January 1914, however, shoppers in Chatham were startled when a naked man suddenly appeared in their midst. Nobody had actually seen him appear; he simply was there where a naked man hadn't been before.

Over the last couple of decades there have been hundreds of reports of animals either unknown to zoology or not known to be indigenous to the place from which they are reported. There have been reports of inexplicable 'things', creatures of human form but with wings and often no head. Hitherto viewed as separate phenomena, the similarities in these reported creatures — their elusiveness, ambiguity, and the way in which they have related to the period and society — suggest that they represent a single phenomenon manifesting itself in different ways. A fresh assessment of both appearing and *vanishing people might provide some answers to many of the complex questions surrounding the paranormal.   PB

Bermuda Triangle

The Bermuda Triangle is an area of the western Atlantic contained within an imaginary triangle connecting Bermuda, Puerto Rico and the coast of Florida. Hundreds of ships and aircraft are said to have vanished there in mysterious circumstances, leaving no wreckage and no survivors. In some cases garbled, inexplicable radio messages have been received, telling of weird fogs, strange behaviour of equipment, unaccountable loss of power, the sea looking different. According to several authors the number and circumstances of the losses exceed what can be accounted for by the natural hazards of the sea, mechanical malfunction and human error. In short, it is claimed that some hitherto unknown and currently unexplained force is causing the losses, and that the authorities, unable to explain the phenomenon, are operating a cover-up. However, there is no shortage of theories, and these range from death rays from lost *Atlantis and interdimensional voids to *UFOs and unspecified electromagnetic anomalies.

Although it is said that the region has been shrouded in mystery and superstition since the days of Columbus, interest really began as a result of an event in 1945. Five US Navy aircraft vanished after the control tower had received a series of strange messages from the flight leader: 'We seem to be off course, we cannot see land ... we are not sure of our position ... everything is wrong, strange ... even the sea doesn't look as it should ... it looks like we are entering ...' The mystery was heightened a few hours later when an aircraft participating in the search operation also vanished without trace.

Further losses over the years attracted the attention of several sensationalist writers, most of whom called the area by different names. It was not until 1964 that Vincent Gaddis in an article coined the name 'Bermuda Triangle'. Ten years later Charles Berlitz's bestselling *The Bermuda Triangle* made the name a household word, and the region became the subject of or inspiration for numerous books, novels, feature films, documentaries, a short-lived television series and even a children's board game.

The 7th District Coast Guard, which has jurisdiction over the area, has always denied claims that the Bermuda Triangle is a danger zone and that some 'supernatural' phenomenon is active there. It is, they say, one of the busiest regions in the world, crossed by military and commercial ships and aircraft and by thousands of private pilots and boat owners, many of whom are inexperienced and do not take adequate precautions to cope with conditions they might meet. Moreover, the region is prone to sudden and dramatic changes in weather, and is the home of the Gulf Stream, a fast-moving body of water which can carry a disabled vessel or unwary boater miles off course, and disperse wreckage over a wide area within hours.

Proponents of the view that some unknown, inexplicable force is operating in the area acknowledge the Coast Guard view, but do not believe it explains the very odd circumstances of the losses — no wreckage, no survivors.

On analysing the Bermuda Triangle disappearances, however, several researchers have concluded that few of the losses happened as described, that facts have been distorted, research has been shoddy, and prosaic explanations scrupulously avoided. They found many of the details about the US Navy aircraft incident in 1945 — the famous case of Flight 19 — were grossly inaccurate. They found that the crew was inexperienced. The flight leader believed that they had flown off course (which in fact they had not) but was uncertain about where they were. Radio communications grew bad and the leader was not informed of his error. The weather deteriorated, a storm blew up and the sea became rough. It grew dark and finally the aircraft ran out of fuel. The chance of successfully ditching in heavy seas at night was negligible, particularly for inexperienced pilots; even if the crew succeeded, it is doubtful if they would have survived long in the prevailing seas. The search operation did not get under way until after dark, and was little more than a token gesture, because darkness made it almost impossible to detect any wreckage, and by dawn any debris which might have survived the ditching would have been dispersed by the sea. As for the baffling radio messages, there is no evidence that they ever took place and they cannot be traced beyond an article published in 1962. Of the missing search aircraft, it was seen to explode twenty minutes after take-off.

A key story in the Triangle collection is the case of the Japanese freighter *Raifuku Maru*, which is said to have vanished after radioing: 'Danger like dagger now ... come quick ...', and thereby giving rise to speculation as to what kind of danger looks like a dagger. In fact the message logged by receiving stations was: 'Now very danger, come quick', and a vessel which went to the freighter's aid found her engulfed by a violent storm.

The Triangle account of the bark *Freya* is an example of the gross misresearch conducted by sensationalist writers. Featured in almost every book on the subject, she is said to have been found inexplicably abandoned in the Triangle. In fact, records show that she was abandoned at a time of submarine volcanic activity — and in the Pacific, which is far from the Triangle, even considering the elastic boundaries given to the area by many writers.

Research has revealed prosaic explanations for most of the Triangle disappearances. Some evidence does seem to exist for unexplained magnetic aberrations in the region, but these are not likely to cause anything to disappear. In fact, research has shown that the only thing connected with the Triangle which is in danger of abruptly vanishing is the Triangle myth itself. PB

Elementals

Today we think of fairies as fluttering little creatures with gauze-like wings; once, the fairy was regarded as a formidable force.

What is a fairy? Webster describes 'an imaginary being supposed to be able to assume human form, usually tiny, and to meddle in human affairs'. One encyclopedia limits them sharply: 'A legend of the British Isles, supernatural beings similar to humans and usually beautiful but having magical powers and generally ill disposed towards men.'

The roots of the legend are distant and deep. Evans Wentz, author of *The Fairy Faith in Celtic Countries*, wrote: 'There seems never to have been an uncivilized tribe, a race or nation of civilized men, who have not had some form of belief in an unseen world, peopled by unseen beings.' He maintained that 'fairies actually exist as invisible beings or intelligences' and concluded that Fairyland is as real as our own visible world, which is immersed like an island in an unexplored ocean peopled by species of living beings beyond our comprehension.

This belief in invisible beings who can be seen might explain why fairies are accepted in Ireland, where the gift of seeing such spirits remains in the unspoilt countryside. Yeats asked, 'Are they "the Gods of the earth"? Many poets and all mystic writers in all ages and countries, have declared that behind the visible are chains and chains of conscious beings, who are not of heaven but of the earth, who have no inherent form but change according to their whim, or the mind that sees them.'

They change according to their environment, too. In the soft mists of Connemara they are known as the 'good people', but in the harsher climate of Scotland they can be malignant, like the dreaded water kelpie or the nuckelavee, a particularly nasty 'spirit' found in the Lowlands with a head ten times larger than a man's, a mouth like a pig's, no hair on his body (because he had no skin), and a breath that destroyed crops and sickened animals — and presumably provided a useful scapegoat.

The redcaps dyed their caps in the blood of travellers, and the *baobhan sith* looked like beautiful women but sucked the blood of the men who fell in love with them — both revealing vampiric tendencies (see *vampires). More agreeable are the trooping fairies of Cornwall, mischievous but benevolent. As any summer visitor to Cornwall will confirm, the shops abound with souvenir pixies, also known as 'piskys', and in some parts the white moths that emerge at twilight are still known as 'pisgies'. Pixies were handsome little people with such an obsession with cleanliness that Cornish housewives kept their homes spotless. Their mischievous nature was expressed in blowing out candles, kissing servant maids, and flying long distances to find wine cellars — hence 'pixy led' or 'pixilated', good-humouredly drunk.

'Elfs' or 'Elves' was an Anglo-Saxon word for spirits, described by Scott as 'sprites of a coarser sort ... and more malignant temper ... than the Fairies'.

The hobgoblin could cure whooping-cough, and parents brought their sick children to chant, 'Hobhole Hob! My bairn's got kincough. Tak't off!' In *A Midsummer Night's Dream* Shakespeare mixed him up with Puck, but they might well have been the same. Hob may be the diminutive of 'Robin', and Robin Goodfellow, supposedly the son of Oberon, a King of the Fairies, has been associated with Robin Hood, always dressed in the favourite green. 'Puck' comes from 'pook', an elf or sprite, from the Dutch 'spook', the Welsh 'puca', the Icelandic 'piki' and the Irish 'pooka', which assumed the shape of animals (it seems reasonable to assume that 'pixie' is yet another version). Puck is also synonymous with Will-o'-the-wisp and Jack-o'-lantern.

The imp is the worst of hobgoblins, and comes straight from Hell. In sixteenth-century paintings it is portrayed as a little devil with a round cap, pointed shoes and a bushy tail; startlingly, its hands are naked feet.

The typical fairy is not sympathetic: quick to take offence, so snobbish he insists on being referred to as 'gentry', paralysing men and cattle with fairy darts and kidnapping human children. But he can be bribed with a saucer of milk left on the windowsill overnight. And some fairies are actually grateful — for example, the leprechaun, who works as a shoemaker, and the Scottish brownie, a small but industrious creature who refuses payment for such services as the settling of a swarm of bees.

It is significant that the word 'fairy' comes from 'fey', a romantic quality that is part of the Celtic nature. But this does not explain the persistent belief in fairies, nor such documentation as the Cottingley Fairies reported in 1917 by two intelligent girls of ten and thirteen who took photographs of fairies at the bottom of their garden in the Yorkshire village of Cottingley. In spite of photographic tests, these were never exposed as fakes and were accepted by Conan Doyle, who published the story under the sensational title 'An epoch-making event ... fairies photographed'. Even so serious a character as Air Chief Marshal Lord Dowding claimed they were genuine. However, the fairies were *exactly* what we would expect, with the conventional wings, and both Doyle and Dowding were convinced spiritualists and *wanted* to believe.

This desire is part of the legend. Wentz claimed 'the germs of much of our European religions and philosophies, customs and institutions' are found in this belief. 'It is one of the chief keys to unlock the mysteries of Celtic mythology.'

There is, also, the Pygmy Theory: that fairies are a *folk memory* of a people who really did inhabit the Earth and now are seen as ghostlike images. Writing on romances in the West of England Robert Hunt refers to the Small People 'believed by some to be the spirits of the people who inhabited Cornwall many thousands of years ago ... long, long before the birth of Christ'. Persisting today, as glimpses of the invisible? DF

Giants

How big are giants? A race of exceptionally tall men, suggested by the 8ft 2in skeletons found on Lundy? Or men of truly enormous proportions?

Folklore has an abundance of giant legends. The giant Ymir, in Norse mythology, was the first man and created the human race. The Indians of north-west America had stories of primeval giants who were cannibals. Greek mythology gave us the Titans and the Gigantes who had serpents for feet. And British mythology claimed that the island was inhabited by giants until they were defeated by Brutus, who seized the last two giants, *Gog and Magog.

The subjection of a giant by an ordinary man is a favourite theme, reflected in 'Jack the Giant Killer' and 'Jack and the Beanstalk', still popular in pantomime. More plausible is the biblical story of David and Goliath. As the Champion of the Philistines, Goliath was alleged to be 'six cubits and a span' in height, about 10ft. To be so tall implies a certain physical weakness and — with the further handicap of armour (weighing 208 lb) — it is believable that the giant was slain by a stone from David's slingshot.

A Welsh giant decided to take his revenge against the mayor of Shrewsbury by damming the River Severn so that the town would be flooded and the people drowned. He set off with a vast shovelful of earth and lost his way. He met a cobbler who was returning from Shrewsbury with a bag of old shoes to be mended. The giant asked directions, but when the cobbler realized his customers might be drowned he assured the giant he would never reach the town that day, or the next. As proof he opened his bag: 'Just look! I've come from Shrewsbury myself and worn out all those shoes on the way.' The disenchanted giant lost heart and threw his spadeful of earth on the ground beside him, creating the hill now known as the Wrekin. Another example of the stupid giant outwitted by a man of ordinary size.

Yet there are benevolent giants, too, and the legend of the giant is not necessarily of a monstrous or ferocious creature. There is a latent admiration for the power of such a godlike creature who uses thunder to convey displeasure, and has the superhuman strength to make islands by flinging rocks into the sea, valleys when he lies down to rest, and mountains with shovels of earth.

Landmarks with such names as the Giant's Leap or the Giant's Causeway pay compliment to such colossal strength; while *megalithic monuments and Egypt's *Pyramids are proof of Man's own capacity for building monuments on a truly gigantic scale. DF

Kaspar Hauser

A boy aged about sixteen, Kaspar Hauser, appeared in Nuremberg in 1828. He was unable to say how he got there or tell anything about himself except that for as long as he could remember he had been confined in a small, dark room and had lived off bread and water. He had never seen his captor. Adopted by the city, he was for some time lionized until doubts began to be expressed, following the discovery of Kaspar unconscious and his subsequent claim that somebody had tried to kill him. Many believed that he was a fraud, his mysterious assailant an invention, and his wounds self-inflicted, all in an attempt to stay in the limelight. Others maintained that those who had imprisoned him were trying to kill him. The argument, never resolved, has succeeded in obscuring many of the facts.

In 1833 he was wounded and claimed that he had been stabbed. The wounds proved fatal and he died on 17 December.

At the time, gossip connected him with a complex and barely believable conspiracy involving the baby hereditary Prince of Baden. If his story was true, whoever kept him incarcerated for sixteen years must have had exceptional reasons. On the other hand, if his story is untrue, it is difficult to see what Kaspar hoped to gain. In the final analysis, Kaspar Hauser's story is riddled with doubt, but if he was a fraud he was a particularly clever one, and if not ...

We shall probably never know but, if his death was a mystery, his birth was and is an even bigger one. PB

Lycanthropy

The word 'lycanthropy' suggests that there is no such animal as a werewolf, for the lycanthrope is, literally, someone who *thinks* he is a wolf. Yet werewolves have been reported since before Christ. Ovid described the transformation of a king: 'In vain he attempted to speak; from that very instant his jaws were besputtered with foam, and he thirsted for blood, as he raged amongst flocks and panted for slaughter. His vesture was changed into hair, his limbs became crooked; a wolf, yet he retained traces of his ancient expression. Hoary as he was before, his countenance rabid, his eyes glittered savagely, the picture of fury.' This offers a clue: possibly his 'rabid' appearance was due, literally, to rabies.

A century later Petronius gave a further account which is less explicable but has the classic elements of the legend. The servant of an officer on a journey was shocked to see him strip and change into a wolf. When the servant reached a farmhouse, he was told that a wolf had broken in, killing cattle until driven off by sword. Hurrying back to the roadside he saw the soldier's clothes had gone, in their place a pool of blood. At home he found his master being attended for a sword wound on the neck.

A similar tale was repeated in 1558 in Auvergne. (Just as vampirism erupted in Eastern Europe in the eighteenth century, so central France was the hunting ground for werewolves 200 years earlier: 30,000 cases of *loups-garoux* were listed between 1520 and 1630.) In this case ,a hunter promised to bring a nobleman some of his game but was attacked by a savage wolf which he drove off by slashing one of its paws. He called to tell his friend of the incident, producing the severed paw from his hunting-bag as proof, only to find it was now a delicate female hand. His horror was surpassed by that of his friend, who recognized a ring on one of the fingers and raced upstairs to see his wife bandaging the stump of her wrist. After confessing, she was burnt.

Confession was surprisingly frequent; doubtless many innocents were tortured and condemned. Seldom was the obvious suggested, that the attacker really *was* a wolf! Equally, the legend could have been encouraged by parents anxious to warn their children not to wander in the forest at night, as East Enders scolded theirs: 'If you don't behave, Jack the Ripper will get you.'

And, of course, there are proven cases of abandoned children brought up by wolves. The Wolf Children of Midnapore, rescued by the Reverend Singh in 1920, and the 'wild boy' discovered in a French forest in 1797, are famous examples of such protection; if such a human shape were seen running on all-fours with the wolf pack, the legend would have been supported.

Yet dressing as and identifying with animals is a primeval instinct — from the hunters who donned the pelts of animals to today's lady in mink. The Berserkirs of Scandinavia wore bearskins to intimidate the villagers during their raids. The Leopard Men persisted in the Congo until recently, exploiting a similar fear.

In his *Book of Werewolves, Being an Account of a Terrible Superstition*, Baring-Gould said the legend was so persistent it had to be based on fact. He claimed: 'Half the world believes, or believed in werewolves.' That was written in 1865. If the legend is no longer credible today, clearly it continues to fascinate.   DF

Sea Monsters

If we had never seen an elephant before, how astounded we should be by such a discovery today. Now that every corner of the Earth is explored, there seems little chance of finding new 'monsters' on land. But monsters of the deep, concealed in the unexplored regions of the ocean bed, remain credible.

The discovery of the coelacanth confirms their possibility. Fossil evidence suggested the fish had died out 70 million years ago, but the living beast was fished up off South Africa in 1938, and others since. If this 'extinct' species survived, earlier legends of sea monsters might be true. Sailors have reported such sea serpents ever since they first set sail. And, if early explorers were appalled by the sight of gorillas when they went ashore, describing them as giant men or 'serpents with beards', it is not surprising if mariners were equally inaccurate in their accounts of monsters which were glimpsed only for seconds.

The Kraken is the most famous serpent. Among the many reports is one in 1734, testified to by a Danish missionary, who saw such a creature off the coast of Greenland: 'The monster was of so huge a size that, coming out of the water, its head reached as high as a mainmast; its body was as bulky as the ship, and three or four times as long. It had a long pointed snout, and spouted like a whale; it had great broad paws; the body seemed covered with shellwork, and the skin was very ragged and uneven. The under part of its body was shaped like an enormous huge serpent and when it dived again under the water, it plunged backward into the sea, and so raised its tail aloft, which seemed a whole ship's length distant from the bulkiest part of its body.' The man was a reliable witness and there is no cause to doubt his story. But there is every reason to suspect that this and similar sightings concerned a giant squid or octopus. The largest authenticated such creature was caught off Newfoundland in 1878 with a 20ft body and one tentacle stretching 35ft. This explains the fleshy, red 'serpent' floating on the water noticed by a US ship's Captain which proved to be the arm of an octopus, 45ft long, with suckers, and $2\frac{1}{2}$ft thick. Henry Lee illustrated his *Sea Monsters Unmasked* to show how easily a partly submerged squid could be mistaken for a monstrous serpent. Depending on the angle, the thicker end of a tentacle rising from the surface could resemble a tail, suggesting a huge, solid form underneath, longer and larger than the ship itself.

Another explanation is seldom offered: that another species could be in the same area, adding to the confusion. Migrating whales, for example, are often closely followed by large black sharks.

But the ocean is vast, and the coelacanth proof of our limited knowledge. The two UK soldiers who rowed the Atlantic in 1966, Ridgway and Blyth, were baffled by a midnight encounter when they '... suddenly saw the writhing, twisting shape of a great creature. It was outlined by the phosphorescence in the sea as if a string of neon lights were hanging from it. It was an enormous size, some 35ft long, and it came toward me quite fast. I must have watched it for some ten seconds ... I reluctantly had to believe that there was only one thing it could have been — a sea serpent.'

If a giant squid is the explanation at sea, a giant eel is the likeliest for the monsters of the lakes. These are legion. In British Columbia, where an arm pulled down a horse into Lake Onegan in the last century, the monster was known as Naitaka to the local Indians and Ogopogo to the white settlers, who reported him so often that the name was celebrated in a music-hall song: 'His mother was an earwig,/his father was a whale;/A little bit of head,/And hardly any tail./And Ogopogo was his name.' Ogopogo was described by an American in 1949 as having 'a long sinuous body, 30ft in length, consisting of about five undulations (each about 5ft long) apparently separated from each other by a 2ft space'. In 1952 a woman saw it clearly as it rose three times before it disappeared, and thought it 'beautiful'; it had a head resembling that of a cow or horse. In 1959, the publisher of the *Vernon Advertiser* was cruising down the lake at 10mph when he saw the Ogopogo travelling faster. This time the head was snake-like but the five humps were plainly visible.

The Ogopogo, and similar lake monsters such as Slimey Sim in Lake Payette, Idaho, or the beast of Bear Lake, Utah, prove there is nothing new under the Sun, and parallel the many sightings of the Loch Ness Monster, the most famous of all. Reported in 1880, the creature was seen again in 1933 and appeared to have a long neck, tiny head, and heavy body. A photograph taken by a London doctor a year later seemed to confirm this, and the hunt was on.

Sir Peter Scott accepted the flashlit underwater photographs taken by the team led by the US scientist, Dr Robert Rines, as genuine, suggesting a neck roughly 10ft long: 'I would stake all my knowledge of human relations that this is no hoax.' But sceptics have pointed out that the name given to the monster, *Nessiteras rhombopteryx*, can be twisted into an anagram — 'monsters hoax by Sir Peter' — although there is no reason to believe he is a hoaxer.

However, so many sightings by reputable witnesses suggest *something* is there, although patterns of light on moving water, and rhythms of currents, can be deceptive. A study of the map reveals how easily a sea monster might have been cut off from the Moray Firth. David Attenborough has suggested that, if such a monster exists, it could be a giant eel, returned from the ocean and able to go on land, as 'Nessie' was supposed to have done in 1933, lumbering out of the bracken with a lamb in its mouth. Like other naturalists, he discounts the theory of a reptile, such as a plesiosaur (like the coelacanth thought to have become extinct about 70 million years ago), which would have to surface every half hour to breathe and would find it hard to survive in such extreme cold.

Another, totally different, theory expounded by Colin Wilson in *Mysteries* is based on the first-hand studies by F.W. Holiday in the 1960s. 'Nessie' could be a 'manifestation': '... [noting] the frequency of *UFO sightings above lakes where there are reports of monsters he came to the conclusion that he was not dealing with dragons or discs, but with some archetypal symbol of good and evil.' Wilson adds that a *ley line runs down the middle of the loch. DF

Spring-Heeled Jack

With talonlike fingers, curious protuberant eyes which 'burned like coals', the ability to spit fire and to jump extraordinary heights (in fact he seems to have bounded considerable lengths), Spring-Heeled Jack caused commotion in suburban London by attacking unsuspecting travellers. His principal reign of terror was in 1837–8, when three Penny Dreadfuls helped develop his legend, but reports of his activities — or of the activities of those who assumed his mantle — continued until the turn of the century.

His most celebrated appearance was in 1877. Three sentries were attacked at Aldershot Barracks. They fired at him several times, giving rise to the legend that he was impervious to lead; but it seems that the guards were using blanks.

He was last reported in 1904 in Everton where, according to a contemporary report in the *News of the World*, hundreds of people saw him leaping from rooftop to pavement, finally executing a tremendous bound over the rooftops and vanishing, forever. Sadly, this grand exit never happened: the story stems from gossip about a supposedly haunted house.

As early as 1838 the authorities seem to have had information that a scapegrace young nobleman, Henry, Marquis of Waterford, had invented Jack in an effort to cause the death of thirty people through fright and thereby collect £3,000 wagered on the issue by his companions. PB

Tunguska Event

Exactly what caused the explosion that occurred in a remote part of Siberia just after 7am on 30 June 1908 is not known. For various reasons the site was not properly inspected until nearly twenty years later, and almost certainly much evidence must have been lost. Investigators have had to rely on what was left at the site — spectacular enough evidence in itself — as well as on eyewitness accounts.

According to these an elongated object, brighter than the Sun and trailing clouds of multi-coloured smoke, sped across the sky with an ear-splitting roar to explode in the region of the Stony Tunguska River. Witnesses stated that there appeared a pillar of fire, followed by clouds of black smoke that ascended to a height of some $12\frac{1}{2}$ miles. The explosion was indeed a mighty one, estimated to have been of the order of 30 million tons of TNT, which puts it on a scale with the largest hydrogen bombs. The shock waves in the atmosphere travelled twice around the world before dissipating, and seismic waves were detected as far away as Washington. For some time the aurora borealis was especially prominent, and magnetic disturbances in the atmosphere were detected several thousand miles away. Across much of Europe high-altitude 'silvery clouds' were observed, and luminosity in the night sky was for some time bright enough to cause panic as far away as London; closer to the affected region, people could take photographs at midnight.

Russia was then in the midst of the political turmoil that would result in the Revolution of 1917; moreover, the area of the explosion was remote, and travel to it hard. So it was not until 1921 that a scientific expedition was sent out to investigate the region. It was led by Leonid Kulik, an expert in meteorites from the Mineralogical Museum at Petrograd; he had read the accounts and assumed that the event had been the impacting of a giant meteorite. This expedition did not visit the actual site, and everything that Kulik discovered persuaded him that he had been right in his assumption. He returned in 1927, and this time he *was* able to reach the site. What he found was astonishing.

Over an area of some 1,200 square miles devastation had reigned. Trees were scorched — many showing signs that their branches had been instantly incinerated — and thrown flat on the ground, their roots pointing towards what had obviously been the centre of the blast. But at the centre of the site, to Kulik's amazement, there was no meteorite crater. There were, however, many shallow holes a few yards deep and up to a few dozen yards across. Could it be that the meteorite had burst into pieces in the air, the fragments impacting individually? But, if so, why were there no meteorite remains?

What was it, then, that had caused the explosion? In the early 1930s it was suggested that it was a cometary nucleus. The chances of such a thing hitting the Earth are small but reasonable. Under certain circumstances a cometary nucleus could explode in mid-air and create the observed effects.

But, with the appearance of the atomic bomb at Hiroshima and Nagasaki, a number of scientists pointed out that the Tunguska explosion was rather remarkably like an atomic one; for example, the mushrooming cloud of smoke immediately after the explosion. Much of the energy output of the explosion was in the form of concussion, heat and light — again a characteristic of a nuclear explosion. The temperature of the blast was deduced to be several million degrees; surely only a nuclear explosion could create such temperatures. There was some evidence pointing to the possibility of radiation sickness among domestic animals in the region, and plant life, too, showed possible signs of genetic damage.

Soon after World War II Aleksander Kazantsev proposed that the explosion had indeed been nuclear; it had been caused by the failure of the atomic engine powering a spacecraft from *Mars. At the time this was not a totally unrespectable idea. Kazantsev suggested that the dying race of Mars had come to Earth in search of water, and pointed out that the explosion had occurred near Lake Baikal, the largest body of fresh water on Earth. (Why they should not have chosen the Antarctic icecap, a much larger body of fresh water — albeit frozen — and even more remote, we are not told.)

In the 1940s it was suggested that the Earth had been struck by a lump of *antimatter. But such an explosion in the atmosphere would result in the generation of a great deal of radioactive carbon; a survey made in the region made antimatter seem unlikely.

A small *black hole? This could indeed hit the Earth, go right through and continue on its way. But it would not make a big enough bang while so doing, and it would leave a crater.

Rather striking evidence has emerged that would seem to be in favour of the exploding-alien-spacecraft hypothesis. Collating the accounts of eyewitnesses as to the direction they saw the object travelling in, and considering also the locations of the eyewitnesses, it appears that the object seems to have taken, not the simple path from south-east to north-west that had been assumed, but a course which took it in the directions south-south-west to north-north-east, *then* west-south-west to east-north-east, and then *finally* east-south-east to west-north-west. Could this not indicate that the alien crew, realizing their spacecraft was about to explode, made manoeuvres to try to be over the most sparsely inhabited region possible when it did so?

The alterations in direction could indeed have been course corrections, and the hypothesis is not unreasonable. But there are other explanations. Meteorites sometimes do funny and unpredictable things as they plunge through our atmosphere: if ordinary meteorites can act in this way, would not a more unusual object, such as a cometary nucleus or an antimatter meteorite, possibly act even more strangely? As an irregularly shaped antimatter meteorite, say, hurtled on its destructive way it is perfectly conceivable that the bumps would cause smaller explosions (as were reported by some eyewitnesses) before the main blast, and these could easily result in changes of flight path.

Currently, the consensus of opinion has it that the Tunguska object was indeed the nucleus of a comet, but there is still uncertainty in the evidence. Until this uncertainty is cleared up, there must remain doubt as to what the object was. It could even have been an alien spacecraft.

JG

Vampires

There may not be such things as vampires, but people have believed in them since the beginning of time. This belief was so prevalent in Eastern Europe in the middle of the eighteenth century that it was virtually an epidemic in itself. In 1746, Dom Calmet wrote: 'We are told that dead men ... return from their tombs, are heard to speak, walk about ... injure both men and animals whose blood they drain ... making them sick and finally causing death ... Nor can the men deliver themselves unless they dig the corpses up ... and drive a sharp stake through these bodies, cut off the heads, tear out the hearts; or else they burn the bodies to ashes. It seems impossible not to subscribe to the prevailing belief that these apparitions do actually come forth from their graves.'

The astonishing claim in this last sentence is confirmed by Rousseau: 'If ever there was in the world a warranted and proven history, it is that of vampires: nothing is lacking, official reports, testimonials of persons of standing, of surgeons, of clergyman, of judges; the judicial evidence is all-embracing.'

It is this documentation that is so baffling to the sceptic. It does seem, as Colin Wilson wrote in 1974, that: 'There must have been a reason that these vampire stories suddenly caught the imagination of Europe. Obviously *something* happened, and it seems unlikely that it was pure imagination.'

Certainly the evidence seems irrefutable. A case was recorded in 1732 when a deputation was sent from Belgrade to investigate the report of a vampire in a remote village. This consisted of civil and military officials, a Public Prosecutor, a lieutenant of Duke Charles Alexander of Württemberg's regiment with twenty-four soldiers, and various 'respected persons'. As dusk fell, they went to the grave where the vampire had been buried three years earlier. It was claimed that in the last fortnight he had killed one of his brothers and three of his nieces and nephews. He was starting on his fifth victim, another beautiful young niece whose blood he had sucked on two occasions, when he was interrupted. Now they opened his grave and found the man apparently healthy. His heart was beating, although this sensational revelation is mentioned only casually. When his heart was pierced by an iron bar, white fluid mixed with blood burst out. Then his head was cut off and his body buried in quicklime. After that the vampirism ceased and his last victim recovered.

Another story, vouched for by Calmet, concerned a Hungarian soldier who was billeted in a house where he saw a stranger join the family one evening for supper. He noticed that they seemed frightened. The following morning he was told that his host was dead. The stranger was the dead man's father, who had been buried ten years earlier, and whose arrival had announced and caused the death of his son. The soldier reported this to the Count de Cabreras, the captain of the regiment, who ordered the exhumation of the father. Once again, the corpse resembled a man who had just died — 'his blood like that of a living man'.

Though Calmet was meticulous in recording such case histories, he did not necessarily believe in them. On the contrary, he showed a rare compassion for the unfortunate people who were *thought* to be vampires: 'It suffices to explain how vampires have been dragged from the grave and made to speak, shout, scream and bleed: *they were still alive* [my italics]. They were killed by decapitation, perforation or burning, and this has been a great wrong; for the allegation that they returned to haunt and destroy the living has never been sufficiently proved to authorize such inhumanity, or to permit innocent beings to be dishonoured and ignominiously killed as a result of wild and unproved accusations. For the stories told of these apparitions, and all the distress caused by these supposed vampires, are totally without solid proof.'

Why, then, the persistence and prevalence of this belief? Montague Summers gave an explanation for this particular mid-eighteenth-century outbreak: '... in Romania we find gathered together around the vampire almost all the beliefs and superstitions that prevail throughout the whole of Eastern Europe.' At that time Romania was divided into Wallachia, Moldavia and Transylvania (the setting for Bram Stoker's *Dracula*). Undoubtedly, the superstition that Summers refers to would be rife in this 'land beyond the forest' where vampires — or the belief in them — could be exploited.

At the same time, there are a number of possible explanations that are wholly logical.

Dennis Wheatley suggested that in times of great poverty beggars would break into the mausoleums of a graveyard and make their homes inside, emerging in the safety of darkness to scavenge for food. If they were glimpsed in the moonlight it is hardly surprising if rumours of vampires spread, and grew in the retelling.

But the most obvious explanation is ignorance. People were baffled when bodies were dug up in a perfect state of preservation. This happens in volcanic soil and explains why Santorini (Thera) has such a reputation for vampirism that the Greeks had a sarcastic expression, 'taking a vampire to Thera', implying that there was an abundance there already.

There is confusion also over the state of *rigor mortis*, which reaches completion after approximately twelve hours but passes off after a further thirty-six. In 1974 a gypsy woman in Romania recalled the horror of her father's death when she was a child. As the family lifted his legs and arms to dress him in his burial clothes, they were alarmed to find they were not stiff at all. The villagers, unaware that *rigor mortis* had passed, came to the house with a wooden stake which they plunged through his heart to avoid any risk of vampirism.

But the likeliest explanation is premature burial, and the ignorance surrounding the state of death. It is no exaggeration to say that thousands of innocent people were buried alive. In 1855 the *British Medical Journal* stated: 'It is true that hardly any one sign of death, short of putrefaction, can be relied on as infallible.' As recently as 1973 the 'corpse' whose kidneys were being removed for a transplant operation in Birmingham turned out to be alive. If we can make such mistakes today, how easy it would have been several centuries ago, when the states of trance and catalepsy were not fully understood, particularly during outbreaks of plague when the authorities were anxious to bury the dead as quickly as possible.

There have been cases of grieving relatives returning to find the 'dear departed' breathing. Charlotte Stoker, Bram's mother, told him of a Sergeant Callan who was so tall that the undertaker decided to break his legs to fit him into the coffin. At the first blow the Sergeant returned to life and Charlotte saw him walking about afterwards — presumably with a limp.

In view of these logical explanations, the belief that the dead can return to suck the blood of the living seems all the more extraordinary.

Partly it is due to fear of the unknown. In 1973 Demetrious Myiciura was found dead in Stoke-on-Trent. A policeman realized that the room was a sort of fortress, with salt sprinkled over the bed and a bowl of urine containing garlic on the window-ledge. A visit to the public library for Masters' *The Natural History of the Vampire* confirmed his suspicion that the Pole had lived in fear of attack by vampires, and the inquest revealed that he had choked to death on a clove of garlic which he had placed in his mouth at night as a final safeguard.

There is another psychological reason which may seem glib but helps to explain the appeal of *Dracula* — sexuality. In his *Psychoanalysis of Ghost Stories* Maurice Richardson wrote of *Dracula* that 'from a

Freudian standpoint — and from no other does the story really make sense ... it is a vast polymorph perverse bisexual, oral-anal genital sado-masochistic timeless orgy'.

Bram Stoker was puritanical, and would have been shocked by the unconscious sexuality of his most famous novel. For example, oral sex is suggested when the three vampire women in Castle Dracula 'go down': '... the moisture shining on the scarlet lips and on the red tongue as it lapped the white sharp teeth. Lower and lower went her head ... I closed my eyes in langourous ecstasy and waited ...' Later, Dracula forces Mrs Harker's face 'down on his bosom ... The attitude of the two had a terrible resemblance to a child forcing a kitten's nose into a saucer of milk to compel it to drink.' Christopher Lee refers to the Count's 'strange, dark heroism. He is a superman image, with erotic appeal for women who find him totally alluring. In many ways, he is everything people would like to be ... the anti-hero, the heroic villain.'

The sadomasochistic appeal is indisputable: he demands and he takes not only blood but the life-force itself — energy. This idea is examined in Colin Wilson's novel *The Space Vampires*. He refers not only to the super-vampire from whom no one is safe but also to those weaker people around us who attach themselves like leeches. Most of us know someone like this, who leaves one feeling absolutely *drained*. To this extent, vampires are all around us.

DF

Vanishing People

Every year thousands of people deliberately disappear. Their reasons are as many and as varied as those for which people commit suicide, to which some people choose disappearing as a preferable alternative. Every week as many as ten people — just from London — disappear and are never seen again. Not surprisingly, there are no estimates of the worldwide figure.

The majority of missing people are juveniles fleeing parental authority; the rest are adults seeking to avoid some responsibility or a real or imagined threat to their freedom or security. But there are some cases for which there is no apparent motive, where the person has vanished as if on the spur of the moment, without preparation. To draw a distinction, these people have not just disappeared — they have vanished.

There are several celebrated cases of wholesale vanishing. Perhaps most famous is that of the crew of the *Mary Celeste*. In 1872 the *Dei Gratia* found the *Celeste* drifting in the Atlantic. Stories that fresh food and mugs of warm tea were laid on the galley table, that the aroma of tobacco smoke lingered in the captain's cabin, and that the lifeboats were securely in place, are pieces of fiction. The lifeboat was missing and it was evident that all aboard had abandoned ship, so the fate of the crew demands little imagination to guess. What baffled investigators at the time and has continued to perplex to this day is why the *Celeste* was abandoned. Abandonment is an extreme act and taken only when the danger presents no alternative, yet the ship was in very good condition, carried plenty of food and fresh water, and afforded no clue as to the danger her crew must have believed they were in. Various theories have been advanced, but none take full account of the facts; the mystery of the *Mary Celeste* is unexplained.

More interesting in terms of 'vanishing people' is a case which happened sixty-three years earlier, in 1809. Benjamin Bathurst had stopped at an inn in Perlberg for rest and refreshment. Preparing to continue his journey, Bathurst went into the courtyard of the inn to check his carriage. He was never seen or heard from again and, despite a prolonged and intensive investigation by both his family and the British government, as well as generous help from Napoleon, no clue to his fate was ever discovered.

Considerable mystery surrounds other celebrated cases. No one knows the fate of Ambrose Bierce, who vanished in 1913. Or of wealthy socialite Dorothy Arnold, who was last seen shopping on New York's crowded Fifth Avenue in 1910. And people continue to vanish in the most extraordinary circumstances. Particularly inexplicable cases are regularly reported in the newspapers and sometimes, as in the case of the missing Devon schoolgirl Genette Tate, become the subject of national interest.

An exceptional incident happened in 1975. Jackson Wright and his wife Martha were driving to New York. They stopped their car in the Lincoln Tunnel to clear snow from the windows. While Jackson was clearing the windscreen, Martha went to wipe the rear window, and vanished.

Even with careful preparation and detailed planning it is not easy to disappear successfully, especially from modern society, but to vanish on the spur of the moment like Martha Wright and thousands of other people seems beyond belief, and it is not surprising that such events are eventually linked to whatever superstition or myth is popular at the time — that the people were claimed by the Devil, abducted by fairies, or kidnapped by *UFOs.

Despite fairly extensive research, no case of a disappearance in front of witnesses — other than by a *ghost, *doppelgänger, or something similar — has been substantiated, but several accounts appear in books of the 'stranger than fiction' variety. Perhaps the best known is the tale of David Lang, a Tennessee farmer who is supposed to have vanished in 1880 in front of five people while crossing a field. Most of these tales do not survive close examination. In the Lang case (see page 12) the story seems to have originated with a salesman named Joe Mulhattan or McHattan. There is at least one claim, however, that he based the Lang story on a real event, the disappearance of Orion Williamson in Selma in 1854.

Although nobody has been proven to have vanished in front of witnesses, there is a substantial amount of material to the effect that people and creatures have *appeared* (see *appearing people); and one theory popular among the authors of sensationalist books is that of the *parallel world or other dimension of reality. It is hypothesized that a sort of doorway exists between our world and other dimensions and that sometimes people pass through.

An interesting story (if true!) about a man who may have passed into a parallel world is that of a Chilean army corporal, Armando Valdes. On 25 April 1977 he apparently vanished in front of six of his men; fifteen minutes later he reappeared. His men noticed that the calendar on Valdes' watch had advanced five days and that he had grown a five-day beard. Unfortunately, Valdes could remember nothing of the abduction, nor of what happened during the fifteen minutes/five days he had been missing.

The phenomenon of vanishing people has been given little attention by researchers, and stories should be received with open-minded scepticism, particularly those as sensational as the Valdes incident; but since it cannot be denied that people have vanished and continue to vanish in extraordinary circumstances, it is almost impossible not to seek solutions in the paranormal. And the interest is intensified by stories told by people who, like Valdes, disappeared and came back. None of these stories has been proven to everybody's satisfaction, largely because acceptance eventually boils down to whether or not you believe the people who told them. Sceptics have not even been convinced by the use of hypnotic regression techniques or the employment of lie-detectors, as in the case of Travis Walton, who disappeared for five days in 1975 after five colleagues had seen him struck by a peculiar light from a *UFO; but that these stories are told and do have some corroborative backing perhaps provides the only clue to the enigma of those people who go out and never come back. PB

Zombies

Haiti is the home of the Zombie, and the location explains the legend. When slaves were transported from the Congo, they brought their superstitions with them. In the eighteenth century, up to 30,000 slaves landed each year; as the island was a French colony, their native religions were banned, and grew all the stronger in secrecy. Revolution was inevitable; and when Haitian independence was declared in 1804 *voodoo replaced Catholicism as the new religion.

The illegality of superstition in those intervening years had encouraged the sense of dangerous romance in ancestor worship. As a form of the undead, the Zombie could be revived by a sorcerer, who broke into the grave before the body rotted and led it away to become his slave. Zombies, therefore, were useful possessions. Although many graves had heavy boulders placed on top, and were guarded by relatives until the body did rot, numbers of Zombies were forced into service.

There is a strong possibility that the abject, shuffling creatures described in 1918 by William Seabrook, being led to the canefields to work, were under the influence of an unidentified drug made from indigenous plants. Although their eyes were those of a dead man — 'not blind, but staring unfocused' — Seabrook concluded that they were simply 'poor, ordinary demented human beings, idiots forced to toil in the fields'. Article 246 of the old Haitian Penal Code states: 'Also to be termed intention to kill, by poisoning, is the use of substances whereby a person is not killed but reduced to *a state of lethargy*, more or less prolonged.' This could explain the Zombie.   DF

Evolution: 3

One of the most important aspects of terrestrial evolution, so far as we are concerned, is that it has given rise to our own intelligence, our own consciousness. Whether intelligence is an inevitable product of evolution we do not know.

Perhaps the most overt manifestation of consciousness is that it has a sense of time. To most animals, and even to the new-born child, life is a succession of nows: the past is forgotten and the future unconsidered. But does our sense of time reflect reality? Is there genuinely such a quality as time?

These are the questions asked in the next section.   JG

PART FOUR
TIME IN DISARRAY

Introductory: 4

The name of Paul Kammerer is known to posterity largely because he committed suicide when one of his experiments to prove the inheritance of *acquired characteristics was shown to have been faked (probably by one of his assistants) — Koestler has told the story in *The Case of the Midwife Toad*. But Kammerer is remarkable for another reason; he became intrigued by 'odd coincidences', and began making notes of them. Rather than give an example from Kammerer, I can offer one of my own from the past few days. When I wrote the article on the *pineal eye for this book I found myself wondering idly how long it has been known as the pineal *gland*. It has been proved to be a gland only since 1958; but I had a vague idea at the back of my mind that Descartes had referred to it as a gland. That evening, I opened a volume of the complete novels of Smollett and began reading his *Adventures of an Atom* — to discover, on page 2, a reference to the 'pineal gland'. (The novel dates from 1769; there are also some staggeringly perceptive comments about the role of atoms — Dalton's atomic theory dates from 1803.)

*Jung called this kind of *coincidence 'synchronicity', and I mention it here because *if* it has any significance — beyond mere chance — then it is a form of mildly 'paranormal' experience that just about everybody — even the most determined sceptics — has encountered. (*The Challenge of Chance* by Hardy, Harvie and Koestler is the only full-length study of this odd phenomenon.)

Which leads on to another interesting question connected with 'chance': why is it that important discoveries are so often 'in the air', and get made at the same time by several people? Spectacles, the telescope, photography, the theory of evolution and the discovery of Neptune are just five examples of these simultaneous discoveries. They seem to be a large-scale equivalent of small-scale synchronicities like my 'pineal gland' experience. We may, of course, continue to insist that such things are pure chance, like a gambling machine producing a whole row of lemons. But when the odds against are astronomical, surely it is more sensible to admit that there is probably more to it than that, even if we haven't the vaguest idea of what it is?

It is, of course, tempting to ask *who* is 'causing' such 'coincidences'. In *The Occult* I discuss the cybernetician David Foster, who has suggested that cosmic rays could be information-carriers, designed to 'programme' us in the direction of evolution; his theory posits a 'cosmic intelligence' of some sort. But, even if we reject anything so 'anthropomorphic', there is still the interesting possibility that there is in nature some mysterious factor which favours the acquisition of knowledge, and which somehow arranges that our discoveries come in clusters. Vallée has even suggested that the purpose of *UFOs could be somehow 'heuristic' — a deliberate attempt to open our minds to new possibilities.

At all events, this section may be regarded as a natural transition between the realms of the incredible and miraculous and that of scientific possibility.   CW

Astrology

No one would deny that there is something preposterous in the idea that the stars can influence human destiny — or even human personality. Yet anyone who has taken even the most casual interest in astrology will have noticed that, contrary to all commonsense, it actually seems to work. Our personal characteristics are supposed to be governed by first the 'Sun sign' of the month in which we were born (Aries for April, Taurus for May, Gemini for June, etc.), and second the constellation coming up over the horizon at the moment of birth (the 'rising sign'). And character assessments based on these factors can be remarkably accurate.

If we are sufficiently open-minded to refuse to dismiss it because it *ought* to be nonsense, the next obvious step is to attempt some kind of scientific assessment of the evidence. This is, in fact, an idea that occurred to Paul Choisnard, a French artillery officer trained in engineering, who attempted to 'prove' astrology by statistics around the turn of the century. His work influenced a Swiss mathematician named Krafft, who preferred to call the subject 'astro-biology'. Krafft's *Treatise on Astro-Biology* appeared in French in 1939, and was largely ignored. But Krafft achieved sudden recognition in the same year when he wrote a letter to a member of Himmler's Intelligence Service predicting that Hitler's life would be in danger from 'explosives' between 7 and 10 November. In fact, Hitler missed death from a bomb by only a few minutes on 8 November 1939. Krafft was brought to Berlin, and for a time became a kind of semi-official astrologer to the Nazis; but he fell into disfavour and died in a concentration camp.

Experts in the field, like Ellic Howe, seem to be agreed that Krafft's *Treatise* did *not* succeed in 'proving' astrology. He checked the birth data of 2,800 musicians, and argued that there was a relation between their Sun sign and temperament, as well as their family history. These results were shown to be erroneous when a statistician, Michel Gauquelin, fed them into a computer in 1950. But, having disproved Krafft, Gauquelin decided to test some other central propositions of astrology: (1) that people born in the odd months (Aries = 1) are extroverts, while those born in even months (Taurus = 2) are introverts; and (2) that a person's choice of profession is governed by his rising sign. To his astonishment, the computer results agreed with both propositions. The tests have been repeated many times since then, always with the same result.

The professions chosen were sportsmen, actors and scientists. Sportsmen, Gauquelin discovered, showed a tendency to be born under Mars, actors under Jupiter, scientists and doctors under Saturn. The computer showed that three other positions seemed to be important: when these planets were directly overhead, directly 'underfoot', and sinking below the western horizon.

Hans Eysenck checked these results, expecting to find them erroneous; he was startled to find that they seemed to withstand the most rigorous analysis, and has since become one of Gauquelin's most influential supporters.

In his important book *The Cosmic Clocks*, Gauquelin spends a great deal of time assembling evidence that human beings can be influenced by the Sun and Moon — for example, every doctor connected with mental homes knows that a large number of patients *are* influenced by the full Moon (hence the term 'lunacy'). Human blood is influenced by sunspot activity, as Maki Takata discovered when the flocculation index (the rate at which blood albumin curdles) of patients all over the country began to rise. Giorgio Piccardi discovered that various chemical reactions vary according to sunspot activity and Moon cycles. Y. Rocard established that human beings have an extremely delicate sensitivity to the Earth's magnetic field, and he concluded that this sensitivity explains the phenomena of *dowsing. Since Gauquelin's book appeared (in 1967), scientists have established beyond all doubt that the homing instinct depends upon a sensitivity to Earth magnetism.

Here, then, it seems, we have a possible explanation as to why astrology (or astrobiology) works. The Sun and Moon exercise a major influence on Earth's magnetic field. But so do the planets — although, obviously, to a far lesser extent. It has been convincingly argued that the alignment of several planets may cause earthquakes; in *The Jupiter Effect*, John Gribbin and Stephen Plageman predict earthquake and volcanic activity in 1982, when for a while all the planets will be on the same side of the Sun. It seems reasonable that, if it is true that the planets can gravitationally affect the forces at work in the Earth's crust, they can also affect the human nervous system via the Earth's magnetic field.

Of course, many propositions of astrology — the majority, in fact — have not been verified by science. The ecliptic is divided into twelve approximately equal parts by twelve constellations. These zodiacal constellations are, of course, made up of stars, and few astrologers would claim that the stars themselves influence human destiny. They are merely convenient symbols, like the figures around the outside of a clock, which make it easier to tell the time. But it is the planets — the hands — that are important. And since the planets all move at different speeds — so that it would take millions of years for them all to return to the same relative positions — it seems plain that the influence of the Sun sign (for example, whether you are a Cancer, Virgo, or whatever) must vary considerably, if it exists at all. On the other hand, the planets closest to Earth (including the Sun and Moon, which in astrology are regarded as planets) move in regular cycles which form a comparatively short-term repetitive pattern of influence. And Gauquelin's investigations showed that the position of these planets at the moment of birth has a more important influence than the Sun sign.

Astrology also divides the great circle of the ecliptic up into twelve 'houses' — like cutting a cake into twelve segments — each of which is traditionally believed to exercise a different influence on various areas of human life: the first house is related to the personal ego, the second to possessions and finances, the third to communication, the fourth to home, the fifth to creativity, the sixth to work, the seventh to partnerships (both business and marriage), the eighth to sex and death, the ninth to philosophy and ideas, the tenth to career, the eleventh to friends and associates, the twelfth to altruistic service. The astrologer begins by drawing up a 'birth chart' in which the exact positions of the planets are shown in the various houses at the moment of birth, then measures the various angles between the planets, paying particular attention to conjunctions (two planets in the same position), oppositions (two planets on opposite sides of the chart), angles of 90° (squares), 120° (trines) and 30° (sextiles). Some of these are favourable, some unfavourable. Each planet has its own particular influence: the Sun, creativity; the Moon, intuition; Mercury, communication; Venus, feelings and affections; Mars, will, drive; Jupiter, optimism; Saturn, discipline and limitation — these were the original seven planets of traditional astrology. Modern astrology has assigned to Uranus change and disruption, Neptune mysticism and romanticism, and Pluto regeneration, sometimes through violence.

All this sounds nonsensical enough. Yet, again, what surprises the investigator is that the result can often be strikingly accurate. (It can also be highly inaccurate! — astrology is an intuitive science.) At present, science has nothing to say about this aspect of astrology, and Gauquelin and Eysenck preserve a highly sceptical attitude towards it. Yet it is clearly based on a tradition that stretches back many thousands of years — long before the 'breakdown of the bicameral mind' (see page 15). If we assume that our remote ancestors were far more sensitive to the forces of the Earth than we are, then it is arguable that astrology has been part of Man's 'lunar' (or intuitive) knowledge system for the last 100,000 years, and that this explains why Cro-Magnon Man was making careful notes of the positions of the rising of the

Moon 30,000 years ago (see *ancient Man; *ley lines). The purpose of *megalithic monuments might thus be regarded as astrological rather than astronomical, since their architects were basically concerned with the influence of the planets upon the Earth and, through the Earth, upon living creatures.

Astrology is still a very long way from being scientifically acceptable; but the labours of many serious investigators make it increasingly clear that it can no longer be dismissed as merely a manifestation of human gullibility. CW

Card Prediction

The use of playing cards for character reading, divination and prediction is a practice closely associated with gypsies, a people believed to have been of Egyptian origin. The legend goes that when the priestly orders of ancient Egypt were faced with imminent destruction they decided that the best way to convey their teachings to the future was not by way of appeal to our virtuous elements but through our penchant for vice, and thus all their wisdom was embodied in the symbolism of a set of gaming cards, the Tarot. The name is said to be from two Egyptian words, *Tar*, 'road', and *Ro*, 'royal', implying that study of the Tarot is a royal road to knowledge and wisdom.

Our normal deck of playing cards derives from the Tarot. In the eighteenth century the Tarot's wands, swords, cups and pentacles were changed to clubs, spades, hearts and diamonds, probably because a rationalist age rejected the paraphernalia of magic. But recently the recognition of the power of symbols to affect human consciousness, and to give access to levels of the subconscious that possess funds of knowledge and ways of knowing not available to the rational everyday consciousness, has led to a reawakening of interest in the Tarot and its potential.

Although the fairground fortune-teller may work according to a set of rigid rules and principles, in which one thing is automatically associated with another and symbols bear a fixed meaning, the true art of *prediction or divination involves the operation of this subconscious dimension of the mind, and often requires the stimulus of highly suggestive or emotionally charged imagery. The Tarot embodies such imagery. Some of its twenty-one major trump cards — for example, the Devil, the Emperor, the Hermit and the Lovers — are symbols with obvious significances, but the meanings of others — for example, the Hanged Man, the Female Pope, the Juggler and the Stars — are not so obvious, and the contemplation of their meanings and associations and the esoteric traditions from which they derive can open the mind to new dimensions of knowledge.

SH

Causality

Causality is a fundamental theorem of modern understanding, and of plain commonsense. It can be simply described as the rule that cause precedes effect: in order to score a goal I have first to kick the ball; the goal cannot precede the kick.

One consequence of this law is that *precognition is impossible — or so it seems (see *time travel). If you know you will go out tomorrow and be run over, you stay at home, thereby altering the future. At first glance this would seem to violate causality, since the cause (your being run over) has had the effect of making you decide to stay at home. But this seems simplistic: surely we are wrong to say that the cause is your being run over (which anyway will never happen — or, at least, not tomorrow); surely the real cause is *your knowledge* that if you go out tomorrow you will be run over — and this knowledge preceded your decision to stay at home. You may perhaps have altered the future (it is hard to say: we know little of the nature of *time), but you seem not to have violated causality.

One school of thought has suggested that causality is in no way a universal law, but simply a product of our own mental organization. That is to say, we may be misusing the terms 'cause' and 'effect'. It may simply be that we have learned from experience that event B always occurs after event A, in a way that we can describe and apparently understand — within the logical system that we have erected based on causality — so that we say and feel, erroneously, that B has occurred 'as a result of' A. But this seems unsatisfactory: in many fields of knowledge, effects have been perceived and their causes established theoretically before those causes have been located (for example, the neutrino was predicted in 1931 but not detected until 1956). It would seem, therefore, that our logical system corresponds fairly well with the laws of reality, and to say that A does not actually *cause* B is merely to indulge in verbal gymnastics.

There are other areas — for example, *coincidence — where causality appears to have been violated, but even in the most extreme cases it would seem that perhaps, simply, we do not know *why* A causes B.

Nevertheless, causality is an empirical law — and today it is becoming increasingly under threat. In the world of *fundamental particles, for example, there are signs that in certain cases effect may precede cause; it has been suggested that causality need not apply within *black holes; and it is very hard to find a cause for the *Big Bang, since before that event there seems to have been no such thing as time. At the very least, we must begin to question our use of the word 'because'. JG

Clairvoyance

Clairvoyance is a form of *ESP which involves being able to see objects not actually present to the sense of sight. (Similarly, clairaudience means hearing something that takes place elsewhere or at a different time.)

The well known clairvoyant Bert Reese was arrested for 'disorderly conduct' and offered to demonstrate his powers on the spot. He asked the judge to write something on three pieces of paper, fold them into pellets and mix them up thoroughly; then the judge was asked to press each separately against Reese's forehead. Reese was able to state what was on all three pieces of paper ('You have 15 dollars in that bank account'; 'This contains the name of a former governess of your children'). He was acquitted.

It is worth noting that Reese is a Welsh name, and that clairvoyance is more frequently found in the Celtic races than among Anglo-Saxons. The reason, evolutionarily speaking, could be that the Saxons, with their aggressive and pragmatic temperament, have tended to suppress their 'clairvoyant faculties' in favour of practicality; the Celts are traditionally 'dreamers'. (It follows that the coming of North Sea oil to Scotland and heavy industry to Ireland will probably have the effect of suppressing clairvoyance.) Andrew Lang criticized Frazer's *The Golden Bough* on anthropological grounds; but he added the important comment that Frazer was also mistaken in his assumption that all 'magic' is crude superstition; as a child in Scotland, Lang had known many people with 'the second sight' — as well as people who had seen *ghosts — and he pointed out that such people are not imaginative hysterics but 'steady, unimaginative, unexcitable people with just one odd experience'.

It seems to follow that clairvoyance is simply a developed form of intuition — the 'right brain faculty'. Probably its commonest manifestation is when someone 'knows' that there will be a letter from Auntie Hilda in the morning's post, or that a distant cousin who has not been seen in years is going to call later in the day. But then it could be argued that the 'jungle sensitiveness' developed by tiger-hunter Jim Corbett was a form of clairvoyance: something 'told' him when a tiger was lying in wait for him.

If this theory is correct, then that 'other person' who lives in the right cerebral hemisphere is naturally clairvoyant. But his insights are suppressed by the 'practical' ego of the left, which is obsessed with coping with the present. This also means that, in order to activate the clairvoyant faculty, we need only — in theory — suppress left-brain interference by 'soothing' it into quiescence.

The earliest known method for doing this was to stare into water, or into the flame of a candle (a practice known as *scrying). In *Meetings with Remarkable Men* *Gurdjieff has described how, as a youth, he consulted a local 'seer', who sat between two candles and stared into his thumb-nail. He told Gurdjieff that he would have an accident with a fire-arm; this happened a week later when he was out duck-shooting.

Dee had no natural clairvoyant faculty and had to employ various scryers — the best known of whom was Edward Kelley, who used a bowl of water. (The crystal ball became popular only in a later age.)

Clearly, these methods amount to self-hypnosis; so it is not surprising that *hypnosis works just as well. This was discovered in the early nineteenth century, when the discoveries of Mesmer and Puységur had spread over Europe. Puységur, the discoverer of hypnotism, found that hypnosis could induce telepathy or clairvoyance; he would place a girl called Madeleine in a trance, then would stare at some object in the room; Madeleine, with eyes tightly closed, would go and touch it. Rigorous tests convinced sceptics that no fakery was involved. (One of them stared at her for several seconds; then, in response to his mental order, she reached into his pocket and took out three small screws.)

One of the most famous of these hypnotic psychics was Alexis Didier. His father had been hypnotized, and often fell into spontaneous trances; Didier discovered that, if his father were reading the paper aloud when he fell into a trance, the paper could be removed and his father would continue to read. Didier was able to play cards when blindfolded, and played perfectly with the cards face downwards or when a large book was placed on the table so that he was unable to see his opponent's cards. He also demonstrated travelling clairvoyance, projecting himself to the home of his interrogator and describing it in detail. (I have myself witnessed a convincing demonstration of travelling clairvoyance in the Westward Television studios, when a number of subjects, placed in a relaxed semi-trance state by Barney Camfield, were able to describe in remarkable detail various places suggested by the presenter of the programme — including his home.) By the mid-nineteenth century, medical opinion had decided that it was nonsense to suppose that hypnosis could induce paranormal powers — an assertion that can be found in most modern works on hypnosis.

At an early stage in his career, Andrew Lang was convinced that *dowsing was a harmful superstition, until the experiments of William Barrett convinced him otherwise. Dowsers assert that their faculty can be used as a form of 'travelling clairvoyance' — for example, a dowser with the aid of a rough map can often accurately indicate all sources of water at a certain place. Lethbridge was convinced that the pendulum could return accurate answers to all 'yes or no' questions. In fact, the pendulum should be the ideal way of obtaining 'paranormal' information, since it moves through spontaneous contractions of the muscles under the control of the right cerebral hemisphere. Here we move out of the realm of clairvoyance and into the wider area of *ESP. (See also *precognition.)   CW

Coincidence

It is an everyday observation that coincidences seem to happen rather more often than they 'ought' to. But, since it is rather difficult to establish statistically just how often they 'ought' to occur, little research has been done into the matter. (For example, if I travel to the centre of a town of 100,000, see 1,000 people walking around while I am there, one of whom is the only person I know in that town, it may seem that this is something of a coincidence — especially if it happens twice running. But it may simply be that his shopping habits are the same as mine.) Nevertheless, some work has been done.

Paul Kammerer collected and recorded coincidences during the first couple of decades of this century, publishing his conclusions in *Das Gesetz der Serie* (1919). He ascribes three qualities to coincidences, given by Koestler as order, power and their number of parameters: order is the number of successive events composing the coincidence, power the number of simultaneous events, and a parameter is a shared quality between two events — if I see four bearded women in a day this is a fourth-order coincidence; if two friends in different towns did the same that day and told me I would know it to be a third-power coincidence; if it were our birthday the coincidence would have two parameters (bearded women, birthdays). He attempted to explain his recorded coincidences by invoking a fundamental principle of the Universe — acting alongside *causality — which, as it were, correlates like things.

*Jung, too, attempted to step outside causality in his theory of synchronicity, although cause and effect play their part. A fly sitting on the hour hand of a clock might think it a startling coincidence that, every time it passed a numeral, it heard a chiming sound — clearly caused neither by the numeral nor by the hand (nor by the fly!). Similarly, there may be cosmic causes operating of which we know nothing, whose results we cannot really understand, merely observe.

More recently, Koestler has made a distinguished but finally unsatisfying attempt to link coincidence, ESP and frontier physics, suggesting that there is a fundamental law involved in aspects of all three which we do not yet know: as he admits, his essay, *The Roots of Coincidence*, is merely a first step into a darkened room.

Whether or not any researches to date into coincidence have real value is moot — coincidences may be merely coincidences, their apparent over-frequency nothing more than a product of our mathematically unlearned minds. But the researches have at least forced us to question the universal truth of *causality — and that is of genuine importance.　　　　　　　　　　　JG

I Ching

The *I Ching* or *Book of Change* is based on the belief that Man and his cosmic and terrestrial environments constitute an interacting unity. The Universe is held to be made up of two equal and complementary forces, yin and yang. Yang is the active principle and stands for positive qualities; yin is passive but equally important, and stands for the negative. Yang is light, yin is dark. According to the ancient Chinese philosophy, every event results from an interaction between these two.

The *I Ching* contains sixty-four figurations, each a different combination of six broken and unbroken lines known as a hexagram. The broken lines represent yin, the unbroken lines yang. Each hexagram has a symbolic name signifying a different condition of life, and is accompanied by a short explanatory text. There is also a commentary on the text, attributed to Confucius, as well as explanations of the symbolism of the hexagram and the meaning of the separate lines in it.

The philosophy of the *I Ching* is not determinist. It does not regard the future as fixed or purport to tell those who consult it what will happen. Its purpose is to give guidance at the highest moral level, so that an individual can determine in particular circumstances what his right course of action should be. Because this guidance depends largely on perceptive interpretation, it is important for the questioner to approach the book in a serious frame of mind.

To find out which hexagram is relevant, a questioner tosses three coins six times (the original method uses division of a bunch of fifty yarrow stalks). Each toss indicates a line of the hexagram working up from the bottom. For instance, if the first toss produces two tails and one head, the bottom line is an unbroken one. The hexagram formed in this way by the six tosses is the one to be consulted and interpreted in ways too complicated to repeat here.

Since the *I Ching* was first translated into English in 1882, it has gained many Western followers. One was *Jung, who evolved his concept of synchronicity to explain why consultation of the *I Ching* often produces remarkably accurate information and guidance. He proposed 'an acausal connecting principle' between events, that events in no way associated by way of cause and effect (see *causality) may nevertheless be linked by the factors of time and meaning. There must exist, he proposed, a great network of relationships between people, things and events, and the *I Ching* serves as an instrument to enable human consciousness to tune into the network. SH

Numerology

All magic and occult lore is based on the idea that everything is bound together in a great design.

Numerology stems from the assumption that the design is numerical, an ancient concept of which the earliest exponents in the Western tradition were the Pythagoreans. They assigned different properties to the various numbers. Odd numbers were given active, creative characteristics and regarded as male; even numbers were regarded as female and assigned passive, receptive qualities. These distinctions remain the basis of numerology. They are not entirely derogatory of the female, however — for example, 6 is said to stand for the characteristics of dependability, harmony and domesticity, and it is significant to note that this assignment of qualities is not entirely arbitrary, but based upon the mathematical properties of the number. Six is regarded as a 'perfect' number, for it equals the sum of its divisors ($1 + 2 + 3 = 6$), and also it is divisible by both an odd and an even number, and so may be said harmoniously to combine elements of each.

It was the Cabalists who developed numerology as a method of *prediction, character reading and divination. The Cabalists believed a name mystically encodes the essential character of a person or thing as well as information about its destiny. They developed a system, the *gematria*, for reducing names to number values and thus decoding the information believed to be implicit in them.

The method of conversion based on Cabalistic principles gives numerical values to the letters of the alphabet as follows:

1	2	3	4	5	6	7	8
A	B	C	D	E	U	O	F
I	K	G	M	H	V	Z	P
Q	R	L	T	N	W		
J		S					
Y							

To determine your 'name number', add up the numbers for each letter of your full name, then add the digits of the resultant number, and so on, until the addition yields a number below 10. This number represents your essential character. If you similarly add the values of just the vowels you find the nature of the hidden self (the vowels are not written in Hebrew), and if you add the consonant numbers you obtain a pointer to your outward personality. The frequency of particular numbers in a name is regarded as significant, as is the lack of any particular numbers.

The interpretation of the numbers according to this system is: **1**, purpose, action, ambition, aggression, leadership; **2**, balance, passivity, receptivity; **3**, versatility, gaiety, brilliance; **4**, steadiness, endurance, dullness; **5**, adventure, instability, sexuality; **6**, dependability, harmony, domesticity; **7**, mystery, knowledge, solitariness; **8**, material success and worldly involvement; **9**, great achievement, inspiration, spirituality. SH

Palmistry

There is an Indian tradition that when the Buddha was born he was recognized as the 'promised one' by sages who interpreted the lines in his palms. Hand-reading, chirology or palmistry is an ancient occult science based on the study and interpretation of the lines of the palms and of the fleshy pads at the base of the fingers and thumb. Chirologists stress that it is complex, that interpretations are based on a combination of factors, that the length of a line or elevation of a pad is not in itself an adequate ground for judging a person's character or destiny, and that a thorough reading must take into account the characteristics of both hands.

Bearing this in mind, let us now consider the first principles of hand-reading, based on the interpretation of the four major lines etched into the palm of the hand, as indicated in the diagram. Relevant factors are length, depth, whether they run straight or deviate, and whether they are crossed by other lines.

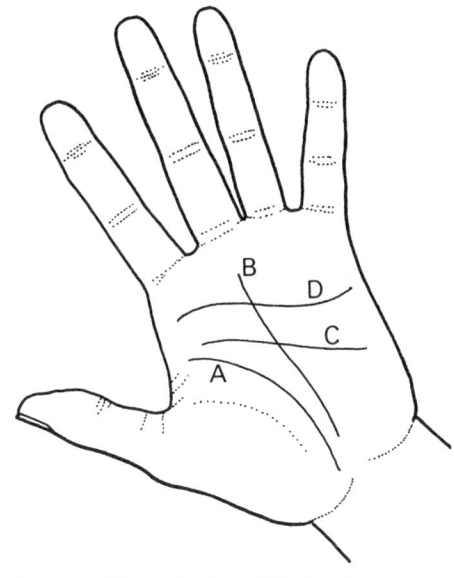

Figure 2 *The major lines of the hand (see text).*

Generally speaking, a long and deeply etched life line (A), curving from about the middle of the palm between the thumb and the index finger to about the middle of the wrist, indicates a tendency to longevity and a strong constitution. If the line runs straight it suggests a cold, selfish disposition, and if it is crossed by other lines these announce the occurrence of obstructions and hindrances in life. Sometimes the line is broken, and this points to the occurrence of serious illnesses in the course of life.

The line of destiny (B) is not found in all hands, and sometimes in only one of a pair of hands. If this one is the left, it indicates that a person will shape his own destiny, and if it is the right hand it indicates that his life will be determined by circumstances and hereditary influences.

When the line of the head (C) goes straight across the palm of the hand, the person will tend to be of a realistic disposition, whereas when it curves downwards he will probably be an imaginative and creative type.

The length of the line of the heart (D) is indicative of the degree of emotional depth and sensitivity of a person. Offshoots are highly significant, those going downwards indicating the occurrence of emotional frustrations and aborted relationships, and those going upwards indicating a tendency to win and keep friends.

This is but a sampling of the interpretative principles of palmistry. The interested reader will readily find books which go into the subject at depth and explain the significance of the secondary lines and of the pads.   SH

Precognition

By all rational and logical criteria precognition ought to be impossible, since the future has yet to take place. But, oddly enough, there is more convincing evidence for it than for almost any other 'paranormal' faculty.

In 1939, S.G. Soal was investigating the possibility of telepathy using Zener cards. His results were disappointing. But a colleague, Whately Carrington, had been carrying out tests in which subjects were asked to draw a 'target picture', and had noticed that some were drawing the *next* picture. So Carrington suggested that Soal should check his own results for 'forward guessing'. Soal found that one of his subjects, a housewife named Gloria Stewart, had made an astonishing number of such 'predictive' guesses. Soal tested her thoroughly and under the most rigorous conditions, and the results were beyond doubt. He later discovered a young photographer named Basil Shackleton with equally remarkable 'predictive' abilities; the experiments he conducted with Shackleton over three years have become classics of paranormal investigation, and most researchers would agree that they place the existence of precognition beyond all possible doubt.

An even more remarkable test was devised by Eugène Osty, in which a medium was asked to 'guess' a future event and place it on record many weeks before it occurred. Osty asked the medium to 'guess' who would be sitting in a particular chair in a certain hall at a date some months hence; he was asked to write details of the person, and to pass on his (sealed) letter to the investigator, who would then arrange a meeting in which the chair would be occupied. When such a test was conducted by the Israeli Parapsychological Society under H.C. Berendt, a psychic named Orlop was asked to guess the identity of the occupant of the chair; he tape-recorded his prediction and mailed it to Jerusalem. Two weeks later, the audience entered the hall and took chairs at random. Then the recorder was switched on, and Orlop's voice said: 'Seat number 14, a lady, height 1 metre 70 to 1 metre 75, age between 40 and 50.' Her profession he gave as 'helping other people to spend their leisure time'. Orlop also mentioned that she had recently injured her knee. In fact, the woman was 42; her height was 1 metre 72; she was an actress; and had injured her ankle, not her knee. This test has been carried out repeatedly — once by the Oxford University Society for Psychical Research under Kevin M'Clure, the 'psychic' being Robert Cracknell; again, the results were of incredible accuracy.

Precognitive dreams were investigated by Dunne in his famous *An Experiment With Time*, and later by Lethbridge, who described his results in *The Power of the Pendulum*. Dunne (see *prediction) made a habit of noting down his dreams in the middle of the night, before he could forget them, and was surprised at their accuracy. But both Dunne and Lethbridge noted that their dreams concerned their own future rather than future events as such. For example, Dunne dreamed of the great volcanic eruption in Martinique of 1902, and that 4,000 people had been killed; he later read of the Mont Pelée eruption in a newspaper, whose headline proclaimed that 40,000 had been killed. (The figure later proved to be quite inaccurate.) He had misread the headline as saying 4,000, and only later discovered his mistake.

In my *Mysteries* I record a remarkable case. It concerned Lord Kilbracken, who began to dream the winners of horse races in 1946; he won several times, and later became racing correspondent of the *Daily Mirror*. The UK Independent Television science correspondent Peter Fairley has described how, after a traumatic period of blindness, he developed the ability to pick out racing winners by simply looking at a newspaper list of runners; he says that when he began to worry about 'getting it right' the ability vanished — although not before he had made a great deal of money.

Fairley's experience obviously suggests that his right brain was responsible, and that when the left began to 'worry' the faculty vanished (see page 19). But this still fails to explain *how* the right brain can know the future. Dunne suggested that, in some sense, the future has already taken place, and that such glimpses are analogous to a gramophone stylus skipping a groove, or to a loop in a film. But this obviously suggests that life is somehow an illusion and the future totally preordained — although this suggestion may arise purely from a confusion over the nature of *time. (We may take a less extreme view and believe that the 'play' is scripted, but that the actors can still improvise.)

In *Patterns of Prophecy* Alan Vaughan has described how he became interested in precognition because of a personal experience (see *seers and prophets). Through experimenting with an ouija board he became 'possessed'; a medium summoned a 'spirit' who forced the invading entity out of the top of his head. In the moment of becoming 'dispossessed', Vaughan said that he could foresee the future, and could have accurately foretold *any* future event. (See also *possession.)

I have suggested the answer to all problems of paranormal cognition may be that we are not one person but a whole *hierarchy* of persons, arranged in the form of a ladder (see *multiple personality). Our present 'self' is simply the rung we happen to have reached; above us are more rungs that we may or may not reach in the future. Yet these higher rungs are, apparently, already there; the 'higher selves' already seem to exist. I have suggested that paranormal cognition is an accidental short-circuit between the 'present self' and one of these 'higher selves'. (See also *clairvoyance.) CW

Prediction
Rudyard Kipling was a man who professed disbelief in any kind of psychic experience. But once he had a dream in which he saw himself standing in a line of formally dressed men in a large stone-floored hall. A ceremony was in progress, which he could not see for the crowd, and, when it was over, a stranger took his arm and said, 'I want a word with you.' Six weeks later he remembered the dream when attending a war memorial service in Westminster Abbey. The place and his situation were exactly as in the dream, and at the end of the service a stranger took his arm and said, 'I want a word with you, please.' In his autobiography, Kipling asked, 'How, or why, had I been shown an unreleased roll of my life film?'

*Time, in our everyday experience, unrolls like a film, sequentially and at a consistent pace, and even if we can make the speculative leap of assuming that the future in a sense already exists, rather as the unprojected frames of a film already exist, we find it very difficult to take the further step of allowing that we can acquire knowledge of future events.

Perhaps we can find a clue as to the nature of prediction in the fact that recorded predictions of disaster or death outnumber predictions of happy events by four to one. This is the finding of Dr Ian Stevenson, who has made a systematic study of predictions of disasters. His study suggests also that there is a precognitive faculty in us that often works at an unconscious level, for it establishes the fact that the number of passengers on accident-bound trains is always fewer than on corresponding trains on other days. The implications are reinforced by the fact that in the week before the *Titanic* set out on its maiden voyage in 1912 an unusually large number of people cancelled their passages. Many were unable to give any better reason than that they thought it unlucky to travel on a ship's maiden voyage, but one, a London businessman named J. Connor Middleton, cancelled because he had had a vivid dream in which he saw the ship 'floating on the sea, keel upwards and her passengers and crew swimming around her' — a precise description of the tragedy.

Stevenson's investigations revealed an impressive number of ostensible predictions of the sinking of the *Titanic*. When the ship was steaming out of Southampton, one of the thousands of people standing on the shore was a Mrs Marshall, who suddenly had a vivid mental image of hundreds of people struggling in icy waters and cried out, 'That ship is going to sink before she reaches America.' At the very hour when the ship did sink, a woman in New York awoke from a nightmare in which she had seen her mother in a crowded lifeboat in mid-ocean, had heard the cries of people drowning and seen a great upturned liner take its final plunge. The woman did not know at the time that her mother had booked a passage on the *Titanic*.

In all cultures and throughout history the prophet or *seer has been respected and consulted, and there exists a wealth of historical cases of prophecies being fulfilled. For example, Nostradamus foretold the French Revolution and World War 1, saying that the latter would be fought by land, sea and air, although the existence of the aeroplane so puzzled him that he could describe it only by analogy as 'a flock of ravens high in the air, throwing fire from the sky on the cities and the soldiers below'.

Alan Vaughan, who has made some remarkable predictions, writes: 'As I become activated enough to lose my sense of ego-identity, then conventional time loses its meaning as I get caught up with extradimensional adventures in the future.' This lends support to the theory of serial time developed by J.W. Dunne in 1929 (see *precognition). Dunne believed there was 'some extraordinary fault' in his relation to reality, something 'so uniquely wrong that it compelled me to perceive, at rare intervals, large blocks of otherwise perfectly normal personal experience displaced from their proper positions in time'. Investigations led him to conclude that he was not unique in having these experiences, and taking a lead from *Relativity he suggested there was a dimension of reality in which space and time were compounded. Under certain circumstances events could be observed as occupying space, spread out so that parts of the past and future were accessible to consciousness as well as the present. This fourth dimension of space-time could not be penetrated by the conscious mind according to Dunne; but the unconscious could on certain occasions, and particularly in dreams, temporarily enter it. (See also *clairvoyance.) SH

Scrying

Scrying is a means of practising *clairvoyance or divination by gazing into a crystal ball. Although the ball is regarded by many as an affectation of the charlatan, there is evidence that crystal-gazing is sometimes and for some people an effective means of acquiring information about things remote in space or time. These people are probably psychically gifted anyway; crystal-gazing is no doubt more often nothing more than an effective way of inducing visual hallucinations.

Some psychologists have pointed out a similarity between scrying and the experience of hypnagogic imagery, the vivid but brief mental pictures some people have in the state between sleeping and waking. The difference appears to be that the scryer's images are more stable and enduring.

The ability to see figures and scenes in a crystal ball is one that many people probably possess without realizing it, although there is no guarantee that what is seen in most cases is due to the operation of paranormal faculty. The method is to put the crystal ball on a dark background, to sit with the light behind you and gaze at the crystal. After up to ten minutes the successful scryer will see the crystal turn cloudy, but this soon gives way to the appearance of figures and scenes. Some recommend the beginner to develop the faculty by gazing first at some prominent object in the room, then trying to transfer its image to the ball, or to recall a vivid memory and try to project it into the ball.

Described visions are of varying degrees of depth and intensity. Some have reported experiencing the complete disappearance of the crystal and finding themselves seemingly projected into the scene. One writer has said that when she experienced 'writer's block' when engaged on a work of fiction she would resort to the crystal because she could see enacted in it what her characters were going to do next.

But perhaps the strangest use of scrying was that of John Dee. With the help of Edward Kelley, he used scrying in combination with a complicated system of numbered and lettered charts to receive, he alleged, dictation from the angels. An angel would appear in the ball and with a wand would point in sequence to numbers and letters on the chart. Dee called the language of these communications 'Enochian', and the curious thing is that it has a consistent grammar and syntax. But whether it emanated from the angels or from Dee's subconscious is a matter of doubt. SH

Seers and Prophets

In *Patterns of Prophecy*, dealing with scientific investigation into *precognition, Alan Vaughan has described how, through a sense of immense relief, he suddenly 'began to sense what was going on in other people's minds and ... I began to sense the future through some kind of extended awareness'. He began to study cases of prophecy, and found them remarkably hard to verify, although he was impressed by the prophecy made by Jeane Dixon which appeared in *Parade* in 1956: 'As for the 1960 election, Mrs Dixon thinks it will be dominated by labour and won by a Democrat. But he will be assassinated or die in office "though not necessarily in his first term".' Kennedy was, of course, assassinated, in his first term.

In the same book, Vaughan speaks of a series of experiments in long-distance telepathy conducted by the UK psychic Mrs A.M. Kaulback with her two sons. Some of her word-pictures corresponded accurately to what her sons were doing at the time, others were of recently past events, and a few were of future events. Mrs Kaulback received these 'pictures' through 'discarnate entities', including her dead husband. On 4 November 1942 'her husband' told her via automatic script that their son Bill was being given command of a battalion, and described how the letter was handed to him by an orderly and how Bill then showed it to a colonel who said: 'I shall be sorry to lose you.' The event occurred precisely as described — but a month later. Mrs Kaulback asked her 'guide' for an explanation of the mistake, and was told that discarnate entities were aware of the future as well as the past, and could easily get them confused.

Lethbridge came to believe that the pendulum could respond accurately to any substance on Earth. And if it were longer than 40in it would respond to a 'timeless realm' beyond death; he believed glimpses of this timeless realm were obtained in precognitive dreams (see *precognition).

It is worth noting that Vaughan's brief ability to 'sense the future' was accompanied by the ability to sense what was going on in other people's minds. It seems clear that the power of prophecy, or precognition, is not a specialized psychic faculty, but is part of a more general paranormal ability which makes no clear distinction between past and future. It is also worth noting that 'psychic' abilities often develop as a result of trauma or strain, as if some apparatus that would normally exclude them had been damaged or misaligned.

The career of Michel de Nostredame, the most famous of all 'prophets', is a case in point. Born at St Rémy in 1503 into a family of physicians, Nostredame first proved his medical skill in a plague in Provence in 1525. He settled in Agen, married, and became highly successful; but in 1534 a casual remark about his dislike of statues led to accusations of heresy. In the following year, plague again broke out, and his wife and two children died. He left Agen and once more became a wanderer; it seems to have been now that his psychic powers appeared. At the age of forty-four he again settled down, in Salon. His reputation slowly spread across Europe. In 1555 he published the first edition of his prophecies, called *Centuries* because they appeared in sets of 100 stanzas (the first edition contains 300). It contained a prophecy that brought him widespread notoriety: '*Le lyon jeune le vieux surmontera/En champ bellique par singulier duelle;/Dans cage d'or les yeux lui crevera,/Deux classes une, puis mourir, mort cruelle.*' (The young lion shall overcome the old on the field of battle in single combat; in a cage of gold he will pierce his eyes, two wounds in one, then he dies a cruel death.)

Four years later, in 1559, during marriage festivities, Henry II broke lances with Montgomery of the Scottish guard; Montgomery's lance splintered, and the end pierced the king's golden helmet, entering his eye; he died ten days later. Another prophet, Luc Gauric, had warned Henry that his reign would begin and end in duels, and the first had taken place soon after he was crowned.

This quatrain demonstrates the problem of interpreting Nostradamus. Montgomery *was* younger than Henry, but only by seven years. Henry sometimes used a lion in his emblem, but Montgomery did not. The quatrains speak of 'eyes' being wounded, but it was only one eye. Some interpreters suggest that '*deux classes une*' ('two breaks one') means that this was the first of two blows that would destroy the house of Valois — the second being the assassination of Henry III. But it can be seen why sceptics also feel that Nostradamus' prophecies could mean practically anything.

But many others are more convincing. One speaks of two married persons who would come through the forest of Reines by a circuitous route to Varennes — then there would be tempests, blood and beheading (*trancher*, 'to slice'). Varennes appears only once in French history, when Louis XVI and Marie Antoinette were arrested there in flight from Paris.

One quatrain states that in July 1999 'the

great king of terror will descend from the sky'. This has been interpreted as a prophecy of an invasion from space, the hydrogen bomb, or simply the landing of a world dictator by aeroplane ... We may take comfort from the fact that Nostradamus' most accurate prophecies concern his own time, and that he becomes more inaccurate as he speaks of the distant future.

Mother Shipton was his contemporary; her birth is thought to have been in 1488, near Knaresborough — although her life is so badly documented that there is even doubt as to whether she really existed. It is said that she prophesied that Cardinal Wolsey would never enter York, although he would see it. In fact, Wolsey saw York from the castle tower at Cawood, eight miles away, then was called to London by a message from the king, and died en route at Leicester. To Mother Shipton is attributed a piece of doggerel, published in 1641, beginning: 'Carriages without horses shall go, / And accidents fill the world with woe. / Around the Earth thoughts shall fly. / In the twinkling of an eye ...' and prophesying that iron would one day float in the water 'as easily as a wooden boat' (steamships) and that men should fly in the air. But the prophecy ends by announcing that the world 'to an end shall come / In eighteen hundred and eighty one'.

The execution of Mary, Queen of Scots, was described in remarkable detail by many Highland seers.

The best known British prophet is probably Kenneth Mackenzie, the Brahan Seer or Warlock of the Glen (*Coinneach Odhar Foisaiche*). Again, precise dates are lacking — it is known only that he was born early in the seventeenth century on Lewis in the Hebrides. He worked as a labourer at a farm near Brahan Castle, in Ross and Cromarty, and was apparently subject to trances when he stared at bright objects (see *precognition). Most of his prophecies concerned local events and families. He predicted 150 years before the building of the Caledonian Canal that ships would sail behind Tomnahurich hill, near Inverness. Offended by the Mackenzies of Lochalsh, he told them that they would have to dispose of their estates to an Englishman of great liberality, who would have one son and two daughters; and after his death the property would revert to the Mathiesons, who would build a castle at Balmacarra. Again, it was 150 years before the prophecy was fulfilled in detail.

Crossing the site where the Battle of Culloden would take place a century later, he predicted that it would be stained by the 'best blood in the Highlands', and that no quarter would be given on either side — a prophecy that appeared in records long before it was fulfilled. He also predicted that the bridge spanning the Ness would be destroyed by flood waters as a man and woman were crossing it; this happened in 1849 — although only one arch collapsed, and the man was not, as Mackenzie predicted, on horseback.

The seer's powers led to his death. Asked by the wife of the third Earl of Seaforth what her husband was at present doing in Paris, he admitted that he could see him with his arm around a lady's waist. Lady Seaforth sentenced him to be burnt as a witch. Mackenzie made long and precise prophecies about the future — and downfall — of the Seaforths, which again proved astonishingly accurate.

Inevitably, the most violent events are foretold most frequently. Cagliostro has several accurate predictions to his credit, including one that the king would lose his head and that Marie Antoinette would be imprisoned and beheaded; this prophecy was made at a masonic gathering through *numerology. Cazotte prophesied the French Revolution in detail in 1788 at a dinner given by the Duchesse de Gramont, telling Condorcet that he would take poison to cheat the executioner, that Bailly would die at the hands of a mob, that Chamfort would cut his own veins but die months later, and that the Duchess herself would be executed. All this was taken down in detail by a sceptic, Jean de la Harpe, among whose papers it was found in 1803.

In *Patterns of Prophecy* Alan Vaughan advances the theory that certain basic motifs or 'archetypes' of life are repeated from generation to generation; they look like *coincidence but are, in fact, forms of synchronicity (see *Jung) — recurring *patterns*. Individual lives also have a 'blueprint', Vaughan believes, but this nevertheless permits considerable basic freedom — in the way that a blueprint of a house would determine its rooms, but not the way that the owner decides to furnish it.   CW

Time

H.G. Wells can be regarded as the first writer to treat *time travel in fiction, although some earlier writers (like L.-S. Mercier and W.H. Hudson) had sent their heroes into the future by making them fall asleep, like Rip Van Winkle, for a few decades or centuries. The hero of Wells' *The Time Machine* argues that time is no more than an extra dimension of space — anticipating the Einstein-Minkowski notion of space time. Consider a number of photographs of a man at different ages, he says; these are three-dimensional representations of a four-dimensional being — slices or cross-sections of a being which extends into an invisible dimension.

This sounds a possible explanation for the baffling phenomenon of *precognition (see also *time slips), but it has one logical defect. The time traveller could travel back to meet his self of the previous day. In fact, he could collect as many previous (or future) 'selves' as his machine would hold, and invite them all back for dinner. In short, the notion of time travel contains the hidden supposition that there are thousands of parallel universes (see *alternate universes, *parallel worlds), each a fraction of a second ahead or behind this one in time. But then each universe would either have to be 'frozen' or have its *own* past and future — a contradiction of the original assumption of time as an 'extra dimension'.

In fact, a little analysis reveals that the idea of *time travel in the Wellsian sense is an impossibility. We do not really experience 'time'; we experience process. Time is an abstraction from the fact of things *happening*. We might imagine, for example, a man born on a train who invents a word — 'zyme' — to describe the movement of objects past the windows; so that when the train stops in a station he says that zyme is standing still. We, who have not been born on trains, can point out to him that 'zyme' does not exist; what really exists is the train and the landscape, and their relative motion. But we *are* born in time; we cannot imagine ourselves apart from it. So we make the same kind of logical error.

J.W. Dunne, whose *An Experiment With Time* achieved immense popularity in the 1930s, attempted to construct a theory of time based upon Einstein's notion that time is the 'fourth dimension'. If time 'flows', he says, then we must have a sense of some other kind of time to measure it by — he calls this 'Time Two'. But then the same must apply to Time Two, creating an infinite number of Times. This implies an infinite number of 'me's.

In *Man and Time* J.B. Priestley made the penetrating suggestion that this 'infinite regress' of selves is unnecessary. He suggests that self-observation tells us that there are three 'me's. The first is the 'me' who is present when I observe the world passively — half asleep, as it were. The second 'me' comes into being when I wake up fully and focus my attention. This 'me' is active. But when I am launched into purposeful activity there is still another 'me' who can observe it in a detached way. If 'self two' is miserable and worried, 'self three' may note this and feel slightly contemptuous. These three 'selves', Priestley argues, explain all our normal experience. He goes on to argue that there are also three kinds of time: 'ordinary time' which passes as I stand in a bus queue; 'inner time' which I experience in moments of serenity and contemplation; and 'creative time' which artists occasionally experience in moments of great intensity (Priestley says that he once wrote four difficult plays at top speed, 'like a man watching himself run at a headlong pace across a minefield'). He feels that this third 'time' is experienced by the unconscious. (Split-brain experiments seem to indicate that the right brain has little or no sense of time.) In *The Dramatic Universe* J.G. Bennett also has suggested that time may have three dimensions, like space.

In *The Occult* I coined the term Faculty X to cover what Priestley calls 'time two'. He mentions that these contemplative glimpses 'across' time may come when he hears someone say 'France' or 'eighteenth century'. Proust described in *Swann's Way* how he had a similar vivid glimpse of his own childhood as he tasted a cake dipped in herb tea. *À la Recherche du Temps Perdu* describes his attempts to recapture these moments in which other times and places become as vivid and real as the present. Toynbee has described how the idea of his *A Study of History* came from a number of similar 'glimpses' in which the past suddenly became as real as the present. Clearly, we possess the power to achieve these glimpses, but our vitality is normally too low. It is as if there is a 'muscle' in the brain that must be galvanized by sudden intensity or emergency before we can achieve glimpses of 'Faculty X', the power to grasp the reality of other times and places. But, since a muscle can be developed, there seems to be no reason why we should not eventually learn to use 'Faculty X' at will. The basic condition is that we should cease to live 'mechanically', that we should consciously attempt to use Priestley's 'self two' and 'self three'; which, in turn, requires the recognition that we possess freedom and are capable of exercising it. This is Howard Miller's recognition that we possess a 'unit of pure thought' which presides over consciousness, a 'transcendental ego' (see page 20). Our chief problem is our tendency to drift with the stream, to fail to use our powers of choice.

It seems clear, then, that even though we may be unable to grasp the nature of time analytically, we are, in another sense, capable of rising 'above time'. Dostoevsky attached immense importance to the quotation from *Revelation* that 'there shall be time no longer'; he said it corresponded to his own experience of mystical ecstasy on the point of epileptic attacks. Lethbridge, too, had some interesting speculations on the nature of time. This recognition — that time is intimately, and inversely, associated with freedom (and that therefore freedom may be conceived as a kind of fifth dimension) — suggests that, contrary to all common sense, human beings may one day be capable of grasping the nature of time 'from above'.

(For other ideas on the nature of time, consult the Directory-Index.) CW

Time Reversal

The arrow of time appears always to point in the same direction — from past through present into future. Indeed, we would probably all lose our minds if it did not.

This has important consequences and manifestations. For example, common sense dictates that cause precedes effect (see *causality): I hit you *before* you fall over. At the frontiers of modern experimental physics, this law appears to be a universal one. But is it?

Elsewhere in this book we find suggestions that *antimatter particles could be ordinary particles for which the arrow of time is reversed; that succeeding universes may be characterized by the direction within them of the arrow of time (see *alternate universes). If *tachyons exist, one can do no more than hazard a guess as to which direction the arrow of time points for them.

Our *Universe appears to be expanding. This does not mean simply that all the galaxies are scurrying away from an initial point in space where they erupted into being; it means that spacetime as a whole is expanding. If there should ever come a point where the Universe begins to contract then it seems plausible that, since at that point space and time too will begin to contract, the arrow of time will reverse: *time will begin to run backwards* (see *time-symmetric Universe). JG

Time Slip

The phrase 'time slip' has come into being in recent years to describe experiences in which people have apparently found themselves 'in the past'. The notion sounds like science fiction; yet there are a number of well authenticated examples.

Best known is undoubtedly the experience of two English ladies, Charlotte Moberly and Eleanor Jourdain, at Versailles. On 10 August 1901 they were walking in the Trianon park, and were surprised to encounter a number of people in eighteenth-century dress. They passed a woman in old-fashioned dress who was drawing, but only Moberly saw her. Yet it was not until a week later that they compared notes and decided there was something strange about the experience. Jourdain returned alone to Versailles the following January, and again saw oddly dressed people — this time labourers in bright tunics — and again felt 'as if I had crossed a line and was suddenly in a circle of influence'. Yet, when the two ladies returned three years later, everything had changed. A study of books on Versailles convinced them that they had seen the place as it was in the reign of Marie Antoinette, and that she was probably the sketching woman.

The story, told in *An Adventure*, became famous and was widely discussed. Speaking about it in his *Guide to Modern Thought*, C.E.M. Joad used the phrase 'the undoubted queerness of time'. (This was also the period when Dunne's theories were being widely discussed; see *time, *precognition.) But, in a biography of Robert de Montesquiou, Philippe Jullian suggested that the ladies had merely witnessed a fancy-dress party organized at Versailles by Mme Greffulhe. Yet the fancy-dress party he describes took place seven years too early, and Mme Greffulhe was actually in London on the day the two ladies had their 'adventure'.

In *Mysteries* and *The Book of Time* I recorded a 'time slip' that came accidentally to my notice. Jane O'Neill witnessed a serious accident, and was so shocked that she had to take several weeks off work. After this she had odd flashes of '*clairvoyance'. One day, she visited the church at Fotheringhay with a friend and was impressed by a picture behind the altar. She mentioned it later to her friend who said she had not seen the picture. Later, to settle the matter, they returned to the church, and to O'Neill's surprise, it was apparently a completely different place; it was smaller, and the picture was not there. She corresponded with an expert on the church, who told her that the church she had 'seen' was the church as it had been 400 years ago, before it had been rebuilt in 1553.

In both cases, the most striking thing is the apparent 'normality' of the experience. Moberly and Jourdain recorded an 'odd feeling', but still had no sense of hallucination.

In *The Masks of Time* Joan Forman has described many 'time slips'. Perhaps the oddest concerns a Mr Squirrel, who in 1973 went into a stationer's shop in Great Yarmouth to buy some envelopes. He was served by a woman in Edwardian dress, and bought three dozen envelopes for a shilling. He noticed that the building was extremely silent — there was no traffic noise. On visiting the shop a week later, he found it completely changed and modernized; the assistant, an elderly lady, denied that there had been any other assistant in the shop the previous week.

The envelopes disintegrated very quickly. Forman heard of the case and interviewed Squirrel; he was able to produce for her one of the remaining envelopes. Forman wrote to the manufacturers, who said that such envelopes had ceased to be manufactured fifteen years before. However, Forman admits that 'as a genuine time dislocation this case is not proved by the evidence'. And, certainly, the actual existence of the envelope places the story in a completely different category from the Versailles or Fotheringhay incidents.

The simplest explanation is probably the psychometric hypothesis. In the mid-nineteenth century, Dr Joseph Rodes Buchanan of the Covington Medical Institute performed experiments that convinced him that certain of his students could distinguish different chemicals when they were wrapped in thick brown paper. Then he discovered that some of these 'sensitives' could hold letters in their hands and accurately describe the character of the writer. He became convinced that all objects carry their 'history' photographed in them (see *ESP). His friend William Denton, a professor of geology, experimented with his own students, and obtained striking results with geological samples; they were often able to describe with astonishing accuracy where the sample had come from. Buchanan wrote: 'The past is entombed in the present ... The discoveries of psychometry will enable us to explore the history of Man as those of geology enable us to explore the history of the Earth ...' Both he and Denton were convinced that they had founded a new science which had no connection with *Spiritualism or the 'occult'. In modern times, their 'science' has reappeared as 'psychic archaeology', and has produced some remarkable results.

Clearly, psychometry may be seen as a form of 'time slip'. Yet the dividing line between this and a case like Jane O'Neill's seems at present too sharp to allow them to be merged — even in theory. CW

Time Travel

In principle, it is easier to travel into the distant future than to travel *one second* backwards in time. *Relativity permits two ways of travelling into the remote future. The first is to travel far enough and fast enough. Bodies moving at velocities close to that of light experience a marked time dilation — their clocks run slow as compared with that of a 'stationary' observer. This effect becomes apparent only at extremely high velocities: to halve the rate of the clocks one must travel at 87 per cent of the velocity of light. But one can travel 10,000 years into the future by undertaking a twenty-year space voyage at 99.9 per cent of the velocity of light, or even a two-year voyage at 99.99 per cent light speed.

The second possibility is to use the intense gravitational field of a *black hole. Just as high velocity produces a time dilation effect, so does the presence of a strong gravititational field. Thus, one could in theory take up a close orbit around a black hole — or, more realistically, 'skim' close to it several times — and then emerge to find that thousands of years had passed.

If one *could* travel back in time, a number of intriguing paradoxes would emerge. One could, for example, use one's time machine to travel back to tell one's younger self how to build a time machine. Such paradoxes are taken to indicate that travel into the past is impossible — or that at least there is some fundamental law whereby one cannot convey any information to (that is, change) the past (see *causality). For example, it has been suggested that antiparticles (see *antimatter) may be equivalent to particles travelling in a reverse time direction; the fundamental law would dictate that we cannot affect these antiparticles such as to make them convey information (for example, modulate them, as we do radio waves).

Invoking a fundamental law in order to avoid paradoxes is a practice with a poor history. Knowledge has often profited substantially from the investigation of apparent paradoxes and the discovery that they are not paradoxical at all but are manifestations of a law previously unknown. Moreover, if we cannot convey information from the present into the past, it follows that we cannot receive information from the future — yet there certainly seems some reality in the phenomenon of *precognition.

Where, then, are the travellers from the future? Either, like the members of the hypothetical *Galactic Club, they are perhaps being careful not to interfere with us or, of course, Man may not have a long enough future left to him to allow him to invent time machines. Or, and this must remain the most reasonable explanation, time travel into the past really is impossible.

JG

Evolution: 4

The following three sections of this book are concerned, quite fundamentally, with three different aspects of present and future human evolution.

It is perhaps a truism to say that we are on the brink of a major evolutionary step forward. However, it would seem that there are two factors involved. The first is our growing awareness of the untapped powers of the human mind — a theme that has turned up many times during the earlier parts of this book. In evolutionary terms, it is to a certain extent irrelevant whether we are rediscovering or newly discovering the 'forgotten' right brain, for in either case we have never been in the position of using both halves of our brain in integrated fashion in the near-future cultural and technological environment.

And it is this environment which is at once both a cause and an effect of the second major factor involved: as we reach out in our minds to embrace concepts that challenge all our accepted knowledge, so our minds must needs become more competent, more versatile.

In the following sections we shall see how the two superficially disparate strands of this book are in fact one.

JG

PART FIVE
INNER SPACE: MIND AND BODY

Introductory: 5

This section of the book is perhaps the most controversial, because its individual articles are more closely connected than in earlier sections. It should become clear, to begin with, how the speculations about the right and left brain in the Introduction (see pages 13–22) throw light on a tremendous mass of apparently unrelated material. The section on *multiple personality — the central topic of my *Mysteries* — also raises some new complexities; I have suggested that we are *all* 'multiple personalities', and that our 'selves' may be arranged in the form of a ladder.

Both multiple personality and *reincarnation seem to offer a direct challenge to the view of John Taylor that personality is a product of our brain functions. Again and again in the literature of multiple personality, doctors mention that as soon as they enter a patient's room they can tell which 'person' is in charge of the body. Mothers feel that their babies are distinct personalities from the moment they are born. (This, of course, does not conflict with the view that the personality is a product of brain-functions; but it conflicts with the common-sense view that personality is formed by things that happen to us and our response to them.) And the case of Jasbir Lal seems to suggest clearly that a 'person' exists quite independently of the body — a man who had just died seems to have 'moved in' to Jasbir's body when he was on the point of death or had actually died. What we do not know — and what would be tremendously interesting to know — is whether the 'old' Jasbir was able to co-exist in the body with the new personality. The literature of multiple personality seems to suggest that it could be so.

Another interesting question arises from this matter. In multiple personalities, one personality is often able to slip out of the body, leaving another to take over some awkward or embarrassing situation. This raises a fundamental question. *What* is it precisely that prevents 'me' from simply vacating my body in the face of some problem? According to Cleve Backster, plants 'pass out' when they are severely shocked — which may be their equivalent. And yogic tradition affirms that yogis *can* vacate the body at will. Lyall Watson, in *The Romeo Error*, writes about the 'death trance' — the fact that when people are close to death they seem to become serene and cheerful about it — and may even resent being dragged back to life. Is it conceivable that we all possess this power to vacate the body at will, but that there are powerful inhibitory mechanisms in us to prevent us from doing it too easily?

This, and many other questions raised in this section, would no doubt strike scientists as unanswerable, if not nonsensical. But then, their attitude is irrelevant in the present context; the aim of this book is to present *possibilities*. No question can be answered unless it has first been raised. CW

Acquired Characteristics

The doctrine of evolution by acquired characteristics (for example, that a man who had built up his muscles could pass on his strength to his children) is now regarded as totally discredited. Yet it remains a burning issue, simply because the alternative view — rigid Darwinism — leaves no place for free will. (Samuel Butler remarked that Darwin had 'banished God from the Universe'.)

The doctrine of evolution was first propounded by Benoit de Maillet, who in 1715 wrote *Telliamed*, which suggested that life originated in space as a germ (see *panspermia), and developed on Earth into marine organisms, which came ashore, and in turn slowly developed into animals and birds. Buffon and Goethe took up the theory. Lamarck suggested that evolution takes place because, when some individual develops a useful characteristic through effort, it passes it on to its children. So, for example, the giraffe developed its long neck by striving to reach higher and higher branches, and individuals passed it on to subsequent generations of giraffes.

Darwin's *Origin of Species* propounded survival of the fittest through natural selection. According to Darwin, a giraffe that 'accidentally' had a longer neck would be able to reach more food when food was scarce than would short-necked giraffes. Over generations the balance would shift in favour of longer necks. Yet Darwin believed that 'Lamarckism' too played its part in evolution. His followers disagreed: 'survival of the fittest' seemed to them a perfectly adequate mechanism, whether or not it reduced life to a mere spectacle in which free will (if it exists) could play no active part. Their view was apparently confimed by the discovery by Mendel that the unit of inheritance is the gene, and that genes alone determine whether a man is strong or weak, stupid or clever.

In his preface to *Back to Methuselah* Shaw denounced rigid Darwinism and asserted his own view that living creatures evolve through effort, and that this effort can somehow be passed on to future generations. He was dismissed as a 'vitalist' (see *vitalism). But it is only since World War II that many biologists have shown themselves doubtful about the philosophical implications of rigid Darwinism. The controversy was complicated by Stalin's enthusiastic espousal of Lamarckism (as taught by Lysenko) because Stalin wanted to believe that Man can become stronger and more intelligent as his environment is improved. His persecution of Darwinian biologists led to a strong reaction in favour of Darwin. Yet in 1968 a gathering of eminent scientists at Alpbach all expressed their feeling that 'reductionism' — the attempt to 'explain' Man in terms of mechanical responses — has ceased to be credible. The chairman, Arthur Koestler, talked about the 'totalitarian claims of Darwinian orthodoxy'.

It has yet to be proved that genes can be influenced by the will or 'education' of the individual. A more convincing approach, perhaps, is to attempt to show that certain species cannot have evolved certain abilities by a purely Darwinian mechanism — for example, the ability of colonies of flattid bugs to form themselves into a semblance of a perfect flower which does not exist in nature. (Darwinian evolution affects individuals by favouring or eliminating them; there is no obvious way in which it could lead to a colony 'accidentally' imitating a flower and so avoiding predators.) In *The Case of the Midwife Toad*, Arthur Koestler has attempted to rehabilitate Paul Kammerer who apparently proved inheritance of acquired characteristics in the laboratory, but who committed suicide when it was discovered that one of his assistants had 'cheated'.

An interesting light is also thrown on this problem by new discoveries in *biofeedback. In *The Living Stream*, Sir Alister Hardy mentions the amazing behaviour of a flatworm called *Microstomum*, which eats a polyp called *Hydra* for the sake of its defence system. *Hydra* has certain stinging capsules to keep off predators, but they do not work against *Microstomum*, which swallows and digests the *Hydra*. Then the stinging bombs are picked up in the lining of the flatworm's stomach, passed through it to another set of cells, which in turn carries them to the flatworm's skin, where they are mounted, pointing outward, for defence. The *Microstomum* does not eat the *Hydra* for food, but only to steal its 'bombs'. Darwinians have so far failed to explain how such an elaborate system came about by 'chance' or natural selection, and one scientist was even driven to 'postulate a group mind among the cells of the body' to account for it. However, biofeedback reveals that we can learn to control the autonomic nervous system, and even our 'automatic' physical functions. Human beings possess consciousness, which has cut them off from their 'deeper' levels; clearly, the *Microstomum* does not have this problem, and can move its cells around as easily as we move our fingers. But if items at the cellular level can be influenced by the will, then presumably — although it is a giant leap — so can the genes, and the inheritance of acquired characteristics should be possible after all.

In the 1980s, it looks as if these problems may be acquiring new relevance. *The Times* for 24 June 1980 carried a report headed 'Immunology: Lamarckian inheritance reopened'. Its second paragraph states: 'Dr R.M. Gorczynski and Dr E.J. Steele, working at the Ontario Cancer Institute in Canada, have used a well known technique for inducing mice to tolerate grafts of foreign tissue instead of rejecting them, and have shown that those mice seem to pass on their acquired tolerance to some of their young.' This may be passive immune transfer (antibodies passed from mother to child providing a temporary immunity) but it may not.

Lamarck may have the last word yet.

CW

Acupuncture

Acupuncture ('pricking with a needle') is a traditional Chinese method of healing in which needles are inserted into the skin. It seems to have developed from a recognition that parts of the body become tender during various illnesses. The Chinese believe that there are about 1,000 points which may be stimulated to cure disease. Various points lie on 'meridians'. The philosophy underlying acupuncture is the notion that the body is covered with currents of vitality. It is also related to the Hindu idea that vital energy (*prana*) is picked up from the atmosphere around us and is then distributed through definite pathways over the body.

An acupuncture point may appear to have no direct connection with the part of the body it governs. The point associated with the heart lies in the little finger; the 'liver point' is in the big toe. (But the point associated with headaches lies at the base of the skull, at the back of the neck.) The toboscope, invented by Viktor Adamenko, can register the body's 'L-fields' (see *aura), and it lights up as it passes over acupuncture points.

Acupuncture appears to be superior to Western medicine in many respects — for example, Western television cameramen have filmed a major operation in which the patient was fully conscious, anaesthetized by a single needle in the relevant acupuncture point.

CW

Aura

Living creatures are surrounded by an electrical energy field. In the 1930s, Harold Saxton Burr succeeded in measuring the 'fields of life' by means of electrical apparatus, and was able to show that the life-field (or L-field) of a tree fluctuated according to sunspot activity and the lunar phases. In the late 1930s the Kirlians (see *Kirlian photography) were convinced that they had succeeded in photographing these L-fields.

The notion of a vital 'aura' dates back many millennia: the ancient Egyptians sometimes show haloes around the heads of the gods or important human beings; so did the Hindus, Greeks and Romans; Christian saints, of course, are traditionally shown with a halo. For many centuries, occultists and mystics have described a halo surrounding the whole human body. Phoebe Payne describes (in *Man's Latent Powers*) how as a child she could see living creatures surrounded by coloured emanations, and assumed that everyone else could see them too. Dr Shafica Karagulla, a psychologist who became interested in the healing powers of Edgar Cayce, began to investigate what she called 'higher sense perception', and became convinced that a large number of ordinary general practitioners had the power to see the 'life field' of the patient and to diagnose what was wrong with it.

In the nineteenth century, the notion of a vital aura became for a brief period scientifically respectable when von Reichenbach published his *Researches in Magnetism* in which he described his tests on 'sick sensitives', all of whom could see a red light emanating from the south pole of a magnet and blue from the north. His sensitives could detect the presence of a magnet through thick walls, and even when asleep. Reichenbach discovered they could also see light streaming from crystals and from finger-ends. The book was taken very seriously; its English translator, Dr John Ashburner, duplicated Reichenbach's experiments and confirmed his results. But the 'psychic craze' which began in the late 1840s as a result of the 'Hydesville rappings' had the effect of causing a tidal wave of 'tough-mindedness' among scientists, and within a decade Reichenbach's 'odic force' (the name he gave to this energy) was regarded as a joke.

At about the same time, Dr Joseph Rodes Buchanan had discovered that his students could correctly name chemicals wrapped in brown paper parcels (see *jinxes and curses, *time slip); he assumed this 'sixth sense' was due to some nervous force, which he called the nerve aura.

In the 1880s, Dr Charle Féré spoke of a 'neuropathic aura' he had observed in various patients — for example, an orange-coloured glow around the head and hands of a hysterical female patient.

Around 1900 Dr Walter J. Kilner of St Thomas's Hospital, London, tried to study the 'aura' scientifically. He claimed that if a human being stands against a black background, and is viewed through glass stained with dicyanin dye, the aura surrounding the body can be seen in three distinct layers. He invented 'Kilner goggles' which were supposed to enable anyone to see this aura. Kilner said that the body is surrounded immediately by a dark layer, the 'etheric double', beyond which can be seen the 'aura proper', in two layers. After his death in 1920, his work fell into disrepute.

Dr Shafica Karagulla concluded that the body is surrounded by a physical energy field, then by an emotional field, extending about 18in, then by a mental field, extending another 6in. One doctor who possessed 'higher sense perception' could see vortices of energy associated with the glands. (Oddly enough, the five 'vortices' associated with the endocrine glands corresponded to the five 'chakras' of Hindu philosophy.) Dr Edward Aubert, commenting on Karagulla's book, remarks: 'It seems that we live in a vast ocean of interlacing energies... Each person appears to have his own method of selecting energy.' This again corresponds closely to the Hindu view of the 'chakras' as energy transmitters. In this view, Man could be regarded as an energy transformer, picking up his energy in the same way that a radio aerial picks up signals from the surrounding 'aether'.

Scientific evidence points increasingly to the real existence of the 'aura' — although it should be emphasized that this has no 'occult' implications. Kilner insisted that it was simply some form of electrical envelope. On the other hand, such writers as Arthur E. Powell accept the 'etheric double' as a distinct entity which can be separated from the physical body (although this induces unconsciousness). Its function is to absorb *prana*, vital energy, and distribute it to the physical body (yoga is the power of distributing this vital current at will). But it should not be confused with the 'astral body', the 'body' which becomes separated from the physical body in *out-of-the-body experiences. Powell states, however, that the German term for etheric body is *Doppelgänger*, which in turn suggests that 'phantasms of the living' are projections of the etheric body. (If so, then they should be accompanied by unconsciousness in the 'projector', and this does not appear to be so.)

In *The Romeo Error*, Lyall Watson cites William Tiller of Stanford University as believing that the 'somatic system' (our physical energy system, as studied by Burr) is supplemented by at least one other. He then goes on to suggest that the 'human ensemble' might be separated into seven levels: the 'somatic system', the 'etheric double', the astral level, three levels associated with the mind, and finally a 'spirit' level.

Perhaps the most interesting possibility raised by Watson is the notion that *poltergeist activity may be due to powerful magnetic activity of the 'second level' — which, according to Nelya Mikhailova, has registered a magnetic field ten times as great as that of the Earth. This could suggest that the energy used in poltergeist activity is 'picked up' by the 'etheric body' and then projected.   CW

Automatic Writing

Writing and speaking while in a trance-state became popular in the late eighteenth century as a result of the spread of mesmerism (see *hypnosis). Even then, pre-Freud, it was recognized that much of the material came from the writer's unconscious (or subliminal) mind. But some of the writings purported to be the dictation of spirits — for example, *Nature's Divine Revelations* by Andrew Jackson Davis and *The Pilgrimage of Thomas Paine* by C. Hammond, in which the well known agnostic described his experiences after death.

In 1852 Planchette invented a pencil on wheels to facilitate automatic writing, and this became immensely popular. The ouija board, a tripod on rollers which moved around under the pressure of the hand to indicate various letters, was also much used (it had been known since the fifth century BC). It was an ouija board that, at a 'sitting' in St Louis in 1913, announced it was a spirit named Patience Worth; it dictated several interesting historical novels whose insight into past eras intrigued historians who felt that it was beyond the capacities of the 'medium' through whom it was received. Like so much automatic writing, the novels of Patience Worth are probably of interest chiefly as evidence of the remarkable powers of the unconscious.

One of the most remarkable cases of automatic writing in the history of psychical research is undoubtedly that of the 'cross correspondences'. In 1904 Mrs Verrall 'received' a script containing the words 'record the bits, and when fitted together they will make the whole'. And in fact four ladies operating independently — Mrs Verrall, Mrs Fleming, Mrs Forbes and Mrs Piper (see *mediums) — each produced fragments which, fitted together, made rather complex conundrums. The 'spirits' responsible claimed to be the three deceased founders of the SPR, Henry Sidgwick, Frederick Myers and Edmund Gurney.

A typical 'conundrum' is as follows. In 1906 Mrs Fleming produced a message with the words 'dawn', 'evening' and 'morning', a reference to bay leaves and the name Laurence. Six weeks later, Mrs Verrall produced a message referring to laurel and to a library. Mrs Piper came out of a trance speaking of laurel, 'nigger' and of 'more head'. Mrs Fleming produced more scripts referring to night and day, evening and morning, and to Alexander's Tomb with laurel leaves. Eventually, the answer was discovered — the tomb of the Medicis in the Church of San Lorenzo in Florence, designed by Michelangelo and containing his sculptures of night and day, evening and morning. Lorenzo de Medici's emblem was the laurel, and near the tombs is the Laurentian Library. Alessandro de Medici was half-negro; after his murder, his body was hidden in the tomb of Giuliano. 'More head' should have been 'Moor head' — a negro's head. This conundrum was solved only four years after the first 'clue'. There can be no question of telepathy since the mediums themselves did not understand the clues.

It seems appropriate that the founders of the SPR should have invented this incredibly complex way of 'proving' life after death. Yet if the three men really were the 'communicators', they partly defeated their own object since the various conundrums are so complex and erudite that it takes a scholar to understand them. CW

Biofeedback

Biofeedback is basically a recognition that animals, including humans, can control functions usually considered 'automatic', like heartbeat, temperature and, more especially, brain rhythms.

In the 1960s Neal E. Miller, a professor of psychology at the Rockefeller Institute, discovered that rats could be trained to control their body temperature with traditional techniques of 'conditioning'. Psychologists like Joe Kamiya and Elmer Green discovered that if patients could actually see their brain rhythms on a screen they could learn to control them (see *healing). Most civilized people are so tensed up that they cannot go into alpha-rhythm states for more than a few seconds at a time; then some anxiety 'starts up the engine'. Kamiya discovered that when patients studied their own EEGs they soon learned to recognize *how* they induced relaxation; many quickly learned how to induce what Maslow called '*peak experiences'.

Biofeedback research has shown that nearly all diseases are 'psychosomatic' — are caused by either 'stress' or the body's failure to deal with the illness because the mind is not co-operating. There has even been startlingly successful cancer treatment by persuading the patient to deliberately mobilize his forces (often by a kind of visualization — 'Stand by to repel boarders'). The consequences are startling, and still largely unexplored. CW

Dianetics

In the late 1940s, John W. Campbell Jr, the science-fiction editor, was suffering from chronic sinusitis, and allowed himself to be treated by a writer named L. Ron Hubbard; he was so impressed that he printed in *Astounding Science Fiction* (May 1950) an article by Hubbard on his new method of treatment, dianetics.

Hubbard says that he had observed that people often finished sentences with odd *non sequiturs* — for example, 'I don't know, you can never tell about things like that.' On investigation, he claims to have discovered that the person who habitually used that expression had been in an accident and heard the 'phrase' while he was unconscious — a reply to 'Will he be permanently damaged?'.

Hubbard came to believe that such accidental 'engrams' (a word borrowed from Felix Semon, meaning an imprint of an experience) remain stuck in the unconscious mind, until 'triggered' by some similar word or experience — in fact, a variant on the Freudian theory of neurosis. In dianetics, free association is replaced by a similar process, 'auditing'. The auditor's job is to root out the engram by dragging it into the light of consciousness. He does this by having the patient sink into a 'dianetic revery' in a semi-darkened room; he then attempts to take the patient back in time — to the womb or even earlier, to previous lives.

Hubbard later changed the name to 'scientology' and declared it a religion, a form in which it flourishes. CW

Dowsing

Dowsing, detecting water or other materials by means of a divining rod or pendulum, is probably as old as mankind; Australian Aborigines can often detect water in the desert even without the aid of such instruments. In the nineteenth century it became the subject of much scepticism so that, for example, S. Baring-Gould has a chapter on it in *Curious Myths of the Middle Ages*; he tells a typical story of a Swiss dowser, Jacques Aymar, who tracked down the murderers of a Lyon wine merchant and his wife using his dowsing rod. Andrew Lang began as a sceptic but was converted by evidence presented by Sir William Barrett, and owned dowsing to be 'a fact, and a very serviceable fact'.

Sir William Barrett published the result of his own studies in *The Divining Rod*. He considered the theory that dowsing is simply some form of natural response to a 'vibration' given off by water, but maintained that dowsing is a paranormal faculty — what Charles Richet called 'cryptesthesia': 'By means of this cryptesthesia, knowledge of whatever object is searched for enters the dowser's subconsciousness and is revealed by means of an unconscious muscular reaction.' This is consistent with the theory suggested in my Introduction (page 14) that dowsing is a right-hemisphere reaction communicated to the muscles.

In that case, the ability should be natural to all human beings. My own experience is that nine out of ten people can dowse, and that the tenth person is usually convinced in advance that 'it won't work', and suppresses the ability through left-brain tension.

After World War II Guy Underwood investigated dowsing; he wanted to check a theory that barrows and other prehistoric sites were crossed by underground streams. He found this to be true; he found also that underground water caused a pull on the left-hand side of the divining rod. But he noticed, too, a force which caused a pull on the right hand, and this seemed to be an underground magnetic force (see *ley lines).

T.C. Lethbridge had always been a good dowser, once locating blindfold all the volcanic dikes in a particular area. After his retirement he began experimenting with a pendulum. Many dowsers use the 'short pendulum' — any kind of bob on the end of a short piece of string or cotton. Most people find that such a pendulum goes into a circular swing when held over someone's hand — that it rotates clockwise over the right hand and anti-clockwise over the left. Lethbridge experimented with a longer thread, and quickly concluded that the pendulum reacts to different substances at different lengths. He became convinced also that the pendulum reacts as well to ideas as to substances. (This, again, is what might be expected if the right cerebral hemisphere has access to 'paranormal' information.) He found, for example, that sling stones from an Iron Age site reacted at both 24in and 40in. Ordinary stones from a beach reacted at neither. But when he had thrown the stones against a wall they reacted to a 24in pendulum; those thrown by his wife reacted at 29in — suggesting that 24in was the 'rate' for maleness and 29in for femaleness. He concluded that the 40in response was due to the fact that the stones had been used in war, and that 40in was the rate for anger. Lethbridge's ideas are still not widely accepted, even among dowsers, yet his various books like *Ghost and Divining Rod*, have a refreshing air of pragmatism and common sense.

Another contemporary dowser, Robert Leftwich, is convinced that the mind can 'tune in' to any substance the dowser wishes to search for; so that he could, for example, distinguish between coins and playing cards hidden beneath a carpet, or between water and minerals. Leftwich has successfully dowsed for minerals from an aeroplane.

The word 'radiesthesia' is sometimes used as a synonym for dowsing, although it is more usual to confine its application to the use of a pendulum (or divining rod) for medical purposes, or for finding lost objects.   CW

Dreams and Visions

In March 1893, V. Hilprecht of the University of Pennsylvania was struggling to decipher a cuneiform inscription on two small fragments of agate. He went to bed, exhausted, and had a dream in which a priest of Nippur led him to a treasure chamber in which were a wooden chest and, on the floor, scraps of agate and lapis lazuli. The priest told him that the two fragments he had published on two separate pages of his book actually belonged together; but they were not finger rings. They were ear-rings, cut from a votive cylinder presented by King Kurigalzu to the temple of Bel; and, said the priest, there was a third piece of the cylinder somewhere. Hilprecht woke and rushed to his own book. Sure enough, on the two pages mentioned he saw two fragments that *did* fit together; moreover, the inscription confirmed what the priest had said.

Here we apparently have an example of the power of 'unconscious observation' in dreams — Hilprecht's unconscious mind had noted that the two fragments fitted together. But this theory leaves one odd fact unexplained. Later that year, at the museum in Constantinople, Hilprecht found the third fragment. It seems conceivable that his unconscious had seen the relation between the two earlier fragments; but how did it know that there was a third?

Freud's recognition that dreams were manifestations of the unconscious was a fundamental breakthrough. But the later recognition of the different functions of the right and left hemispheres was perhaps even more important, for it also involved recognition that, while the 'you' lives in the left hemisphere, the 'right-ego' is, for all practical purposes, *another person*. Moreover, there is evidence to support the view that this other person has access to paranormal information and can exercise paranormal powers (see *dowsing, *poltergeists, and page 13).

The so-called power of 'vision' is obviously closely connected with dreaming. William Blake claimed to be able to see his sitters — even purely imaginary ones like the ghost of a flea — just as clearly as if they were present. Similarly, Tesla was able to do calculations on a blackboard inside his head, and visualize his inventions so clearly that they seemed quite concrete. In both cases, the powers of the right brain (of gestalt or pattern recognition) were abnormally developed — or possibly the left interfered less. Tesla almost died of a serious illness in childhood, and it is worth noting that many psychics have achieved their powers through serious illness or accidents — as Ramakrishna achieved his first 'vision of God' through a suicide attempt (see *ESP, *yoga).

Precognitive dreams have been widely studied (see *precognition), and at the Maimonides Institute in New York a study in ESP cognition during dream-states showed positive results (see *Dream Telepathy* by Ullman and Krippner).

P.D. Ouspensky became interested in problems of 'the occult' because of a childhood interest in dreams; he discovered it was possible to remain in a semi-waking state in which dreams continued and could be observed (this is the hypnagogic state). It was Ouspensky's recognition that dreams can actually continue while we are apparently 'wide awake' that prepared him for *Gurdjieff's doctrine that human beings are basically 'asleep', even when they think they are awake.

Ouspensky records also (in *A New Model of the Universe*) a number of 'lucid dreams' — that is, dreams that seemed totally real, yet in which he was aware he was asleep and dreaming. An important study of these was presented to the SPR in 1913 by Frederik van Eeden. He said his own lucid dreams were often preceded for several nights by dreams of flying. In one of the lucid dreams, in which he saw magnificent scenery with a sense of total reality, someone told him that he would be robbed of a large sum of money, a prediction that proved accurate. Van Eeden noted also that when he dreamed that he was lying on his stomach — while knowing that he was in bed on his back — he woke himself slowly, and experienced a sensation of slipping from one body — in which he was on his stomach — into another. This convinced him of the existence of what he called the 'dream body'.

It has also been suggested that lucid dreams may lead to '*out-of-the-body experiences'. Hugh Calloway, writing as Oliver Fox, describes in *Astral Projection* how, in 1902, he dreamed that he was standing outside his house, but noticed that the paving stones were laid the wrong way, whereupon it struck him that he must be asleep. He began trying hard to induce lucid dreams by thinking hard about it before he fell asleep; soon he learned how to, and became convinced his 'dream body' actually visited other places in these states. Eventually, Calloway learned the trick of 'astral projection' while he was awake, beginning by inducing a trance state, and trying to hurl himself against an imaginary trapdoor which he called 'the pineal door'.

In *Windows on the Mind: The Christos Experiment* the Australian writer G.M. Glaskin describes how he and two friends came upon a typescript called 'The Christos Experiment' which gave a recipe for 'astral travel' in a fully conscious state. He describes how he lay on the floor, while one friend massaged his forehead vigorously and the other massaged his feet; when he began to feel dizzy, he was ordered to imagine that he was taller, which worked immediately, then that he was swelling. Finally, wide awake, he was able to describe in detail a waking dream in which he was in ancient Egypt and was inspecting his own sarcophagus. The book details experiences in which others were able to 'travel' to Roman times, nineteenth-century Norway, etc. He admits that this is no proof that his friends were seeing previous existences. One man described a homosexual experience in a Roman brothel, and said his name was Trimalchio; it is, perhaps, coincidence that the *Satyricon* of Petronius describes homosexual acts and has a character named Trimalchio. Glaskin himself speaks of the Christos technique simply as a method of experiencing waking dreams; but in a second book, *Worlds Within*, he describes how, on a trip to London, he visited the British Museum and was fascinated to discover how much his own vision of ancient Egypt corresponded to the actuality. It is, of course, possible that his 'waking dream' was merely a 'replay' of some book about Egypt read long before and forgotten; but, if so, the book he read must have been remarkably accurate and full of striking minor details of Egyptian life.

Lethbridge (see *dowsing) was convinced that there are a number of dimensions or realms beyond the physical world — all accessible to the 'power of the pendulum' — and that the 'next' realm beyond our physical world is a timeless realm — the world beyond death, as well as the world we visit in dreams. He also concluded from his pendulum researches that the level of energy vibrations on this level is four times that of Earth. His speculations are so complex that they need to be studied in his books, particularly *The Power of the Pendulum*.

The shaman is traditionally supposed to inhabit this realm midway between sleep and waking, or life and death — so that, for example, Sir Arthur Grimble described the magician in the Gilbert Islands 'summoning the porpoises' by sending out his 'dream body' when asleep. Modern paranormal research is increasingly preoccupied with such matters as the experimental control of dreaming and the possibility of using dreams deliberately for creative purposes; while modern medical researchers are calling upon the aid of lucid dreamers in their investigations of the dream state. CW

ESP

The term 'extrasensory perception' (ESP) was invented by J.B. Rhine, the pioneer of scientific paranormal research, and was used by him as a book title in 1934. He meant it to refer to such faculties as *clairvoyance and telepathy; but he also recognized that it was closely — indeed, inseparably — connected to psychokinesis (PK), the ability to move physical objects with the mind.

Since the formation of the SPR in 1882, scientists had been trying to devise foolproof tests for telepathy, precognition, and so on. Sometimes, as in Osty's test for *precognition, the method seemed foolproof; yet there was always the remote chance of collusion between the individuals involved to 'cook' the results.

In 1927 Rhine managed to persuade Duke University to set up a Parapsychology Department, where ESP would be investigated by strictly scientific methods. He extended a method already used at Groningen University, of having the 'sender' and 'receiver' sitting in different rooms, under observation. He also developed a set of five 'Zener' cards with simple symbols on them — star, circle, cross, square and wavy line — to simplify the sending and receiving. His results were exciting: some subjects showed an ability to score well above chance under strictly controlled conditions.

But Rhine's most fruitful period began in 1934 when a young gambler walked into his office and announced that he, like all good gamblers, believed he could control the fall of the die. Tests conducted over eight years produced hundreds of pages of statistics, and these showed a curious result. On a 'first run', a gambler might often show an extremely high score, far above chance. On a second run, the score fell suddenly; on a third run, it fell even more steeply. In other words, the gambler could best influence the dice when he was fresh and interested.

This is quite characteristic of paranormal powers: they seem to operate best when the conscious ego is relaxed. The harder the subject 'tries', the less successful he is likely to be — for example, in the case of Peter Fairley (see *precognition). Felicia Parise, who has demonstrated remarkable powers of psychokinesis, tells how she started trying to develop her powers after seeing a film of the USSR PK expert, Nina Kulagina. At first she obtained no result; then one day she received a telephone call saying that her grandmother was dying — a severe emotional shock. As she reached out for a small plastic bottle, it moved away. The trauma had released her PK powers.

Why? Presumably because she had already developed the powers by her intense efforts of concentration; but they remained 'in check' since the effort had also increased the powers of the critical ego, the left brain. The shock upset the balance, and the powers could suddenly find expression.

It is important that paranormal powers often seem to be associated with traumas. Uri Geller has stated that his own metal-bending powers developed after he had received a severe electric shock from his mother's sewing machine; Matthew Manning has mentioned that his mother received a severe electric shock when she was carrying him. (In both cases, the paranormal powers seem to be some form of *poltergeist effect — that is to say, PK on a larger scale than usual.)

One of the most significant experiments in the history of ESP (or 'psi') research was conducted by Dr Gertrude Schmeidler in 1942 — the famous 'sheep and goats' experiment. Schmeidler asked a group of her students to submit to tests using Zener cards. Before the experiment she asked which of them believed in 'psi' and which thought it nonsense. She classified the 'believers' as 'sheep' and the sceptics as 'goats'. The results showed that the 'sheep' had scored significantly above average. Equally exciting was that the 'goats' had scored *below*. This was impossible on a chance basis, and meant that they had somehow suppressed their natural 'psi' powers to support their own intellectual convictions; that is to say, the left brain simply countered the right brain's attempts at ESP, but in so doing left its fingerprints all over the experiment.

This result could well explain why so many scientists have totally failed to obtain results in various tests for psi abilities. Professor John Taylor is a case in point. When Geller first demonstrated his spoon-bending abilities on UK television in November 1973, Taylor was one of two 'experts' asked to scrutinize the tests (Lyall Watson was the other). Many children who watched tried spoon-bending and found it worked. Their parents contacted the BBC, who put them on to Taylor. Taylor conducted a thorough investigation into Geller and the spoon-bending children, and announced his conclusions in *Superminds*. He had no doubt of the genuineness of the phenomena. His scientific colleagues greeted his conclusions with derision. And his experimental results — for example, with *Kirlian photography — became steadily more disappointing. Eventually, in *Science and the Supernatural*, he announced that he had concluded that 'psi' was non-existent, that whenever psi effects were examined closely they simply melted away. Yet there was no suggestion that he felt Geller and the children were frauds. In fact, he made no attempt to explain how he could have been so convinced earlier. And the book is full of accounts of many exceptionally convincing cases, recounted without any attempt at detailed criticism, producing a strangely ambiguous effect, as if he wants to say that the evidence for 'psi' is powerful, but that he personally has had no success in pinning it down. A comparison of *Superminds* with the later book suggests that we may here be dealing with a more complex version of the 'Schmeidler effect'.

Yet works like the massive *Handbook of Parapsychology* (ed. Wolman) make it clear that, whatever the opinion of individual scientists, ESP has now been established beyond all reasonable doubt. CW

Games Theory

For most, work has become so mechanical and repetitive, or so worrying and obsessive, that it does not provide fulfilment and satisfaction. The hands work while the mind sleeps, or the mind works while the body gets ulcers. To consider games and sports which combine physical and mental activity gives us the chance to examine experiences demanding the whole person.

The rules under which games are conducted mark them off from normal life and give them intensity within a convention. A game has many characteristics of life itself — hardship, uncertainty, emotional involvement, accident and so on — but its rules and its time limitation give it a structure which is clearly perceptible and therefore more digestible and meaningful than everyday life. In this it resembles art but, since it is free interaction, it is more fiercely real in experience than art, and closely resembles a living drama in which the dénouement is always in doubt.

A player fully extended both physically and mentally in a game is not as a rule conscious of delight and satisfaction. Nor, normally, is he conscious of himself. He is conscious only of the game — for example, of the relation of players, including himself, to the ball and to other players. If he is good he is conscious of the overall pattern made by this relationship, and it enables him to alter the pattern to the advantage of his team. But when I say 'conscious' I do not mean 'reflectively conscious': a game may move at such a pace that deliberate reflection is not possible during play; yet one may choose with intuitive certainty and at lightning speed to move to 'the right place at the right time'. The more often one does this and the less often one thinks, 'Where shall I go and what shall I do?', the better one is likely to be playing.

We may train for games by applying will to concentrated practice and the acquirement of correct technique. But concentration, technical skill and set determination are not enough. The state of mind for which deliberation is unnecessary, when a player plays at his best and experiences the deepest satisfaction that a game can give, is known as being 'in form', and one of the peculiarities of this state is that it cannot be willed. Someone out of form cannot will himself back into it; he can only play himself back into it. He is as technically competent as he was yesterday, but today he plays poorly. Why?

To be in form, a mind of no-interruption, no-lassitude is essential, a mind which can respond immediately to whatever is presented to it. Being out of form is being so assailed by the world that room is left for interruption from a quarter not in vital relationship with the occasion. Doubts, worries and preoccupations relevant to some other part of a man's life interfere between question and answer, stimulus and response, ball and stroke. One reason for the importance of games today is that a person who almost never experiences the state of being in form in everyday life can experience it on the games field, and can banish preoccupation nowhere else.

In games, flickering thoughts are fatal. In cricket, for example, most close fielders tend to make an anticipatory movement born of apprehension, eagerness and the effort to avoid the grab of too-lateness. This causes a slight misplacement in time and space which may mean a missed catch. But the best close fielders flow from a relaxed position of readiness; it is as if they moved without moving, and the ball is accepted with an immediacy and ease that makes a supremely difficult catch look simple. The mind of such a fielder is not fixed and concentrated but attentive, still and alight.

This may appear to be instinctive reaction. But what, in such sophisticated circumstances, can 'instinctive reaction' mean? It might also be called a 'learned skill'. But this type of learning is not the grooving of a set of movements by constant practice. It involves choice. Nobody can move like this to precisely the right place at precisely the right time without being alertly aware of what he is doing — yet he is not thinking about it, for there is no time to think. Moreover, the will is not pliable enough to determine this immediacy, and emotion is beside the point because fully absorbed in the game (any direct manifestation of emotion is unsettling and leads to loss of form).

Concentration is valuable as a corrective to self-consciousness, but in all the great ball games it must be concentration on the ball to be hit, and not on 'I hitting it'. Something more than and different from concentration is involved. For one in form there is an ease, swiftness and inevitability of response for which the word concentration is too intense. A state of calm attention and alert awareness absorbs and replaces concentration.

Anyone who has experienced being in form will recognize that, not only is it different from the soldier's automatic response to a command, it is at the opposite end of the scale from the reduction of man to robot. It is fulfilment, not limitation. And this fulfilment is the true justification for games which become a discipline and a rite that enable the whole person to live in the physical activity itself.

To be in form is to move at once, without calculation. This sense of ease is something other than self-confidence. The self and its confidence are irrelevant. And the self-loss experienced in a team game feels like self-fulfilment when relived in memory. Moreover, there are moments in such self-loss when awareness of detached joy in unity comes upon one as if by surprise, a wondering realization of existence: 'So this is what the world is like, and here am *I* in it!' The 'I' is not the everyday self, which interferes between ball and response, and which seeks to impose itself upon a recalcitrant world. At this point we are aware of an accepting witness which simply sees what is present to be seen. The necessary precondition for realization of the witness is the state of being in form, and the necessary precondition for being in form is unity of mind.

JBP

Gurdjieff, Georgei Ivanovitch

There have been so many prophets and messiahs in the past century — *Blavatsky, *Steiner, *Crowley, Eddy, Alice M. Bailey, Thomas Lake Harris, Hubbard — that sensible people are rightly suspicious of anyone with a large and enthusiastic following. Gurdjieff differs from most of these in that he never demanded 'belief'. What he had to teach was a scientific method of self-exploration, and he expected his followers to decide whether it was true or not by testing it.

The basic assertion of his 'philosophy' (although he would have rejected the word) is that humans are almost entirely mechanical. They are elaborate robots or computers. Yet they are also capable of a degree of freedom. Consciousness can be extended far beyond its present limits. But this can be done only by studying the 'computer' and attempting to reprogramme it.

Gurdjieff was born about 1873 in Alexandropol; his father was Greek, his mother Armenian. Because of the Russo-Turkish war (1875–8), his part of the world was highly unstable; he became a wanderer in his early teens and remained so for most of his life.

In the autobiographical *Meetings With Remarkable Men* he describes his early encounters with the 'occult' — table-rapping, *healing, *precognition — and his determination to try to understand such phenomena. He also tells how, in the ruins of an ancient city, he and a friend, Pogossian, discovered an old parchment that spoke of a mysterious 'Sarmoung Brotherhood'. They went in search of the Brotherhood; whether they found it is not clear, but what Gurdjieff *did* find was a monastery in the northern Himalayas, where he spent three months and learned of 'the law of three' and 'the law of seven' — concepts that became central to his thinking. According to the late James Webb, he spent some time in Lhasa as a kind of Russian spy. What seems clear is that he spent the years 1890–1910 wandering all over central Asia and the Mediterranean and picking up much 'esoteric knowledge'.

Around 1909 he returned to Russia, married one of the Tsarina's ladies-in-waiting, and began to teach what he had learned.

Part of his 'system' is esoteric — concerning Man's 'seven centres' (physical, intellectual, emotional, instinctive, sexual — and higher intellectual and emotional centres), the 'ray of creation' and other such difficult matters. Yet its essence was extremely simple. When we wake in the morning, we assume we have now entered 'waking' consciousness. In fact, says Gurdjieff, we remain *asleep*, and are so for most of our lives. We do not really 'live'; we react, like penny-in-the-slot machines.

Yet we all experience certain moments in which we feel 'more alive', in which freedom seems an exciting reality. These are not an illusion. But we cannot take advantage of them because 'mechanicalness' descends almost instantly, and we feel unable to do anything to re-create — or even understand — the sense of freedom.

One thing is clear: it is in moments of crisis or excitement that we are galvanized to unexpected effort; *then* we experience a sense of freedom. A soldier under fire for the first time is 'free' (as Sartre says, 'freedom is terror'). But can we create a kind of 'artificial crisis' that will galvanize us into freedom?

Gurdjieff devised various 'exercises' that demand extreme concentration; some require the student to do something different with each hand, each foot and his head, all at the same time. These were basically a training in alertness. Gurdjieff might appear in the dormitory in the middle of the night and snap his fingers; all the followers were expected to be out of bed and in some complicated position within seconds.

There were also mental exercises, chief of which was 'self remembering'. We can close our eyes and become aware of 'ourselves', or we can look at external objects and become aware of them. But it is incredibly difficult to look at some object — say, your watch — and to be conscious of yourself looking at it. Within seconds you either forget to be aware of the watch or forget to be aware of yourself looking at it. 'Self remembering' — which happens spontaneously in moments of happiness (that feeling: 'What, *me, here?*') — must be practised in all situations. Also, we must observe ourselves and our reactions to people and situations to note the mechanical nature of responses we assume to be spontaneous.

What we call 'the mind', Gurdjieff said, is almost non-existent in most of us, a *response* to events. But it can be strengthened and controlled. His view might be summarized by saying that people are like grandfather clocks driven by watchsprings; the problem is to strengthen the spring.

Gurdjieff's attempt to set up an 'Institute for the Harmonious Development of Man' was frustrated by World War I. Escaping from Russia during the Revolution, he eventually set up his Institute at Fontainebleau, in a château. His chief 'disciple', P.D. Ouspensky, had meanwhile set up his own school in London, where he, too, taught the principles of the 'war against sleep'. For a while Gurdjieff's Institute prospered, with such eminent students as A.R. Orage, J.G. Bennett and Katherine Mansfield (who died there). In the late 1920s a serious car accident caused him to close it down. He began to write his books: *Beelzebub's Tales to His Grandson*, *Meetings With Remarkable Men*, and the final, unfinished, *Life Is Only Real Then When 'I Am'* — whose title in itself summarizes the essence of Gurdjieff's 'philosophy'. He went to the USA in the 1930s and set up various groups, but spent World War II in Paris where, among other things, he seems to have made a living on the black market. He returned to the USA after the war. His death in 1949 was probably hastened by his vast intake of food and drink — he gave elaborate lunches and dinners at which guests had to drink endless toasts in brandy or vodka, the aim being to get them to reveal their 'essence', to drop the guard of the personality.

During his lifetime he was regarded by many as a charlatan — an image he went out of his way to foster, since he wanted his students to test his ideas rather than accept him as a messiah. The best exposition of these ideas can be found in Ouspensky's *In Search of the Miraculous*. The appeal of Gurdjieff lies in his logic and psychological penetration. Whether or not he discovered his 'teachings' in ancient monasteries (as he was inclined to allege) he was undoubtedly one of the greatest psychologists of this century. And although Gurdjieff 'groups' are now more widespread than ever, he remains the 'Outsider's philosopher', the thinker whose appeal is basically to 'non-joiners', to those with an obsessive need to think for themselves.   CW

Homoeopathy

This medical method was founded by Christian Hahnemann, who believed that diseases can be cured by small doses of drugs that produce similar effects; he is said to have discovered the principle when he noticed that a dose of quinine gave him symptoms like malaria. Similarly, a spider poison, *Latrodectus mactans*, produces symptoms similar to angina, so it is given in small doses for angina.

The basic notion is that we possess within ourselves a *healing force which needs only to be stimulated — a view increasingly accepted by modern medicine.

Inevitably, Hahnemann encountered bitter opposition. The motto 'Like cures like' (*similia similibus curantur*) became a popular medical tag during his lifetime. But, in spite of the resistance, he was highly respected by the time he died. In Vienna, during the cholera outbreak of 1836, homoeopathy was tried in one hospital, and the death rate there dropped by two-thirds. It again proved its value in outbreaks in Edinburgh in 1848 and London in 1854.

It was his pupil Frederick Quin who was responsible for its success in England. When the figures on homoeopathic cures were suppressed in a parliamentary report, Quin managed to have them published openly.

In the early twentieth century homoeopathy lost ground because of the successes of orthodox medicine. But, as modern practitioners become increasingly aware of the disastrous side-effects of many drugs, it is enjoying a slow but steady return to favour.   CW

Hypnosis

One day in 1780 the Marquis de Puységur, a student of Mesmer, was attempting to cure a peasant of some minor ailment by 'magnetizing' him, in accordance with Mesmer's method (see *healing). The twenty-one-year-old shepherd, Victor Race, was tied to a lime tree, and Puységur was making passes over his head and body with a large magnet — the aim being to cause a certain mysterious vital energy to flow around the body. (This was the essence of mesmerism.) To Puységur's surprise, the shepherd fell asleep. Puységur ordered him to wake up and untie himself; Race proceeded to untie the ropes without opening his eyes. Puységur could see that he had induced a trance state, but its nature baffled him.

He had, of course, discovered 'hypnotism' (from the Greek *hypnos*, sleep). And, as far as the medical profession is concerned, its nature is still a mystery. Yet the recognition that there are literally two different people living inside our heads — one in the left half of the brain, one in the right — seems to offer the obvious explanation. Clearly, during hypnosis the conscious ego — the 'you' (which is situated in the left cerebral hemisphere) — falls asleep. The fact that there is still 'someone there' to carry out orders suggests just as clearly that it is that 'other' person who lives in the right hemisphere.

During the nineteenth century hypnotism fell into such disrepute that any medical man who dared to take it seriously ran the risk of being made a laughing stock. This was partly because it was still associated with the name of Mesmer and his belief that all space is pervaded by an unknown fluid, and that the same vital fluid flows through our bodies. When the flow is unimpeded, we are healthy; when it gets blocked, we become ill. The idea sounds simplistic, and Mesmer's belief that ordinary magnets could unblock the flow undoubtedly *was* simplistic; yet followers of *Reich regard Mesmer as his most interesting predecessor because Reich's own major 'discovery', orgone energy, is undoubtedly the 'mesmeric fluid'. Moreover, *acupuncture also teaches that vital nerve-currents flow through the body, and that their stimulation (with needles, not magnets) can cure illness.

The rejection by the medical profession was due partly to the belief of occultists and 'spiritualists' that hypnosis could produce almost magical effects. It was believed to induce *clairvoyance, and there is very strong evidence that it does just that. Towards the end of the nineteenth century, J.M. Charcot became interested in hypnotism, chiefly because he thought it was a form of hysteria. Undoubtedly, the results are curiously similar. (For example, a patient might suffer from hysterical paralysis of the right side; Charcot found that he could induce precisely the same thing by hypnotic suggestion.) Freud studied briefly under Charcot in the early 1880s and was immensely impressed by his hypnotic demonstrations; Freud recognized immediately that both hypnosis and hysteria revealed that there is a far more powerful part of the mind than the conscious will. A woman could not consciously will her stomach to swell up in 'phantom pregnancy'; yet a powerful desire to become pregnant *could* cause it. Freud decided that this unknown mind was the 'unconscious'. And he made another important assumption: that, if the unconscious mind is far more powerful than the conscious mind, the unconscious must be the real master — the unknown self who makes the puppet dance, so to speak. The assumption became the basis of psychoanalysis, and was responsible for its pessimistic orientation. It apparently never struck Freud that a ship is far more 'powerful' than its captain, or an elephant than its driver.

Is the right cerebral hemisphere the seat of the unconscious mind? Stan Gooch thinks not, believing that the 'unconscious' lives in the cerebellum, part of the 'old brain'. Yet it seems very clear that the right brain is, at the very least, the gateway to the unconscious.

What *does* seem clear is that the right brain is Man's intuitive half and, as such, seems to be in control of his energy supply.

When one is tired from a hard day at the office (left-brain work) one needs to 'unwind', perhaps listening to music (right-brain work) or in some other way persuading one's gestalt faculty, the power of recognition of pattern and of purpose, to exercise itself. Five minutes of deep 'absorption' can restore vitality and energy.

After Charcot and Freud, hypnosis ceased to be unmentionable in the medical profession. In recent years it has been discovered that about 5 per cent of people are 'deep trance subjects' and that the most startling hypnotic effects can be induced in such subjects — for example, that their warts can be cured by suggestion. What seems odder still, a subject who believes he has been touched by a hot iron may develop a blister; while one who *is* touched by a hot iron, but is told that it is only an icicle, may not develop a blister. In short, it seems that Man actually has a basic control of his somatic system and his autonomic nervous system, although this control is not conscious. (See *biofeedback, *healing.)

If, therefore, certain paranormal faculties, like clairvoyance, or *poltergeist phenomena, are associated with the 'unconscious mind', then there is nothing illogical in the notion that they could be induced by hypnosis. In which case we may well have to revise our dismissive opinion of some of those nineteenth-century experimenters who were convinced that hypnosis was somehow linked with the 'supernatural'.

In any case, the most interesting and exciting thing about hypnosis is that it clearly indicates that we possess powers not normally accessible to our 'personal' control. Yet they *are*, apparently, accessible to the hypnotist. Why? The answer, clearly, is that he is an external 'authority figure' and that, when *he* tells that 'other self' (what George Groddeck called the 'It') that it has access to tremendous powers, it promptly does his bidding. So why will it not obey our left-brain ego when *it* tries giving similar orders? *Because it doesn't believe it.* The left brain is too weak; it lacks confidence.

It would seem that writers like D.H.

Lawrence and Henry Miller are mistaken when they declare that modern Man possesses too much 'head-consciousness' (i.e., left-brain control). Quite clearly, he doesn't possess enough. CW

Jung, Jungianism

The 'analytical psychology' of Carl Gustav Jung developed originally in opposition to Freud's psychoanalysis, with its fundamentally deterministic outlook.

Jung was born in Switzerland in 1875, the son of a pastor; after taking his medical degree, he worked at the Psychiatric Clinic, Zurich University. His thesis, 'On the Psychology and Pathology of So-called Occult Phenomena', was a study of a female cousin who was a case of *multiple personality. Freud's studies of dreams and the unconscious excited him and he became a Freudian disciple — at one point, Freud seems to have regarded him as his 'heir'. But between 1907, when he met Freud, and 1912, he became increasingly sceptical about Freud's 'sexual theory', feeling that Freud was too rigid, narrow and materialistic. In his autobiography *Memories, Dreams, Reflections* he describes a remarkable episode in which he and Freud argued about 'paranormal phenomena', Freud taking the view that such things were pure superstition. Jung had an odd sensation 'as if my diaphragm were made of iron and were becoming red hot'; a loud report sounded from the bookcase. Jung told Freud this was an example of a *poltergeist effect; when Freud pooh-poohed this view, Jung predicted that there would be another in a moment; as soon as he had spoken, there was another loud report from the bookcase.

Jung felt that Freud's sexual theory reduced the mystery of the human psyche to a problem of sexual pathology; Freud's concept of the 'unconscious' seemed to be of a kind of damp cellar full of rats and centipedes. Jung saw it as far bigger and far more mysterious, like the Earth itself, with its layer upon layer of strata containing all its past history. He came to believe that below the 'personal unconscious' of the individual there is the far greater 'collective unconscious' of the race, perhaps of all living creatures.

Jung broke with Freud in 1912 and came, for a period, dangerously close to mental breakdown. In 1913 he had dreams of blood, which he later came to believe were premonitions of World War I.

One day, sitting at his desk, he experienced a kind of dream while wide awake; he descended into a twilit cave, where there was a dwarf with a leathery skin; in a stream he saw the floating corpse of a blonde youth with a head wound, followed by a black scarab, then a rising Sun.

This, and other similar experiences, led Jung to develop a method that he called 'active imagination'; he asserted that it was possible to 'descend into the unconscious' while wide awake, to conjure up a scene with a sense of its total reality, and to explore it consciously.

Jung's reputation as an 'analytical psychologist' was founded on his book *Psychological Types* in which he makes his famous distinction between 'extroverts' and 'introverts', and divides mental processes into four categories: sensing, feeling, intuiting and thinking. Since people of these 'types' may be introverts or extroverts, this gives eight basic psychological types. Modern Jungians are inclined to regard these rigid categories as less important than Jung's recognition that the 'collective unconscious' contains material that is not derived from the individual's own experience. For example, the scarab and the Sun he observed in the waking dream are both Egyptian religious symbols, and Jung was convinced that the collective unconscious contains all the fundamental religious symbols, and is the repository of Man's religious aspirations. Neurosis, he thought, was the result of trying to live 'within too narrow a spiritual horizon'. The personality needs to expand beyond its narrow personal range, and neurosis is a form of meaning-starvation. The symbolic motifs of the collective unconscious are known as archetypes. In a famous paper on *UFOs he suggested that they are, in effect, a religious archetype that has forced itself into consciousness, a waking dream or 'psychological projection'. (But a niece of Jung's has asserted that he changed his mind before he died, and was inclined to believe that they are genuine physical objects.)

In 1928, Jung came upon a Chinese alchemical treatise containing a mandala symbol, a symbol he had often noticed in the drawings of patients. He came to believe that alchemy should be regarded as a metaphor for spiritual integration, or 'individuation', as he called it. This notion of *alchemy as a symbolic search for 'salvation' is not entirely borne out by the texts themselves, but it is a good illustration of Jung's tendency to regard psychology as the study of the *suprapersonal* contents of the mind.

Jung's own personal experience convinced him of the reality of psychic phenomena. In his autobiography he describes various 'poltergeist effects' that occurred in his own home (he believed these effects were caused by the cousin who suffered from multiple personality). In 1920, he slept in a haunted cottage, and woke one night to find half a woman's head on the pillow beside him, looking at him from one open eye. It vanished when he lit a candle. So Jung was altogether more open than Freud to the possibility that the mind may be a repository of unknown powers. (Yet even Freud was willing to admit, in later life, that his view of 'occult phenomena' might have been too narrow and rigid.) Jung's important paper on 'synchronicity' — meaningful '*coincidences' — added a new word to the language. His acceptance of synchronicity led him to accept also that such ancient methods of divination as the *I Ching could provide genuine information.

In practice, Jung's psychology continued to lean heavily on Freud; and some Jungian disciples, like John Layard, seem to be more Freudian than Freud in their search for sexual symbols and motifs in mental life. Jung's importance lies primarily in his originality as an innovator, and in the intuitive 'anti-reductionism' that made him regard the human psyche as an unfathomed mystery rather than as a mere by-product of Man's physical and sexual evolution.   CW

Kirlian Photography

When Semyon Kirlian was visiting a hospital in Krasnodar, USSR, in 1939, he watched a patient receiving treatment from a high-frequency generator, and noticed that, as glass electrodes were brought close to the patient's skin, there was a tiny flash, not unlike that in a neon tube when the light is switched on. In an attempt to investigate this phenomenon, Kirlian and his wife Valentina tried taking photographs of human skin in a powerful electrical field. They set up two metal plates, on one of which was the film, and passed a high-voltage current; then Kirlian placed his hand between the plates. The result was a photograph of Kirlian's hand surrounded by a kind of glowing *aura. It was not until 1970, with the publication of *Psychic Discoveries Behind the Iron Curtain* (Ostrander and Schroeder), that news of this experiment reached the West.

There were various other phenomena. If the newly cut stem of a flower were photographed it seemed to be emitting sparks. The Kirlian photograph of a torn leaf showed a dim outline of the missing section. The 'aura' of a man's hand after he had taken a glass of vodka became brighter — it was literally 'lit up'.

It looked, then, as if the Kirlians had found a method of photographing the 'life field' of living creatures. The torn-leaf phenomenon was in no way 'psychic'; it meant merely that the electrical field of the missing portion still bridged the gap.

Sceptics quickly dismissed the whole phenomenon. The flow of a high-frequency current in a condenser is not constant, so the photograph might actually be 'blurred' by the fluctuations; moreover, when a change of voltage occurs in a photographic plate, the result is a tree-like pattern known as a Lichtenburg figure. Researchers like Dr Thelma Moss and Max Toth replied that such purely electrical patterns would be constant, and that there would be no difference between, say, the fingertip of a tired man and the same man after a stiff drink. Experimental results have been contradictory. Moss's *The Probability of the Impossible* shows Kirlian photographs that substantiate Kirlian's original result; but John Taylor tried similar experiments and announced negative results (see *ESP).

In his introductory article to *Galaxies of Life*, Toth makes it clear that no one believes that Kirlian photography is in any way connected, for example, to the psychic photography so popular in the nineteenth century. Living beings possess electrical fields, as Burr showed in the 1930s, and Kirlian photography is probably an electrical phenomenon caused by the interaction of the two electric fields; Toth compares it to St Elmo's fire, which is due to static electricity. But, if the electrical fields of living creatures vary with health (as, for example, acupuncturists assert), it seems that Kirlian photography might be used as a diagnostic aid. CW

Levitation

Levitation is the ability to rise from the ground or to raise objects by paranormal means. Hindu fakirs have been demonstrating it for centuries, but many cases have been observed in the West.

St Joseph of Copertino one day floated up into the air in a state of ecstasy and landed on the altar. From then on, for the remainder of his life, he would float into the air whenever in a state of rapture. These floating fits occurred almost daily, and often in front of many witnesses, including Leibniz. Daniel Dunglas Home not only floated in and out of windows but could cause articles of furniture to rise into the air; again, this happened in broad daylight, and dozens of scientists witnessed it and signed depositions.

It is difficult to produce a theory that can even begin to explain levitation in scientific terms. In saints and mystics it seems to be associated with ecstasy. In many cases, 'radiance' streams from the face — an actual physical light. Yet, since we know that '*poltergeists' can cause objects or even people to levitate (as in the case of Douglass Deen), and that poltergeists are an aspect of the right brain, the question may really amount to what physical forces the mind could draw upon to produce these effects. CW

Life After Death

The problem of life after death is encapsulated in F.W.H. Myers' *Human Personality and Its Survival of Bodily Death* — a cornerstone of psychical research. We are all aware that 'personality' is formed by experience and social contact and is therefore, so to speak, an 'artefact'. So why should it survive death? On the other hand, any mother is aware that the personality of her child is inherent from the moment it is born. And one of the most interesting arguments for 'survival' is that in cases of *multiple personality totally different personalities can inhabit the same body, which suggests that personality is not simply a product of bodily processes.

All civilizations have believed the 'spirit' survives death. In 1848 the 'Hydesville rappings' inaugurated the worldwide nineteenth-century interest in *Spiritualism, and the SPR was founded in 1882 by a number of eminent scientists and intellectuals, including Myers. Many eminent *mediums were studied, perhaps the most remarkable being Mrs Piper. Most serious investigators concluded that she was genuine and that 'spirits of the dead' really spoke through her. The chief problem associated with mediums is that, even if genuine, they could, in most cases, be obtaining their information telepathically from the sitter. Yet in a few cases this seems impossible. In *The Paranormal*, Stan Gooch cites a case recorded by Nils Jacobsen of a man who was run over by a truck and died three days later without regaining consciousness. In a séance some years later the man's brother was told by the medium that his brother was present. The dead man told the sitter that he had died not from the skull injury but that it 'came from the bones'. Many years later the facts were checked through hospital records, and they revealed that death was due to a brain embolism caused by lower bone thrombosis. Here telepathy seems almost impossible.

Another founder of the SPR, Sir William Barrett, made a study of deathbed visions, having discovered that many people on the point of death are convinced that dead relatives enter the room to 'help them to the other side'. He was particularly impressed by a case in which a woman died after childbirth in a Clapton hospital; she had not been told that her sister had died since she entered the hospital, yet, just before her death, she stared in astonishment, claiming that her deceased father had entered the room with her sister, whom she thought to be alive.

Raymond A. Moody made an extensive study of people who have been on the point of death — sometimes pronounced medically dead — and have then 'returned'; again and again such subjects are convinced they have left their bodies, that they see weeping relatives, etc., and that they are aware of their continued existence 'out of the body'. Many cases resemble that of J.L. Bertrand, the Protestant pastor of Neuilly-sur-Seine, whose story was recorded in the SPR *Proceedings* for 1892. Bertrand was climbing in Switzerland with a party and allowed the others to go on to the summit without him while he sat down for a smoke. He had underestimated the cold and suddenly realized he could not move. He sat there as all sensation left his body, then observed himself floating into the air, attached to his body by a kind of string. He could see the others climbing the mountain, and noticed that they had taken a different path to the summit from the one he had recommended. Also, he saw the guide surreptitiously taking swigs of Madeira and stealing a leg of cooked chicken. In due course, the party returned and found him 'dead'; they revived him by rubbing his body with snow. Bertrand was annoyed to be brought back to life — a reaction that is surprisingly general in such cases; he had enjoyed being 'dead'. Once revived, he was able to tell the party that they had disobeyed his instructions about their route, and to confront the guide with the theft of the chicken leg. He had also 'seen', in his 'dead' state, that his wife in his absence had made a trip to Lucerne a day earlier than intended; this he was able to verify when he arrived home.

This is not, of course, proof of 'survival'; it may be proof only that Bertrand experienced an *out-of-the-body experience. Yet such cases certainly strengthen the evidence that some form of 'survival' is possible.

In 1960 Karlis Osis, Director of Research at the Parapsychology Foundation in New York, decided to investigate 'deathbed hallucinations', and sent questionnaires to thousands of doctors and nurses. He discovered that these 'hallucinations' do not vary from culture to culture. Most people seemed to experience a state of peace and happiness, beginning about two hours before death; in many cases, the patient was convinced that dead relatives had come to the bedside. Osis answered the objection that this might be wish fulfilment by pointing out that many of them strenuously objected to being taken away by their dead relatives.

It is a pity that the notion of 'survival' has been made unacceptable to many by the naïve enthusiasm of 'spiritualists' who seem to turn the Christian doctrines of heaven and hell into something cosy and comfortable, with dead relatives advising their survivors not to forget to feed the canary. Yet much of the evidence is impressive. In 1936 the Archbishop of Canterbury, Cosmo Lang, appointed a commission of eleven distinguished churchmen and -women to attempt to decide whether 'communication with the dead' could be taken seriously by the Church of England. In 1939 the commission reported that the claims of *Spiritualism are probably true, and that there is nothing in the idea of communication with the dead that contradicts the beliefs of Christianity. Yet Lang chose not to publish the findings, and the report was not released until March 1979. His caution underlines one of the basic problems of Spiritualism: that the belief that we shall all spend eternity under pleasant circumstances not unlike a seaside holiday may do more harm than good by inducing a kind of complacent literal-mindedness. Most sensitive people feel that there is an element of illusion about life: not that life itself is an illusion, but that we live it in a state of illusion and stupidity. Naïve 'survivalism' seems to be a desire to perpetuate the stupidity forever. CW

Mediums

Mediums (or sensitives) are believed by Spiritualists to be intermediaries between the living and the dead — the same role shamans play in primitive societies. John Dee employed various mediums or 'scryers', most notable of whom was Edward Kelley. The result was *A True and Faithful Relation of What Passed for Many Years Between Dr John Dee and Some Spirits* (1659). Kelley seems to have gone into a light trance, sometimes through *scrying, and contacted 'spirits', often via a 'guide'. Dee assumed these were all angels.

The Fox sisters were the first acknowledged 'mediums' of the modern era, although D.D. Home began to give 'sittings' soon after the Fox sisters achieved notoriety. Many of Home's abilities — for example, *levitation — sound like '*poltergeist effects' — which, psychical researchers later realized, originate in the unconscious mind of living individuals. Yet Home himself was totally convinced his powers came from the spirits of the dead, and there is much to support this belief. For example, he conversed in a room in an Italian villa with a '*ghost' that spoke Italian; but Home's Italian was poor, and he had to have the spirit's remarks translated for him. (It identified itself as a murderer.)

Leonora Piper realized she was 'psychic' as a child when a voice spoke inside her head, identifying itself as 'Aunt Sara' — who was later discovered to have died at precisely that moment. In her early twenties she consulted a clairvoyant doctor, fell into a spontaneous trance, and scrawled words on a sheet of paper which she handed to a judge who was in the room; it was a message from his dead son. Her fame spread quickly, but she refused to get involved in mediumship until the mother-in-law of William James contacted her. Her results were so remarkable that James became interested, and was 'converted' by her obvious genuineness. When James ceased to supervise her séances, Richard Hodgson came from England; he was a keen fraud-hunter and sceptic, and even had Piper followed by a private detective to make sure that she could not obtain information 'normally'. She was not allowed to see newspapers and most of the 'sitters' were unknown to her. She passed all tests. Later, she came to England, and was involved in the famous 'cross correspondences' (see *automatic writing).

Could mediums be obtaining information telepathically from their sitters, or even from people not present? It is difficult to draw a line between clairvoyants and 'paragnosts', like Croiset and Hurkos, who can handle an object and produce 'paranormal' information, and mediums like Piper. Yet after studying accounts of the careers of famous mediums *and* paragnosts, it is very hard to see why a dividing line needs to be drawn; *all* the phenomena seem to deny natural explanation. CW

Multiple Personality

The phenomenon of multiple personality is one of the oddest mysteries in psychology. Some of the earliest observed cases are mentioned in William James' *Principles of Psychology*. In 1811, a girl named Mary Reynolds fell asleep, and woke without any memory of her past; it took another five weeks for her to learn to speak again. Then one morning she woke up with her old memory restored, but with no memory of the past five weeks. For many years the two personalities alternated. The two 'Marys' were quite different: 'Mary one' was cautious and timid; 'Mary two' was vivacious, lively and determined.

This pattern can be observed in most such cases. Two of the most remarkable were those of Christine Beauchamp, recorded by Morton Prince, and of 'Doris Fischer', recorded by Walter Prince.

Christine was a depressive, neurasthenic girl who, under hypnosis, turned into 'Sally', lively, mischievous but childlike. A third personality, more mature and responsible than either, also emerged. Sally enjoyed playing tricks on Christine; she might, for example, walk miles out into the countryside, then 'abandon' the body. Significantly, in spite of sharing the same body, Sally was energetic and healthy, Christine a victim of fatigue and lassitude.

The case of Doris Fischer is even stranger; she split into five distinct personalities, the 'original Doris' being number three in the hierarchy. Doris knew about her two 'lower' personalities but not about the two 'above' her. This also seems a common feature of such cases: the personalities seem to be arranged in the form of a 'ladder', with the topmost self aware of all those underneath, then the next aware of those below *but not the one above*, and so on.

In the case of 'Sybil', described by Flora Rheta Schreiber, the patient had no less than sixteen personalities, some male. Dr Schreiber makes the amazing observation that EEG tests revealed that each personality had a different brain rhythm — as paradoxical as discovering that the same person has different sets of fingerprints.

It should be emphasized that in most of these cases the personalities are just as distinct as any assortment of individuals one might encounter; both Walter and Morton Prince could tell which personality was 'inhabiting' the body merely by looking at the patient's face.

In most cases, patients suffering from multiple personality have had a traumatic childhood, and tend to be timid and depressed. And since the 'secondary personality' is usually far more vital and mischievous, it seems likely that a whole 'suppressed' section of the personality is fighting for its freedom. This in turn suggests that personality is not simply a slow accretion of habits, but is in some sense 'already there' — as an oak tree is already present in the acorn — and needs to develop according to its own inner laws. The process of development should also be a process of fulfilment, accompanied by successful problem-solving.

The central problem is how such a wide range of personalities could form out of the basic substance of the 'self'. It looks amazingly like what was known in the Middle Ages as 'demoniacal *possession'. Yet much of the evidence suggests that the personalities *are* different facets of the same 'person'. The actual 'split' is usually caused by some severe shock — for example, with Doris Fischer the first of the secondary personalities, 'Margaret', came into being after Doris had been snatched from her mother's arms and flung to the ground by her father; a later personality appeared when her mother died suddenly. The 'split' may not be immediately apparent. Christine Beauchamp's 'trauma' occurred when a man she trusted implicitly — an old friend of the family — made a sexual advance; but 'Sally' appeared only later, under *hypnosis.

It has often been pointed out that the 'controls' of *mediums bear the hallmarks of secondary personalities — which may seem to suggest that mediumship can be dismissed as a mental illness of the same type as multiple personality. But another striking feature of many cases of multiple personality is that one or other of the personalities often possesses genuine psychic powers; in *Eve* Christine Sizemore cites a number of convincing examples of second sight: how, for example, she persuaded her husband to stay at home one day because she had a premonition that he would be electrocuted at work; the man who took over his job was, indeed, electrocuted.

This raises the possibility that there may be some at present unsuspected connection between multiple personality and 'paranormal' powers. In *Mysteries* I suggested that we are all, in a sense, multiple personalities, but that the firm control of the central ego prevents this from becoming apparent.

Another implication seems to emerge from such cases: that the 'ladder of selves' includes personalities who will (or could) evolve at some future date, but have not yet had time to do so (this is implied also in the 'acorn' theory). The 'highest' personality to emerge was more mature than the 'original' Christine or Doris — in fact, seemed in every way a more balanced and fulfilled human being. This also raises the interesting possibility that the 'clairvoyant' powers sometimes exhibited may be associated with one of these higher personalities. But the association of paranormal powers with the right cerebral hemisphere — and the 'self' associated with it — may render this theory superfluous.

Pierre Janet observed many cases of multiple personality, and observed that they are often connected with hysteria. The personality of a patient suffering from hysterical anxiety seemed to 'shrink' so that the field of attention was narrowed down to what lay under his nose. It was difficult to attract the attention of such a patient. Yet if Janet gave some order in a low voice — for example, 'Raise your hand' — the patient would do it automatically; if Janet then attracted his attention to the raised hand, the patient was surprised. This in turn seems to suggest that what we think of as a 'normal' personality may be suffering, relatively speaking, from this hysterical 'narrowing'. Again, we are confronted by the recognition that the structure of personality may be more complex than any psychologist has so far suspected.

We are probably *all* multiple personalities.   CW

Out-of-the-Body Experiences

The experience of having an existence separate from one's physical body, and even being able to stand apart and see one's own body as an independent object, is strange indeed but remarkably common. Celia Green received some 400 replies when she broadcast an appeal for first-hand accounts, and her analysis of these brought out patterns that not only prove the authenticity of the experience but also suggest that there must be some truth in the ancient belief that a component of the human personality is independent of the physical body and survives it.

OOBEs cannot be dismissed as mere hallucination or fantasy, because often a person has been seen by others while travelling in his or her 'second body' (see *doppelgängers) or has been able to give verifiable evidence of having acquired information from a physically remote location. For example, a woman who was in the habit of projecting out of her body on one trip located her dream-house. Over a year she returned to it often, and each time it pleased her more. She and her husband were planning to move and she thought that the house would suit them ideally, if only she knew where it was. They went house-hunting in London — on the ordinary physical plane — and to her delight found the house she knew so well. Everything, down to the furniture and the decorations, was as she had seen it. Furthermore, the place was remarkably cheap because it was said to be haunted. When the prospective buyer met the owner, the latter stared at her and screamed, 'You're the ghost!'

Most OOBEs are simple experiences of autoscopy — that is, seeing oneself from a distance. The view is normally from above and usually occurs during sleep, frequently after childbirth or an operation. Those who experience it are always firmly convinced that they have seen themselves as never before, clearly, distinctly, vividly, and in detail from outside. Travelling OOBEs are rarer, but many psychically gifted people have developed the facility to practise what is known as astral projection. The OOBE, whether it occurs only once and spontaneously or frequently and deliberately, always leaves those who have it convinced that they possess a second body or double not subject to the limitations of the physical body. Most become convinced that some kind of personal identity survives death.

In 1929 Hereward Carrington cooperated with a young psychic named Sylvan Muldoon to write *The Projection of the Astral Body* in which many examples were given of Muldoon's obtaining correct information about distant events by travelling out of his body. More recently, researchers have devised ingenious controlled experiments to test the hypothesis that such travel is possible.

At the Stanford Research Institute Harold Puthoff and Russell Targ conducted some successful experiments in which the subject was required to project out of his body to the ceiling of the laboratory and identify objects and geometrical shapes placed on a platform high above his head. One subject, Ingo Swann, after scoring highly, suggested another experiment in which the target would be not a physical object but a location on the Earth's surface identified by latitude and longitude.

In one test, he was given a coordinate and responded: 'I see what seems to be a mountain sticking up through some clouds; no, not just a mountain, it must be an island.' The experimenter said he was wrong, the location was in the middle of the southern Indian Ocean. Further checking revealed, however, that there was an island at the indicated location, with mountains rising at its eastern end. Swann continued his probe, and drew a sketch of a part of the island which was later found to correspond with the actuality.

Thousands of accounts have been collected and analysed by Robert Crookall. Over several decades he has carefully investigated, checked and collated accounts from correspondents around the world. Here is a typical case.

A young Englishwoman had just married and was travelling with her husband to the USA, where they were going to live. She was terribly seasick during the first day of the voyage. Her mother, sitting in her kitchen in England, was thinking about her daughter at the time. Suddenly she felt that she was out of her body and flying over the ocean. Finding the right cabin, she went in, took her daughter's hand and told her that she would feel better if she washed, dressed and went on deck. Then she flew back home. She noticed that only five minutes had elapsed. A few days later she received a letter from her daughter that confirmed every detail of the strange meeting.

Tales like this generally bring forth a polite smile or an unbelieving shrug. But the systematic, controlled research that parapsychologists and physicists are devoting to OOBEs today is steadily reducing their improbability.   SH

Paranormal Photography

Soon after the discovery of photography in the 1820s it was realized that it is possible to record more than one image on the same plate; but not until the 1860s did photographers begin to claim to have photographed the spirits of the dead. The first to capitalize on this was William Mumler, a Boston jewellery engraver, who was tried for fraud (and acquitted). Nevertheless, there are thousands of 'spirit photographs' from the nineteenth century.

In 1910, a Japanese researcher, Tomokichi Fukurai, was trying to find out whether a *medium could 'see' the image of a calligraphic character on an undeveloped film plate, and found that another plate in the room became impressed with the character. He conducted many experiments and discovered that mediums could often influence photographic plates and imprint mental images on them.

The best known psychic photographer of modern times is Ted Serios who has been extensively tested by Jule Eisenbud. Serios began with experiments in 'travelling clairvoyance' in search of hidden treasure, then tried to obtain pictures of the sites with a box camera. To his own surprise, photographs of unknown places began to appear. He discovered later that he could do it in front of witnesses with a polaroid camera. Eisenbud's *The World of Ted Serios* is full of remarkable photographs which Serios took by simply staring into a camera lens with a cap taped over it. A much publicized 'exposé' of Serios by Charles Reynolds has been discredited.

Uri Geller, too, produced a remarkable series of 'thought photographs' in 1974.   CW

Peak Experience

This is a phrase invented by Abraham Maslow to describe sudden moments of almost mystical joy and affirmation. He believed that all psychologically healthy people have 'PEs' fairly often. He developed the notion in the 1950s after writing a paper, 'Self-Actualizing People, A Study of Psychological Health' (1950), in which he pointed out that some form of 'creative' activity seems natural to healthy human beings whose 'deficiency needs' (i.e., for food, security, sex) have been satisfied.

He explained that, as a psychologist, he got bored with studying sick people and decided to study the healthy instead. He quickly noted that his 'alphas', or self-actualizers, were prone to sudden experiences of bubbling happiness — although he was careful to emphasize that these should not be regarded as in any way mystical. He felt that they are a part of the 'human norm'. Moreover, when he discussed PEs with his students, they not only began recalling PEs they had experienced in the past *but not really noticed at the time*, they also began having more PEs. That is to say, the PE is a function of normal health and sense of purpose. People might be compared to cars whose batteries run down if they are left unused but charge up the moment they experience a sense of enthusiasm and purpose. His psychology is based on the idea of 'higher ceilings of human nature' — the notion that creativity and PEs are as 'natural' as Freudian sexuality. CW

Pineal Eye

In Hindu mythology, each man has a 'third eye', the channel of his occult powers; it is supposed to be situated in the centre of the forehead.

In fact, the 'third eye' is an anatomical reality; it is the pineal gland, lying roughly in the centre of the brain. In birds and animals (whose cerebrum, the top part of the brain, is small or non-existent) it actually lies immediately under the skull, and *is* sensitive to light. Its existence has been known to doctors for centuries; Descartes believed that it is the point at which the mind and body are joined together.

The pineal body is a tiny grey mass only $\frac{1}{4}$in long, weighing $\frac{1}{30}$oz. It has always intrigued anatomists because, while the rest of the brain is 'double', the pineal body has no duplicate. As long ago as the fourth century BC Herophilus described it as the organ which regulated the flow of thought — he compared it to a sphincter.

The pineal gland was, apparently, once an eye. In the *Tuatara* lizard of New Zealand there is a cleft in the centre of the skull, and there is a transparent membrane with the scales arranged around it in a rosette; under this is a vestigial eye, complete with pigmented retina and a kind of lens. It lacks connecting nerves and seems to serve no purpose. Nineteenth-century anatomists showed that this body was identical with the pineal eye which has become 'buried' in the brains of men and animals. In 1958 two zoologists from the University of California discovered that removal of the gland made the escape reactions of lizards much slower — so it undoubtedly has survival value.

Also in 1958, the hormone secreted by the pineal body was finally isolated; it was called melatonin — 'darkness constricting' — because when it is injected (or fed) into various creatures it turns them a lighter colour.

In 1898, Otto Huebner reported a case of a boy suffering from a cancer of the pineal gland whose sexual organs were overdeveloped. It looks as if the secretion of the pineal gland influences sexuality. Virginia Fiske discovered that rats exposed to constant light show premature sexual development and that their pineal gland grows smaller.

Melatonin is manufactured by the pineal gland through the action of a hormone upon serotonin, a chemical messenger which transmits nerve impulse across synapses. The primates have higher serotonin levels than any other creature, which seems to explain their late sexual development. Only a tiny portion of the body's serotonin — less than 1 per cent — is contained in the brain, but it appears to be of immense importance. Schizophrenics have been discovered to have far less serotonin in the brain than other people. It begins to look, then, as if melatonin and serotonin could be somehow connected to Man's higher functions — which would certainly seem to confirm the Hindu belief that the third eye is Man's 'spiritual' centre. (We might also note that the figs of the *Ficus religiosa*, or Bo tree, under which the Buddha is traditionally supposed to have sat, has the highest serotonin level of all fruit, although bananas and plums also have large amounts.)

Psychedelic drugs like mescalin and LSD have some chemical resemblance to serotonin, and LSD-25 is a powerful opponent of serotonin. There are several theories about how LSD acts upon the brain to produce 'psychedelic' effects. One could be summarized as follows: The brain is a kind of Frankenstein's castle, full of hidden rooms; if all were unlocked at the same time, we would probably go insane. Serotonin is the jailer who has the keys at his belt; his job is to make sure that the cells are opened in an orderly manner. LSD paralyses the jailer and opens the doors with its own skeleton keys, causing hallucinations. And, depending upon what happens to be locked in the dungeons, the result is either a good or a bad 'trip'.

But serotonin, or melatonin (or both), seems to play an important part in the evolution of our higher functions and to act as an inhibitor of lower functions, like sex. As a chemical messenger, for example, it could be involved in the control processes of *biofeedback, where the action of our 'automatic' somatic systems can be controlled by the conscious ego. When the brain cells are deprived of serotonin, we become incapable of rational thought. All this seems to suggest that serotonin could be the key to human *evolution; in other words, a saint or superman ought to be distinguishable from the rest of us by his higher serotonin levels. In the present state of medical knowledge it is difficult to know how we might make use of this possibility.

CW

Plant Communication

The experiment that started the controversy about whether 'plants can read our minds' took place in February 1966 in the office of Cleve Backster, a lie-detector expert. A polygraph, or lie detector, works by registering the increase in skin moisture in a subject when he experiences increased tension. It entered Backster's mind to wonder if a plant's leaves would show a similar change when it was watered, so he poured water into the pot of a *Draecaena* plant. Oddly enough, the graph showed *decreased* tension (equivalent to emotional satisfaction). He tried dipping a leaf in his hot coffee; it had no effect. He wondered what would happen if he burned a leaf — and before he could do so he saw the graph suddenly swing upward, as if in alarm. When he returned to the room with matches it again soared.

He began a systematic study of all kinds of plants, and was soon convinced they are somehow tuned in to the life around them. If he chased a spider, the plant reacted to the spider's alarm. When live shrimps were dropped into boiling water the needle jumped. It even reacted when Backster put iodine on a cut on his finger, as the iodine killed living cells. One of his assistants was asked to kill another plant in the office by tearing it up and trampling on it. Later, all the assistants were paraded in front of the plant, and it reacted powerfully to the 'killer'. When a particular scientist was present, the plants all failed to react, but did so after he had left the office. Backster discovered that part of the scientist's job was to roast plants in an oven. His plants were reacting by 'fainting'. He concluded that this is a frequent reaction. Unlike humans, the plants do not seem to be able to cut themselves off from what goes on around them, and if something shocks them too much they 'pass out'.

His experiments caused widespread excitement and were repeated by many others. In some cases, the experiments were unsuccessful, which Backster believes may be due to this 'fainting' reaction.

An interesting variation is described in Stuart Holroyd's *Prelude to a Landing on Planet Earth*; it happened at the May Lectures (on parapsychology and related subjects) in London, 1974. Backster had lectured on communication with plants, and Marcel Vogel on his own experiments, suggesting that the actual medium of communication between plants may be ultraviolet radiation. An Indian healer, Tommy Wadkins, then took part in an experiment to transmit healing, via a plant, to someone across the Atlantic. He stood before the plant and, according to Vogel, proceeded to pour out healing radiations which were to be transmitted to a glaucoma patient who was meditating and trying to receive them. After some minutes, Wadkins began to shake — apparently this was normal for him when healing — but Vogel, unaware of this, went over and seized his shoulders. Wadkins groaned and convulsed; the transformer connected to the lie detector blew out (although it was connected to the plant, not to Wadkins), and people in the audience experienced a kind of electric shock. In California, a patient meditating with the glaucoma patient died of a heart attack, although this may or may not have been connected with the events in London. (Later, 'psychic communicants' who, allegedly, were communicating through Wadkins stated that he had disobeyed their injunction that he should have no metal on him — he had coins in his pocket and wore a ring; when checked this proved true.)

Backster's original results caused widespread controversy, and *The Secret Life of Plants*, by Peter Tompkins and Christopher Bird, became a bestseller; but the general consensus of scientific opinion seems to be that Backster's results are unsubstantiated. Yet the experiments *have* been successful so many times that it seems unreasonable to dismiss 'the Backster effect' just because many scientists have failed to duplicate it. *If* confirmed, it would support the important idea advanced by Bergson and Broad and popularized by Aldous Huxley in his *Doors of Perception*: '... that the function of the brain and nervous system and sense organs is in the main eliminative and not productive. Each person is at each moment capable of remembering all that has ever happened to him and of perceiving everything that is happening everywhere in the Universe. The function of the brain and nervous system is to protect us from being overwhelmed by this mass of largely useless and irrelevant knowledge ...' In short, our senses are *filters*, intended to keep things out rather than let them in. And we have such filters because we are so much more organized than plants. (There is also evidence that animals are more 'psychic' than the average human.)

The basic picture that begins to emerge is similar to that suggested in Whitehead's 'philosophy of organism', in which nature is seen as a single living organism. We can conceive nature as a vast system of intercommunication in which Man originally played an intimate part. The deliberate development of filters, probably associated with the left brain, has cut us off from this network, yet also has presented us with the possibility of *grasping* both mind and nature from a detached standpoint; it is this detachment that has led to the creating of modern civilization and its major product, science.

Perhaps the oddest possibility to emerge from Backster's research is the notion that, in some sense, plants do not 'mind' being eaten. Shredded plants responded to the electrodes just as well as ordinary leaves. Backster speculated that the ritual performed by kosher butchers before slaughtering an animal may be intended to tranquillize it. (Watson's *The Romeo Error* contains some fascinating material on the 'death trance'.) This led him to the speculation that 'plants and succulent fruit might *wish* to be eaten, but only in a sort of loving ritual, with a real communication between the eater and the eaten — somehow akin to the Christian rite of Communion — instead of the usual heartless carnage'. Which suggests the further possibility that life ingested from other things may somehow contribute to the life of the ingestor, rather as cannibals believe that eating the brain or other organs of an enemy can endow the eater with his courage. CW

Poltergeists

Accounts of 'rattling ghosts' date back to long before the Christian era. They cause bangings, *levitation of objects, and all kinds of other annoying disturbances; they have been described as 'the knockabout comedians of the psychic world'. But it was not until the late nineteenth century, when serious psychic research was undertaken in Europe and the USA, that it was realized that these are not 'ghosts' at all, but manifestations of unconscious mental disturbance, usually in children or teenagers. The 'phantom drummer of Tedworth', described in *Lord Halifax's Ghost Book*, caused loud drumming noises in the house of Mr Mompesson, a magistrate who had gaoled a begger, William Drury, and confiscated his drum. Drury admitted to someone who visited him in prison that he was somehow causing the disturbances — a rare case of conscious control of such powers by an adult. The famous Cock Lane Ghost, investigated by Dr Johnson, was clearly a poltergeist emanating from eleven-year-old Elizabeth Parsons in whose father's house it caused the usual bangings and levitation of objects. Her father was sent to prison as a result of the widespread controversy, it being assumed that he was responsible.

The 'Hydesville rappings' in the home of the Fox sisters — which case, in the late 1840s, inaugurated the history of modern *Spiritualism — were almost certainly poltergeist phenomena, and were therefore no proof of *life after death.

Poltergeist occurrences can also bear an uncannily close resemblance to 'demonic *possession'. The 'Amherst mystery' of Nova Scotia is a case in point. Esther Cox lived with her sister and brother-in-law, Mr and Mrs Daniel Teed. In 1878 her boyfriend seems to have made a half-hearted attempt to force sexual intercourse on her, then fled the area in alarm. Soon after, rustling noises were heard in the bedroom she shared with another, unmarried, sister, then loud bangs. Finally, Esther inflated like a balloon and rose into the air, while, in the presence of witnesses, an unseen hand scratched into the plaster of the wall the words 'Esther Cox, you are mine to kill'. The poltergeist activities became more violent; a knife flew through the air and stabbed Esther in the back; iron spokes placed in her lap became too hot to touch; unexpected fires broke out. Suspected of arson, Esther was finally jailed for four months, and the manifestations ceased. It seems clear that Esther's sexual frustrations were the root of the problem, as with the nuns of Loudon. The words traced on the wall, the stabbing with a knife, all show a masochistic desire to be 'possessed' — sexually, not demonically.

The puzzling thing is *how* it is possible for a person to be 'responsible' for such destructive activities and yet be totally unaware that he or she is the cause. Sperry's discovery that we literally have two different people living in our heads (see page 13), and that the person living in the right cerebral hemisphere is the 'not-you', suggests the explanation. Yet the disturbed children involved in poltergeist cases are not 'split-brain' patients. And this, in turn, underlines something that we are all aware of: that we *are* self-divided, and that the 'other self' is inclined to go its own way. (Hesse, in *Steppenwolf*, speaks of the two aspects as 'man' and 'wolf'.)

This still leaves the question: how does that 'other self' cause objects to fly through the air or metal to become red hot? The answer could lie in the observation that some dowsers can be thrown into convulsions when they stand above underground springs. If we assume that it is the right brain that is sensitive to various Earth-fields, then it seems conceivable that the right brain has access to some powerful energy source, either in the human body or, possibly, in the Earth itself (in which case it could be regarded as a kind of transformer). This still fails to explain how it can produce *action at a distance, and we are left to suppose that we are dealing with energy fields at present unknown to science.

A remarkable experiment carried out in Toronto by a group led by Dr and Mrs George Owen seems to confirm the 'unknown self' theory of poltergeists. The Owens' group decided to invent a *ghost, and then try to 'summon' it. They worked out the life history and background of a character called Philip, a contemporary of Cromwell, who had an affair with a gypsy girl; the girl was burnt at the stake, accused of witchcraft, and Philip killed himself. For months the group tried to 'raise' Philip, with no result. One evening, as they were relaxing after a session, there was a rap on the table. They questioned the 'rapper' in the usual way (1 rap = yes, 2 = no), and verified that this was Philip, who repeated the story they had invented for him. 'He' was later able to make a table waltz around the room; once, in front of television cameras, he made it climb a flight of stairs. We may, of course, prefer to believe that the being who called himself Philip was an alien entity with nothing better to do; but a less far-fetched hypothesis is that the unconscious mind of the group had finally obliged them and created a 'ghost'.

All this suggests another tempting hypothesis: that all paranormal occurrences are evidence not of 'the dark side of nature', but of 'the dark side of the human mind'. Such an hypothesis can be made to fit most, but not all, cases of hauntings or apparitions (see *ghosts). It seems more probable that the real answer may lie in a far wider and more comprehensive theory of the paranormal. cw

Reich, Wilhelm

The astonishing career of Reich came to an end in November 1957 when he died of a heart attack in prison — he had been sentenced for selling, in effect, quack remedies. The remedy in question was his 'orgone box', a cabinet made of alternate layers of wood and metal that was supposed to trap a mysterious life-energy, orgone energy, rather as a greenhouse traps infrared rays.

The strangest thing about his career is that he began as an arch-materialist, a fanatical disciple of Freud; he ended as something very like a mystic, yet still convinced he was an orthodox Freudian.

He was born in Austria in 1897. When he was thirteen, he discovered that his mother was having an affair with a resident tutor and told his father. His mother committed suicide. This event probably gave him a lifelong guilt complex, as well as a profound mistrust of women. World War I ruined the family fortunes. When Reich left the army he went to medical school in Vienna, where he completed a six-year course in four years and was acknowledged to be one of the most brilliant students of his generation.

While still a student he attended a lecture on psychoanalysis and became an instant convert. Freud was impressed by him and soon let him become a member of the Psychoanalytic Society. For a while it even looked as if Reich might one day become Freud's chief successor — Reich certainly hoped so. But he aroused much dislike among his colleagues, being regarded as too ambitious. Freud himself soon began to regard Reich as a liability. And this, oddly enough, was because Reich was, in a sense, more Freudian the Freud. He took the sexual theory literally, believing that health is the result of the free flow of 'libido', life energy, and that the natural expression of libido lies in the orgasm. Freud was just beginning to gain respect and acceptance as a psychological innovator, and Reich's revolutionary orgasm theory was an embarrassment. In 1927, Freud quarrelled with him, and Reich was so shattered that he developed tuberculosis and had to spend some time in a sanatorium.

When he came out, he moved to Berlin, joined the Communist Party, and for a while became its chief sexual theorist. He preached that Fascism was the outcome of sexual repression and that its leaders maintained their power through keeping the masses frustrated. Soon the Communists, too, began to feel that he was a liability since he seemed to be encouraging an identification of social revolution with promiscuity. Again, he was rejected by those he considered 'his own'.

After Hitler came to power in 1933, Reich spent some time in Sweden, but failed to get his visa renewed; he moved to Norway in 1934. By this time he had made what he considered his great discovery: the basic unit of living matter, or 'bion', a blue cell which, he claimed, is visible under the microscope. He announced that if a completely sterile solution of beef tea (*bouillon*) is sealed hermetically, bions will still begin to appear, since the blue life-energy streams through all space.

Reich moved to the USA. In 1940, on holiday in Maine, he noticed blue patches between the stars that twinkle and seem to give off light. This, he was convinced, was the basic life-energy, orgone. He invented his 'orgone box' which, he was convinced, would cure most illnesses, even cancer, although he soon came to recognize that a sudden improvement could be followed by a relapse, due to a radiation overdose. As persecution by journalists, and later the authorities, increased, Reich, who had always been slightly paranoid, became convinced that he was a world-saviour, like Christ, and would probably be destroyed for the same reason. He invented a kind of orgone-ray gun (called a cloud-buster) for inducing rain, and became convinced that his activities had attracted hostile *UFOs. Finally the authorities pounced, declaring that Reich had to stop selling his orgone accumulators — and literature — outside the state. One of Reich's assistants deliberately infringed this order; Reich was tried and sent to prison, where he died.

Reich's 'orgone energy' seems to have been the force that modern scientists refer to simply as bio-energy; and he may be seen as a distinguished member of a line of discoverers that includes Mesmer, von Reichenbach, Kilner (see *aura) and more recent figures like Harold Burr, Semyon Kirlian and Thelma Moss (see *Kirlian photography). cw

Reincarnation

Belief in reincarnation is common in the East, particularly among Hindus and Buddhists, but altogether rarer in the West. There is, however, a great deal of favourable evidence, even though the problem, by its very nature, can hardly be investigated experimentally.

One of the best known cases is that of Shanti Devi, born in Delhi in 1926. When she was seven, she told her mother that she had been alive before, in a town called Muttra. During the next two years her memories seemed to increase, until she was telling her parents about her previous husband, their house, and her three children. When she was nine, a stranger came to the door to discuss business with her father and Shanti claimed that she recognized him as her husband's cousin. The man *did* live in Muttra and agreed that his cousin's wife, Ludgi, had died ten years earlier. The husband came to visit her; she flung herself into his arms, recognizing him immediately. Taken to Muttra, she was able to direct the carriage to Ludgi's house and identified her father-in-law sitting in front of it. She also recognized her two eldest children, but not the youngest, whose birth had cost Ludgi her life.

This story, although well documented, was not investigated with scientific rigour. But in India Professor Hemendra Banerjee, of Rajasthan University, has devoted many years to studying cases with the kind of thoroughness that was first advocated by the SPR; while in the USA Ian Stevenson has published detailed studies of many cases: his *Twenty Cases Suggestive of Reincarnation* covers India, Brazil, Alaska and Lebanon, while a later immense project, *Cases of the Reincarnation Type*, begins with a volume covering ten Indian cases. These usually bear a family resemblance to the case of Shanti Devi. Three-year-old Jasbir Lal Jat, of Uttar Pradesh, 'died' of smallpox; as it was late, his father decided not to bury him until the next day. A few hours later, the child stirred, and then revived. It was some weeks before Jasbir was able to express himself clearly again, and then he seemed completely changed. He said that he was the son of a Brahmin named Shankar of Vehedi village and declined to eat food in his new home because he was of a higher caste than his father. A Brahmin lady solved that problem by agreeing to cook for him; this lasted for two years. The child described how, in his previous existence, he had been given poisoned sweets, and had fallen off a cart, suffering a head injury from which he died. In 1957, a Brahmin lady from Vehedi visited Jasbir's village, Rasulpur, and Jasbir recognized her as his aunt. She confirmed that a young man named Sobha Ram, aged twenty-two, *had* died of smallpox. Jasbir was taken to Vehedi under supervision and was able to lead the way — a complicated route — to his former home; he demonstrated a detailed knowledge of the family and its affairs. He subsequently went back often to spend his holdiays in Vehedi. The 'poisoning' was never satisfactorily cleared up.

The astonishing feature in this case is obviously that Sobha Ram died after Jasbir was born. It seems that the 'spirit' of Sobha Ram 'moved into' Jasbir's body. Was Jasbir actually dead at the time? Stevenson, whose careful investigation was exemplary, nevertheless forgets to mention whether Jasbir clearly recalled his earlier life, before the 'takeover'.

In *The Shape of Minds to Come* Professor John Taylor states the standard 'scientific' view of personality: '... we recognize personality as a summation of the different contributions to behaviour from the various control units of the brain.' In fact, most mothers would insist that children reveal a distinct personality from earliest babyhood. And cases like that of Jasbir would, if proven, demonstrate the falsity of Taylor's view. Cases of *multiple personality point in the same direction.

In the West, cases of reincarnation seem rarer. Nevertheless, the Lurancy Vennum case (see *possession) is unusually convincing. So is the case of 'Mrs Smith', described by Guirdham in *The Cathars and Reincarnation*. Mrs Smith's experiences convinced her that she was a Cathar who was burned for heresy around 1244. Her dreams of the period were full of precise detail about the Cathars, and Guirdham was able to check their accuracy by corresponding with French experts. She asserted that Cathar priests wore blue, not black, and this proved to be correct. She stated that she had given her lover loaf-sugar when he was ill, which struck Guirdham as unlikely. But careful research revealed not only that loaf-sugar could be obtained at the time but that it was regarded as a medicine.

Even so, there is plenty of ammunition for sceptics in Guirdham's story. He himself came to believe that he had been a Cathar, and had been, in fact, the lover recalled by 'Mrs Smith'. Once he began to recall this previous incarnation, he seems to have had memories of other incarnations — as a Napoleonic soldier, a Roman, and as a Cretan in the thirteenth century BC. If we can accept the likelihood of reincarnation, and of certain people having detailed memories of previous lives, then all this is perfectly possible. But this flood of relatively unchecked material about 'previous lives' is bound to raise precisely the kind of doubts that *The Cathars and Reincarnation* undermines so convincingly.

Another point is that most of Stevenson's cases of reincarnation appear among people who accept it as part of their religion — Hindus, Eskimos, Tlingit Indians, etc. But then a little research reveals there have been a number of recorded cases in Europe and the USA — Patience Worth, Joan Grant, Edward Ryall, Ann Ockendon, and many investigated by 'regression hypnotists' like Arnall Bloxham and Joe Keeton. It may be simply that, in a cultural climate unsympathetic to the idea of reincarnation, past cases have tended to go unrecorded.   CW

Revelations, Mystical

In his essay 'A Suggestion About Mysticism', William James makes the fundamental statement: '... states of mystical intuition may be only very sudden and great extensions of the ordinary "field of consciousness".' The suggestion is important because the word 'mysticism' is often used to mean vague and imprecise thinking. But this notion is in itself based upon a failure to recognize that 'everyday consciousness' is essentially limited in its nature, like tunnel vision.

Everyday consciousness is essentially *selective*. It is governed by the need for self-preservation, for coping with the complexities of our experience. It tends to be directed towards 'the next thing to be done', ignoring things on either side.

So, in a sense, what we experience on holiday is a type of mystical consciousness — that sense of freshness, of reality, the feeling that the world is a more interesting and complex place than we had realized. This in turn makes us aware that our senses 'filter out' an enormous proportion of our experience. Huxley gives clear recognition to this insight in *The Doors of Perception*, in which he describes how mescalin produced a kind of mystical perception in which everything he looked at was 'more real'. He talked about the 'is-ness' of things — the recognition that they *really exist* — a point Sartre had already made in *Nausea*: 'Never, until these last few days, had I understood the meaning of *existence*. I was like the others ... I said with them: The ocean *is* green, that white speck up there *is* a seagull, but I didn't feel that it existed ...'

Recognition of the differing functions of the right and left sides of the brain (see page 13) throws important light on this observation. The left brain, the 'you', is the 'coper'; it deals with the problems of existence; the right brain looks inward; it deals with intuition and feeling. So 'my' experience is, by its very nature, 'symbolic' and two-dimensional. It is only when I deeply relax that my right brain is allowed to contribute its own experience of 'depth', of feeling, of a 'third dimension', to my consciousness. It seems likely that, if we could get inside the brain of a cow, we would discover that its consciousness is 'mystical' all the time. But it would also have the disadvantage of being static. Nietzsche comments that it would be pointless to ask the cow why it is so contented, because it would have forgotten the question before it could give the answer. The 'flatness' is the price we pay for our ability to deal with the complexity of human experience.

Yet a wider form of consciousness lies very close to our everyday awareness. William James speaks of several personal experiences of 'extended awareness': 'In one instance I was engaged in conversation, but I doubt whether the interlocutor noticed my abstraction. What happened each time was that I seemed all at once to be reminded of a past experience; and this reminiscence, ere I could conceive or name it distinctly, developed into something further that belonged with it, this in turn into something further still, and so on, until the process faded out, leaving me amazed at the sudden vision of increasing ranges of distant fact of which I could give no articulate account.'

Most of us have had similar experiences. It seems that focusing upon our everyday problems requires a kind of 'close-up' awareness, like a narrow-angle lens in a camera; yet when we feel relaxed and interested we can somehow slip in a wide-angle lens and grasp a far wider area — James' 'increasing ranges of distant fact'. (The crucial word here is 'fact'.)

Closely related is deep relaxation — the kind of thing we may feel when some anxiety is suddenly relieved or a crisis is solved: a sense of being perfectly happy to rest in the present moment, with no sense of haste or compulsion. (The left brain contains our 'time sense'; the right appears to have little sense of time.) But, if we attempt to slip into this state when we have nothing else to do, we find it oddly difficult to achieve. The left brain declines to relax and go off-duty. Our state of tension is automatic, mechanical, and we cannot switch it off at will. Yet *biofeedback demonstrates that we can achieve control over 'automatic' functions. There is, in fact, no good reason why we should not learn to achieve these states of deep relaxation, with all their sense of enriched experience, at will.

In *The Occult* I suggested the term 'Faculty X' for this state of 'enriched consciousness'. Ordinary, left-brain consciousness lacks the sense of 'real existence', as Sartre said. We say 'That speck is a seagull' or 'This time last year I was in Italy', yet in a sense we do not *believe* it, even though we know it is true. Yet in moments of '3-D consciousness', when the two dimensions of the left are enriched by the right's sense of meaning, we can say it and *know* it is true. Proust and Toynbee described similar experiences (see *time). Proust wrote: 'I had ceased to feel mediocre, accidental, mortal ...' An experience near Victoria Station, when for Toynbee *all* history became real for a moment, seems a perfect illustration of William James' belief that mystical experience is simply a glimpse of 'distant horizons' of fact.

The chief problem of mystics has always been how to induce the mystical experience. Their 'glimpses' make them dissatisfied with the limitations of ordinary consciousness, yet efforts to achieve a wider consciousness are usually abortive simply because it is the 'left-brain self' that tries to make them and, the harder it tries, the less it succeeds, since what it really needs to do is to hand over control to the right. Yet the discovery of *biofeedback, and the recognition of the different roles of the right and left brains, hold out the promise of a new degree of control over our states of consciousness — the possibility of the deliberate cultivation of 'Faculty X'. CW

Rosicrucians

In 1614 a pamphlet called *Fama Fraternitas of the Worthy Order of the Rosy Cross* was published at Kassel. It declared that a man called Christian Rosenkreuz (who had lived to be 106) had spent his life wandering around the East in search of occult wisdom; having found it, he formed an order called the Brotherhood of the Rosy Cross. He was buried in an unknown tomb, surrounded by inextinguishable candles, and lay there for 120 years before a Brother of the Order found his tomb. That was the signal for the Brotherhood to declare its existence openly and invite the learned men of Europe to join. A year later came another Rosicrucian pamphlet, the *Confessio Fraternitas*, which spoke of a reformed world, and hinted at some marvellous occult knowledge.

'Interested parties' had only to make their interest known, said the *Fama*, and they would be contacted. Naturally, many people went to the trouble of having declarations of interest printed; as far as is known, none ever heard from the Brothers. But in the following year, a third Rosicrucian document was published, this time a kind of short novel called *The Chemical Wedding of Christian Rosenkreuz*, a curious allegorical work in which the narrator becomes a guest of a king and queen at a wedding at which various weird and obscure events occur — the symbolism owes much to *alchemy. Scholarship has established that the author of this work, and probably of the other two, was a Tübingen minister named Johann Valentin Andreae (see *Utopia), who had written *The Chemical Wedding* about ten years earlier.

This is all we know about the Rosicrucians. They were probably a group of intellectual idealists who gathered in Tübingen; they felt things ought to be changed. In his will, written in 1634 (when he was forty-eight), Andreae wrote: 'Though I leave the Fraternity itself, I shall never leave the true Christian Fraternity, which, beneath the Cross, smells of the rose, and is quite apart from the filth of this century.' Like most men of most times, they felt they lived in a corrupt age when things were going from bad to worse. It was also an age that still believed in magic — Dee was still alive when Andreae wrote *The Chemical Wedding*, and Newton would later devote much time to researches into alchemy.

The Rosicrucians have continued to exercise a powerful influence on 'occult philosophy' down the centuries (although the modern order of Rosicrucians in California — AMORC — has nothing to do with the tradition), largely because this notion of a secret society possessing occult knowledge has a powerful emotional appeal. *Steiner, for example, was strongly influenced by the Rosicrucian idea: *A Rosicrucian Anthology* contains several of his essays on the subject, as well as the three major Rosicrucian documents. In spite of its vagueness, Rosicrucianism remains an idea of extraordinary force and durability. CW

Spiritualism

The nineteenth century was ready for the Spiritualist movement. Industrialism was slowly creeping across the landscape and, for the first time in centuries, Christianity could be openly challenged in Christian countries without danger of the stake or the dungeon.

The notion of disembodied spirits was not new. Dee performed ceremonies to raise spirits (see *scrying). Cagliostro, who died in the Inquisition's prison as recently as 1795, used children as scryers — they usually went into a light trance gazing into water. Dr Johnson, who helped investigate the famous Cock Lane Ghost in 1759, concluded that it was a hoax — actually, it was a *poltergeist, and no one then realized that poltergeists originate in the unconscious. At the same period, Swedenborg propagated his own version of Christianity, based on what he had been told by 'spirits'; and a number of well authenticated anecdotes reveal that he had remarkable psychic powers. The doctrines of Mesmer led to much interest in *clairvoyance and occultism. And one of the most widely read books of the first half of the nineteenth century was *The Seeress of Prevorst* by Justinus Kerner, an account of Frederica Hauffe, who had frequent *out-of-the-body experiences and conversed with spirits. A later bestseller was *The Principles of Nature* by Andrew Jackson Davis, a shoemaker's apprentice who had been hypnotized, and who later dictated this remarkable work while in a trance. (Like many 'spirit teachings' from Swedenborg onward, it emphasized that Man must do penance in the afterlife for sins committed in this one, but that there is no hell and no vicarious atonement on the cross for the sins of mankind.)

Davis prophesied in his book that the truths of the spirit would soon present themselves to the world as a 'living demonstration'. He proved basically correct. In 1847, a Methodist farmer named John Fox moved into a small house in Hydesville. In March 1848, rapping noises began to be heard in the family bedroom. There were two daughters, Margaret, fifteen, and Kate, twelve. Kate challenged the 'spirit' to answer when she snapped her fingers, and it obliged by rapping. Neighbours were invited in and one asked the 'spirit' questions (with a code of one rap for yes, two for no). They ascertained that the 'spirit' was of a pedlar who said that he had been murdered in the house and buried in the cellar. Attempts to dig in the cellar were at first unsuccessful because of flood water, but later in 1848 some teeth and hair were dug up; and as late as 1904 human bones were found behind a wall, together with a pedlar's tin box.

The Foxes moved to Rochester, and the rapping continued; in 1849, the girls began to demonstrate their powers in public. What then happened may be compared to what happened in 1947 after the first *UFO sighting was reported: hundreds of people began to hear mysterious raps. Spiritualist 'mediums' sprang up all over the place. Rappings had occurred in the house of two brothers named Davenport as early as 1846; in 1850, they tried 'table-turning' and were soon obtaining very remarkable manifestations — *automatic writing, *levitation and the untying of ropes with which they were bound. A 'spirit' named John King became their 'guide'. The Fox sisters began causing misty figures to materialize. Daniel Dunglas Home, a Scot who had moved to the USA, began giving public 'séances' in 1851; he was certainly one of the greatest mediums of all time, able to cause heavy furniture to levitate to the ceiling, while he himself could wash his face in blazing coals and float in and out of windows. (Browning satirized him as 'Mr Sludge the medium', but Home, unlike 'Sludge', was never 'exposed'.) The Eddy brothers specialized in causing ghostly figures to materialize in the room. In 1873, Madame *Blavatsky arrived in the USA, and soon demonstrated her own remarkable mediumistic powers. One young admirer, Charles Johnston, described how she was idly tapping her fingers on the table, then, without thinking, raised her hand in the air and continued the movements; the tappings continued. Aware of his interest, she turned to him and 'transmitted' the taps across the room onto the back of his hand — he said that it felt like little spurts of electricity. This story is interesting because it underlines an important point: many 'mediums', from the Fox sisters onward, were really producing *poltergeist phenomena*. And these are probably related to the right cerebral hemisphere and, possibly, to the 'Earth forces' that dowsers respond to. The nineteenth century leapt from these phenomena to the belief in *ghosts and spirits without being fully aware of the role of the unconscious in such manifestations.

In 1882, the Society for Psychical Research was founded in England, made up basically of sceptical scientists. They formulated precise, rigorous rules for the study of 'psychic phenomena'. Yet it soon became clear to everyone concerned that, despite a certain amount of self-deception and some wilful trickery, an enormous percentage of psychic phenomena had to be accepted as genuine. Moreover, with such remarkable mediums as Mrs Piper, Mrs Leonard, Eusapia Palladino and the Schneider brothers, it began to seem likely that psychical research was on the point of some great breakthrough, and that death would cease to be the 'undiscovered country from whose bourne no traveller returns'. Sadly, these hopes proved illusory. In the twentieth century, the age of the great mediums seemed to come to an end, although there are undoubtedly more good mediums now than there were a century ago when the SPR was founded. Spiritualist churches continue to flourish, although, on the whole, investigators would no longer take them as seriously as in the days of Home and Palladino. Psychical research has become more concerned with the study of *ESP and with attempts to understand the unknown powers of the human mind. A remarkable modern 'psychic', Robert Cracknell, left the Spiritualist movement because he felt that it contains an enormous amount of self-deception; he takes the view that psychic powers probably have nothing to do with 'spirits' or *life after death. While there is some powerful evidence to the contrary — a few 'spirit communications' seem to pass every test for genuineness — his view is worth bearing in mind as an antidote to what might be called 'simplistic Spiritualism'. CW

Steiner, Rudolph

Steiner was born in 1861. Intellectually precocious, he might easily have become a scientist or mathematician, had it not been for a powerful perception, which he claims was always with him, of the 'spiritual world'. Like Boehme or Swedenborg, he was a natural clairvoyant. He edited Goethe's scientific works at the age of twenty-three, then went to work in the Goethe Archives at Weimar. He moved to Berlin in his mid-thirties, editing a literary magazine and working in the theatre. There he encountered Theosophy, and became a follower of *Blavatsky.

In 1909, at the age of forty-eight, he broke with the Theosophical Society and founded his own Anthroposophical Society. A brilliant lecturer, he gained an immense following, and in the years immediately following World War I supervised the building of a 'Goetheanum' at Dornach, Switzerland. This was burned down in 1922, possibly by nationalist rowdies who detested Steiner's philosophy of spiritual brotherhood. Another Goetheanum was begun soon after, but Steiner never saw its completion. He died, basically of overwork, in March 1925, aged sixty-four.

It is difficult to assess his achievement. Probably most educated people today would dismiss him as another crank 'messiah', a man who wrote books on *Atlantis and Lemuria and taught vaguely spiritual doctrines. Anyone who takes the trouble to read his books soon discovers that his was too keen an intellect to be dismissed in this manner; he remained, as he began, a scientist. But his attempt to blend occultism and science was far from successful. Probably, from his own point of view, his life work should be regarded as a failure, a realization that may have contributed to his death. More than fifty years later we are better able to grasp his real importance, that he was a scientist who felt that there should be no conflict between science and the paranormal. Two years after his death, J.B. Rhine began his researches into *ESP at Duke University. In the 1970s, the books of Lyall Watson argued convincingly that science now offers a great deal of support to the basic assertions of 'occultism'. But in Steiner's lifetime the gap still seemed unbridgeable; his remarkable work may be seen as an heroic attempt to throw a rainbow-bridge of imagination and intuition across the gulf. CW

Stigmata

Marks on the hands or feet resembling the nail holes of the Crucifixion are known as stigmata; when they occurred in well known saints they were accepted as a sign of heavenly grace. There are hundreds of recorded examples: well known is that of St Francis of Assisi, who developed 'wounds' on his hands and feet after an ecstatic vision. More recently, St Gemma Galgani of Lucca developed wounds in her hands — deep cavitities filled with blood — every Thursday evening; these healed up and vanished during Friday.

Charcot's researches into hysteria and *hypnosis in the late nineteenth century made it clear that stigmata were basically hysterical symptoms. In 1932 Adolph Lechler encountered an Austrian peasant girl who had been deeply affected by a film about the life of Jesus. Under hypnosis, he suggested that wounds would develop in her hands and feet, where she was already experiencing aches. Wounds appeared and were deepened by further suggestion; he also made appear the 'Crown of Thorns' on her forehead and a sagging of the shoulder where the cross had been carried. After photographing these effects, he healed them by counter-suggestion.

It might be argued that this ability of the mind to produce such remarkable physical effects is in itself as miraculous as the stigmata were once believed to be.   CW

Tantrism

Tantrism is a Hindu religious philosophy based upon sexual disciplines; it derives from texts known as the Tantra. The notion that sex lies at the heart of religion may be said to be implicit in Hinduism with its notion that the Universe is pervaded by the male and female forces, Shiva and Shakti (also known as Kali). In Hindu mythology, Shakti was the mother of Shiva whom she subsequently married. (In her form as sexual energy, Shakti is known as Devi.) Tantrism, although regarded as a scandalous aberration by most orthodox Hindus and Buddhists, is a genuine form of *yoga, whose aim is to make use of the sexual energy instead of allowing it to waste itself in the orgasm. It involves breath-control, and the partners remain almost motionless, the woman maintaining her partner's erection by means of her vaginal muscles.

Similar techniques were to be found also in China, here specifically associated with *alchemy. In the West, too, there is evidence that sexual intercourse was part of the secret alchemical tradition and, in his introduction to the works of Thomas Vaughan, Kenneth Rexroth argues convincingly that Vaughan believed the ultimate secret of alchemy to be sexual in nature. Aleister *Crowley practised tantric forms of magic, and the current revival of interest in Crowley has led to a widespread interest in 'sexual occultism', particularly in the USA.   CW

Transcendental Meditation

TM is a technique of meditation brought to the West in 1958 by the Maharishi Mahesh Yogi. The individual is given a mantra — usually a meaningless word — to repeat, while he attempts to sink into a state that combines relaxation and alertness, and to move downwards towards 'the pool of Bliss lying within'. Books on TM insist that it can be learned only through personal guidance, but this may be doubted.

Its starting point is that of all meditation techniques: the mind is by nature mechanical and 'wandering', and spends most of its time over-reacting to trivial problems of everyday existence. So *any* deliberate attempt to control it is going to have beneficial effects.

*Crowley obliged a film actress, Elizabeth Fox, to sit for a month on a cliff-top with only a rude tin shelter, living on bread and water. At first she suffered agonies of boredom; then, towards the end of the month, she sank into a state of ecstatic serenity in which the sea and the sky seemed to become infinitely fascinating. All that had happened is that her overtense left brain had relaxed its neurotic grip and allowed the right free expression. When the left-brain ego relaxes there is a delightful sense of endless time-to-spare, and of the immense interestingness of everything. All meditation — or conscious mind-control — has this effect.

TM has been valuable in making large

numbers of people in the West aware of something that should have been obvious but, regrettably, was not: that, in the depth of his being, Man possesses a source of power.   CW

Yoga

The popular notion of the yogi as a skinny Hindu lying on a bed of nails is by no means inaccurate. In fact, 'fakirs' (or jogis) are practitioners of only one narrow aspect of yoga, the science of spiritual, mental and physical control. Yogis have performed, under test conditions, such feats as suspending their breathing until it is undetectable (and being buried alive for weeks at a time), displaying different pulse rates in each wrist, and walking on fire. While such accounts once struck Westerners as incredible, they can now be understood in terms of *hypnosis and *biofeedback control of the autonomic nervous system: in *Beyond Biofeedback*, Elmer and Alyce Green described the feats of Jack Schwarz, who is able to withstand beating, burning and stabbing not only without pain but also without injury. What is slowly becoming apparent is that our ability to control the body and the autonomic (automatic) nervous system is greater than Western medicine has ever imagined.

Yoga is basically a Hindu form of self-discipline, although most religions have their own counterparts. There are many different forms. The physical yoga that has become so popular in the West is Hatha yoga, which may be regarded as the basic form since Hindus accept that spiritual discipline must begin at the level of the body. It involves exercises in breathing — which is of fundamental importance in controlling the vital energies, *prana* — and in posture.

Other forms are Bhakti yoga, the yoga of prayer and devotion; Dhyana yoga, that of contemplation and meditation (which is essential to all forms of yoga, including Hatha); Jnana yoga, rooted in the study of sacred texts; Karma yoga, the yoga of good works; and Raja yoga, the 'royal way', which deals with the upper reaches of spiritual development. Jnana yoga probably comes closest to the Christian intellectual tradition, as embodied (for example) in Aquinas.

The ultimate aim of all yoga is *samadhi*, trance-like union with God. The clearest exposition of the aims of the yogi is to be found in the *Bhagavad Gita*, the Song of God, part of the Hindu epic *Mahabharata*. The Prince Arjuna objects to battling with his kinsmen; the Lord Krishna explains to him that it is not possible for Man to completely withdraw from the world and ignore it, but he can perform his physical tasks with total mental detachment, his mind only on enlightenment, the condition of ultimate freedom. The fundamental aim is this ultimate freedom. The soul of man, the Atman, is identical with God, Brahman. Man spends his life involved in trivial aims and emotions which create in him a false sense of identity. His task is to rise above this false self through the practice of detachment and meditation, until he realizes that the soul *is* God, *Tat tvam asi* — 'That thou art'. Buddhism, in which this state of ultimate detachment is called Nirvana, is a natural offshoot of Hinduism. But while the spiritual depth of such teachings is undeniable, it is worth bearing in mind that they are based upon the notion that human existence is something to be rejected, involving illusion, involvement and suffering. Buddhism, in particular, is closely related to the doctrines of the Manichees (or Dualists) who believed that the world was created by the Devil and is entirely evil; salvation can be found only by totally rejecting matter and turning towards spirit. The Western observer may sense a similar attitude underlying the disciplines of yogis who have sat in the same position for many years until their muscles have become locked and immovable, or who have held their fingers against their palms until the nails have grown like claws into their hands.

Christianity decisively rejected Dualism on the grounds that God created the world 'and saw that it was good'.

The basic aim of yoga is, nevertheless, identical with the aim of saints and mystics of all times: to gain control over the body and emotions, to enable the mind to move inward toward the 'source of power, meaning and purpose' which lies deep inside everyone.

There seems no doubt that these practices often result in miraculous powers. A French lawyer, Louis Jacolliot, who was in India in the early 1860s, described many such examples in his *Occult Science in India*. He describes how one fakir was able to cause a pawpaw seed to sprout into an 8in plant in two hours by meditating above it; another was able to cause a small table to stick to the floor so firmly that all Jacolliot's attempts to move it only broke it.

But yogis hold such 'miracles' in low esteem, insisting that they are merely 'tricks', irrelevant to salvation. What is important is *samadhi* — as attained, for example, by the nineteenth-century Hindu saint Ramakrishna who was about to plunge a sword into his breast, out of despair, when 'the Divine Mother revealed herself', causing a sensation of being overwhelmed by waves of light. Thereafter, Ramakrishna could always induce *samadhi* simply by talking about Krishna or the Divine Mother Kali.

Yet even here it is possible to begin to understand something of the mechanisms of what happened. The 'Ramakrishna' who was obsessed by his search for the Divine Mother was the 'false ego' — the left-brain 'self'. The suicide attempt violently shattered this false self-image, plunging him into the 'other mode of consciousness' which seems to lie side by side with 'this' one — the mode that produces flashes of the feeling of 'absurd good news', or even Proust's revelation, tasting a cake dipped in herb tea, of suddenly ceasing to feel 'mediocre, accidental, mortal'.

This is perhaps one of the most exciting developments in psychology in the late twentieth century — its increasing ability to understand such traditional religious disciplines as yoga, and to explain them in a 'non-reductionist' manner which seems to promise an end to the traditional 'warfare between science and theology'. CW

Zen

Zen is a Japanese (and Chinese) offshoot of Mahayana Buddhism. Buddhism emphasizes 'enlightenment', the sudden moment of realization when the mind rises above illusions. It also states that all men have the 'Buddha nature', rather as Hinduism states that Atman, the soul, is identical with Brahman, God. Zen is also related to Taoism in which the 'way of Tao' must be followed with intuition, with a combination of quiescence and concentration. The relation between Taoism and Zen emerges very clearly in Eugen Herrigel's *Zen in the Art of Archery* in which he describes how his Zen master taught him to use a bow 'intuitively'; when the master himself drew the bow, his action seemed casual — yet the arrow flew straight to the bull.

Westerners find it hard to grasp the Eastern disapproval of the ego. Freud's recognition of the unconscious was an immense advance, while the more recent recognition that the right and left hemispheres are two different people is even more important. Zen may be seen as an attempt to persuade the left-brain ego, with its logic and practicality, to recognize the importance of its partner and allow him to do half the work. Zen emphasizes that truth cannot be grasped with logic, and that it cannot be found merely by turning away from what is false. Man has developed this powerful logical ego because his basic attitude towards existence is one of mistrust; he is always prepared for the worst. His basic strategy is to 'play safe', and Western civilization is a monument to his success — Western science likewise. Yet a scientist who mistrusted his intuition would be a bad scientist. And a religious man who tried to find 'salvation' by obeying the letter of the scriptures would be in a similar position. Both would be guilty of a kind of laziness, like someone afraid to walk across the centre of a room, preferring to support himself against the walls. Zen, like all mysticism, is a recognition that the essence of religion is *freedom*, the ability to cross the room directly. Man is never merely 'what he is' — his body, his emotions, his history; he contains an element of pure potentiality. When the mind is tired, or lazy, this is almost impossible to grasp; we seem to be 'what we are', just as a table is 'what it is'. Yet when we are full of delight and anticipation we are clearly aware that the basic difference between a man and, say, a table is one of freedom.

How can the mind be galvanized into this grasp of freedom? The Zen master tries to throw the mind off its logical tracks with 'koans' like 'What is the sound of one hand clapping?'. Or he may, like the Buddha, give a 'sermon' by remaining silent and holding up a flower. Or by answering a silly question with a kick. The aim is to make Man aware that his essence is not 'Man' but freedom, potentiality. This results in a state of serene enlightenment, *satori*. 'Man' is the tip of the iceberg; the rest is potentiality. The visible part is the left-brain ego; if one is conscious of oneself merely as this ego, one is a prisoner of one's own idea of oneself. A 'free' person would be aware of the vast bulk of potentiality below the water-line. Zen appears paradoxical only if this is not understood. CW

Evolution: 5

We shall probably never be able to pinpoint the origin of intelligence, or to trace its early evolution. Cultural evolution over the last few millennia gives us some clues, and for a few million years before that there are occasional artefacts, but clearly intelligence must have emerged on Earth long, long before that.

Strangely, then, we are almost in a position to understand more about the future evolution of intelligence, of the mind, than we do about its past. In this section we have examined some of the exciting developments that seem to be taking place at a mental level; in the next we shall review some of the more staggering areas of modern knowledge, the very frontiers of our understanding. These two elements, together, form an integrated whole, as noted on page 23. And, together, they give us a basis on which we can found our speculations concerning the nature of our descendants. JG

PART SIX
OUTER SPACE: THE UNIVERSE AT LARGE

Introductory: 6

'The most beautiful and most profound emotion one can experience is the sensation of the mystical. It is the source of all true science.' The author is not William Blake or Madame *Blavatsky, but Albert Einstein. He also said: 'I believe with Schopenhauer that one of the strongest motives that leads men to art and science is to escape from everyday life, with its painful crudity and hopeless dreariness, from the fetters of one's own ever-shifting desires. A finely tempered nature longs to escape from personal life into the world of objective perception and thought; this desire may be compared with the townsman's irresistable longing to escape from his noisy, cramped surroundings into the silence of high mountains, where the eye ranges freely through the still, pure air and fondly traces out the restful contours, which look as if they were built for eternity ...'

These comments make it plain that the basic motive behind science is the motive that led the Lake poets to seek out the great hills of Cumberland and Westmorland. That arch-rationalist Bertrand Russell wrote in a letter: 'I must, I *must*, before I die, find *some* way to say the essential thing that is in me, that I have never said yet — a thing that is not love or hate or pity or scorn, but the very breath of life, fierce and coming from far away, bringing into human life the vastness and the fearful passionless force of non-human things.' At first it seems incredible that this was said by one whom Blake would have accused of 'single vision and Newton's sleep'. But this is only if we fail to grasp the basic identity of the psychological drives that produce science *and* poetry. If there could be any further doubt, then it might be dispelled by the last line of Blake's *Vala, or the Four Zoas*: 'The dark religions are departed, and sweet Science reigns ...'

What Blake and Russell have in common is a recognition that we waste most of our lives preoccupied with the trivial. Concentrating grimly on the problems in front of our noses, we fail to look at the distant horizon. Yet Man is most himself when he is concerned with this vast, impersonal horizon.

The truth is that there are no real opponents of this view — Russell or Newton or anybody else. The men who believe that 'the proper study of mankind is Man' — like Pope and Maugham — usually turn out to be rather nasty, oversensitive little characters who are trapped in the horizons of the personal by their own wounded self-esteem and self-pity. Ted Morgan's admirable biography of Maugham shows him as a man who had his glimpses of the 'distant horizon' but lacked the kind of self-confidence that made Einstein set out cheerfully to reach it on foot.

And now, at last, we are beginning to see the rise of a new physics that is willing to come to terms with the reality of the poet and mystic. Anyone who feels prepared to take the vertiginous plunge should get hold of books by 'hard scientists' like Paul Davies and John Gribbin, or some of the new 'scientific mystics' like Fritjof Capra and Gary Zukav. Those of a philosophical turn of mind may prefer to begin with Michael Polanyi (whose *Personal Knowledge* is the major classic in this field) or Sir Karl Popper. While those who wish to try the water for temperature could do worse than read the following two sections.[1]

CW

---

[1] It is an interesting example of the artificial barriers erected within modern culture that the 'common-sense metric' system of units used in the following two sections is not considered suitable for the earlier sections. JG

Alternate Universes

There are a number of considerations which suggest the plausibility of there being universes other than our own.

1 Our four-dimensional expanding *Universe has often been likened to the two-dimensional expanding surface of a balloon which is being inflated: as the balloon is blown up, so points on its surface move apart in the same fashion as distant galaxies are observed to recede from us. Carrying the analogy further, a number of cosmologists have asked, in effect, 'What is on the *inside* surface of the balloon?' The answer, if there is an answer, is 'an alternate universe'.

2 Matter falling into a *black hole disappears from our Universe. Where does it go to? There are three choices: (a) it just disappears; (b) it reappears in another part of our Universe, perhaps gushing forth from a *white hole; (c) it reappears in an alternate universe. Ignoring (a), in (b) it is interesting to note that there may be no apparent relationship between the time of entering the black hole and the time of emergence from the white hole: in everyday terms, one may emerge from the white hole before, while or after entering the black hole. If one emerged from the white hole *before* entering the black hole then, for a period, our Universe would contain a little more 'stuff' than usual, which would seem to violate established laws of conservation. Of course, there may be some unknown mechanism which prevents this from happening; or the Universe may make some compensation which we do not know about; or, even, the short-term breaking of such laws may be tolerable, in accord with many of the ideas of modern physics. But a perfectly tenable hypothesis is that black holes and white holes maintain a balance via the medium of alternate universes. Thus, if one entered a black hole one would most probably emerge in an alternate universe; but if, by chance, one emerged in our own Universe a short time before entering a black hole, then this would be compensated for by something else of the same mass disappearing into an alternate universe. We can liken this to two salt solutions of equal strength separated by a porous membrane: while individual particles may travel to and fro through the membrane, the concentrations of the two solutions remain the same. Of course, if one uses the black hole/white hole mechanism to travel to alternate universes, one has the intriguing problem of working out how to let those at home know that the experiment has been a success.

3 At any particular moment in our lives we are faced with a number of choices: you can continue to read this sentence, stop reading it, tear up this page, die, etc. The atoms in a lump of radioactive carbon-14 have a choice, at any particular instant, of decaying to give atoms of nitrogen-14 or of not doing so: over a period of about 5,730 years half the atoms in the lump will have decayed, but we cannot predict *which* these atoms will be, nor the particular moment a particular atom will choose to decay. If all the *other* atoms in the lump had chosen to decay over 5,730 years, while those that had chosen to decay had decided against, we would be unable to tell the difference between the two situations. Everything in our Universe, then, has at any moment a plurality of choices. We live in a Universe determined by innumerable choices made in the past, and innumerable choices being made in the present. It has been suggested that each of those choices may give rise to an alternate universe. For example, in a 'nearby' alternate universe an atom of radiocarbon may just have decayed, while in our Universe it will not decay for another second yet: in that universe there is a virtually identical 'you' reading from an almost identical page to this one. 'Further away', 'you' may not exist, or the Earth may not exist, or . . .

4 In *oscillating Universe models, each successive link in the 'chain' of universes may be considered an alternate universe. While it is conventionally held that there is no relationship between the links — i.e., no information survives the 'Big Crunch' and *Big Bang to be passed from one universe to the 'next' — this may not be the case. If the suggestion is correct that universes of matter are succeeded by universes of *anti-

matter (which are succeeded in turn by universes of matter, etc.) then it is possible that in very real terms there may 'have been' countless universes. There is an uneasiness about tense in this paragraph; in a 'Big Crunch' not only matter but also space and, even more importantly, time would be annihilated, and so to say that there may 'have been' countless other matter universes is rather to juggle with the dimensions. It is equally meaningful to think of those universes coexisting with our own. (See also *parallel worlds.) JG

Antigravity

Since our knowledge of the nature of gravity is so limited, it is perhaps a vanity to attempt to speculate on the possibility of there existing such a 'force' as that science-fiction writer's dream, antigravity.

In terms of *Relativity, gravity can be thought of using the familiar analogy of objects lying on a taut rubber sheet: the heavier the object, the deeper the dent it makes; the paths of objects are affected by the 'dents' caused by other objects. To extend the analogy, antigravity would involve hummocks in the sheet, and passing objects would be deflected not towards but away from the centres of these. It is hard to conceive what might produce such hummocks!

That said, it is appealing to speculate that there might be a force of antigravity which attracts *antimatter particles to each other (possibly repelling matter particles, which might explain why there is so little antimatter in our part of the Universe — but see *Big Bang); and, of course, if *white holes exist, they may be considered regions of huge 'negative gravity' — or antigravity. JG

Antimatter

Matter is made up of particles. The fundamental building-block of matter, the atom, is made of three principal particles, the positively charged proton and the neutral neutron, found together in the atomic nucleus, and the negatively charged electron (but see *fundamental particles).

In a stable atom the number of protons in the nucleus is equal to the number of electrons orbiting the nucleus so that the atom is overall electrically neutral. But this stability could equally well be achieved if protons were negatively charged and electrons positively charged — and indeed, the positively charged electron, the positron, was the first antiparticle to be discovered, in 1932.

Other properties of particles include spin, which can be viewed as the angular momentum of the particle as it rotates (just as the Earth has angular momentum owing to its rotation). Particles spin in one direction, antiparticles in the opposite one.

Antimatter is, then, an analogue of matter built of antiparticles rather than of particles. There is very little of it in our region of the Universe since matter and antimatter annihilate each other explosively on contact, but there is no reason to believe that some of the galaxies we see in our telescopes are not made of antimatter, obeying the same laws as matter and hence indistinguishable. Another theory suggests that in the *Big Bang almost equal quantities of matter and antimatter were produced but that, by chance, there was just a little more matter than antimatter; the Universe as we see it represents this small excess, since the remaining matter and antimatter would have been annihilated.

In 1949 Feynman suggested that antiparticles were particles for whom the arrow of *time was reversed — i.e., they were travelling from future into past. This rather neatly accounts for their rarity and their short-livedness: modern physics supposes that, while large numbers of particles (or waves or events) statistically conform to the known laws of the Universe, individual particles may for a short time flout them.

Another suggestion is that antimatter is truly rare throughout our Universe and that the arrow of time truly points in one direction only (apart from the occasional 'sport' particle). However, in terms of the *oscillating Universe model, our Universe is only one of a chain — could it be that the universes 'before' and 'after' ours are antimatter universes in which the arrow of time is reversed? This is elegant and appealing since it implies that the Universe, which in spacetime terms is a closed system, is part of a 'multiverse' which is itself closed (see *alternate universes). We may have been here before. JG

Ball Lightning

Ball lightning is extremely rare — until quite recently orthodox science did not recognize that it existed at all. Because of this, little is known of its nature or of the circumstances that give rise to it.

The lightning takes the form of a glowing ball, close to the ground; the ball generally disappears in an explosive flash. Tales of the behaviour of these items are profuse: they are said to follow nearby telephone wires (behaviour often ascribed to *UFOs, and it is suggested that many UFO reports may arise from sightings of ball lightning); and in one instance a ball is said to have progressed silently down the centre of the table at a military dinner, harming in no way the startled officers on either side.

Ball lightning is occasionally called upon as the basis of a mechanism for spontaneous combustion. JG

Big Bang

Theory suggests that the *Universe originated a finite time ago in a hot, dense exploding fireball of matter and radiation. The observed rate of expansion of the Universe, indicated by the mutual recession of the galaxies, implies that the time which has elapsed since the Big Bang is between 10 and 20 billion years.

According to the 'standard model', the sequence of events was as follows. In the first instant, the Universe emerged from a singularity — a state of infinite compression concerning which we cannot even speculate intelligently. After about one millionth of a second the Universe consisted of a primeval 'soup' of particles of matter and particles of radiation (photons), the density being so high that particles and their antiparticles were forming and mutually annihilating in a continuous process (see *antimatter, *fundamental particles).

As the expansion continued, the rate of particle creation rapidly declined, and only those which avoided mutual annihilation survived to make up the present matter content of the Universe. The numbers of protons and neutrons were settled in the first hundredth of a second, while the electrons' numbers were determined by about ten seconds after the initial event. Some basic imbalance may have ensured the apparent dominance of matter over antimatter.

By the time the Universe was about three minutes old, the temperature had dropped to about a billion Kelvins (K) and conditions were favourable for the formation of helium; very quickly, the basic matter content of the Universe was converted almost entirely to a mixture of hydrogen and helium (nuclei) in much the same proportions which we see today (roughly 70 per cent hydrogen to 30 per cent helium). Thereafter, the primeval soup continued to expand and cool until, after about 700,000 years, the temperature had dropped to about 4,000 K, when electrons and protons could come together to form electrically neutral hydrogen atoms. Up to this time, the Universe had been opaque (i.e., radiation could not travel far before being absorbed), but with the formation of hydrogen atoms the primeval 'fog' cleared, and light was able to travel freely throughout the Universe.

The radiation released at that time had the same character as the radiation emitted by a hot body at 4,000 K to 3,000 K (i.e., it was blackbody radiation), but since then, because of the expansion and redshift, the radiation has cooled to about 3 K and shifted in wavelength from the visible to the microwave part of the spectrum (see *Universe, theories of).

Although the Big Bang is the most popular current theory, and is favoured by the balance of evidence, doubts and difficulties remain. IKMN

Black Holes

Black holes are theoretical objects believed to represent the ultimately compacted state of matter. In the immense gravitational fields of such objects, light and other forms of electromagnetic radiation — infrared, ultraviolet, radio, X-rays — are permanently trapped. Because light cannot escape, the objects are termed 'black holes'. This term refers to a physical condition rather than a true colour because black holes have *no* colour.

The concept is not a recent one. Black holes were first described — in terms of pure mathematical theory — by Laplace. He suggested that there might be bodies so massive and yet so compacted that the escape velocity at their surface might be greater than that of light. (The escape velocity of an object is determined by the object's mass and by its radius: the smaller the radius of a body with a given mass, the greater its escape velocity. Thus, if the Earth retained its present mass but shrank until it had only a quarter of its present radius, its escape velocity would double.) While Laplace was working with the physical laws as described by Newton rather than as described by Einstein, his basic idea is not unlike that held today.

In post-Einstein days, it was Karl Schwartzschild who first applied relativistic principles to massively compressed bodies. In 1917 he showed that such objects possess a critical radius: were it to be compressed further, the object would have an escape velocity equal to that of light, so that neither matter nor radiation could leave the object; once within this distance of the object everything would be eternally trapped.

This theoretical distance is generally known as the 'Schwartzschild radius'; the term 'event horizon' is often used for the surface defined by this radius since, if light cannot escape, an outside observer will be able to tell nothing about anything that occurs within it. If he dropped an object towards the black hole, all that he would be able to detect, at best, would be the frozen image of the object 'stuck' to the event horizon, lingering almost forever as the 'particles' of light struggled to free themselves from the gravitational field. (This is a 'thought experiment': the light would be infinitely redshifted.)

The degree of compression required to produce a black hole can be judged from the event horizons that the Earth and the Sun would have if they became black holes. The Earth has a mass of approximately 6,000,000,000,000,000,000,000 tons; nonetheless, were the planet to become a black hole, all this would be crammed into an 'object' a little under 2cm across. Even an object as large as the Sun would be, as a black hole, only about 6km 'across'.

If an object as compact as this were composed of solid matter the figures would be impressive enough: our hypothetical black-hole Earth would have a density of around 1,500,000,000,000,000,000,000 tons per cubic centimetre — the size of a sugar lump. But this is not the case. The size of a black hole is determined by its Schwartzschild radius; but the matter within does not fill the sphere so defined — indeed, there is, in fact, no matter there at all, for at the centre of the black hole all the matter that formed it in the first place has been crushed out of existence in a single point, the singularity. And all subsequent matter is similarly doomed. But the gravitational field *behaves as though the matter were still there*.

How, then, do black holes come about? The classic case is that of an exploding massive star — a supernova. When the star explodes the outer layers are given a tremendous 'kick' into space, where they form a pretty nebula such as that known as the Crab. Simultaneously, the inner layers are given a great 'kick' inwards; they may collapse uncontrollably until they pass the Schwartzschild radius for their mass.

There are other mechanisms for black-hole formation. The colossal pressures involved in the *Big Bang can hardly have failed to give rise to black holes. Even more important, black holes tend to coalesce: if you put two black holes close to each other you find that, after a while, they have swung together to form a single, larger, black hole. This has given rise to the suggestion that at the centres of galaxies, including our own, there are 'super black holes', arising from the combination of countless black holes formed as stars went supernova. Even more depressing is the thought that, possibly, the end of the Universe might be as a lightless hell of enormous black holes, all the stars and planets at last swallowed or their matter scattered isotropically through space. Of course, these black holes might combine to form one single unimaginable black hole, a description not unlike those of the original cosmic egg.

In the Big Bang there is no reason to believe that mini black holes were not formed: these might have the mass of, say, Mount Everest — about a billion tons, near enough — and a diameter somewhat less than that of a proton.

The idea that nothing escapes from a black hole has recently been modified by Stephen Hawking. He showed that particles *could* escape from black holes by a process known as quantum tunnelling: in its simplest terms, the intense gravitational field may be considered as 'grainy', possessing random patches which are weaker or stronger than average; particles which accidentally find themselves following a fortuitous succession of weak patches can tunnel their way through. In other words, while the *average* strength of the gravitational field is immense, there are below-average places where the occasional particle can sneak through. The overall result is indistinguishable from the one whereby 'particles' of heat leave a red-hot poker — although, in the case of a black hole, the effect is much less intense.

Hawking was further able to show that the event horizon of a massive black hole was disproportionately larger than that of a 'mini' black hole: that is, if you increase the mass of a black hole by a factor of x, the event horizon will increase by a factor of something more than x. This might suggest that larger black holes are losing a greater proportion of particles than smaller ones. Nevertheless, small black holes lose particles just like larger ones, and because the event horizon is disproportionately smaller these particles must be more energetic — i.e., hotter — in order to escape. So we can deduce that small black holes are very much hotter than large ones. For obvious reasons, they also have very much shorter lifetimes.

When the appropriate figures are worked out, a black hole of solar mass would have a surface temperature only one tenmillionth of a Kelvin above the Absolute Zero of cold; its lifetime would be some 50 billion billion billion billion billion billion times the 'currently accepted' age of the Universe. But a black hole with a lifetime comparable with that of the Universe — about 15 to 20 billion years — would have a mass about that of Mount Everest; at its event horizon, however, temperatures would be of the order of 120 *billion* Kelvins.

Well, if mini black holes have a lifetime approximately the age of the Universe, shouldn't we be able to find some evidence of their exploding as they die? For various reasons, we might be able to detect these cumulative explosions in the form of microwave radiation; unfortunately, searches have failed to detect such radiation, so far.

Larger black holes — of mass, say 0.5 to 100 times that of the Sun — are believed to arise from the supernova explosions of giant stars ranging in mass from about 5 to about 200 times that of the Sun; with stars of up to about 3 times the mass of the Sun, a *pulsar may be formed, but, if the star has a greater mass than this, it is thought that the core collapses so extensively that a black hole is formed.

It is obviously difficult to detect such an object. Or is it?

Although the content of the preceding paragraphs is still largely theoretical conjecture, there are good grounds for believing that the radio astronomical source Cassiopeia A is just such a remnant. It is known to have passed through the supernova stage comparatively recently, c AD 1668, and yet there are no contemporary records of what should have been an easily visible event in the night skies. Ioseph Shklovskii has suggested that this particular 'supernova' collapsed almost immediately to a black hole without any intermediate explosion and consequent observable (to us) outburst of light. He estimates that the original star must have had a mass about 20 times that of the Sun: at the collapse (and explosion) this would have decreased by about half — the other half being blasted off into space — so that there might be a mass about 3 times that of the Sun now trapped in the central regions. His theory is being examined with interest.

Nevertheless, if little or nothing can escape from a black hole, how can one possibly hope to detect one? Well, matter falling into a black hole is believed to give off radiation — its final protest, as it were. In particular, it should, according to theory, give off X-rays.

And another black-hole candidate is Cygnus X-1. This object is now known to be a binary star system. The visible component is a blue giant star of mass about 30 times that of the Sun, but it is orbited by an *invisible* component whose mass is about 8.5 times that of the Sun. This invisible object is far too massive to be a white dwarf star or a *pulsar and, moreover, the system is a prolific source of X-rays. The emission of X-rays is thought to be from material which has been 'sucked' off the visible star to form a flat accretion disc around the black hole companion — think of the waters around the centre of a whirlpool — until it finally vanishes down the black hole's gravitational throat, in just the same way that bath water disappears.

Several other such systems have been detected, but the invisible component of the binary star system Cygnus X-1 remains the best candidate to date.

We have mentioned already super black holes. Enormous black holes of mass 100 million or so times that of the Sun may be responsible for the gigantic energies that power *quasars. And we have mentioned the idea that galaxies may have giant black holes at their centres: at the heart of our own Milky Way there appears to be an unusual X-ray source. Martin Rees, who considers that it might be a black hole about a billion kilometres in diameter, describes it elegantly as 'a unique object in a unique place'.

The intense spacetime distortion produced by black holes has led some authorities to consider them as 'gravitational gateways' linking one part of the Universe with another. The reasoning is roughly as follows. If you fall into a stationary black hole there is only one possible destination: the singularity at its centre, where you will be crushed out of existence. However, stars spin and so it seems reasonable to assume that black holes spin also. A spacecraft heading into a spinning black hole can adopt a course which does not take it to the singularity. In Iain Nicolson's words: '... if the spacecraft falls in and does not get crushed up, yet cannot re-emerge from the black hole into our own Universe, it must end up somewhere else!' That 'somewhere else' could be a distant region of our Universe, in which case we have instantaneous *interstellar travel. (Or it could be in an *alternate universe, which is perhaps even more exciting. But there are grave doubts about the models.)

At one end of the 'tunnel' or 'wormhole', then, would be a black hole, at the other a *white hole, a cosmic gusher out of which would pour the matter and energy which is busily vanishing down the gullet of the black hole. If the spacecraft and its crew survive the colossal gravitational whirlpool, they face two further problems. Firstly, at a white hole objects would be mutually repelled at a velocity approaching that of light. Our crewmen would thus face the rather daunting prospect of finding their constituent atoms spread equally all over the Universe.

Assuming this problem is circumvented, there is still a second one: how does the crew get home? Unless there is a black hole near to the white hole from which they have emerged — a coincidence difficult to contemplate — they will just have to remain in whatever part of the Universe (or multiverse) they find themselves in, with the knowledge that any message sent home to describe their position will possibly take millions of years in transit. Some writers — for example, Adrian Berry — have suggested that the solution to this problem lies in the building of black holes, an idea which is not beyond the bounds of conceivable technology: push enough interstellar material together using modified ramjets, allow gravity to play its part, stand well clear, and you have a black hole. Simple — well, in theory.

But surely Einstein said that faster-than-light travel was impossible? Yes, but Einstein's *Relativity was dealing with 'normal' space and time. The properties of the interior of a black or white hole are largely matters of conjecture — especially since *white holes, which should be rather noticeable, have yet to be detected — but conditions should be sufficiently different from those of ordinary space to allow faster-than-light or even instantaneous travel as perfectly respectable concepts.

Almost all of our discussion has been based on the supposition that black holes exist. Although a number of likely candidates are known, the hypothesis has yet to be finally proven. Much work remains to be done before the existence of black holes is confirmed. However, both theoretical and practical advances continue to be made in this, one of the most exciting areas of frontier cosmology. The possible existence of black holes is rapidly becoming an overwhelming probability. ATL & JG

Continuous Creation

The Steady State Theory of the *Universe relies upon the hypothesis that everywhere matter is being created out of nothing. This may seem improbable, but is it any more in conflict with common sense than the suggestion that the Universe erupted into existence from nowhere in a single event (see *Big Bang)? Moreover, the amount of newly created matter required is not very great; Hoyle's classic *Frontiers of Astronomy* stated: '... one hydrogen atom must originate every second in a cube with a 160 kilometre side; or stated somewhat differently ... about one atom every century in a volume equal to the Empire State Building.' Hoyle regarded the process as actually being *responsible* for the recession of the galaxies: as matter came into existence, space itself was forced to stretch to accommodate.

While the Steady State Theory is aesthetically appealing, it seems to have failed a number of crucial tests — tests which alternative theories have passed — and is now not generally accepted. Evolutionary theories of the *Universe do not require continuous creation so, by Occam's Razor, it seems highly unlikely that the process occurs.

However, theory does suggest that there *is* a mechanism whereby matter can pop into existence from nowhere. It is called pair creation (see *fundamental particles). The process is believed to occur only rarely, if at all, and certainly could not be responsible for matter creation on the scale required by the Steady State Theory; but it does show that our common sense misleads us when it makes us reject out of hand the creation of matter 'from nowhere'. JG

Cosmologies, Unorthodox

For the purpose of this article, let me define 'unorthodox cosmologies' as those models of the Universe which appear to have no basis in accepted scientific fact. This is not to say that those models are necessarily totally fallacious — a medieval scholar would consider our *Big Bang model highly improbable — but simply that these cosmologies have no place in our established body of knowledge.

In historical terms, the most important early model of the Universe was the geocentric one. There were various versions of this, but typically the Earth, which lay at the centre of the Universe (and generally was flat — see *flat Earth), was surrounded by a number of concentric spheres in which were embedded the various celestial bodies. Seven of these were associated with objects in the Solar System — closest was that of the Moon, then those of Mercury, Venus, the Sun, Mars, Jupiter and finally Saturn (the planets Uranus, Neptune and Pluto were not discovered until very much later). Beyond was the sphere of the fixed stars.

All of these spheres rotated about the Earth in their own peculiar ways, and considerable effort was expended in calculating their motions. Moreover, the motions of Mars, Jupiter and Saturn displayed an alarming oddity: every now and then, the planet concerned would halt in its

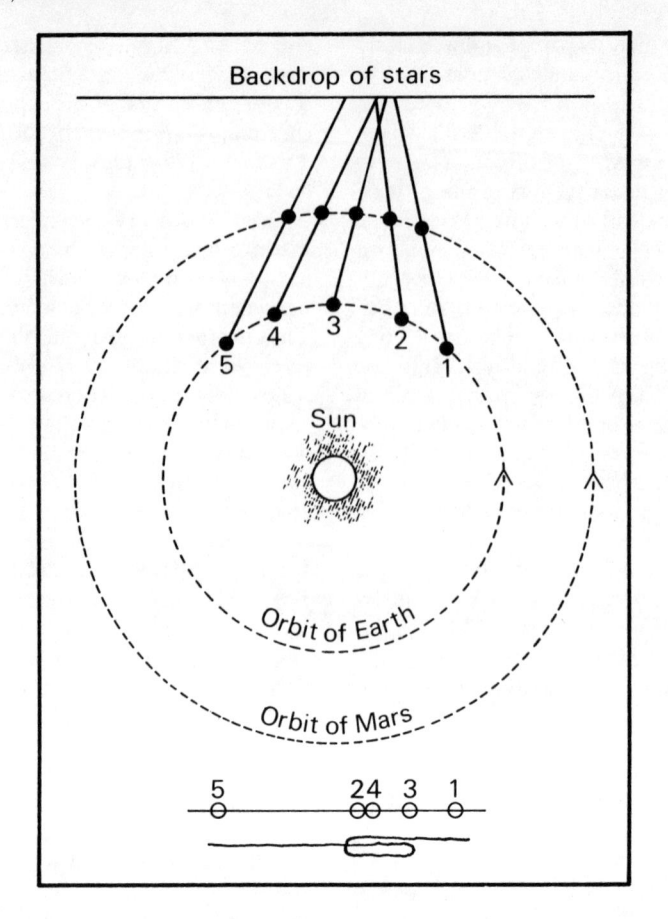

Figure 3 *Why the outer planets sometimes appear to 'loop' in the sky, as seen from Earth. Earth travels more swiftly around its orbit than does Mars, so that at the five positions shown in the upper part of the diagram the position of Mars against the backdrop of stars is as shown in the lower part of the diagram — and thus the planet appears to be moving, for a while, in a retrograde direction before turning once again to continue in its customary direction.*

steady progress across the background of the fixed stars, travel in the opposite direction for a while, and then continue along its previous path. In order to explain this, it was proposed that the planets concerned moved on epicycles, small circles whose centres lay on the rotating spheres. By adjusting the proposed speeds of rotation of the epicycle and of the sphere, reasonable approximations to the motions of the planets could be obtained. When these were not enough, it was suggested that the centre of each of the large circles be set at a little distance from the Earth.

This sort of system was not the only model in the ancient world. Leaving aside such notions as the flat Earth supported on the backs of elephants, we have the suggestion of the Pythagoreans (or so it seems — they were a secretive and mystic lot) that the Earth and other planets travelled around the Sun, which itself travelled around a 'central fire' at the centre of the Universe; and the surprisingly modern proposals, some 200 years later, of Aristarchus, which were not dissimilar from those of Copernicus. In addition, the Pythagoreans, who were obsessed with music and with number and ratio, proposed that the spheres were at distances proportional to the harmonic lengths of a vibrating string — hence the idea of the music of the spheres.

In most of the ancient cosmologies there were two fundamental axioms: while the Earth was the region of transient phenomena, sin and decay, the heavens were eternal, pure and uniform; and, since the heavens had this nature, the only allowable type of motion to be displayed was uniform and circular. It was for this reason that the increasingly complicated systems — more and more epicycles had to be invoked — were adhered to. It is interesting to note that Copernicus' heliocentric system initially required *more* epicycles than the best of the contemporary geocentric models.

There are still a few, a very few, subscribers to such ideas; most modern proponents of unorthodox cosmologies pay at least lip service to more realistic theories of the *Universe.

But not all. In his entertaining *Can You Speak Venusian?* Patrick Moore details a number of extremely unconventional ideas of the Universe. In one, the stars are merely an optical illusion. The Universe is bordered in all directions by, as it were, crumpled baking foil. The only star is the Sun, but we can see its reflections in the crumpled foil; some of these reflections are extremely distorted, while others are, of course, apparently at different distances because the light from the Sun has been reflected several times off different crinkles in the foil before returning to us.

That particular cosmology has few supporters. Others have been more influential. The World Ice theory of Hörbiger was of considerable importance in Nazi Germany. It claimed that the majority of the free matter in the Universe is in the form of frozen water. Chunks of this ice quite frequently fall into stars, and the result is an immense explosion; the material cast out from the star in such an event is available to form a planetary system. Moreover, he held that smaller bodies do not orbit larger ones in the way that we accept, but that they slowly spiral inwards. Thus the Earth has been subject to periodic catastrophes as moons which it has captured have crashed down to the surface; the next, and rather major, cataclysm will occur when our present Moon impacts. It seems hardly surprising that these ideas were greeted enthusiastically by Hitler and Himmler, anxious to discredit the theories of *Relativity put forward by the Jewish Einstein.

Another theory which has had intermittent bursts of popularity over the decades is that the Earth is hollow, ingress to the interior being possible via holes at the poles (in recent years a montage of satellite photographs of the Earth's north polar regions has been triumphantly acclaimed as showing such a hole; in fact, the apparent 'hole' is due to the fact that none of the shots showed the extreme northerly parts of the region, so that in the photomontage there is a blank space in the middle). The idea in its modern form probably originated with John Cleves Symmes in the early nineteenth century; he crusaded in the USA for his theory, and was probably the author, as Captain Adam Seaborn, of a novel called *Symzonia: A Voyage of Discovery* (1820) which told of a utopian civilization within the hollow Earth. (Earlier fantasies which used the device of the hollow Earth include Casanova's *Icosaméron*.) Supporters of the theory today are far more numerous than one might expect; some believe that the interior of the Earth, rather than outer space, is the source of *UFOs.

An extremely interesting variant was proposed by Cyrus Reed Teed (also called 'Koresh'). In this we live on the inside, not the outside, of a sphere, which contains also the Sun and the planets. The idea is an entrancing one, if rather swiftly disprovable. On the basis of it, Teed founded a quasi-religious organization of 'Koreshan Unity' which survived until after World War II. (Once again, the Nazis toyed with this theory.)

The number of unorthodox cosmologies is probably almost equal to the number of what Patrick Moore calls 'independent thinkers'. Some are worked out in considerable detail: every publisher in the world several times a year receives (lengthy) new expositions of 'the Truth' — most of which never see the light of day.

To select just one that did. In his *The Radiant Universe* George Hill, accepting that the idea of the luminiferous aether is defunct, is nevertheless unable to accept that the Universe can carry on without *some* such medium. According to him: 'A form of radiation, (energy propagation), is a reality throughout all space whether such space is occupied by matter or not. This radiation is of a texture, (frequency and amplitude), exceedingly fine. The very existence of this radiation is undetectable due to restrictions imposed upon us by the nature of matter. This radiation cannot be isolated as it permeates all space, all matter, and is the reservoir from which all energy is drawn and to which all energy is eventually returned. All else is but a manifestation of change of this energy. Matter itself is but the position of change of this radiation to forms of greater wavelength. All other forms of radiation are effects of the functioning of this basic property of matter as the seat of change in this Basic Radiation and this radiation is maintained by all other forms of radiant energy. Hence Basic Radiation maintains matter; matter maintains Basic Radiation.' This is typical of the opacity of many unorthodox cosmologies.

One, however, has in this century produced several best-selling books and has millions of supporters. The ideas of Immanuel Velikovsky seek to explain events recorded in mythology or in the scriptures in terms of violent and catastrophic events in the Solar System. He suggests that Venus was originally a comet erupted a few thousand years ago from Jupiter. As this comet fell towards the Sun it became gravitationally involved with the Earth several times; swooping backwards and forwards, it naturally affected the Earth — for example, at one point the Earth ceased in its rotation (explaining the section in *Joshua* where the Sun and the Moon stood still); the Red Sea was divided; and the desert was showered with hydrocarbons, which the Israelites ate and called 'manna' (presumably Velikovsky intends carbohydrates, or cannot tell the difference.

His first book, *Worlds in Collision*, was the subject of an almost hysterical scientific rejection, and this no doubt contributed more than anything to its popularity.

In the Preface to a much later edition of this book Velikovsky states that his thesis has passed two vital tests: he had predicted that Venus would be anomalously hot because of its extreme youth, and had been proved correct; and he had said that its atmosphere should be rich in hydrocarbons (carbohydrates?), an idea proved correct when *Mariner 2* flew by the planet at the end of 1962.

His prediction of Venus' high surface temperature *was* correct, although he had not been the first to make it. But his reasons are flawed in that, while Venus *may* be rather younger than the other planets, it is nevertheless over 4 *billion* years old, not a few thousand — its formation thus antedates the appearance of life on Earth, let alone the appearance of the Israelites. And his second prediction failed the vital test: *Mariner 2* did *not* detect the presence of a thick hydrocarbon layer in Venus' atmosphere, although, owing to a misunderstanding at a press conference, it was widely and erroneously reported that it had.

That Velikovsky's ideas should have so many supporters despite their being quite blatantly inaccurate is an interesting comment on our society. Do we seek in pseudoscience a new form of religion? Or do we simply enjoy thinking that perhaps all those scientists are wrong? JG

Extraterrestrial Intelligence

The idea that there exist intelligent beings elsewhere in the Universe has a long history. The most frequently cited early writing in which intelligent extraterrestrials appear is *The True History* of Lucian of Samosata, from the second century AD: in this satirical 'fantastic voyage' there is a war between Endymion, King of the Moon, and Phaeton, King of the Sun. It would be impossible to list all the works produced since then which have, for satirical, philosophical or other reasons, postulated inhabitants of other worlds. As the

Earth lost its uniqueness and it was realized that other planets were, indeed, other worlds, so the enthusiasm and unselectiveness with which intelligent beings were allocated to the various celestial objects (especially to *Mars) increased. Sir William Herschel, a notable astronomer, declared that even on the Sun there was life — intelligent life, organized in a society much like Earth's! And Constantine Rafinesque, in an edition of Thomas Wright's *An Original Theory and New Hypothesis of the Universe* published in 1837, described 'worlds of bliss, where Beings fly through the dense atmosphere, as birds do in our Aerial one, or we conceive Angels may — where they and WE ALSO may assume every variety of lovely shapes, the agency of GOD himself being the vehicle that carries there our immortal souls, through unfathomable Space and Time, in the lapse of a moment, to be happy forever'.

Modern students of xenobiology are less inclined towards flights of fancy. They consider it compellingly likely that there exist many other technological civilizations in the Universe, basing their arguments on astrophysics, biochemistry, evolution and statistics.

Before one can consider how solar systems form, it is wise to try to find out if other stars do, indeed, possess planetary retinues. Such investigations have been carried out, the best known being Peter Van de Kamp's studies of Barnard's Star. This star, about 6 light years distant and of brightness only about 0.00045 that of the Sun, has a very high component of motion across our line of sight. Van de Kamp has carried out numerous studies of the wobbles in the star's track, and ascribes these to the existence of two large planets, one of roughly the same mass as Jupiter, the other about half that. (Various other estimates exist.) Similar studies of other stars suggest that planetary retinues are the rule rather than the exception.

Theoretical models of the events taking place inside a gaseous nebula as it collapses to form a star and planetary retinue suggest that other solar systems may be not unlike our own. As the cloud contracts it adopts a disc-shaped configuration, spinning rapidly. The outer regions are extremely cold, and here particles of ice, frozen gases and rocky materials aggregate to form large bodies of rock and ice like the planets Uranus and Neptune. Closer in the gas is warmer, so that rocky fragments have lost their associated frozen gases; the larger fragments travel more swiftly than the smaller ones, since they are less affected by drag within the gas, and 'sweep out' an area of the cloud to form a large rocky body surrounded by gases pulled from the cloud by straightforward gravitational attraction. Jupiter and Saturn are such bodies. Still closer in the gas is yet warmer, and convection interferes with the process of accumulation, so that smaller rocky bodies, unable to cling to much of the primordial gases, are formed. These are planets like Mercury, Venus, Earth and Mars, whose atmospheres are mainly formed by secondary processes after the initial planetary formation.

If such models are correct, we can expect most single stars to have planetary retinues which are not unlike the Solar System. This implies that there are many planets which are not wildly dissimilar from the Earth in terms of composition and distance from the primary star. In other words, there are concentrations of the elements essential for life as we know it to be found in environments where temperatures are suitable for the operation of life processes.

But, just because there are so many bricks lying around, can we confidently expect to find a wall? The answer seems to be yes. A number of experiments have been carried out in which mixtures of gases (typically hydrogen, methane, ammonia and water), thought to resemble the mixture present in the Earth's primitive atmosphere, have been subjected to electric discharges (analogous to lightning). The various organic compounds which have been thus produced include, notably, amino acids, as well as fatty acids, monosaccharides and porphyrins. (More recently, it has been proposed that the Earth's primeval atmosphere was probably largely carbon dioxide and water, and the experiments have been repeated, with similar results, using such a mixture.) Further experiments with amino acids have demonstrated that from this starting point 'proteinoid microspheres' can be produced. Sidney Fox has examined the behaviour of solutions of amino acids evaporated on a bed of hot lava and subjected to various indignities, and has discovered that spherical structures not unlike living cells are produced. Moreover, suitable treatment can cause these globules to grow and divide (although it should be stressed that they are *not* living cells). Further evidence that this pre-life chemical evolution is common has come from meteorite studies (discussed under *panspermia).

It may be thought a long leap from protolife to life: it is all very well producing cell-like proteinoid microspheres, but why can't these experiments produce cells? The reason is, of course, time; give the exobiologist a few hundred million years and he will produce cells galore.

If Earth-like planets are abundant, and the elements present on them make it probable that life will emerge, can we expect intelligence automatically to result? Here we are on far shakier ground. Clearly, intelligence is an evolutionary survival factor — witness ourselves and the dolphins — but it is only one of many. What we *can* assert with a degree of confidence is that it is such a powerful survival factor that, once it has appeared, it has a good chance of surviving — assuming it does not develop a technology with which to wipe itself out.

We have absolutely no idea as to how many intelligent civilizations with a technology comparable with or superior to ours, and with whom communication may be possible, currently exist in the Galaxy. But attempts *have* been made to derive possible figures, the best known being the equation concocted by Frank Drake:

$$N = R_* f_p n_e f_l f_i f_c L,$$

where N is the number, R_* the average rate of formation of stars in the Galaxy, f_p the fraction of stars which have planetary retinues, n_e the number of planets per retinue where there is an environment suitable for life, f_l the fraction of such planets where life actually does appear, f_i the fraction of those planets where intelligence emerges, f_c the fraction of civilizations which develop the ability and desire to communicate with others, and L the average lifetime of such civilizations. Clearly, our estimates of each of these terms become vaguer as we move from N to L. Indeed, one must question the equation's value, since it is perfectly possible that there are other important factors of which we know nothing; moreover, values for most of the terms can be more or less randomly ascribed — varying L alone gives values for N anywhere from millions down to one: us.

Assuming for the moment, and for no logical reason, that communicating civilizations are abundant enough for their separations to be of the order of a thousand light years, we are faced with the problem of how to communicate with our neighbours (see *CETI, *SETI, *von Neumann probes). Even if we are successful in our search for the right radio frequency, or whatever medium They may be using for communication, there are two far greater problems, two colossal barriers to communication.

The first of these is concerned with the nature of intelligence, something of which we know little. It is almost certainly Earth-chauvinist to suggest that there is some sort of universality about the nature of intelligence — i.e., that there is only one 'type' of intelligence. If we accept one of the briefest of the many attempted definitions of intelligence, 'the general ability to solve problems', we can hope that different 'types' of intelligence can at least have common ground in that there must be shared problems, and the solutions to any particular problem depend not only upon the nature of the intelligence discovering the solution but also upon the problem itself. For example, if the problem is to get from one side of a wall to the other, there is a finite number of solutions, one of which *must* be selected by the intelligent entity (assuming he is material and can recognize a wall when he sees one); the solution he selects will, to a certain extent, mould the nature of his intelligence. That said, it is, nevertheless, fairly safe to assume that alien intelligences will be exactly that — of a nature entirely alien to our own. In particular, we have no reason to believe that extraterrestrial intelligences have any desire to communicate with each other or with us. (See *CETI.)

The second difficulty is that we must be one of the youngest, if not *the* youngest, civilization in the Galaxy with the ability and desire to communicate. We have possessed the ability for only a few decades, while it is likely that some civilizations gained it as much as several *billion* years ago (assuming they still survive). Consider that you could go back to speak with your parents at the time of your birth; clearly, you would have very great difficulty describing the world of today to them, because progress has been such that many axioms have changed. And that is over a few decades! Attempts to communicate with a civilization 1,000 years 'ahead' of us may prove to be difficult to the point of impossibility, and yet such a civilization may be a close neighbour to ours on the developmental time-scale. Even if there is some sort of universal 'uniformity of mind', time itself may prove an insuperable barrier.

Could machine intelligences act as intermediaries? That is, could our computers speak with Their computers, and deliver comprehensible data to us on the one hand and to Them on the other? This is possible, since it is difficult for us to evaluate the extent to which computer design is affected by the nature of the intelligence responsible for constructing the computer. This slender chance is the basis for the idea of the *von Neumann probe.

Our conclusions must then seem, superficially, rather depressing. Either we are alone in the Universe, in fact or in effect, or the Universe is teeming with intelligences of our 'type', in which latter case we are one of the most junior and negligible of all.

Yet this should not divert us from the quest. The search itself cannot fail to lead us to a greater understanding of the nature of that most alien creature of all, ourselves. If we find that we are, indeed, alone in the Universe then we will be forced to realize our own importance and the sanctity of the gift which we have been given, to forget our childish toys and concerns. And if we should ever make contact with another civilization, then the mere encounter may well be the most important and beneficial event to affect mankind since first we descended from the trees. JG

Flat Earth

In 1895 a Scottish faith-healer named John Alexander Dowie founded the Christian Apostolic Church in Zion, Illinois; ten years later he was forcibly removed from office and replaced by Wilbur Glenn Voliva, a man with paranoid delusions of grandeur, who insisted that the Earth was flat because the Bible seems to say so. Voliva claimed the Earth is a flat disc with the North Pole in the centre and the South Pole spread around the edges; a wall of ice and snow prevents ships from sailing off the edge. He insisted the Sun is only about 5,000km away, and about 50km across.

Nevertheless, the town of Zion seems to have flourished under his direction, and it became a multimillion dollar industry. He predicted the end of the world on a number of occasions, and was apparently unconcerned when it failed to materialize; he also predicted that he would live to be 120 — in fact, he died in 1942, in his seventies.

The ancient Greeks knew that the Earth was a globe (see *cosmologies, unorthodox). Yet St Augustine and Luther both objected that the Earth must be flat, or those living on the underside would not see the descent of Christ on the Day of Judgement. Even today, in the age of the space rocket and round-the-world jet, a small band of flat-Earthers maintains the views of Voliva, and rejects 2,500 years of science. CW

Fundamental Particles

The problem of subatomic goings-on arose late in the nineteenth century; the discovery of the *electron* (1897) and *proton*

(1898–1910, though not named until 1920) first hinted at the complexity underlying the simple concept 'atom'. By 1911 we had the notion of a central nucleus with orbiting electrons, only requiring the *neutron*'s 1932 discovery to give a new understanding of atoms as being composed of protons, neutrons and orbiting electrons ...

But by then theorists were predicting new particles. The massless *neutrino* was predicted in 1931–4 and appeared in 1956; the *positron* or anti-electron, predicted in 1930–1, was found in 1932; to explain strong proton-neutron interactions, the *meson* was requested in 1935 and duly discovered in 1936 — only it proved to be the wrong sort and was dubbed the *muon*, the required *pion* being found in 1947. Such unwanted particles kept appearing; in 1962 a new neutrino was found which was somehow linked with muons, as normal neutrinos were linked with electrons. It also became apparent that every particle had its *antiparticle* (see *antimatter). Thanks to high-energy accelerators, which slam particles together to synthesize new ones, subatomic species were appearing faster than theory could account for them.

Fresh quantum numbers were proposed to 'explain' why some particle interactions mysteriously failed to occur. For example, one of the older and more trustworthy quantum numbers is 'baryon number': heavy particles (*baryons*) like protons and neutrons had baryon number 1, antiprotons and antineutrons were −1, lighter particles like electrons scored zero; and the overall baryon number should stay constant. So two protons (combined baryon number $1+1=2$) colliding with sufficient force could spawn three protons and an antiproton $(1+1+1-1=2)$ but never two protons and an antiproton $(1+1-1=1)$. Other quantum numbers, with whimsical names like 'strangeness', operated less simply.

In this chaos it was hoped that all particles might obey simple, underlying laws. In 1961 the 'eightfold way' classification was suggested, whereby particles were arranged into groups of 1, 8 (most often — hence the name), 10 or 27 members. New particles were required to fill blank spaces in the proposed patterns; one was obligingly filled by the *omega particle* in 1964. Sometimes it seemed that physicists were creating the subatomic universe around them, forcing new particles into existence to obey their theories.

Further simplification came in 1964 with the invention of three *quarks*, hypothetical particles with hitherto unthinkable fractional charge and baryon number, which with their antiparticles could be assembled in various ways to construct all known baryons and mesons. A fourth quark was added to explain new anomalies; this introduced the delightful quantum number 'charm'. Further speculations required that the four quarks come in three different 'colours'; simplifying theories were themselves becoming labyrinthine while, despite promising experiments, no one could definitely locate a lone quark.

The present tentative 'bootstrap' theories avoid the need for quarks by merely suggesting that particles behave *as though quarks existed*. Each particle is defined by the interactions of all the others. There is no underlying 'reality'; the theory holds itself up by its own bootstraps.

But what *is* a particle? Perhaps only a ripple in something called the quantum field, with as much separate reality as an individual ocean wave. An early quantum-theory discovery was that particles could, indeed, behave like wave motions. Interactions involve 'virtual' particles, imaginary quantum-field ripples which, under certain conditions, can become particles in their own right: virtual pions play this part in baryon interactions, and in high-energy collisions can escape as real ones. Virtual particle-antiparticle pairs are constantly appearing and disappearing (pair creation) and can become real: high-energy gamma radiation passing through matter can generate electron-positron pairs; while it seems that intense gravitational fields near small *black holes can force virtual particles into reality, effectively by grabbing one member of the pair so the other cannot recombine with it and vanish.

Loose ends still abound ... *Tachyons

are hypothetical particles travelling faster than light. Neutrinos, by definition massless, may prove to have a tiny mass after all, with vast cosmological implications: much of the Universe's mass could be locked up in neutrinos. *Antimatter, made wholly from antiparticles, seems strangely rare, and this casts new light on events during the *Big Bang. And *black holes are bad news in that almost all quantum number conservation laws break down within them — to the vexation of those who thought the laws universally true. DRL

Galactic Club

If there are extraterrestrial civilizations, where are they all? One answer is that, if They know about us, They might deliberately refrain from replying. Ronald Bracewell has suggested that there may exist a Galactic Club, an alliance of intelligent lifeforms quite accustomed to the emergence of new civilizations. Being accustomed, they would also be expert, and would be concerned not to destroy an emergent civilization by too early a contact: there are numerous examples in our own, recent, history of primitive cultures being destroyed by contact with more advanced ones. It has been suggested that, if the Galactic Club is aware of us, it may be waiting until we can cope with problems such as population growth and our bellicosity, either of which may destroy our civilization, before considering us fit for contact (see *CETI), just as people must achieve certain educational standards before qualifying for entry to a university. JG

Hyperspace

This idea probably dates back to 1934, when the term was used by John W. Campbell Jr in his story *The Mightiest Machine*. It was introduced in an attempt to make faster-than-light travel more credible. Hyperspace is a 'type' of space in which objects are far more closely separated than they are in our 'normal' space: thus, one could switch one's ship into hyperspace, travel a short distance, re-emerge into 'normal' space, and therefore have made the journey in a short time without apparently having violated Special *Relativity. In fact, one would have violated *causality. Nonetheless, the idea is not a useless one, especially since it is now realized that within the event horizon of a *black hole there lies a special 'type' of space to which Relativity need not apply.

JG

Mars

That Mars, in common with all other celestial objects, including the Sun, might be the home of civilization is an old idea: when in 1609 Galileo saw, using the newly invented telescope, that the Moon was a world and inferred that the other planets were also, it rapidly became common belief that *all* celestial objects were inhabited by intelligent beings. Herschel and Arago were two eminent scientists who went on record as saying that they thought that the Sun was inhabited by civilized beings.

But it was Schiaparelli who threw the cat among the pigeons. Observing Mars between 1877 and 1881 he became convinced that on the planet's disc he could see a complex pattern of straight lines. These he called *canali*, channels, which was mistranslated into English as 'canals'. Although many astronomers observing Mars could not see the lines, the idea that a dying Martian civilization, desperate for water, had built enormous canals to transport water from the polar icecaps caught on, and remained popular for a remarkably long period of time (see *Tunguska event). Flammarion and Lowell were the two most notable proponents of the idea.

Already, in 1971, when the NASA probe *Mariner 9* approached Mars, the existence of a Martian civilization seemed a lost cause. This probe sent back photographs which showed that the surface of Mars is inhospitable in the extreme — craters, extinct volcanoes, deserts, endless areas of dust. But there are features which look like dried-up river gorges. Could there have been past life on Mars? Could there still be lowly life on Mars? The likely widespread existence of water in the past makes both ideas tenable.

In 1976 two *Viking* craft landed on

Mars, one of their priority experiments being the testing of the soil for microbial life. The results are controversial in that some tests indicate a total lack of life whereas others point to lifeforms with extremely rapid metabolisms — the sort of muddled results one might expect when dealing with organisms not of this Earth.

Are there Martians? Possibly, but not the ancient civilized race that Lowell and the others envisaged — they might be not unlike terrestrial bacteria. One recalls H.G. Wells' *The War of the Worlds*, in which terrestrial bacteria successfully account for the invading Martians (Orson Welles' 1938 radio adaptation caused widespread panic): could Martian bacteria devastate we invading Earthmen? JG

Neutron Soup

The atom is made up mostly of empty space: according to one popular analogy, an atom the size of an Olympic stadium would have a nucleus the size of a pea. When stars collapse (see *black holes, *pulsars) enormous gravitational forces come into play, and these may be great enough to squash the atoms of collapsing matter so thoroughly that this empty space is eliminated: electrons are rammed onto the protons (see *fundamental particles) and their charges cancelled out, forming neutrons; thus the collapsed matter is packed into a small ball of 'neutron soup'.

Neutron soup is so dense that a piece the size of a sugar cube would have a mass of nearly 1,000,000,000 tons — about the same as a decade's production of the US automobile industry. JG

Oscillating Universe

Will the *Universe continue to expand forever? Or will it eventually begin to contract and finally end in a Big Crunch?

The answer depends on the relationship between two factors: the amount of matter in the Universe; and Hubble's Constant (the rate of recession of one galaxy from another divided by the distance between them). The more matter there is in the Universe, the greater the gravitational forces working to slow down the expansion; the lower the value of Hubble's Constant, the less effective are these gravitational forces (the further away you are from a gravitational field, the less will be its 'pull' on you). Oscillating *Universe theories suggest that the amount of matter is high enough and Hubble's Constant low enough for the Universe eventually to collapse in upon itself, this to be 'followed' by a new cycle, initiated by a new *Big Bang. Values for the two factors are still not well known, and so oscillating models have in recent years periodically enjoyed favour and suffered rejection. (See also *alternate universes, *time-symmetric Universe.)

In 1980, a team of Russian scientists announced that the neutrino (see *fundamental particles), hitherto thought to be massless, might actually have a *very small* mass. If this is the case then, since neutrinos are very common, it would seem that there is enough mass in the Universe to validate the oscillating model. JG

Ozma, Project

In 1960 a team of US radio astronomers led by Frank Drake at the National Radio Observatory, Green Bank, 'listened' to the stars Tau Ceti and Epsilon Eridani for signs of intelligent radio transmission. (Tau Ceti is just under 12 light years distant, and has a luminosity a little less than half that of the Sun's; for Epsilon Eridani the figures are 10.7 light years, 0.3 of the luminosity.) The equipment was sensitive enough to detect a transmission of 1 million watts beamed through a 200m dish at those distances; the researchers were 'listening' at the 21cm hydrogen wavelength. Total listening time was under 200 hours.

No one expected a positive result, and there was none. The purpose of this small, inexpensive, initial experiment was merely to demonstrate the principle of an idea. Sadly, it did not mark the start of a planned (and funded) search using more sensitive equipment and examining further stars (see *SETI).

The project was, of course, named after Oz, the magic land created by L. Frank Baum. JG

Continued on page 193

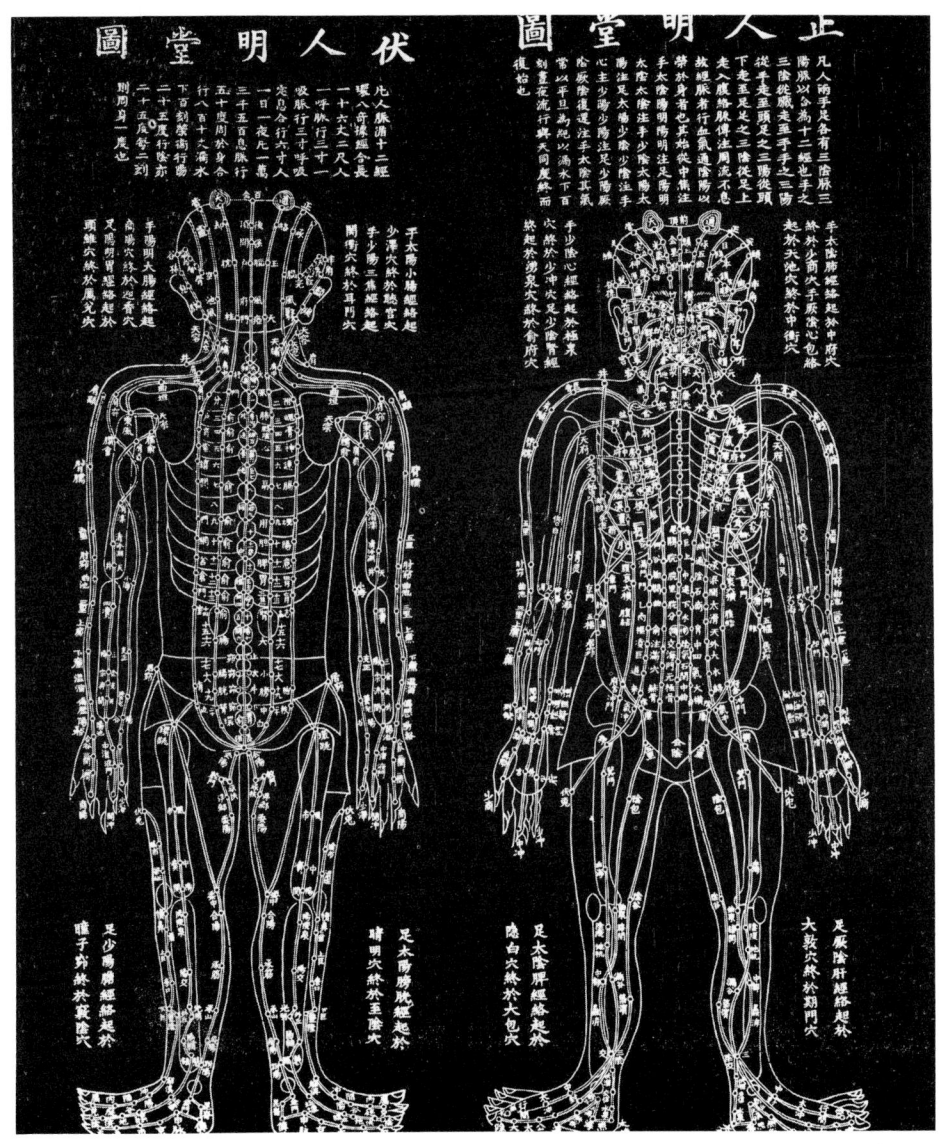

The ancient oriental science of acupuncture involves the placing of needles at various 'nerve centres', of which there are a large number distributed about the body. This Chinese version of a chart whose precise antiquity is unknown maps the various points on the front and back of the body. (See page 123.)

Left, above and below: That automatic writing (see page 125) actually occurs is indisputable, but whether it is merely an unconscious action or, as is more frequently claimed, a means of receiving communications from 'beyond' is a matter of some debate. *Above:* the medium (see page 140) Geraldine Cummins in the process of automatic writing; *below:* script produced in 1898 by Hélène Smith, who claimed that the writing was Martian (see page 175).

Right: Reports of human beings being able to lift themselves bodily from the ground come from all ages. By far the most rigorously documented levitator must be the nineteenth-century medium Daniel Dunglas Home, who counted levitation as but one of his many dramatic feats (see page 138).

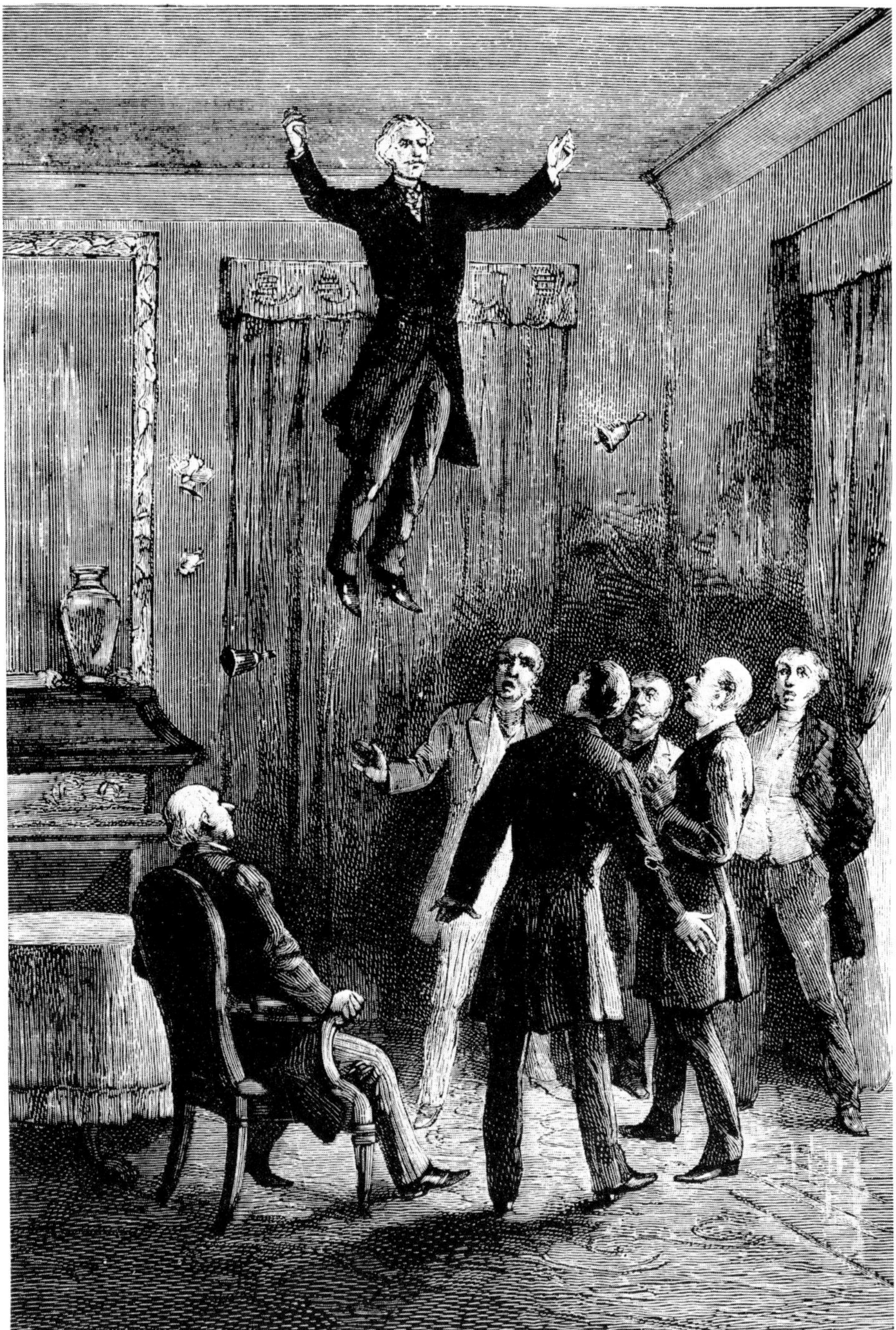

Although the term 'peak experience' was coined in the 1950s by Maslow, the concept has been known in various guises to many other thinkers, both before and since. This attempt to portray the intense feeling of a peak experience — 'The Self in Ecstasy' by Austin Osman Spare — dates from 1909; the figure at the back is that of the artist himself. (See page 143.)

Above: Poltergeists are extremely well documented phenomena, and there are a number of extant photographs of their activities. Although these photographs could in theory have been faked, it seems unlikely that so many independent photographers, many of them from the press, should be part of a single conspiracy. This photograph, taken in 1970, shows some of the disturbances centring on a sixteen-year-old typist working for a company in Leeds, Yorkshire. (See page 146.)

Left: A photograph taken in 1867 by William Mumler which shows Lincoln's wife with, behind her, what appears to be the ghost of Lincoln himself. Lincoln died, of course, in 1865. (See page 152.)

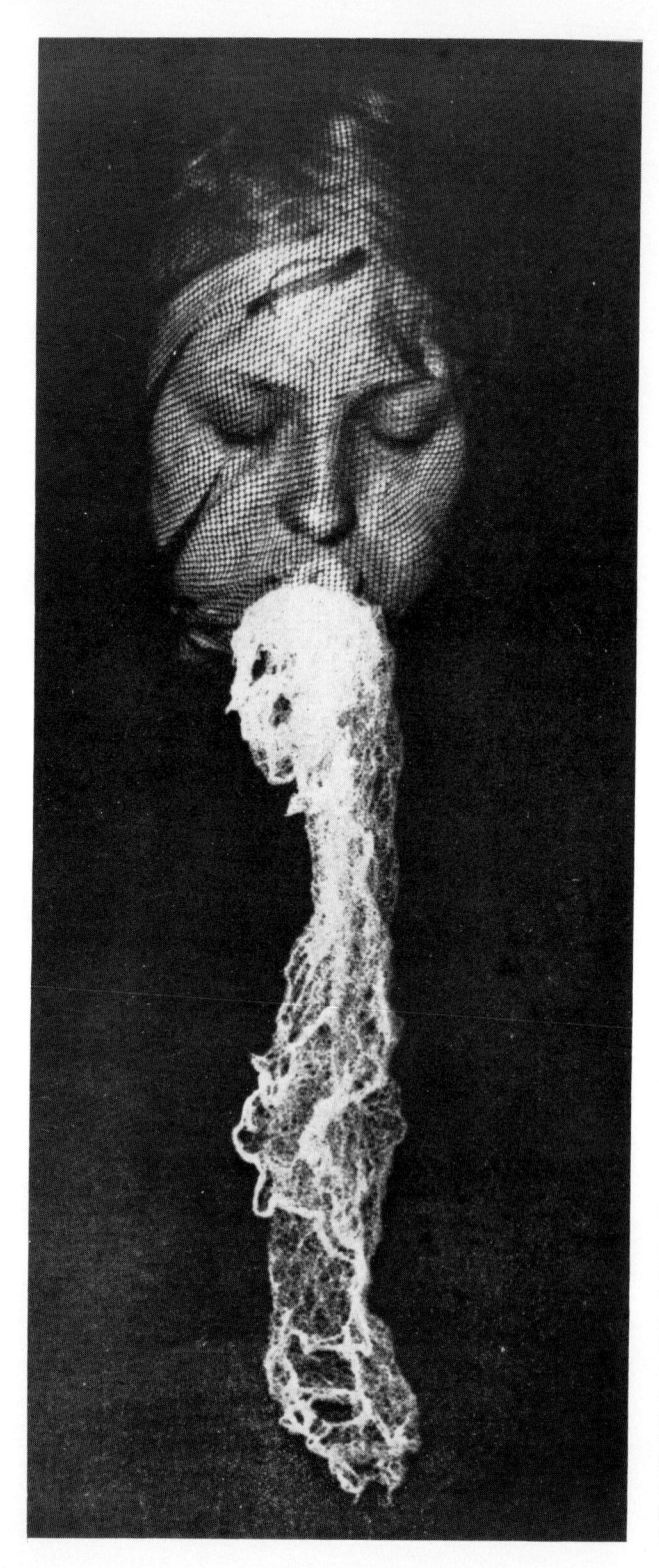

Left: While the very word 'ectoplasm' is enough to prompt many a music-hall joke, mediums have been able to produce the 'substance' under the most rigorous of conditions. Here the medium Stanislava P. emits ectoplasm from the mouth, through the mesh of a net wrapped around her face. This photograph was taken in Munich in 1913. (See page 140.)

Right: Each Friday Thérèse Neumann (1898–1962) lost about one Imperial pint of blood from her stigmata, which corresponded to those of St Francis of Assisi; by the following Sunday her recovery was complete, and she had also regained by then the eight pounds which she had lost during the course of the manifestation. Allegations of trickery were never proved. Here she is seen apparently weeping tears of blood. (See page 154.)

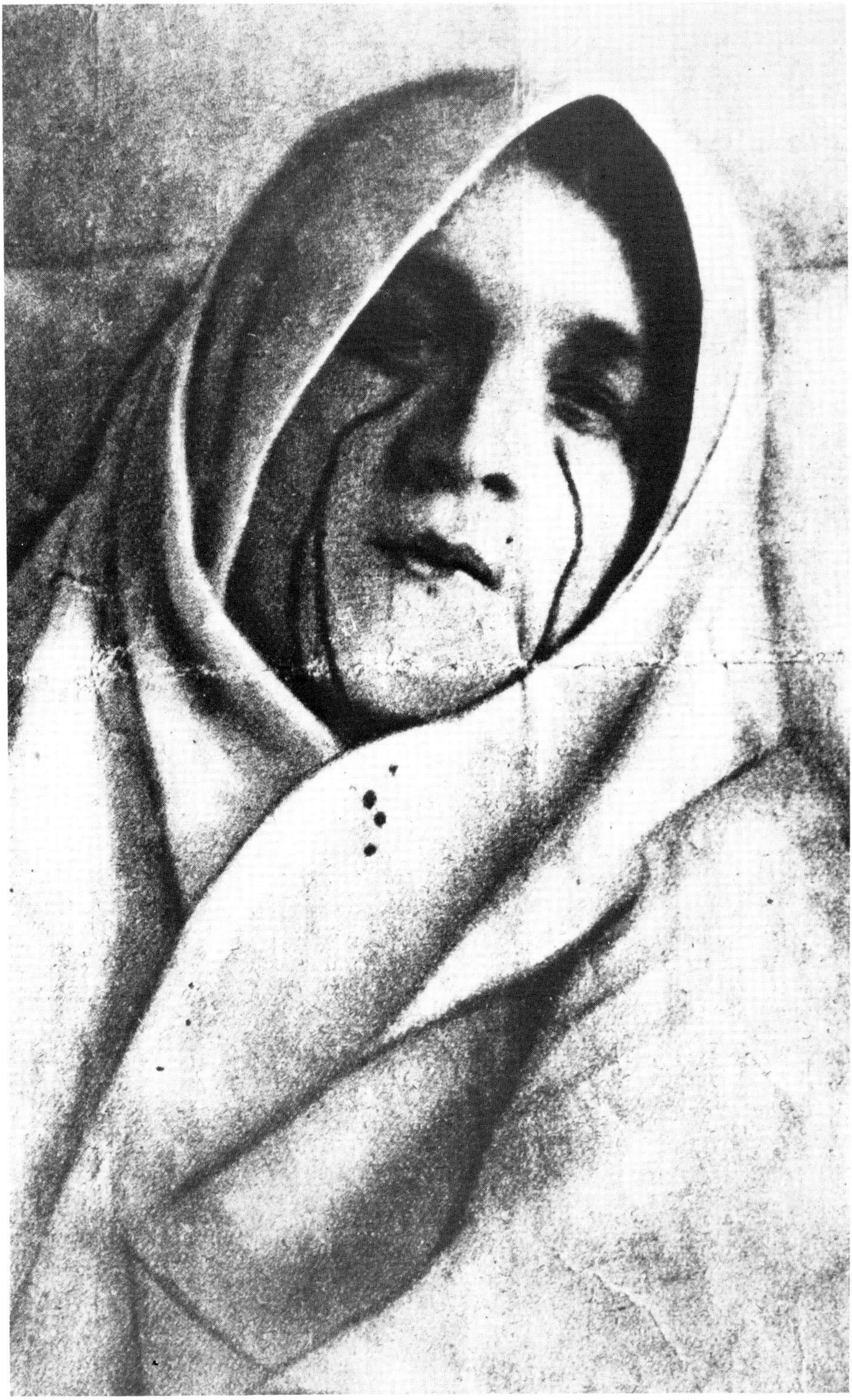

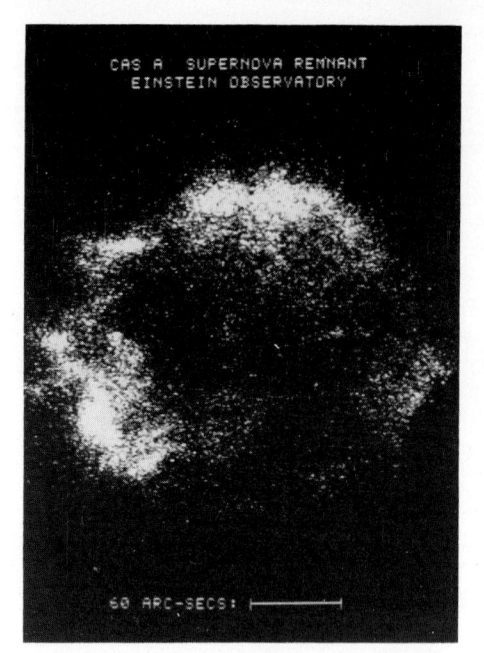

Bizarre objects such as black holes and pulsars can be formed in the cataclysmic explosions of stars — supernovae. This is an X-ray photograph of the expanding shell of gases and other material from a supernova thought to have occurred in about 1657 in the constellation of Cassiopeia: the object is visible only at X-ray and radio frequencies, visible light from it being obscured by surrounding dust. (See pages 163 and 194.)

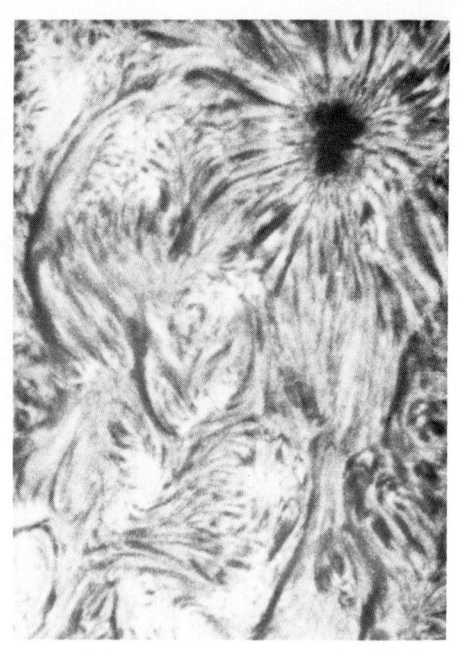

The Sun's surface photographed in hydrogen alpha light, showing a sunspot at upper right. In the early days of debate about extraterrestrial intelligence, Sir William Herschel claimed that sunspots were holes in the solar atmosphere, through which the darkly vegetated surface beneath could be seen (see page 171).

Right: The Great Nebula in the constellation Orion with, above, its satellite nebula. Interstellar nebulae are vast clouds of gas and dust; out of them form new stars and planets — in this nebula new stars can actually be detected in the process of formation. In recent years it has been discovered that such nebulae are quite rich in organic compounds, such as the alcohols, and this has profound implications for our expectations of finding life elsewhere in the Universe. (See page 193.)

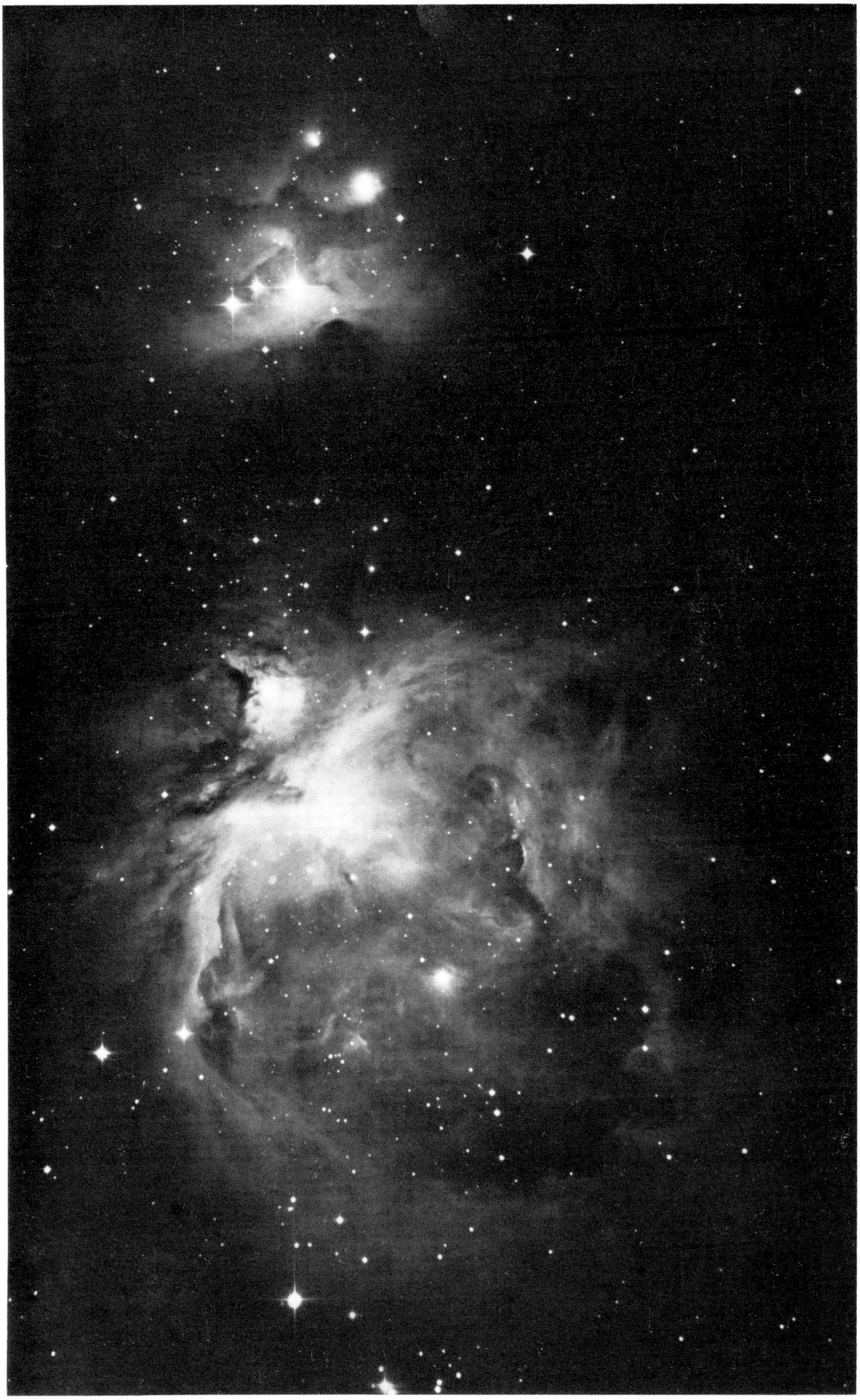

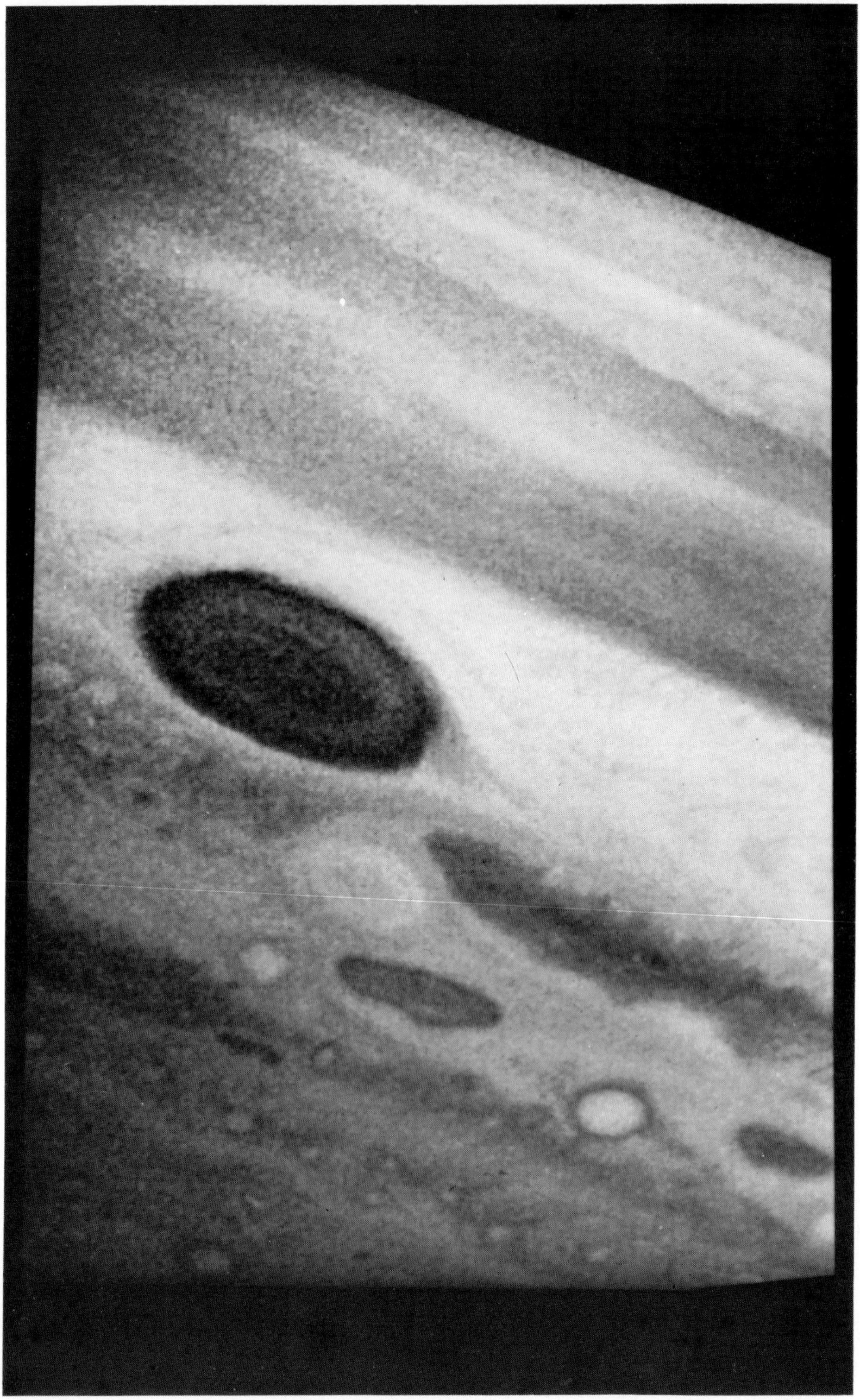

The idea that Mars is inhabited by an ancient race of canal-builders has attracted many writers. *Above:* The Mars of which Ray Bradbury wrote in his eloquent *The Martian Chronicles*, with its crystal cities and its placid blue canals. *Below:* The Mars which *Viking* has revealed has far less obvious glamour, but the new knowledge of the planet which we have gained over the last few years lays fair claim to being as exciting as our earlier dreams. Both of these paintings are by Ed Buckley. (See page 175.)

Left: Part of the surface of Jupiter, photographed by *Pioneer 11* from a distance of about 350,000 miles; the famous Great Red Spot (which is large enough to swallow three Earths) is prominent. SETI enthusiasts claim that gas-giant planets like Jupiter are likely homes for lifeforms whose chemistry requires, for example, ammonia in the same way that ours requires water (see page 197). Clearly communication with such hypothetical beings would be a problem.

Above: Recently it has been suggested by Hoyle and Wickramasinghe that the interiors of the heads of comets may be an environment suitable for the development of complex biochemical compounds and even simple lifeforms (see page 193). But, for obvious reasons, comets are hard to study in close-up. It has been proposed by NASA that on the next visit of Halley's Comet, in 1986, an ion-drive craft (see page 215) be sent 'comet chasing'. Such a craft would draw part of its power from large solar panels, perhaps up to 8m by 40m in size.

Right: A UFO at 1,200m, photographed by Shinichi Takeda of Fujisaw, Japan. Opinions vary about what UFOs actually are: alien spacecraft, products of the mind, or simply cases of mistaken identity? (See page 198.)

At first glance this might appear to be a UFO of the traditional flying-saucer pattern (see page 198). In fact, it is an artist's impression of a space station, and comes from a 1927 German astronautics magazine; Arnold's famous sighting did not take place until twenty years later. Such 'precognitions' lead one to wonder whether UFOs (if spacecraft) are saucer-shaped because that is a rational shape for spacecraft to be or, conversely, if it is merely a case of our *expecting* spacecraft to look like saucers, so that we automatically assume that any unidentified saucer-shaped aerial phenomenon could be a spacecraft.

Above: One suggestion put forward by radio SETI enthusiasts is Project Cyclops, the building of a huge array of large radiotelescopes; and it has been further proposed that the ideal site for such an array would be on the far side of the Moon, since much artificial background 'noise' would then be avoided. (See page 197.)

Right: Two views of a simple hologram, showing the parallax effect. Until quite recently, holograms were 'marvels'; it is a sign of the rapid pace of technological advance that they can be bought at reasonable prices from many outlets. Simple holograms such as this one can be made by the enthusiastic amateur; the cost of the equipment used (including the laser) is about that of a reasonable photographic outfit. (See page 219.)

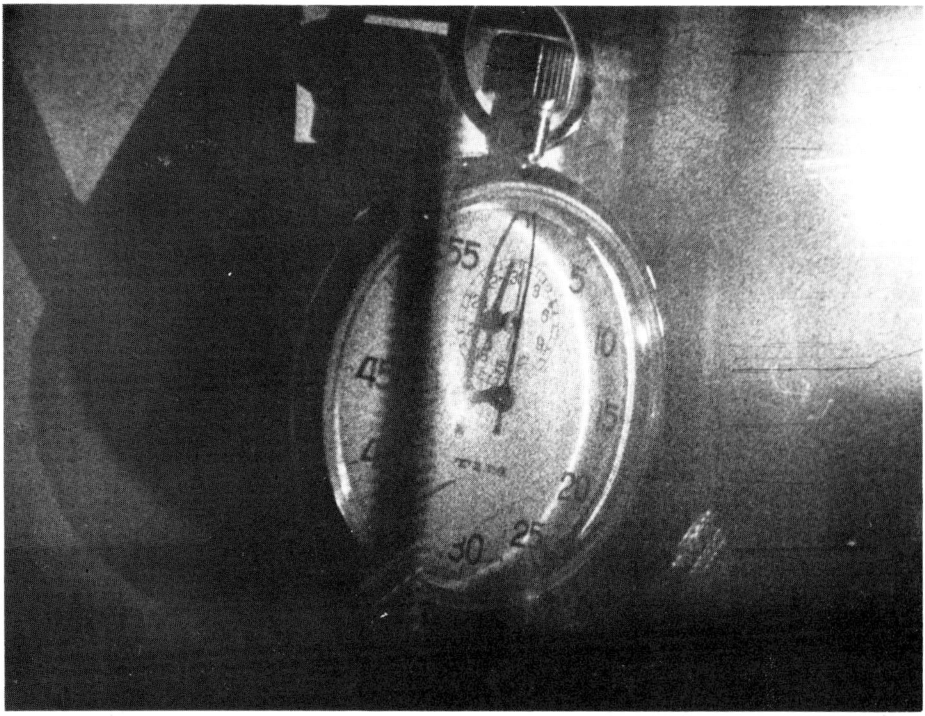
55
5
10
15
20
25
30
45

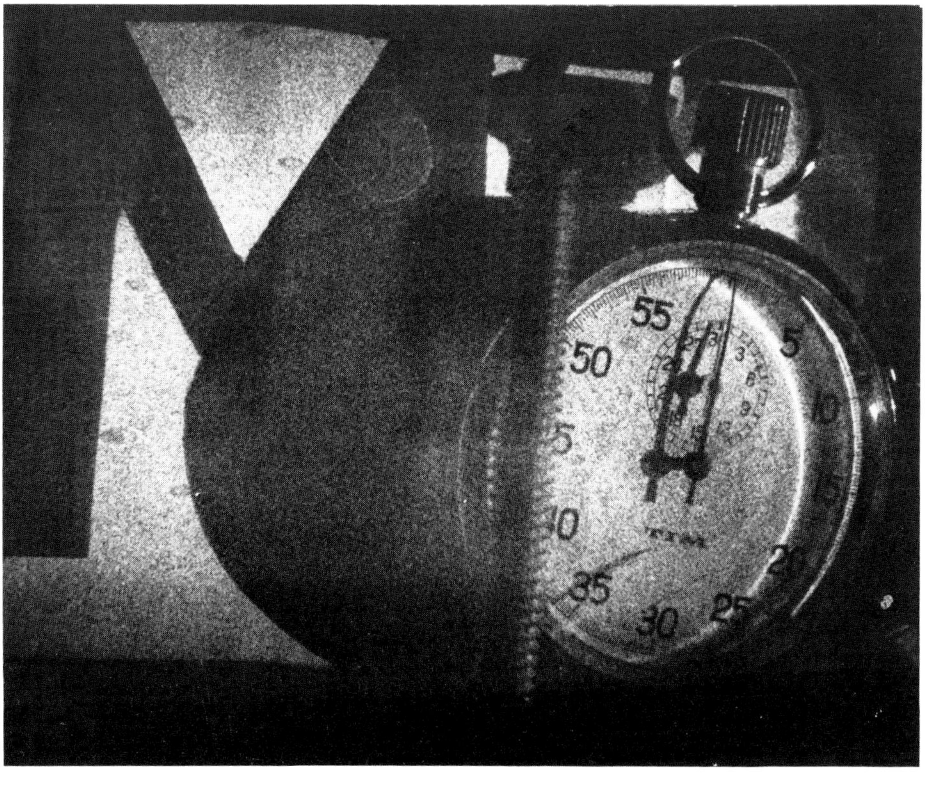
55
50
5
10
20
25
30
35

One idea for space colonies (see page 219) is the Stanford torus. In this NASA painting is shown such a toroidal colony; we see the interior of the colony through 30m strip windows. This colony, which could hold about 10,000 people (its internal diameter is approximately 150m), would rotate once every minute to provide the sensation of gravity. While the initial investment required to build such colonies is large — according to one writer, it would be about the same as the cost of one Vietnam War — they could very soon become self-sufficient, and after a fairly short time show profits.

Panspermia

The panspermic hypothesis suggests that the seeds of life are everywhere present throughout the Universe; these seeds are in the form of spores.

The first rigorous formulation was presented by Arrhenius in *Worlds in the Making* (1908). He suggested that the spores were driven from star to star by the radiation pressure of light — an extremely small driving force but one which could act continuously over long periods, so that the spores could eventually attain high velocities. He pointed out that bacterial spores can survive prolonged intervals in vacuum and conditions of extreme cold; on return to more favourable conditions they 'come to life' again. He suggested that from time to time spores were captured by a planet, such as the Earth, where, if conditions were right, they could flourish, so starting life on that planet along its long evolutionary history.

Unfortunately, his hypothesis did not really explain the origins of life. Where, after all, did the spores come from? Moreover, while they can withstand vacuum and cold, bacterial spores are vulnerable to high-energy radiation, which they could hardly fail to encounter in vast quantities as they journeyed through space. As better and better possible explanations for the origin of life from simpler chemical building blocks were proposed, so the panspermic hypothesis became less and less attractive.

However, in recent years a variation of it has been put forward by the distinguished cosmologists Professors Sir Fred Hoyle and Chandra Wickramasinghe.

By observing spectroscopically the light from celestial objects one can tell a great deal about the elements and compounds present there — whether the particular object is a star shining by its own light or a nebula (a cloud of gas and dust) shining because of hot stars within it; even examining light from beyond that has passed through a nebula will tell one a great deal about what is present in the nebula. For some time it has been known that among the types of molecules present in nebulae there are several which are organic; these include formaldehyde, formic acid, hydrogen cyanide, and methyl and ethyl alcohols — indeed, one nebula close to the centre of our Galaxy contains the equivalent of enough neat whisky to fill the hollowed-out Earth 1,000 times over.

Hoyle and Wickramasinghe, with others, examined the infrared light from typical nebulae and became convinced that this betrayed the presence in the nebulae of rather complicated organic molecules called polysaccharides, most notable of which is cellulose, the commonest organic substance on Earth and, of course, one of the fundamental components of plants. They suggested that biochemicals such as these could form in the gas that outpours from the surface of a hot, luminous star.

They turned their attentions to meteorites and comets. Certain classes of meteorites contain fossilized assemblages of organic material which seem not unlike fossils of living cells — except that in not all cases are the 'cells' like anything known on Earth. Meteorites of this class are thought to have had their origins as fragmented particles of the nuclei of comets; and, indeed, Hoyle and Wickramasinghe point out in *Lifecloud* that the materials which have been detected in the gaseous parts of comets are perfectly consistent with the nucleus itself containing large amounts of biochemical matter; for example, polysaccharides.

Comets are thought to originate from a halo of nuclei surrounding the Solar System at a distance of perhaps a light year from the Sun. Every now and then, owing to some gravitational pull or push, a nucleus falls in towards the Sun; as it swings in towards our star, around it and away again, evaporation of the outer layers of the nucleus produces the characteristic cometary tail. Because comets thus belong less to interplanetary space, more to interstellar space, Hoyle and Wickramasinghe propose that they reflect in their composition the chemicals present in interstellar gas clouds; and they point out that the interior of a cometary nucleus, warm but protected from extremes of heat, is in fact a far more favourable environment for the origin of life than was the primitive Earth.

Indeed, they suggest that the Earth's waters as well as many other of the important constituents of the Earth's surface layers probably came from comets: if, as seems certain, comets were more common in the early days of the Solar System, many must have hit the Earth (see *Tunguska event) giving up their water — and, of course, any primitive lifeforms they bore.

So Hoyle and Wickramasinghe trace the earliest forms of life from the gaseous outpouring of hot stars to interstellar clouds of gas and dust to the cometary halo of the Solar System and finally to Earth. If their theory, which is currently controversial but which has yet to be fundamentally undermined, is correct then Arrhenius' panspermic hypothesis will have at last justified itself.
JG

Parallel Worlds

One popular conception of parallel worlds is based on the idea that all the possible events which might take place in every instant of time each 'give birth' to a distinct future (for further discussion see *alternate universes). Attempting to calculate the sheer *number* of 'parallel Earths' created in such a process is a recipe for neurosis.

But there is a certain amount of evidence that parallel Earths might exist. For example, they have been invoked to explain *UFOs and the phenomenon of *appearing people; *dreams in which a peculiar 'realness' persists, or in which the dreamer receives information otherwise unknown to him, could be as a result of his slipping, mentally, into some parallel world, although here the evidence is, at best, subjective.

There is a problem. Today's physics is nowhere near being able to include such phenomena, and is unlikely to be for a long while yet. And it is unlikely that research will be directed towards them, for the evidence in their favour is not nearly strong enough to give anyone justification to argue their cause. If 'hard' evidence should appear, however, then physics might be in for a violent revolution.
JG

Pulsars

In late 1967 a team of Cambridge radio astronomers picked up a weak signal from the skies — weak, but interesting, because it consisted of a series of regular pulses. Further investigations by Anthony Hewish and Jocelyn Bell showed that the frequency of the pulses was indeed extremely regular — so regular that it seemed as if at last signals from another civilization had been picked up.

Very wisely, Hewish and Bell continued their investigations without making an announcement. They found that the pulses could not originate from a planetary surface; if that were the case, the pulses would show a Doppler shift as the planet rotated on its axis and revolved about its parent star, which they did not. It seemed certain that they were of natural origin. Hewish and Bell christened the new discovery a pulsar; to date, several hundred have been discovered.

At the end of their lives, stars have several courses open to them: essentially, they can go with a whimper or with a bang, a supernova. Depending upon the mass of the star involved in a supernova, a neutron star may be formed (see *black holes for fuller discussion). In a neutron star, matter takes on a form that seems bizarre. The atoms have been subjected to such pressures that the electrons have been forced down onto the atomic nuclei, where they combine with the protons to form neutrons; similarly, the space between the atomic nuclei is annihilated. The resulting *neutron soup is very dense indeed; if our Sun were to become a neutron star (a singularly unlikely event), it would have a diameter of under 20km. Much of its matter would have the strange property of superfluidity; that is, there would be no friction within it: superfluids produced in the laboratory (at temperatures close to Absolute Zero) are so 'runny' that they can climb up and over the walls of their container.

Since stars rotate, their neutron-star remnants should also rotate, and very much more rapidly. It is thought also that the remnant has a powerful magnetic field, displaced from the rotational axis just as is the Earth's magnetic field from the planet's rotational axis. As this field, of strength *at least* several million million times that of the Earth, is dragged around by the spinning star it cuts through the cloud of charged particles attracted by the star's powerful gravitational pull. We have, therefore, a cosmic dynamo capable of producing intense electromagnetic energy: at a certain distance above the surface of the star, the magnetic field is passing through the cloud of particles with a velocity close to that of light, allowing energy to be released in the form of photons. Depending upon the intensity of the magnetic field, this radiation may take the form of gamma-rays, X-rays, light or radio. If the beam of radiation should sweep across the Earth, then we detect it in the form of regular pulses.

There are several other models of pulsars, but this one has satisfied a number of critical tests.

The best, and youngest, known pulsar is that at the heart of the famous Crab Nebula; we receive from it about 33 pulses per second (the supernova which gave it birth was observed in 1054). Another of considerable interest is the object PSR 1913 +16; here a pulsar forms part of a binary pair, the other component being either another neutron star or a black hole. Another young pulsar is that in the Vela Nebula, rotating 11.4 times per second; the supernova was seen in our skies around 8000 BC.

Because of their regularity, pulsars provide signposts in the Galaxy — versatile signposts for, because they slow down according to rigidly prescribed rules, they can be used to pinpoint positions not only in space but in time. On *Pioneer 10*, currently heading out of our Solar System, there is a plaque which pinpoints the Sun by giving reference to fourteen pulsars; if the craft is ever found by an *extraterrestrial intelligence it will be able to deduce both the place and the time of the craft's origin. JG

Quasars

The term 'quasar' is a shortened form of 'quasi-stellar (radio) source'. Not all objects of this type are strong radio emitters but, although the term QSO (quasi-stellar object) is used, 'quasar' is usually applied to all sources which share the following characteristics:

1 They are very compact, appearing almost starlike in photographs. Furthermore, their output of radiation (ranging in some cases from X-rays to radio waves) fluctuates on quite short time-scales, of years, months, or even in some cases hours. Since no source of radiation can vary significantly in brightness in less time than it takes light to cross that source (for no information can be communicated faster than light — see *Relativity), these observations imply the principal energy source in quasars must be smaller than a few light years, light months, or even light days in extent; in some cases the energy source must be smaller than our Solar System.

2 Their spectra show enormous redshifts. Most astronomers assume that these redshifts arise because quasars are receding from us (see *Universe). The largest so far recorded — about 3.5 — correspond to velocities in excess of 90 per cent lightspeed and imply distances of 15–16 billion light years.

If these distances are correct, typical quasars must be emitting roughly 100 times as much energy as an average galaxy. Many hypotheses have been advanced to try to explain how a quasar can release so much energy from so small a volume. The most popular idea at present is that a quasar is the compact nucleus of a galaxy and emits so much energy that the outer regions cannot be seen. The underlying energy source may be a *black hole hundreds of millions of times more massive than our Sun, energy being released by material in the form of gas and disrupted stars spiralling in towards the edge of the hole. The existence of other types of galaxy with compact brilliant and rapidly fluctuating nuclei— for example, Seyfert galaxies and BL Lacerta objects — lends qualitative support to the idea that the only major difference between galaxies like our own, radio galaxies, active galaxies and quasars lies in the mass of the central black hole and in the amount of fuel available to feed it. However, the theory is not proven as yet, and better alternatives may be forthcoming.   IKMN

Relativity

When Einstein was sixteen, in 1895, he speculated idly on what it would be like to travel alongside a beam of light; a man travelling at light-speed would not be able to see his face in a mirror because the light from the mirror could never catch up with his face (or vice versa). By 1904 it had already dawned on Poincaré that it might be impossible to exceed the speed of light and that, if this were so, then a whole new physics would be required.

In 1860 Maxwell had made a suggestion that seems obvious to us but which struck his contemporaries as wildly improbable: that light is an electromagnetic vibration, only a small part of some enormous 'scale' of such vibrations. Infrared and ultraviolet light had been discovered earlier in the century. Later, the discovery of radio waves further 'down' the scale and X-rays and cosmic rays further 'up' confirmed his theory. But the important point was that *all* electromagnetic waves seemed to travel at the same velocity — about 300,000km/s. It looked as if this maximum velocity was a 'law of nature'.

In 1905 Einstein began to brood on his odd notion, and soon had worked out some of its astonishing consequences. If I am travelling on a train which is moving at 100km/h and I throw a ball along the corridor at 100km/h, then the 'total speed' of the ball will be either 200km/h or zero. To get the 'total speed' (i.e., the speed relative to the ground), you add the two velocities. But what would happen if I were on a train travelling at half light-speed and I shone my electric torch toward the engine? To someone sitting on the embankment and measuring the speed of light from my torch, the light beam would be travelling at 1.5 times the speed of light. But if the speed of light is a law of nature, and cannot be exceeded, this is impossible. Something has to 'give'.

And Einstein's Special Theory of Relativity stated that what has to give is space and time. In order to preserve the law of the speed of light, 'space' in the train would concertina, and time would stretch out — it would go slower.

When Einstein tried to work out the 'new mathematics' for the addition of velocities he discovered an interesting thing. The formulae had already been worked out by Lorentz (and, partially, by Fitzgerald); they were known as the Lorentz transformation. But Lorentz had worked it out in a totally different context. If light is a vibration, it ought to be a vibration *in* something — as sound is a vibration in air. Scientists called this something the luminiferous aether. But if the Universe is filled with the aether then we are all travelling through it as the Earth goes around the Sun, the Sun rushes through space, etc. In effect, the aether 'streams' past our Earth. Michelson and Morley set up an experiment to measure the speed of the 'aether stream'. The results of the experiment were negative — there was no trace of the aether. How could this be? Fitzgerald suggested that, since matter is made up of electrically charged particles, perhaps the measuring instruments had *contracted* in the direction of motion; Lorentz worked out just how much they would contract, and produced the Lorentz transformation (which incorporated also the idea that the rate of the passing of *time depended upon one's velocity).

Einstein had now arrived at the Lorentz formula from a totally different viewpoint. Unlike Fitzgerald and Lorentz, Einstein did not think that anything really contracted; the train would only *appear* to contract from the point of view of those in the station. And, similarly, the station would seem foreshortened to the passengers who flew through it on the train. This is equivalent to saying that, in the frame of reference of people standing on the platform, the train *does* contract, and vice versa.

This had some very odd consequences. A train travelling at 75 per cent light-speed would seem foreshortened to the passengers who flew through it on the train. time would also run much slower, so that if a man travelled to a nearby star and back at such a speed he would arrive back appreciably younger than his twin brother who stayed behind. *At* the speed of light, the train's mass would become infinite.

Einstein now decided to try to apply his results to a wider field. If a man were inside a sealed capsule travelling in a straight line at speed he would have no way of knowing that he was in motion; all the laws of physics would remain identical. But if the capsule were swung around on the end of a long rope he would know, since he would be flung against the wall (an acceleration effect). It struck Einstein that such an observer might well believe that he had entered the gravitational field of some planet which was *pulling* him against the wall. Gravity and acceleration are *equivalent*.

This time the attempt to 'balance' the mathematics was far more difficult. Gravitation *is* like acceleration if you happen to be in a lift. But, if the whole Earth were being dragged 'upwards' at a great speed, only the people at the North Pole would experience acceleration as 'gravity'. To remedy this, you would have to envisage the Earth falling into a kind of fourth dimension. But Einstein had no objection to such a concept. Special Relativity had already welded space and time together into a new entity called spacetime; now Einstein suggested that this spacetime could be conceived as a kind of four-dimensional rubber sheet with 'warps' in it. Matter, he said, makes 'warps' in spacetime in the way that a heavy weight would make a dent in a sheet; and light trying to travel from A to B by the 'shortest' route would be forced to 'bend' in such a warp. When such 'bending' was observed during the eclipse of May 1919, the General Theory of Relativity had triumphed. Einstein had replaced 'gravity' with spacetime warps.

His famous $E = mc^2$ (energy equals mass times the speed of light multiplied by itself) was spectacularly confirmed by the atomic bomb. CW

SETI

There may well be a civilization beaming a radio message towards us at this moment, but our chances of detecting it are slight: 1 the number of possible stars from which such a signal might be coming is legion; 2 we would have to be listening on the right frequency. These problems are compounded by the fact that we are making little or no attempt to look for such signals.

It seems, therefore, that radio SETI (*S*earch for *E*xtra*t*errestrial *I*ntelligence) should best be directed towards attempts to eavesdrop on radio 'leakage' from the transmissions which They are making for Their own purposes. We would require extraordinarily sensitive detectors (for obvious reasons, beamed signals maintain greater intensity); but it is worth reflecting that our own domestic radio 'leakage' already fills a sphere some 160 light years across, and radio usage is increasing at such a rate that in a few decades the intensity of radiation leaving the Earth will be, at radio wavelengths, typical of a white-hot body.

In the search for deliberate signals there is the problem of deciding: which frequency? Most popular is the frequency-band known as the 'waterhole', between 1420 megahertz (the absorption frequency of neutral hydrogen) and 1660MHz (that of the hydroxyl molecule): hydrogen (H) + hydroxyl (OH) = water (H_2O), and so this relatively quiet region of the radio spectrum seems an ideal 'meeting place' for water-based lifeforms such as ourselves. A case has been made also for the 'formaldehyde window', between 4260 and 4980MHz.

To date, our SETI attempts have been negligible (see *Project Ozma), shamefully so. Plans have been proposed for an array of over 1,000 radiotelescopes capable of being moved synchronously; Project Cyclops, as this is called, would cost rather less than the *Apollo* project. So far the idea has not been taken further.

(See also *CETI, *extraterrestrial intelligence, *von Neumann probes.) JG

Tachyons

It would seem to be an inescapable conclusion from *Relativity that nothing can travel faster than light. If we look at the mass-increase formula, $m = m_0/\sqrt{(1 - v^2/c^2)}$, it is clear that if the velocity of the object, v, were equal to that of light, c, then the mass m of the moving object would be equal to its rest mass m_0 divided by zero — in other words, m would be infinite. Since it is impossible to have an infinite mass, it seems clearly impossible to propel an object at light-speed; if one cannot travel *at* light-speed then it seems safe to say that one cannot exceed it.

But if we take a velocity *greater* than that of light — say, $v = 2c$ — we have that $m = m_0/\sqrt{-3}$, which can be re-expressed as $m = m_0/1.732i$, where i is the square root of -1. Now i is an 'imaginary number', which means that in common-sense terms it does not exist; nevertheless, mathematicians make use of imaginary numbers in many contexts, and they are a highly satisfactory tool in descriptions of physical reality.

Thus we can conceive of particles, tachyons, which travel faster than light, provided they have imaginary rest masses. Moreover, just as we require more and more energy to propel an ordinary particle up towards light-speed, so tachyons would require more and more energy to *slow down* towards light-speed; i.e., the velocity of light can be seen as a sort of barrier preventing communication between 'our' slower-than-light Universe and the tachyonic one, if the latter exists. For this reason, it seems theoretically impossible ever to detect tachyons — and, indeed, much of modern physics depends upon this fact, since otherwise *causality would be violated.

One line of reasoning runs that, if we cannot detect tachyons, can we not say in accordance with Occam's Razor that they do not exist? There is an analogy with evolution here. It is often said that if an ecological niche exists, then in due course an organism will evolve to fill it. Similarly, it seems tempting to suggest that, if tachyons *can* exist, if there is a 'hole' in the structure of physics which they can occupy, then they do. And, if they can anyway never 'rest', is their imaginary rest mass so ludicrous?

There are a number of *fundamental particles which were initially postulated solely to make the maths work, and which were only much later discovered and accepted. It seems possible that tachyons belong in this category.   JG

Time-Symmetric Universe

This is a concept found in some theories of the *oscillating Universe. Currently, the *Universe is in a state of expansion and the galaxies are receding from each other — i.e., spacetime itself is expanding; we could describe this situation as positive. On the other hand, if the Universe begins to contract, we enter a phase where spacetime is moving in a negative direction; it is contracting. This can be interpreted as meaning that the arrow of *time will point in the opposite direction; everything would run backwards.

One school of thought suggests that this indicates that the whole history of the Universe would be repeated exactly, but the other way round: you would be pulled up from your grave, slowly revive, and spend the rest of your life getting younger and unlearning everything you had known at your 'birth'; finally, you would struggle into your mother's womb and, over nine months, disappear. This seems nonsensical, and for this reason this extreme idea is generally rejected. But it is interesting to speculate that you might see little difference in this situation from the way you live life at the moment; if your life were a process of unlearning, undoing, your past would be a closed book to you but you would 'remember' your future; *causality would be 'reversed', but you might not know the difference. You might well think that you were growing older, and that you lived in an expanding Universe ...

(See also *alternate universes.)   JG

UFOs

The history of modern UFOlogy begins on 24 June 1947. Kenneth Arnold was flying his private plane near Mount Rainier, Washington State, when he saw nine shining discs moving against the background of the mountain. He estimated their speed as about 1,600km/h. He said that they swerved in and out of the peaks of the Cascade Mountains with 'flipping, erratic movements'. He later told a reporter that the objects moved as a saucer would 'if you skipped it across the water'. The next day the story appeared in newspapers all over the nation. People all over the USA began reporting sightings of 'flying saucers', and a US Air Force investigation was initiated; on 4 July, ten days after the sighting, it announced confidently that Arnold had been hallucinating.

On 7 January 1948 a round, white object in the sky was chased by Captain Thomas Mantell in a P-51 fighter; at 9,000m Mantell seems to have blacked out, and his plane went into a fatal dive. This episode probably did more than any other to publicize UFOs in the late 1940s.

The Air Force investigation which, in 1952, became officially known as Project Blue Book, ended in December 1969; its attitude throughout remained sceptical. J. Allen Hynek, an astrophysicist asked to take part in the project, began as sceptic but became convinced that there was a definite residue of cases that could not be dismissed as hoaxes, illusions or honest mistakes. 'Blue Book,' says Hynek in *The UFO Experience*, 'was a cover-up.'

It struck early students that Arnold's sighting was by no means the first. Search through newspaper files soon revealed many earlier ones. As early as 1800 an 'airship' was seen hovering over Baton Rouge. Chapter 26 of Fort's *Book of the Damned* (1919) is devoted to reports of strange lights in the sky; these include the famous 'Durham lights', seen over Durham in 1866, which were investigated by a commission headed by Admiral Collinson. Typically, it 'reached no conclusion'. One of the most convincing sightings, with all the typical features, occurred in 1926 in the Himalayas (see *ancient astronauts).

Josef F. Blumrich, who worked for NASA, was intrigued by von Däniken's assertion that Ezekiel had described something very like a spaceship ('a great cloud, with brightness round about it, and fire flashing forth continually, and in the midst of the fire, as it were gleaming bronze ...'), and made a careful study of the passage in the Bible, concluding that Ezekiel's description *is* remarkably like that of a spaceship.

One important feature of the sightings that later emerged was that the 'objects' were often cigar-shaped rather than circular; and the cigar-shaped objects were larger than the smaller 'saucers'. In fact, many observers have reported seeing the small saucers emerging from the cigar-shaped object, implying that this latter is the parent craft.

Hynek was one of the small number of serious, responsible students of the phenomenon who emerged in the early 1950s; others were Jacques Vallée, Donald Keyhoe, Aimé Michel and M.K. Jessup. Keyhoe, who inaugurated his own study project, is convinced that the 'saucers' are piloted by beings from other planets who have been studying Earth for the past 200 years. He, and many others, pointed out that the first sighting occurred soon after the explosion of the first atomic bomb.

Fred Hoyle is on record as saying that the saucers have been around since the beginning of time. This view is taken also by Raymond Drake, whose *Gods and Spacemen in the Ancient East* (and a companion volume on the West) examines ancient texts for mentions of objects that sound like Ezekiel's wheel of fire.

Some writers are convinced that UFOs are hostile, and that the sightings are basically of reconnaissance vehicles preparing an invasion of Earth. Others, like Brinsley Le Poer Trench, believe that there could be two lots of 'sky people', one friendly and very ancient, the others more recent and more sinister in their intentions. The 'antis' like to point out that car engines and other electrical equipment seem to stall in the presence of UFOs — one writer blames them for the massive New York power failure of 1965.

Inevitably, some of the speculation seems to cross the line into pure fantasy.

Frank Scully, a Hollywood journalist, suggests that the saucers come from Venus and are driven by magnetic propulsion (his book was later denounced as a hoax by *True* magazine). George Adamski claims that he has shaken hands with a charming Venusian in the California desert and been taken for a trip into space. Antonio Boas, a Brazilian farmer, claims that he was taken on board a saucer where two 'little men' took blood samples, and a beautiful naked girl with no lips seduced him — obviously for scientific purposes. Adamski himself states that most 'contactee' claims are imagination — giving precise figures of 800 'genuine' cases out of 3,000. Many 'contactees' have reported hearing the voices of spacemen inside their heads; while Dr George Hunt Williamson's *Secret Places of the Lion* describes how spacemen contacted him through *automatic writing, telling him they arrived on Earth 18 million years ago, and built the Great Pyramid 24,000 years ago — a spacecraft is hidden under its base, according to Williamson.

Even so, many contactee stories are oddly convincing. In September 1961, Mr and Mrs Barney Hill were driving home from Canada when they saw a UFO, then both blacked out. Two hours later they woke up in their car. Under *hypnosis, both recalled being taken aboard a 'saucer' and examined. John G. Fuller's book about their experience, *The Interrupted Journey*, is one of the more convincing 'contactee' records, with its precise transcripts of hypnotic sessions.

As UFO reportings have continued, most of them from ordinary people with no desire for publicity, there has been increasing public acceptance that the phenomena are not *pure* delusion. *Jung, who began by advancing a theory that the saucers were 'projections' from the collective unconscious, ended by recognizing that they seemed to be more 'factual' than that. In 1969, Air Marshal Sir Victor Goddard lectured in London and suggested that UFOs could come from a *parallel world; this view has become increasingly popular. Many writers on *ley lines have pointed out that UFOs are seen most frequently at the crossing point of leys — for example, there have been hundreds of sightings over Warminster, to which a whole book has been devoted by Arthur Shuttlewood. Shuttlewood, like John Michell in *The Flying Saucer Vision*, points out the association between UFO sightings and ancient sacred sites. In *The Dragon and the Disc*, F.W. Holiday notes the similarity of shape of 'disc barrows' and saucers, and also points out how frequently UFO sightings are associated with '*ghosts' — as when a blood-soaked figure staggered out of a hedge near Warminster and vanished. In *The Undiscovered Country*, Stephen Jenkins conducts a lengthy and highly convincing investigation into the connection between UFOs, ley lines and 'supernatural' occurrences. Holiday, too, believes that saucers, like 'lake monsters', should be regarded as some kind of partly supernatural phenomenon, associated with racial memory.

As with 'supernatural' phenomena, one of the most striking things about UFOs is the ambiguity of the whole phenomenon. The evidence looks very convincing; yet all hopes of reaching some final, positive conclusion seem to recede when we try to pin it down. Puharich's *Uri* is a case in point. Puharich describes how Uri Geller went periodically into trances, and how voices of 'extraterrestrials' spoke through his mouth, identifying themselves as members of 'the Nine', space-people whose aim is to guide the Earth through a difficult period in its history and prevent Man from destroying himself. There is much solid evidence that the phenomena really took place, and Puharich himself has a high reputation as a scientific investigator; yet the events themselves seem so weird and inconsequential that it is difficult to take them seriously. After Puharich's break with Geller, the communications continued, and are recounted by Holroyd in *Prelude to a Landing on Planet Earth*: the 'alien communicators' declared that they intended to land on Earth in force, and were anxious to prepare mankind for this event ... but the date for the landing passed without incident. John Keel, another investigator of UFO phenomena, speaks a great deal about the 'men in black' who often warn people to keep silent about their glimpses of UFOs. Again, his books are full of 'hard evidence' — names, dates, signed statements. It seems clear that 'something is going on'; but whether that something is contact with *extraterrestrial intelligence seems doubtful.

In *The Invisible College* Jacques Vallée suggested that the phenomena may be basically 'heuristic' — intended to 'educate' the human race to a new consciousness. He points out that it is impossible to decide whether UFOs are genuine or not; or whether, if they are genuine, they originate in outer space, in 'other dimensions', or in the human mind itself — a kind of super-poltergeist effect. Yet the repetitiveness of the phenomenon and its unpredictability seem to prepare the human mind for something startling; or, at the very least, prepare us to remain openminded. (*Zen koans serve the same function, so the 'intelligence' behind UFOs could be trying to produce a kind of enlightenment.) Alternatively, it could be a manifestation of the human unconscious (right brain), trying to prevent us from becoming jammed in a two-dimensional left-brain reality. CW

Universe, Theories of the

It seems certain that the Universe is expanding; moreover, it is expanding in a regular way.

Until 1924 it was generally believed that the Universe consisted of a single conglomerate, the Galaxy. In 1781 Messier had made a catalogue of various celestial objects which were certainly not stars, presenting as they did a fuzzy appearance; he was interested in these objects, nebulae, purely because he was an enthusiastic comet-hunter, and was tired of being misled by objects which appeared superficially comet-like. In 1912, Vesto Slipher analysed the spectrum of the most prominent of these, the Andromeda Nebula, and discovered by means of the Doppler Effect that it was approaching us at a rate of about 200km/s; by similar analyses of other nebulae he discovered that this velocity towards us was an exception, that the nebulae were receding from us at various rates, some of them very high. And in 1924 Edwin Hubble, using the 250cm (100in) Mount Wilson telescope, was able to resolve individual stars in the Andromeda Nebula, showing that it was a galaxy beyond our own: the galaxy contains Cepheid variables, whose period of variation is proportional to their absolute luminosity, so that by comparison of their variation period with their apparent luminosity (as seen from Earth) he was able to work out (in fact, wrongly) their distance.

Hubble examined other galaxies, and discovered that the Doppler redshift in the spectra of their stars, compared with the apparent luminosity of the galaxies, showed that there seemed to be a relation between the velocity with which they were receding from us and their distance: a galaxy two units from us recedes twice as fast as a galaxy one unit from us. Hubble established Hubble's Constant as a measure of this: the galaxies receded at 150km/s for every million light years that they were distant from us. Unfortunately, his estimate of the distance of the galaxies was too low, and a more acceptable figure today is 25km/s per million light years. But the *exact* value of Hubble's Constant has still to be definitely established, and this has given rise to the two principal theories of the Universe under consideration today (but see *cosmologies, unorthodox).

Making the very probable assumption that the *Big Bang began the Universe, and that it is as a result of that explosion that the Universe continues to expand, there is an obvious question: will the gravitational attraction between the galaxies be sufficient to pull them all back together again, so that the Universe collapses in upon itself to die in a Big Crunch? There are three possible answers: 1 the Hubble Constant is large enough that the Universe will continue to expand forever and until it reaches infinite extent; 2 it will continue to expand forever, but the rate of expansion will slow down such that it will forever have only finite extent; 3 the Hubble Constant is not large enough to prevent the Universe collapsing in upon itself (see *oscillating Universe). The subject is still a matter of controversy.

Another theory, popular until recently, is that the galaxies are, indeed, receding from us but that the Universe cannot be said to be expanding in that it is infinite in extent and is of infinite age. This Steady State Theory, proposed by Bondi, Gold and Hoyle, suggests the *continuous creation of matter in space, which 'pushes' the galaxies apart while at the same time allowing for the formation of new galaxies, so that the average density of the Universe has remained constant throughout time.

There is an obvious way of checking. Because light has a finite velocity, when one looks further into space with a telescope one is looking backwards into time. If the Steady State Theory were correct, then, no matter how far back into time one looked, the Universe would appear much the same. Unfortunately, this is not the case. Moreover, in 1965 Arno Penzias and Robert Wilson discovered a cosmic background microwave radiation, equivalent to a temperature of 3K, which can be explained only as the residual radiation from the *Big Bang, perhaps 15 billion years ago; the Universe would seem not to have yet cooled down from that cataclysmic eruption. Thus, it would seem that the Steady State Theory has fallen by the wayside.

The two remaining possibilities are: the open, ever-expanding Universe; and the *oscillating Universe. However, within these possibilities there is still considerable speculation as to the Universe's real nature; rival theories, worthy of consideration either because they fit the framework of *Relativity or because they propose a serious challenge to it, occasionally emerge; and the Steady State Theory, as modified in recent years by Hoyle and Narlikar, cannot be said truly to have died.

It is unfashionable to add that none of these theories rules out the existence of God. JG

White Holes

There is an elegance about the idea of *black holes having counterparts, white holes, with opposite properties; and this elegance is reflected in the mathematics, which suggest that black holes may be 'connected', via 'wormholes' which transcend spacetime, to white holes elsewhere and, possibly, elsewhen.

We have, then, a picture of the white hole as a vastly luminous entity from which stream large quantities of energy and matter in their most chaotic forms. But, in this case, should not white holes be rather noticeable? Yet none have been detected, and there are no likely candidates.

In *White Holes* John Gribbin suggests that we have, indeed, discovered such phenomena, but do not realize that we have. Noting that there seems to be a firm, evolutionary relationship between *quasars and 'normal' galaxies, via, for example, Seyfert galaxies, he suggests that all (except irregular) galaxies have at their cores white holes — 'cosmic gushers' — which, as it were, 'power' the galaxies and supply further materials for the construction of stars. However, it now seems virtually certain that the vigorous energy sources at the hearts of galaxies are black holes, not white ones.

Another suggestion is that what we call the cosmic egg in *Big Bang theories was — or even *still is* — a white hole; possibly, the Big Bang was not a sudden eruption but the sudden appearance of that white hole, which may, indeed, still be gushing; perhaps we have misinterpreted the background microwave radiation (see *Universe). Moreover, are we correct when we say that white holes should be highly visible? Their outpourings would be very strongly blue-shifted; an extremely distant, and small, source of gamma radiation might well have gone undetected so far.

Such speculations are intriguing but, sadly, one has to conclude that there is as yet no evidence in favour of white holes — and that in itself is strong evidence that no such phenomenon exists. JG

Evolution: 6

And so we near the end of our voyage of discovery.

It is a truism that cultural evolution can be traced solely through artefacts — whether these be paintings, litter or spearheads — and so we make no apology for the fact that the majority of the articles in the next, and final, section of this book are concerned with technological advances. These predicted 'artefacts' enable us to draw a picture of future cultural evolution, which in turn acts as a mirror to future mental evolution.

The world of tomorrow would be, for us, a very strange place to live in. Let us hope that, despite our fears of 'future shock', our descendants do not find it so.

JG

PART SEVEN

THE WORLD OF TOMORROW

Introductory: 7

This last section of the book may strike readers as preposterous; yet all these possibilities have been seriously discussed by scientists in recent years.

When I reviewed the list of contents of this section, I was reminded of a story by Howard Fast, 'The Martian Shop', in which a group of businessmen fabricate some remarkable products whose technology seems far beyond anything possible on Earth, and sell them in three mysterious stores called Mars Products. It is a plot to convince the people of Earth that they may be in danger of an invasion from Mars, and to make them unite in a defensive brotherhood. The products include a 6in-square music box that can play 11,000 pieces, a portable atomic outboard motor, and a computer that takes its orders from the human voice — this is also a 6in cube. The story was written in the late 1950s; what is amusing today is to see that Fast thought a super-computer would have to be so large; if he had known about the microchip he would have made it the size of a pocket diary. Science is overtaking fiction at such a pace that even his music box and portable atomic motor may be with us before the end of the century.

And at this point in history we are surely in a position to see the moral which is beginning to emerge: that the most marvellous new inventions are not really much more important than children's toys. The only scientific discovery that matters at this point in history is how to eliminate poverty. If this could be done, it would hardly matter whether we shall all be driving atomic-powered helicopters or horse-drawn buggies in a century from now. Our Victorian forefathers filled their evenings just as pleasantly with music-making around a piano as we do with our colour televisions. And I have lived just as happily in a cottage without electricity or running water as I do in my present home, with its central heating and solar panels.

The real problem confronting us, at this stage of our evolution, is to achieve a new level of control over our mechanicalness. Robert Graves once remarked that all real poetry is created in the fifth dimension — a remark that baffled me at the time. Several years later, the solution came to me. We seem to be creatures of four dimensions — three of space, one of time. If I look up someone's biography in *Who Was Who*, the words present me with the skeleton of this four-dimensional creature. But if I open *The Divine Comedy* or put on a record of Beethoven, I am being presented with something more — a fragment of the living essence of the man — his freedom. And in order to enter into the meaning of Dante or Beethoven, I have also to turn away from the world of space and time around me, and do my best to kindle an intuition that leaps upward like a spark — upward into this same fifth dimension.

It is difficult to state such a notion in words, because words were invented to describe our spacetime world. Art *can* do it; but if you happen to be in the wrong mood it is like trying to light a fire with damp wood. Our best chance of expressing it still lies in making use of words and ideas and concepts — and in a continual effort to *stretch* them beyond their normal limited meaning. These words lie flat on the page; that is their nature; only you, the reader, can endow them with a fifth dimension.

CW

Bionics

Bionics concerns the copying of living systems, from mechanical models to artificial intelligences.

Popularly, it suggests powered limbs many times stronger and more dextrous than the norm, although today's best limb substitutes are so inadequate that few people are queueing for amputation and replacement. Even if available, unreasonably strong substitutes would be devalued by the law of action and reaction: powered arms capable of punching through brick walls would simultaneously dislocate the owner's collar bone. Popular bionics also ignores the fact that to link machinery to a human body requires flesh and synthetic to be intimately joined, risking infection, allergy, and corrosion of synthetics by salty body fluids, besides the sheer physical problem of gluing live tissue to plastic 'flesh'. Probably bionic limbs can never surpass the real thing; improved crutches remain crutches.

The problem of establishing linkages through the barrier of the human skin is simplest when anchorage can be made to bone, and flesh movement is minimal — suggesting sockets in the skull, leading to electrodes in the brain itself. Equipment might even be enclosed within the skull — a watchdog for the warning signs of epilepsy or other conditions; a built-in calculator, clock, radio or 'memory bank'; in more sinister scenarios, a stimulator of intense pleasure or pain. Every human function involves brain activity which a bionic microcomputer could monitor; every sensation we feel might be electrically imitated by the device. The 'biocomp', with appropriate stimulus-response programming, could sound subjective warning bells in the epileptic's ears, warning of approaching fits; mental formulation of a mathematical problem could cause the solution to be calculated and shown as an overlay on one's vision; mere desire could lead to orgasmic stimulation of pleasure centres, while thinking Wrong Thoughts (as specified in the biocomp's programming) might conversely trigger pain. Returning to limb-substitutes, and not only for the disabled: radio signals from biocomps could enable us to control equipment mentally, from typewriters or robot 'hands' to industrial assembly lines.

Medical biocomps are surely inevitable; detection of Wrong Thoughts perhaps farfetched; electronic ecstasy unpleasantly plausible, countless electrode-equipped rats having chosen to starve rather than stop pressing a 'pleasure' button. Ultimately, feeding computer-generated data into the brain leads to the nightmare wherein we lie unmoving, machine-tended, senses flooded with an unreal but desirable electronic world ... which, if reality is what the senses perceive, would *be* reality.   DRL

CETI

Assuming that one's attempts at *SETI have prospered, how does one set about communicating with an extraterrestrial intelligence? (CETI = *C*ommunication with *E*xtra*t*errestrial *I*ntelligence.) Let us assume that the communication is via radio (but see *von Neumann probes).

By far the most popular suggestion is that one can do so by pictures. Imagine that one is sending a signal consisting of pulses; if one has a 'standard interval' between pulses, one can then send bits of two types: 1 represents a pulse and 0 represents a gap where a pulse ought to have been — i.e., a blank. If in a single message one has, say, 1,271 bits, one may hope that the receivers will realize this number is the product of two prime numbers, 31 and 41, and arrange the bits in an array of, say, 31 across and 41 in depth. (They might try 41 across and 31 in depth, of course, or record the pulses in the array working right to left, or bottom to top, or both; but we will assume that they are patient and get the right answer.) If they do this, making a mark for a 1 and no mark for a 0, they should be confronted by a picture. In this picture there could be representations of ourselves, our Solar System, the number system we use, the important atoms in our make-up, etc.

A similar technique would be to send, between information-carrying sequences of pulses, a sequence giving (say) the 200th

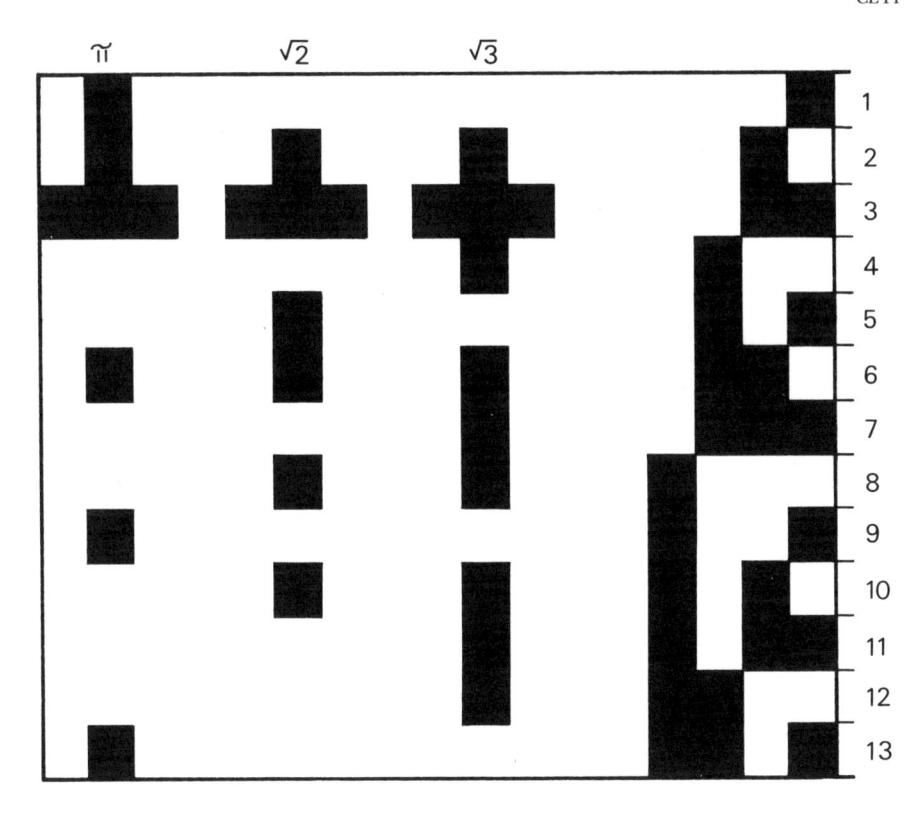

Figure 4 *A simple mathematics lesson for the extraterrestrials. This rectangle is 17 units across and 13 units down (both 17 and 13 are prime numbers). Down the right hand side are the numbers from 1 to 13 in binary notation: the other three columns give approximations, in binary notation, for (from left to right), π, the square root of 2 and the square root of 3 (the horizontal blocks of 3 units represent the 'point'). This could be transmitted as the following stream of pulses (where a 1 indicates a pulse, a 0 a 'gap'):*

0 1 0 0 0 0 0 0 0 0 0 0 0 0 0 1 0 1 0 0 0 1 0 0
0 1 0 0 0 0 0 1 0 1 1 1 0 1 1 1 0 1 1 1 0 0 0 0 1
1 0 0 0 0 0 0 0 0 1 0 0 0 0 1 0 0 0 0 0 0 0 1 0
0 0 0 0 0 0 1 0 1 0 1 0 0 0 1 0 0 0 1 0 0 0 1
1 0 0 0 0 0 0 0 0 1 0 0 0 0 1 1 1 0 0 0 0 0 1
0 0 0 1 0 0 0 1 0 0 0 0 1 0 0 0 0 0 0 0 0 0 0 1
0 0 1 0 0 0 0 0 1 0 0 0 1 0 0 0 1 0 1 0 0 0 0 0 0
0 0 0 0 1 0 0 0 1 0 1 1 0 0 0 0 0 0 0 0 0 1 0 0 0
1 1 0 0 0 1 0 0 0 0 0 0 0 0 0 0 1 1 0 1.

line of Pascal's Triangle; this would define a triangular 'frame' in which the pulses of the information-bearing sequence could be arranged. One disadvantage of the technique would be its cumbersomeness.

Are we, perhaps, assuming too much of our extraterrestrials? Sagan and others have experimented by handing out coded sequences to colleagues, without warning, and asking them to work out the pictures. (This has even been done with a three-dimensional picture.) Not only has the success rate been almost 100 per cent, the speed with which people have been able to work out the result has been astonishing. If aliens think as we do, then they will have no trouble decoding our messages. But is it likely that aliens think as we do?

A strong school of thought suggests that it is unlikely that they do. For example, we have a two-dimensional pictorial convention; but we have no logical reason to believe that *extraterrestrial intelligences have any such convention. Radio CETI enthusiasts say that this is irrelevant: prime numbers are prime numbers the Universe around, and so the message carries the information about its representational convention, which the aliens can learn. And, certainly, if we received a message from the stars which was obviously artificial yet on the face of it made no sense, we would set our finest cryptanalysts on the job and they would not give up until they had cracked the code, however long it might take.

This might seem to beg the question. True, the recipients of the message might understand that they had to set out the bits in a 31 × 41 array, but would they understand what they saw there? Again, the enthusiasts say that they would work it out — and for simple messages this might be true. But think of just a single cultural difference between ourselves and Them: we think the atoms of the basic elements on which our life is based are important; They might not. They might thus interpret our atomic diagrams as showing something important to Them, such as the socially acceptable units in a sexual ménage (i.e., 'family'). The confusion that could arise is interesting to imagine.

In short, and despite such qualms, CETI seems possible — at least for simple messages. Whether *real* communication is feasible is another question. Ignoring even cultural differences, it is quite likely that alien modes of thought are so different from our own that the most important message we shall ever be able to communicate is: 'Hello.' JG

Cybernetics

Cybernetics concerns the theory of communication and control systems both mechanical and biological; current work generally involves computer simulation rather than actual systems, and forms a large part of research into artificial intelligence (AI).

A cybernetic system has five segments, termed programme, control, action, sensors and decision, and achieves the required ends by feedback. Example: a man wishes to squash a fly. Memory (programme) dictates the approximate sequence of muscle movements to reach the target; nerve signals (control) activate arm muscles (action) and set the hand in motion; eyes (sensors) feed back its position; if this fails to meet memory's requirements, the brain (decision) generates course corrections (control again), and so on until the moment of contact. That such involved processes lead, sometimes, to successful squashings shows the effectiveness of human systems; cybernetic models like the above are the first steps towards a mechanistic interpretation of intelligence.

*Bionics simulates living systems using machinery; cybernetics analyses said systems in machine terms, and could ultimately provide a blueprint for AI. The constant increases in computers' speed and number-crunching power must not, though, be confused with AI advances. It is easy to overestimate the present sophistication of machine intelligence, thanks to computer chess-playing masters; in fact, the thought processes of human chess masters are only partly susceptible to cybernetic analysis, and chess programmes tend to 'cheat' by brute-force methods, exhaustively analysing all promising moves and their consequences, so that only a crude ability to assess material and positional strengths is required.

Machines have much more trouble with *go*, where strategy depends on recognition and manipulation of rather subtle patterns of counters; the best *go* programmes rank only as good novices. In the real world, pattern recognition is yet more complex, though heavily researched. Even the task of reading handwriting is complex in machine terms, in terms of the 'programme' segment of a cybernetic loop.

If human intelligence were better understood, one might contrive a 'learning machine' capable of being taught in the same way as people — an AI, in fact. This would require the most elusive of human attributes, the ability to sort out irrelevancies (first define 'irrelevant' . . .) by a sampling procedure — rather as we keep track of a single voice in a crowded room — and to do so very rapidly indeed.

A computer programme to recognize simple shapes, even without distractions, becomes highly complex if it is to cover a fraction of the number of shapes a person can instantly recognize: the programme would go through shape after shape from its memory bank, turning and enlarging or reducing its image of 'circle', 'pentagon', etc., until a stored shape coincided with that percieved. A human, whose nerve impulses travel remarkably slowly, could instantly name the shape irrespective of size, orientation or, probably, distortion sufficient to confuse the computer utterly.

Since the operation of living brains is so obscure, more devious routes to AI seem necessary. Could not a machine be built which could reprogramme itself, in a feedback loop of self-improvement, to approach any desired ideal; a superior learning machine which might acquire 'intelligence' from example, or by trial and error? One hesitates to say 'no', although there remains the vast difficulty of knowing what options, what avenues for self-improvement, to build into such a device, and also what goal to define. 'Become intelligent' is a command with little meaning. 'Recognize patterns more efficiently' is one which could at least be formulated, but again the initial construction of our learning maching is a knotty problem since swift human pattern-recognition may be a function of the peculiar means of information storage within the brain — which, unlike most computers, does not seem to store any specific item of information in any specific place. This is echoed in the more successful pattern-recognition machines, which learn by example and can make quite subtle distinctions without its being at all obvious how they do it.

One day an open-ended learning programme will grope its way to intelligence, only for the builders to discover that its final, intricate state is as impervious to analysis — and incapable of self-analysis — as the human brain. DRL

Dyson Sphere

In 1960 Freeman Dyson suggested that very advanced extraterrestrial civilizations would be capable of dismantling the planets and other material of their solar system in order to build a shell at whose centre lay their parent star. The amount of useful land area made available by such a project is vast: if the sphere had the radius of the Earth's orbit, its inner surface area would be of the order of 300 million billion square kilometres, about 600 million times greater than the surface area of the Earth. It would be a vast engineering project, but would clearly be easier than discovering perhaps a billion new planets for colonization; and so Dyson suggested that in our searches for *extraterrestrial intelligences we might look not for radio signals but for stars apparently going out.

The idea is appealing, especially since the civilization could also make use of the entire energy output of its parent star rather than merely a small fraction. Sadly, however, more recent calculations have suggested that gravitational forces would rather swiftly cause such a structure to disintegrate. JG

Fusion Power

A potted summary of nuclear power systems might run: *fission*, expensive fuel, high hazard, dangerous wastes, economical overall; *fusion*, cheap fuel, minimal hazard, few wastes, does not work. Both take advantage of the variation from element to element of binding energy (BE), the energy input required to extract a nucleon (proton or neutron) from the nucleus. Light elements with few nucleons have low BE, since there is a lack of other nucleons for one to bind to; elements with higher atomic number, iron especially, have higher BE; but those with very high atomic number (for example, uranium) have lower BE again, owing to the large numbers of positively charged protons in the nuclei — their mutual repulsion tends to push the nucleus apart, producing disintegration and hence radioactivity.

BE is an energy *deficit*, an amount which must be supplied to extract a nucleon; if elements with low BE can be transformed into others with high BE, the energy difference is released as useful kinetic energy and radiation. In fission we shatter heavy, low-BE elements into high-BE fragments; in fusion we join light, low-BE elements into others with higher BE; in each case the shift is towards the high-BE peak of the curve, towards highly stable elements like iron.

With fusion the problem is forcing light nuclei together: nuclei are positively charged and thus repel one another with increasing force as they approach — until they're virtually in contact, when strong nuclear forces overcome the repulsion and fusion is achieved. To penetrate this electrostatic barrier, nuclei must be flung together at high velocity, supplied by enormous heat and/or pressure.

Promising methods are *plasma confinement* and *implosion*; a standard fuel is DT mixture, consisting of the hydrogen isotopes deuterium and tritium, which should give useful fusions at relatively low temperatures like 100,000,000 K. Plasma confinement relies on magnetic fields to trap ionized fuel (plasma) in a narrow 'pencil', usually bent into a hoop to avoid problems at its ends; the fuel is heated enormously by radio-frequency induction or by passing a current directly through it, and when a sufficient temperature is achieved the nuclei collide fast enough to fuse, producing a large heat output. (*Some* fusion can be obtained at relatively low temperatures, but the object is to extract significantly more energy from the fusion than is required to power the apparatus — the stumbling block of every fusion reactor to date.) Unfortunately, such speedy nuclei are hard to confine with mere magnetic fields — a feat akin to balancing a stream of water on air-jets, yet necessary since fusion temperatures will melt any tangible walls. Invariably, the plasma stream becomes unstable, collapsing before useful, continuous output can be achieved.

The implosion method sacrifices continuous output to avoid instabilities: here a single, solid pellet of fuel is blasted with twelve or twenty symmetrically arranged, synchronized beams of radiation. In theory, the outer layers boil off so violently that their reaction force (as in a powerful rocket) compresses the remnants of the pellet into a dense, hot mass within which the fusion reaction starts, growing as it heats the pellet still further. A sharp burst of energy is produced, after which another pellet is moved into place and another radiation pulse is fired. If electron beams are used, plenty of radiation power is available but the beam builds up rather slowly, allowing the pellet to boil away before being properly compressed; with *lasers the pulse is swifter but higher power less attainable — the US Shiva Nova laser fusion facility performed disappointingly in trials.

Other methods exist. The 'Z-pinch' pulsed system involves a high-powered electrical discharge which sweeps fuel gas before it into a superheated and compressed state where fusion occurs. A variant has solid fuel in a thin metal tube which is magnetically collapsed by passing immense currents along its length. The speculative 'migma' fusion cell requires a particle accelerator to provide fast-moving nuclei which are then magnetically forced into rosette-shaped orbits wherein they collide head-on with one another.

Each method has produced a number of fusion reactions; none has achieved a net power output surplus to the equipment's needs, and a frequent comment is that twenty years would be required between such success and actual commercial viability.

Moreover, fusion is less clean than advertised, since it produces neutrons which infect harmless materials and make them radioactive; and it is also less cheap, since although deuterium (comprising 0.015 per cent of seaborne hydrogen) is touted as cheap fuel, currently feasible mixtures require also tritium, which must be synthesized at vast expense.

Such pessimism has not prevented grandiose plans for a fusion-powered starship, the nuclear pulse rocket (see *interstellar travel), *Daedalus*. *Daedalus* plans include use of the attractive fusion fuel helium-3, virtually unavailable here but more plentiful in Jupiter's atmosphere. At the ship's rear, within an immense bowl-shaped reflector, pellet after pellet of fuel would be imploded with vast energy releases, the whole resembling a huge, continuous neutron-bomb explosion and accelerating *Daedalus* to 135 million km/h. Turning on this engine near Earth might be one means of sterilizing continents ...   DRL

Genetic Engineering

The techniques contained within this concept mark a major advancement of biotechnology: science has made possible the manipulation, substitution and transplantation of organs and limbs; now we are beginning to reach into the cell, to manipulate and control the chemical instructions — altering the body from within, shaping the idea rather than the flesh.

Three main biotechnologies are commonly referred to as 'genetic engineering': plasmid transfer, DNA recombination, and 'cloning'. Strictly speaking, this last is no more concerned with engineering than is sexual reproduction, for cloning is merely a variety of asexual reproduction (gene replication). The microbiological use of the word 'cloning' to refer to the manufacture of specific genes in bacterial culture invariably becomes confused with the notion that the genetic information in an ordinary cell can be used to fertilize an egg, producing an identical copy of the donor.

Plasmid transfer refers to the crossing, between two bacterial cells, of tiny 'loops' of DNA (usually a single gene) that float free of the central, single huge loop of genetic information. These plasmids code for a single protein, usually an enzyme (a protein that makes possible or speeds up organic chemical reactions). In the early 1970s Ananda Chakrabarty noticed that bacteria which were able to break up the hydrocarbons in oil (and which were used to do just that, in slicks) did so with enzymes produced, not by the main DNA material, but by these discrete, auxiliary parcels of genetic material. Oil is a complex mixture of hydrocarbons and a number of different strains of bacteria were needed to digest it; he discovered that he could transfer plasmids from all the necessary strains into a single, rapid-breeding strain, which could thereafter do the same job alone, and faster.

The second — more sophisticated and more complex — technique is *DNA recombination*, the 'splicing' of a fragment of one DNA strand, containing specific genes for specific tasks, into the DNA strand of another organism, which thereafter treats the implant as its own code, and behaves in response to the code. DNA is a string of millions of nucleotides, four complex organic molecules whose several combinations in groups of three code for the production of *one* amino acid, a basic unit of protein. This string of nucleotides can be cleaved at specific positions along its length using specific enzymes; other enzymes can be used to knit those 'torn' ends together. Currently, the most exciting use of DNA recombination is in the 'industrial' production of the hormone insulin, and of interferon, a chemical produced naturally by cells as part of the body's resistance to viral attack. It takes nearly 40,000 litres of blood to extract just 100mg of interferon; now, by splicing the genes that code for its production into the DNA of the intestinal bacterium *Escherichia coli*, and then growing 'gallons' of the bacterial culture, there is a chance that the chemical may be produced in far greater quantity.

Clearly, this technique will become increasingly applicable to the production of vaccines, hormones, healing chemicals and drugs. Drugs? It will soon be possible to 'construct' genes by simply linking together the nucleotide bases in the correct order, fashioning a gene to produce a specific organic molecule, and placing it into the body of a living organism. The gene for the production of insulin has already been so constructed. The possibilities are boundless, not just in terms of production but also in the field of genetic repair, or correction; consider such 'trigger diseases' as Reiter's Syndrome, where a gene located on human chromosome six (in about 4 per cent of the population) can be activated by bacterial infection and produce a chemical that induces chronic arthritis. Perhaps a gene could be manufactured that would 'displace' the disease-inducing gene from its chromosome; or perhaps the genetic information could be implanted in every cell that permanently 'switched off' the unwanted gene. Carried by benign viral particles to every cell in the body, this would be taking medicine right to the level of the chromosome.

Two things cloud the future of such elaborate and sophisticated techniques: fear of the loss of control of an organism equipped with a terrifying destructive potential; and the Business Mentality.

The first fear is more genuine than scientists, and companies involved in the DNA-recombination industry, would have us believe — as genuine as the fear that *any* cultured virus or bacterial strain might escape rigorous laboratory control. And perhaps more so: while Man tampers with the machinery of evolution, evolution is not necessarily quiescent; any controlled strain of bacteria, subjected to an artificial selection method, may respond with a change of its own. That change could quite easily come during the process of application, say, to an oil slick of hydrocarbon-eating bacteria which are designed to 'die of hunger' when the slick is gone; a simple process of 'gene-jumping' and 'gene amplication' (theoretical processes by which cells may be able to respond rapidly to changes of external environment) could result in that oil-eating strain changing its diet, and continuing to grow.

But it is the fact of the 'industrializing' of this new technology that casts the greatest shadow across its future. That strain artificially contrived in the laboratory to be able to eat all hydrocarbons led to an eight-year battle on the issue of 'patenting' the strain. The Supreme Court decision that a bacterial organism that has been artificially 'reprogrammed' is an 'invention', and can thus be patented, means that such control of life has begun to be localized *within* the human population, and not *to* it. One industry may control a lifeform — a bacterial lifeform, perhaps, but think of where the technique is going.

If a bacterial cell can be made resistant to a specific virus, by equipping it with the DNA that produces the antiviral chemical, then so can a human cell. If a package of genetic information can be carried into a bacterial cell by a benign virus, then it can be so carried to all the cells in a human body. In this event, every cell in the body is an 'invention', and in the future some Industrial Body will 'own' that invention.

And, if that person wishes to reproduce, to have a family, he will pass the 'invention' on, if the 'reprogramming' has been stitched into the main DNA mass of each cell. Will he be asked for compensatory payment, for a *royalty*, for the use of someone else's genetic invention? RH

Heat Death of the Universe

In the language of thermodynamics there is a quantity known as entropy; entropy can be defined in various ways, all of which are equivalent to each other, the simplest being that it is a measure of the degree of disorder of the system under consideration. Another, equivalent, definition is concerned with the amount of information which can be extracted from a system, higher entropy implying a lesser information content: 1kg of oranges has a lower entropy than 1kg of protons.

As we observe the Universe about us we see that in general entropy is on the increase. True, matter is aggregating to form stars, and therefore entropy is locally decreasing; but, having done so, the matter reacts in such a way that much of it is transformed into heat energy; this is an irreversible transformation, and heat energy has a very high entropy.

The idea of the heat death of the Universe is thus that the end-state of the Universe may be its reduction to a uniform state of maximum entropy; a totally disordered assemblage of heat energy which can never become anything else, anything more ordered, because to make it so would require an input of energy from outside — and, of course, there is no 'outside' the Universe.

Recently, the idea has been extended by John Barrow and Frank Tipler, who consider that a penultimate state of the Universe is its being a collection of *black holes, *fundamental particles and background radiation. In the course of time the black holes will evaporate; gravitational fields will all cancel each other out; and spacetime itself (see *Relativity) will have disintegrated. The Universe will see its end as a great uniform sea of motionless particles — and, since the sea is motionless, *time itself will have come to an end, since no further change is possible. At the end, the Universe becomes *nothing*. JG

Immortality

Of all the impossible dreams with which Man has preoccupied himself, perhaps immortality is the most familiar. The fact that immortality is an ecological nonsense did not bother Gilgamesh, who pursued the elixir of youth, and learned the lesson of his own mortality.

There is no immortality. But an extension of lifespan? Yes. So perhaps in the dream there was hidden a basic truth, a way to break down the barrier of those 'three score years and ten' — a lifespan that has remained unchanged for at least 2,000 years: war, plague, accident and starvation merely prevent us from reaching our natural limit which has long been fixed.

The evolutionary arguments against immortality are twofold.

First, the ecosystem of Earth is dynamic, constantly changing; it would not tolerate a significant portion of its biomass being isolated from the flow of life and resources through its sphere. *Evolution has coded into the lifeforms of the Earth self-destruct signals of devastating effectiveness; these signals we witness as the process of ageing.

Secondly, evolution seeks to adapt a species to its environment through a high individual turnover and a variable gene-pool, and not through the clumsy process of adapting individuals themselves. Long-lived individual animals (unless they are denied the reproductive process after their first few years) would cause a shift towards species stagnation, and extinction. Evolution would not allow this.

For much of the human race, of course, there is no question but that they are immortal — their religions do not permit the thought of total death. Indeed, if *reincarnation is not simply a question of hypnosis-induced memory, or induced storytelling, then perhaps there *is* an immortal flow of life through our species.

A little easier to grasp is the naïve theory that our bodies are merely the 'carriers' of the true lifeform: our genetic material. This is a 'chicken and egg' argument. Are our genes dictating to our form, or does our form dictate to our genetic code, changing the code so that the form can be made more adaptable? A single gene codes for a single protein — hardly an advanced lifeform — and gene combinations change from generation to generation — hardly immortality; what remains 'fluctuatingly constant' is the gene-pool itself, but this is manifested as 'the species', so perhaps the species (considered as a single lifeform) can be allocated qualities of immortality, or at least extreme longevity. But a species is an arbitrary division in linear time — when was Man *not* Man? The species that we see around us are really the same organisms they were at the very beginning, specialized and altered to fill the nooks and crannies of the ecosphere. So perhaps the only true immortal in the world is the entire ecology.

Man is one of the few animals that is social *after* it has ceased to function sexually (although it continues to perform). Some primates are social in geriatric time, but few other creatures. The most attractive theory to account for the lifespan of a species is that nothing ill-fitting or fatal that manifests itself *after* reproductive life affects selection by natural means. Thus, the gene-pool of a species can contain a great many fatal auto-immune and cell-failure codings that will never have any effect upon the species and its adaptability, and so will never be weaned out — and will thus represent a barrier to the passage of life. There is an answer offered by this attractive theory to the question: how can we increase our average lifespan? Rather than selecting for *earlier* reproductive ability, if the human population could be made to select for *later* reproductive ability/viability there would be a gradual shift in the upper age-extreme of reproductive potential, and a gradual elimination of those fatal genes from the population. One way to achieve an increased lifespan, then, is to twist evolution to our own ends, allowing it to select, but changing social behaviour into an abnormal pattern.

Will it be possible to circumvent nature, to artificially extend our lifespans? Almost certainly. Recent advances in *genetic engineering give the promise that soon cells will be able to repair their own DNA damage; and it seems likely that human cells will soon be reprogrammable, which means that the build-up of destructive (and age-inducing) toxins might be avoided by programming each cell to metabolize those waste-products.

Laboratory work with fibrocyte cells has proven that *in laboratory conditions* such cells are programmed with a specific number of divisions (about fifty) and after they have used up that division-number they die; this echoes the belief that the heart muscle is programmed with a specific, and absolute, number of beats. Will genetic engineering ever be able to reprogramme dividing body cells every ten years, giving them a whole new division-number? And it is to *genetic engineering that one looks to eliminate such trigger diseases as Reiter's Syndrome... genetic code implants, capable of preventing the gene being activated, will overcome the limit to life imposed by this build-up of non-selectable genes.

Cloning is certainly a possibility for making an individual immortal — as long as the experience of a lifetime, locked in the RNA and electric circuits of his central nervous system, can somehow be transferred to the clone. And if you really want to see the future, despite a limited number of years, you might like to 'freeze hop', live a month a year, and remain in suspended animation for the other eleven. But do not count on this just yet: it seems that every tissue type in your body has a different optimum rate and degree of freezing if it is to be thawed 100 per cent perfect! Short of dissolving your body, the risks attached to freeze preservation are immense — not least being the fact that frozen bodies are fragile and tend to shatter when dropped.

RH

Interstellar Travel

The fundamental problem facing would-be interstellar travellers is the sheer distance involved, which implies intolerably long flight times unless the velocities attained by spacecraft can be made to exceed present-day values by a factor of 10,000 or more.

The nearest star, apart from the Sun, is Proxima Centauri, just over 4.2 light years away. A cornerstone of *Relativity is that no material body can be made to travel at the speed of light. If sufficient energy is available, a body can be made to approach arbitrarily close to that limiting velocity, but it cannot be made to travel precisely *at* the speed of light. If information could be communicated faster than light the fundamental principle of *causality (that cause must always precede effect) would break down, for it would be possible to devise circumstances in which the outcome of an event would be known before the event took place, and steps could be taken to prevent that event happening — an obvious paradox (see *tachyons); for example, the crew of a faster-than-light spacecraft could make their interstellar journey and return to Earth before they had set out, arriving in time to prevent themselves leaving on the grounds that they had already been! The logical contradictions raised by the possibility of faster-than-light travel (or communication) are usually taken to imply that it is impossible.

Studies of the interiors of spinning black holes have appeared to indicate that a spacecraft could enter one and emerge in another, separate, universe. Some have argued that the spacecraft would emerge, not in another universe, but at a different point in space and time in our own Universe, and would, by this means, be able to make virtually instantaneous trips over vast distances. It now appears increasingly likely that the theoretical models which offered this 'back door' mode of transportation were too idealized, and that in practice a spacecraft entering a spinning *black hole would be destroyed.

Given the limitations imposed by the speed of light, there are three basic approaches to interstellar travel:

1 The 'slow' interstellar ark, in which

the flight time is many times longer than an individual lifespan. An entire *space colony of perhaps 10,000 people could be despatched toward a given target in a self-contained biosphere which would have to provide all requirements for the generations of individuals who would live and die before the spacecraft finally reached its destination. If, for the sake of argument, 1 per cent of light-speed could be attained, a star system at a range of 10 light years would be reached after 100 years. Apart from reliability factors in the structure, the major problems surely would be of a psychological and sociological nature.

2 The 'fast' starship. Given that means could be devised to propel a spacecraft at a useful fraction of the speed of light (say, 10–50 per cent), journeys to nearby stars could be attained within the lifetimes of crew members. At 10 per cent of light velocity, Proxima Centauri could be reached in about 43 years, while a round trip at 50 per cent of light-speed to a range of 10 light years could be achieved in 40 years of Earth time. Apart from technological aspects the problems would be motivation and boredom.

3 The 'relativistic' starship. If a speed close to that of light could be attained, almost any journey could be achieved within a relatively small fraction of a crewperson's life. The time dilation effect (see *Relativity) implies that the closer a spacecraft approaches light-speed, the more slowly time will pass aboard it compared to the passage of time here on Earth. If a round trip to a distance of 10 light years were made at 99 per cent light-speed then, neglecting deceleration and turn-round times, 20 years of Earth time would have elapsed, but only 2.8 years would have passed for the crew. At higher velocities the effect would be even more pronounced.

Many different modes of propulsion have been discussed as possibilities for interstellar flight, all of the realistic propositions being based on the familiar rocket principle. The final velocity attained by a rocket depends upon the exhaust velocity (the speed at which particles are ejected) and the mass ratio (the mass of the rocket plus fuel compared to the mass of the empty rocket).

1 The nuclear-electric ion rocket. The principle of the ion rocket is that heavy charged particles (ions) produced in a discharge chamber are accelerated by an electric field and expelled from the rear of the rocket motor at high speeds. In an interstellar vehicle the necessary electrical power would be provided by an on-board nuclear reactor. Present-day ion rockets have exhaust velocities of about 50km/s. An improvement in exhaust velocity by a factor of 20 would allow 1 per cent of light velocity to be attained with a mass ratio of about 20.

2 The fusion rocket. Much research effort is being expended to reproduce fusion reactions here on Earth (see *fusion power). Strong magnetic fields ('magnetic bottles') are used to contain the ultra-hot plasma, but so far it has not been possible to achieve this for long enough periods to produce useful amounts of energy. A fusion rocket would consist, essentially, of a magnetic bottle with a hole at one end out of which plasma would escape with exhaust velocities of perhaps 10,000km/s. A vehicle propelled by this means could attain 3 per cent light-speed with a mass ratio of 2.72, and 10 per cent light-speed with a mass ratio of 20 (a mass ratio of 20 × 20 = 400 would be required to achieve a landing, however!).

3 The nuclear pulse rocket. The vehicle is propelled by a series of explosions, part of the blast from each detonation being absorbed by the spacecraft, so adding an increment to its velocity. The concept originated in 1891 with Hermann Ganswindt, and was examined seriously in the USA in the 1950s under the heading of Project Orion, the idea then being to use a series of nuclear bombs to provide the thrust. A test model, using conventional explosives, was flown. A more sophisticated approach currently under discussion is to use a series of miniature thermonuclear explosions produced by detonating tiny pellets of fuel, the blasts being absorbed by a magnetic nozzle at the rear of the spacecraft.

The British Interplanetary Society, in a study called Project *Daedalus*, has proposed a nuclear pulse rocket system using deuterium and helium-3 pellets (see *fusion power), detonated at a rate of 250 per second, to give a smooth acceleration to a 54,000-tonne spacecraft which, using 50,000 tonnes of fuel, could accelerate its 500-tonne package of scientific instrumentation to a final velocity of about 12.5 per cent light-speed. The nominal target is Barnard's Star, the nearest star for which there is evidence of a planetary system. It would be reached in about fifty years.

4 Interstellar ramjet. A major problem with the rocket is the necessity for it to carry all its fuel with it; as a result, much of the energy content of the fuel is wasted in accelerating the remainder of the fuel. The interstellar ramjet was first discussed in 1960 by R.W. Bussard in an attempt to overcome this limitation, the essential principle being that a magnetic scoop is used to sweep up interstellar gas to be used as fuel in a fusion motor. Bussard estimated that a 1,000-tonne spacecraft should be capable of sustaining 1-g acceleration provided that its magnetic scoop could suck in matter over a diameter of about 100km in a high-density region of space, and some 3,000km in a low-density region. Such a craft could, in principle, approach arbitrarily close to the speed of light. The original calculations were based on highly optimistic assumptions, and today there is dispute as to whether more energy would be gained from the fuel than would be expended in collecting it, but the concept is so elegant that it will surely be tragic if it proves to be infeasible.

5 Ram-augmented interstellar rocket. A magnetic scoop is used to collect ionized interstellar gas purely to act as reaction mass (i.e., material to be expelled by the rocket motor) for a nuclear ion rocket. In effect, a vehicle of this type would be a self-fueling ion rocket.

6 Laser-powered ramjet. Proposed in 1977 by Daniel P. Whitmire and A.A. Jackson IV, this uses a ramscoop to collect interstellar gas to be used as reaction mass, the energy required to expel this material at high velocity from the rocket motor being supplied externally from the Solar System by means of a high-powered *laser beam. Ignoring the obvious technological problems (such as focusing the energy on a spacecraft several light years away!), the scheme has much to commend it since the same beam can be used both to accelerate and decelerate the craft on the outward and inward flights.

7 Laser-sail. A suggestion discussed by R.L. Forward is use of the pressure of light from an intense laser beam to push on a huge sail attached to a spacecraft. The power requirement and the scale of the Solar-System-based laser bank would be enormous, and there would be major (though not insuperable) problems associated with *decelerating* such a craft.

8 Matter-antimatter drive. As used on *Star Trek*'s 'Enterprise', this mode of propulsion has long appealed to writers of fiction. Particles and their antiparticles (see *antimatter), when they meet, mutually annihilate with 100 per cent conversion of mass into energy. Antimatter does not exist in bulk — at least in our part of the Universe — and even if it could be made storage would be extremely difficult. Unfortunately, most of the energy released would be in the form of neutrinos and high-energy gamma-rays; so far, no scheme has been devised, even in principle, for turning such emissions into useful thrust.

9 Photon rocket. Photons obviously travel at the speed of light and, therefore, have the highest possible 'exhaust velocity'. A rocket using pure light might seem to offer the ultimate means of propulsion. Unfortunately, in order to obtain useful thrusts, matter would have to be converted into photons at such a high degree of efficiency that probably only the matter-antimatter reaction, with all its attendant problems, could suffice for this purpose.

Many other, much more speculative, possibilities have been raised, but at a more plausible level it does seem that the best prospects for attaining useful interstellar speeds in the next century lie with the development of the fusion rocket or the nuclear pulse rocket.   IKMN

Invisibility

Invisibility seems to be one of those impossible dreams. There are very few records — outside bad science-fiction stories — of people trying to make themselves invisible. This is quite understandable. If you are invisible, light passes straight through you. Sight depends on the interaction between light and your eyes. If, therefore, you are invisible you are also blind.

This is a thought which does not seem to have occurred to H.G. Wells when he was writing *The Invisible Man* — and it does not seem to have occurred to those who have made movies and television series based on Wells' original.

JG

Laser Science

In various applications lasers are being used because their light travels in straight lines, they can concentrate high energies in narrow beams, they have extremely pure colours, or because they produce well ordered, regular 'coherent' light waves. Some applications utilize all these features.

Surgeons early realized that narrowly focused high-power laser beams could be useful in cutting flesh. The lasers they use work at a wavelength which has the beneficial effect of clotting the blood as the laser cuts, sealing the severed vessels. As a result, the patient loses less blood and the wound heals more quickly. Operating on some parts of the body — for example, removing ingrown toenails — less blood allows the surgeon a better view of the work in hand.

Because of its extremely pure colour, the laser can be tuned to the particular wavelength that excites a specific chemical reaction. Bright light of any sort can speed some reactions — for example, photosynthesis — but the ability to illuminate reactants with laser light of only one pure colour promises the chemist a tool to control which of several possible reactions — each with a different 'activation wavelength' — takes place in a brew of many constituents. Study in this area aims to increase the efficiency with which unused uranium fuel can be recovered from exhausted atomic reactor fuel elements: the activation wavelengths for the useful and not useful isotopes of uranium are different; if a solution of the two is irradiated by light of the correct wavelength the useful isotope is precipitated out and so recovered.

Biologists and medical researchers are starting to use laser-activated 'photochemistry'. Some reactions of biological molecules can be enhanced if the diseased cells are treated with laser radiation of the correct wavelength. Photodynamic therapy is one of the most interesting ideas: the technique may prove useful in treating cancer. It has been known since early this century that some chemical dyes are absorbed to a greater extent by cancer tumours than by healthy tissue. Because the dyes fluoresce, shining ultraviolet light on a patient injected with them causes tumoured areas to glow. In the most recent work using lasers, the fluorescence is being further exploited to go beyond mere detection. A hypodermic is inserted into the cancerous tumour and a hair-thin light-carrying fiberoptic is introduced through the centre of the needle. The fibre is connected to a laser with a tunable output wavelength — colour — which is adjusted to coincide with the absorption of the dye. By increasing the laser power to a predetermined value, the cancerous tissue can be irradiated with sufficient energy to kill those cells, while the surrounding tissue — which does not contain dye, and hence does not absorb the laser's energy — will survive. The technique has yet to cure a patient — tests so far have been with animals and patients in advanced stages of terminal cancer — but there have been promising results.

Lasers can also kill people and destroy machines, either directly, by striking them with a high-power beam, or indirectly, by allowing a front-line military observer to 'mark' a target with a laser spot which a missile or tank shell can home in on. According to unconfirmed reports, the US military has already used a high-power laser to destroy a low-flying incoming missile during tests. Recently, it has been proposed in Congress that laser weapon systems be put in orbiting satellites. Although the *launch* of such satellites is inhibited by international treaties, their preparation and manufacture are not.

Mechanical engineers are finding high-power laser beams increasingly useful for welding, cutting and machining metals and other materials. The beam penetrates deeply, allowing thick pieces of metal to be welded. A hot laser beam can be used to heat-temper the surfaces of metal components which need to be hard-wearing. Semiconductor materials such as silicon can be 'annealed' using laser beams to remove manufacturing faults in their crystal lattices. In laser surface-alloying (or laser-cladding) a mixture of metal powders is sprinkled onto the surface of a light, cheap piece of metal having the same shape as a desired mechanical component; a short pulse of high-power laser energy melts the powders and the top layer of the base metal, forming a hard-wearing, and otherwise expensive, alloy on the component's surface.

High-power laser beams are being used to investigate the possibility of controlled nuclear *fusion. Laser fusion is one of several methods being tried, and the research is slow — a power station using this principle is unlikely to be built until well into the next century — but the prospect of unlimited energy from sea-water provides strong motivation.

Again concerned with the energy problem, high-power laser beams are being mentioned as candidates for the transmission to Earth of energy generated in satellite solar power stations — satellites in geosynchronous orbit carrying acres of solar cells to generate electricity (see also *space colonies). Electricity authorities are examining the possibility also of using laser beams as replacements for cables, not only for national distribution networks but also for providing the energy needed by individual homes — a patent has been issued for the design of a domestic refrigerator powered only by a high-power laser beam. For that application the laser beams might be transmitted through flexible fiberoptics.

Some of us could have a laser in our own home if the launch of the laser-read videodisc — a worldwide marketing exercise being conducted now — is successful. The machine uses a focused laser beam to optically read television programmes recorded as microscopic pits in a finely spaced spiral groove of a gramophone-like disc. The discs are pressed much as are ordinary audio records, and should be cheaper to mass produce than videotapes. The most exciting prospect is that programmes might be originated specifically for videodisc production. That could change our whole attitude to television. Today, television programmes must appeal to a very large audience to justify their broadcast. But with videodiscs it might be economic to 'broadcast' programmes appealing to only a minority interest by mailing, say, 10,000 pressed discs to subscribers of a video 'magazine'. However, the laser-based videodisc has rivals which operate without lasers, and these may be adopted in its place.

Laser light could also enter the home via fiberoptic cables. Made of hair-thin glass fibres, fiberoptics transmit light by bouncing it along their internal walls. Telephone calls, television programmes and inter-computer conversations can all be sent along a fiberoptic by modulating a laser connected to the cable's starting-point; a light receiver at the opposite end converts the signals back to electrical ones. The advantages are several, including the ability to send 'high bandwidth' signals — for example, television — over great distances.

Fiberoptics should make all kinds of communications cheaper and better. Videophones will become possible, allowing us not only to be able to see people a long way away but also to call on banks of 'library' information and entertainment programmes. Videophones and similar services could reduce the need to commute to work, thus saving energy. Fiberoptics could make long-distance telephone cables, and hence calls, cheaper.

Researchers see fiberoptic communications as the tip of an iceberg labelled 'integrated optics', analogous to integrated electronics. The integration of optics will herald a new era in which even smaller chips with even greater computing power will operate by the processing of light signals carried on 'waveguides' within them.

Holography is a method of 3-D photography which exploits the well behaved nature of laser light to produce a recorded image of an object which is similar in many respects to the view we have of the object if we look at it through a window. A coloured, moving 3-D image seems at first to be the ultimate in what holography could offer — at least in terms of pictorial applications — and the development of this is currently being conducted in the USSR. But there are technological difficulties — such as the present lack of lasers with the power outputs, colours and beam qualities necessary to produce the individual 'still' frames — and it is still not clear if the effort involved is justified by the improvement that could be made over the '3-D movies' popular in the 1950s.

Holography will remain primarily a process for producing stills for some time to come, and within that domain, in some mysterious sense, the most interesting holograms will be the ones beyond our present conception.

I would like to propose a simple example. Since a hologram is capable of conveying, to an extent, the impression of looking through a window, it should be possible to make a hologram conveying the visual impression of an observer gazing straight down from the top of the Empire State Building. Now set the hologram in the top of your coffee-table... MW

Space Colonies

Although the idea that Man might build large inhabited structures in space dates back some eighty years to the writings of Tsiolkovskii, current interest in space colonies owes much to the investigations initiated in the 1970s by G.K. O'Neill.

A satisfactory space colony must be able to sustain a pleasant, comfortable and safe environment for a large population, many of whom may live there permanently; it must also be self-sufficient. Solar energy collected by mirrors would be used to generate electrical power, and sunlight beamed in directly would provide natural lighting. Food would be grown intensively with the benefit of controlled illumination, and in a closed system in which recycling would be of the utmost importance. A major factor influencing the structure's mass would be the shielding necessary to protect the inhabitants from harmful radiation — solar X- and ultraviolet rays, particles from solar flares, and cosmic rays, as well as small meteorites. The chance of a colony being struck and destroyed by a major meteorite appears to be negligible.

Artificial gravity would be generated by spinning the colony on an axis, with the result that inhabitants on the inside perimeter would feel themselves pressed against the 'ground' by a centrifugal 'force' indistinguishable, in a large structure, from the force of gravity. By adjusting the rate of spin, the strength of 'gravity' could be brought to any desired level.

If such colonies were to be built, likely locations would be at two of the Lagrangian points, L-4 and L-5, located on the lunar orbit 60 degrees ahead of and behind the position of the Moon itself. A body placed in either of these positions would remain in the same configuration relative to the Earth and Moon, orbiting in the same period as the Moon. The advantage of having colonies at this distance, rather than close to the Earth, is that it requires only about 5 per cent as much energy to transport a given quantity of material away from the Moon as to raise it into space from the surface of the more massive Earth. In energy (and hence in economic) terms it would be far cheaper to use lunar, rather than terrestrial, material for the construction work.

The engineering problems would be formidable, but not insuperable. Lunar rock, comprising 20–30 per cent metals and 40 per cent oxygen, seems well suited to provide both constructional materials and atmospheric constituents. The greatest problems are likely to be physiological and psychological.

An early proposal by O'Neill was for a series of colonies, each consisting of a pair of cylinders, housing from 10,000 to, in the largest form, some 10 million people. The largest cylinders would measure about 35km long by about 6km wide, and structures on this scale would be landscaped to give hills, valleys, rivers, lakes, and separate townships; even clouds would form naturally in the atmosphere. An alternative structure, now favoured by O'Neill, is a sphere ('Bernal Sphere'), which gives the maximum internal volume for the minimum surface area, so minimizing the amount of shielding necessary, and allowing 10,000 people to be housed in a structure 460m in diameter and with a mass of some 3.6 million tons. Other possibilities include a torus, which would eliminate the peculiar sensation of having 'land' and people above one's head; and the hollowing out and conversion of small asteroids, either towed to lunar orbit or used *in situ*.

Colonies would be expensive to build; a basic 10,000-person structure would probably cost several hundred billion dollars at 1980 values. However, studies have indicated that colonies could pay for themselves in a few decades by means of suitable industrial activities. One possibility is the construction of satellite solar power stations, collecting solar energy which could be beamed to Earth in the form of microwaves to be converted into electrical power. In time, space colonies could, in principle, become major factors in the human economic system. IKMN

Utopia

Although the word 'Utopia' was invented by Sir Thomas More (from the Greek, meaning 'no-place'), the notion had been around since Plato's *Republic*: the idea of a reasonable society where people could be happy and at peace. It is an idea that has engaged some of the world's noblest intellects — most, unfortunately, overlooking such basic problems as human aggression and boredom.

Plato's *Republic* is memorable chiefly for its remark that an ideal society will be possible only when kings become philosophers or philosophers become kings. And the famous parable of the cave compared men to slaves trapped in a twilit cave who mistake the shadows on the wall for reality. The philosopher is a man who has been allowed to turn and look into the daylight. But, if he goes back into the cave, he will now be half-blind, and the others will take his words for insane babbling. Plato ended by declaring that poetry was dangerous, because it encourages illusions; so poets would be banned from his ideal republic.

More's *Utopia* (1516) describes an ideal and isolated republic in which all property is communal, all men are workers (although for only six hours a day), and there is no violence or strife.

Johann Valentin Andreae (see *Rosicrucians) in 1619 published his own version of Utopia, *Christianopolis*, another 'artisan democracy'.

Francis Bacon's *New Atlantis* (1627) and Tommaso Campanella's *City of the Sun* (1637) both owe much to Plato, and both are enthusiastic about the benefits of scientific inventions.

The story of men like Fourier and Robert Owen belongs to sociology rather than to the history of utopias; but Owen demonstrated that society did not have to be based on an inhumane system of cut-throat competition; his New Lanark community was a model industrial town. The Lake poets talked of setting up an ideal community — probably in the USA (as did D.H. Lawrence later) — but the plan remained unrealized. There were, nevertheless, a number of attempts in the USA in the nineteenth century to put the socialist, or Fourierist, ideals into practice, and *The History of American Socialism* by John Humphrey Noyes (1870) is one of the best accounts of Brook Farm, Sylvania and other such idealistic projects. Noyes himself founded the Oneida Community in 1848, a form of 'religious communism' whose most striking tenet was the notion of 'complex marriage' (or polygamy) in which unwanted children were to be averted by 'male continence', the male having intercourse without orgasm. It seems to have been remarkably successful, despite intense public hostility, which eventually led to the breakdown of the community.

Later utopian works, such as William Morris's *News From Nowhere* (1890), Edward Bellamy's *Looking Backward 2000–1887* (1888) and H.G. Wells' *A Modern Utopia* (1905) are full of the 'idealistic socialism' that originates in More. Wells' later *Men Like Gods* (1923) is especially revealing because, being poorly written and imagined, and so palpably unreal, it is possible to see how far Wells, like most utopians, allowed himself to be carried away by wishful thinking.

B.F. Skinner's *Walden Two* (1948) is on a higher level. Skinner is a behavioural psychologist, and his attempt to outline a society where a practical science of 'behavioural engineering' has eradicated anti-social urges has a plausibility lacking in most utopian works. But this plausibility only underlines a problem that William James pinpointed in an essay called 'What Makes a Life Significant?'. He had spent a week at the Chautauqua Cooperative Community 'where all conditions are ideal': 'And yet what was my own astonishment, on emerging into the dark and wicked world again, to catch myself quite unexpectedly and involuntarily saying: "Ouf! what a relief! Now for something primordial and savage, even though it were as bad as an Armenian massacre, to set the balance straight again. This order is too tame ..."'

Any *Zen master could tell him why. The world that utopians want to set to rights is this practical world with which the left brain is concerned, a two-dimensional world of orderly meanings. Man's problem is somehow to soar into a third dimension of meaning — what Hesse's Steppenwolf means when he speaks of 'Mozart and the stars'. In banning poets, Plato had made an error of symbolic dimensions. Somehow, the whole Utopian dream needs to be thought through from the beginning, with the recognition that the mind of Man has a basic craving for what Zen calls *satori*, but for which the English word 'freedom' is perfectly adequate.

CW

Von Neumann Probes

In October 1928 three European scientists carried out experiments on long-delayed radio echoes, LDEs. These echoes had been observed quite often before: typically, a radio signal would have on reception an additional series of echoes delayed by three seconds. However, the experiments of the three scientists revealed a startling result: when they sent out regularly spaced pulses the echoes which they received were delayed by intervals of between three and fifteen seconds — had the radio signals been simply reflected off a 'mirror', such as a belt of charged particles, the delays would all have been equal.

The results were an enigma. From time to time it was suggested that the echoes were the response of an unmanned probe from another civilization, lying in Lagrangian orbit (see *space colonies). And in 1972 Duncan Lunan mapped the recorded delay times of the echoes against their sequence, and found that the result appeared to be a map of the constellation Boötes, with one star, Epsilon Boötis, displaced in an apparently rational way. Surely, he argued, it could only be concluded that the echoes were, indeed, the response of a Bracewell probe which came from a planet of Epsilon Boötis. Strong evidence suggested that the probe had arrived in the Solar System some 13,000 years ago; in Lunan's words, it 'compiled its maps, and then ceased operations until we invented radio on Earth'.

Lunan's work has, alas, now been invalidated — for reasons with which he agrees. (That his deductions from the recorded LDEs are perfectly logical provides us with a continuing puzzle.) However, this does not mean that there is *not* a probe in the Lagrangian position.

Such a probe is called a Bracewell probe after Ronald Bracewell, who has championed the idea that attempts at *SETI should employ a long-term strategy involving peppering the skies with robot probes. It may take a very long time to obtain a reply, but at least one is almost certain to be successful, assuming one can send enough probes.

A number of people, notably Chris Boyce, have suggested that the Bracewell-probe idea is too simplistic. Building hundreds upon hundreds of such probes, and launching them, would be prohibitively expensive. Instead, they propose a self-replicating probe (or von Neumann probe, after the US mathematician John von Neumann). Such a probe would arrive in a new solar system, find itself a suitable asteroid, and then build an identical replica of itself; the replica would blast off in search of another solar system while the original remained behind to try to make contact with any technological civilization which might emerge.

Such probes would be to all intents and purposes intelligent. Moreover, as they replicated, surely some measure of evolution by natural selection would begin to play a part (it seems unlikely that the replicas would all be perfect). Boyce has suggested that, should mutually alien intelligences find it impossible to communicate (see *CETI), the *sole* means of intercourse open to them is via their von Neumann probes — all machine intelligences should have some common ground. He envisages a growing galactic population of communicating intelligent probes. If, as he suggests, the von-Neumann-probe strategy is a 'uniquely logical' solution to the problem of interstellar communication, then there should be rather a lot of these probes around.

JG

Evolution: 7

After several billion years of evolution, the Earth bears a creature capable of voyaging to the stars, or of destroying the planet which gave it birth. This creature is at last becoming able to exploit the full potential of its brain — or, perhaps, it is regaining an art which its ancestors fully understood. This creature thinks that it is capable of making contact with intelligences born of other planets; yet it is unable to establish intimate communication with itself.

We live in a time of exciting change. It seems that we are on the verge of taking an important evolutionary step forward — the fusion of the left brain with the right, coloured by the experiences of several tens of thousands of years during which the left brain has played a dominant role. Today we are Man; tomorrow we may be, in a very real sense, Superman.

We live in a time of exciting change. It seems that we are on the verge of taking an important evolutionary step forward — our emergence from being a confined, planetary species; our discovery that we are a creature capable of travel between the stars and, possibly, of communication with other creatures like ourselves. Out there we may find death; but if we do not make the journey, in our bodies or in our minds, then we shall never know the true meaning of life.

Both of these changes are imminent; and they are inseparable. In this book you have explored both; and must realize that what are to us, today, merely possibilities may soon become realities.

In this book, Man's further evolution has been portrayed.

JG

FURTHER READING

A full bibliography to *The Directory of Possibilities* would fill many pages — indeed, such a bibliography exists in the home of one of the editors in the form of index cards, and is many inches thick. What follows is, of necessity, a personal selection of books which may lead the reader onward in the main fields of discussion described in *The Directory of Possibilities*. The courteous and willing help of the staff of Exeter Central Reference Library is a pleasure to acknowledge. JG

General
Cavendish, Richard (ed.): *Encyclopedia of the Unexplained*, Routledge and Kegan Paul, London, 1974
Duncan, Ronald, and Weston-Smith, Miranda (eds): *The Encyclopedia of Ignorance*, Pergamon, Oxford, 1977
Jaynes, Julian: *The Origin of Consciousness in the Breakdown of the Bicameral Mind*, Houghton-Mifflin, Boston, 1977
Sagan, Carl: *The Dragons of Eden: Speculations on the Evolution of Human Intelligence*, Random House, New York, 1977
Yule, John-David (ed.): *Phaidon Concise Encyclopedia of Science and Technology*, Phaidon, Oxford, 1978

Part 1: Mythology and the Ancient World
Ardrey, Robert: *African Genesis*, Collins, London, 1961
Ardrey, Robert: *The Territorial Imperative*, Collins, London, 1966
Ashe, Geoffrey: *King Arthur's Avalon: The Story of Glastonbury*, Collins, London, 1957
Barber, Richard: *The Reign of Chivalry*, David & Charles, Newton Abbot, 1980
Campbell, Joseph: *The Hero With a Thousand Faces*, Bollingen Foundation, New York, 1949
Campbell, Joseph: *The Masks of God: Primitive Mythology*, Viking, New York, 1969
Geoffrey of Monmouth: *The History of the Kings of Britain*, edited and translated by Lewis Thorpe, The Folio Society, London, 1964
Grattidge, Sheila: *The Quest for the Grail* (forthcoming)
Graves, Robert: *The White Goddess*, Faber, London, 1952
Hitching, Francis: *Earth Magic*, Cassell, London, 1976
Malory, Sir Thomas: *Works*, edited by Eugène Vinaver, Oxford University Press, 1971
Renfrew, Colin: *Before Civilization: The Radiocarbon Revolution and Prehistoric Europe*, Cape, London, 1973
Story, Ronald: *The Space-Gods Revealed*, New English Library, London, 1977
Thom, Alexander: *Megalithic Lunar Observatories*, Oxford University Press, 1971
Wellard, James: *The Search for Lost Worlds*, Pan, London, 1975

Part 2: The Occult and Miraculous
Baring-Gould, Sabine: *Curious Myths of the Middle Ages*, London, 1866–8
David-Neel, Alexandra: *Magic and Mystery in Tibet*, Souvenir, London, 1967
Deacon, Richard: *John Dee*, Muller, London, 1968

Eliade, Mircea: *Shamanism*, Routledge and Kegan Paul, London, 1964
Gardner, Gerald: *Witchcraft Today*, Rider, London, 1954
Grant, Kenneth: *Aleister Crowley and the Hidden God*, Muller, London, 1973
Grant, Kenneth: *The Magical Revival*, Muller, London, 1972
Harrison, Michael: *The Roots of Witchcraft*, Muller, London, 1973
Huxley, Aldous: *The Devils of Loudon*, Harper and Row, New York, 1953
Leland, Charles Godfrey (ed.): *Aradia, or the Gospel of the Witches*, London, 1899

Part 3: Strange Creatures and Unusual Events
Begg, Paul: *Into Thin Air: People Who Disappear*, David & Charles, Newton Abbot, 1979
Begg, Paul: *Out of Thin Air: People Who Appear from Nowhere* (forthcoming)
Farson, Daniel: *Vampires, Zombies and Monster Men*, Aldus, London, 1976
Heuvelmans, Bernard: *On the Track of Unknown Animals*, Hill and Wang, New York, 1965 (originally published as *Sur la Piste des Bêtes Ignorées*, Plon, Paris, 1955)
Mackal, Roy P.: *The Monsters of Loch Ness*, Macdonald and Janes, London, 1976
Masters, Anthony: *The Natural History of the Vampire*, Hart-Davis, London, 1972
Napier, John: *Bigfoot: The Yeti and Sasquatch in Myth and Reality*, Cape, London, 1972
Stoneley, Jack, and Lawton, A.T.: *Tunguska: Cauldron of Hell*, Star, London, 1977

Part 4: Time in Disarray
Gattey, Charles N.: *They Saw Tomorrow*, Harrap, London, 1977
Gibson, Walter B., and Gibson, Litzka R.: *The Complete Illustrated Book of Divination and Prophecy* (also published as *The Encyclopedia of Prophecy*), Souvenir, London, 1974
Grant, John (ed.): *The Book of Time* (Consultant Editor: Colin Wilson), Westbridge, Newton Abbot, 1980
Koestler, Arthur: *The Roots of Coincidence*, Hutchinson, London, 1972
Mackenzie, Alexander: *Prophecies of the Brahan Seer*, Constable, London, 1970
Priestley, J.B.: *Man and Time*, Aldus/Allen, London, 1964
Vaughan, Alan: *Patterns of Prophecy*, Turnstone, London, 1973
Whitrow, G.J.: *What is Time?* (also published as *The Nature of Time*), Thames and Hudson, London, 1972

Part 5: Inner Space: Mind and Body
Bennett, J.G.: *The Dramatic Universe*, Hodder & Stoughton, London, 1956
Gooch, Stan: *The Paranormal*, Wildwood, London, 1978
Green, Elmer and Alyce: *Beyond Biofeedback*, Delacorte, New York, 1977
Gurdjieff, G.I.; *Meetings with Remarkable Men*, Routledge and Kegan Paul, London, 1973
Myers, F.W.H.: *Human Personality and Its Survival of Bodily Death*, London, 1903
Watson, Lyall: *Lifetide: A Biology of the Unconscious*, Hodder & Stoughton, London, 1979
Watson, Lyall: *Supernature: A Natural History of the Supernatural*, Hodder & Stoughton, London, 1973
Wilson, Colin: *Mysteries*, Hodder & Stoughton, London, 1978
Wilson, Colin: *The Occult*, Hodder & Stoughton, London, 1971
Wolman, Benjamin R. (ed.): *Handbook of Parapsychology*, Van Nostrand, New York, 1977

Part 6: Outer Space: The Universe at Large
Bernal, J.D.: *The Extension of Man*, Weidenfeld & Nicolson, London, 1972

Boyce, Chris: *Extraterrestrial Encounter: A Personal Perspective*, David & Charles, Newton Abbot, 1979
Boyce, Chris, and Grant, John: *Extraterrestrials: Life in the Universe* (forthcoming)
Bracewell, Ronald: *The Galactic Club*, Freeman, New York, 1975
Calder, Nigel: *Violent Universe: An Eye-Witness Account of the New Astronomy*, BBC, London, 1969
Clark, David: *Superstars: Stellar Explosions Shape the Destiny of the Universe*, Dent, London, 1979
Davies, Paul: *The Runaway Universe* (also published as *Stardoom*), Dent, London, 1978
Eiseley, Loren: *The Unexpected Universe*, Gollancz, London, 1970
Goldsmith, Donald, and Owen, Tobias: *The Search for Life in the Universe*, Benjamin/Cummings, Menlo Park (Ca.), 1980
Gribbin, John: *White Holes: Cosmic Gushers in Space*, Paladin, St Albans, 1977
Hoyle, Fred: *Ten Faces of the Universe*, Freeman, New York, 1977
Hoyle, Fred, and Wickramasinghe, N.C.: *Lifecloud: The Origin of Life in the Universe*, Dent, London, 1978
Hynek, J. Allen: *The UFO Experience*, Abelard-Schuman, London, 1972
Koestler, Arthur: *The Sleepwalkers*, Hutchinson, London, 1959
Lawton, A.T., and Grant, John: *The Limits of Light and Dark* (forthcoming)
Lunan, Duncan: *Man and the Stars* (also published as *Interstellar Contact*), Souvenir, London, 1974
Moore, Patrick: *Can You Speak Venusian?*, David & Charles, Newton Abbot, 1972
Moore, Patrick, and Nicolson, Iain: *Black Holes in Space*, Ocean, London, 1974
Nicolson, Iain: *Gravity, Black Holes and the Universe*, Westbridge, Newton Abbot, 1981
Shklovskii, I.S., and Sagan, Carl: *Intelligent Life in the Universe*, Holden-Day, San Francisco, 1966
Smith, James H.: *Introduction to Special Relativity*, Benjamin, New York, 1965
Sullivan, Walter: *We Are Not Alone*, Hodder & Stoughton, London, 1965
Wilson, Colin: *Starseekers*, Hodder & Stoughton, London, 1980

Part 7: The World of Tomorrow
Asimov, Isaac; *Today and Tomorrow and ...*, Abelard-Schuman, London, 1974
Berry, Adrian: *The Next Ten Thousand Years*, Cape, London, 1974
Brunner, John: *The Sheep Look Up* (novel: many editions), 1972
Brunner, John: *The Shockwave Rider* (novel: many editions), 1975
Brunner, John: *Stand on Zanzibar* (novel: many editions), 1968
Calder, Nigel: *Spaceships of the Mind*, BBC, London, 1978
Gabor, Dennis: *Inventing the Future*, Secker and Warburg, London, 1963
Langford, David: *War in 2080: The Future of Military Technology*, Westbridge, Newton Abbot, 1979
Morgan, Chris: *Future Man: The Further Evolution of the Human Race*, David & Charles, Newton Abbot, 1980
Nicolson, Iain: *The Road to the Stars*, Westbridge, Newton Abbot, 1978
Ponnamperuma, Cyril, and Cameron, A.G.W. (eds): *Interstellar Communication: Scientific Perspectives*, Houghton Mifflin, Boston, 1974
Rosen, Stephen: *Future Facts*, Heinemann, London, 1976
Thompson, Alan E.: *Understanding Futurology*, David & Charles, Newton Abbot, 1979
Toffler, Alvin: *Future Shock*, Bodley Head, London, 1970
Wenyon, Michael: *Understanding Holography*, David & Charles, Newton Abbot, 1978

ACKNOWLEDGEMENTS

The editors and publishers would like to thank the following for permission to use copyright material:

Paul Barnett (Editorial): 77; Mir Bashir: 79; Bibliothèque Nationale, Paris: 68 (below); Janet and Colin Board: 66 (below), 68 (above); Ed Buckley: 187 (above and below); John Chard: 67 (below); CSIRO: 184 (right); Mary Evans Picture Library: 78, 80, 177, 178 (below), 179, 182; Mary Evans Picture Library/Andrew Green: 71, 181 (above); Mary Evans Picture Library/Harry Price Collection, University of London: 183; Mary Evans Picture Library/Society for Psychical Research: 178 (above); Fortean Picture Library: 74, 75 (below), 76 (above and below), 188 (below); Kenneth Grant: 65, 69, 70, 72, 180; Duncan Lunan: 67 (above); Chris Morgan: 189; NASA: 184 (left), 186, 188 (above), 190, 192; Royal Astronomical Society: 185; Theosophical Publishing House: 75 (above); John Topham Picture Library: 73, 181 (below); Michael Wenyon: 191 (above and below).

The following gave particular help in the obtaining of certain illustrations, and to them the editors wish to express especial gratitude:

Mir Bashir, author of *The Art of Hand Analysis*, and others; Anne-Marie Ehrlich; Hilary Evans, co-author of *The Picture Researcher's Handbook* and author of *The Art of Picture Research*, and others; Kenneth Grant, author of *The Magical Revival, Aleister Crowley and the Hidden God, Cults of the Shadow, Images and Oracles of Austin Osman Spare, Nightside of Eden* and *Outside the Circles of Time*; Richard Knox, author of *Discover the Sky with Telescope and Camera, Foundations of Astronomy*, and others; A.T. Lawton, author of *A Window in the Sky* and co-author of *CETI*, and others; Roy Harley Lewis of Bookfinders, author of *The Book Browser's Guide, Antiquarian Books: An Insider's Account, A Cracking of Spines*, and others; Duncan Lunan, author of *Man and the Stars* and *New Worlds for Old*; and Iain Nicolson, author of *The Road to the Stars, Gravity, Black Holes and the Universe*, and others. Jane Barnett, aged two, did not help in the obtaining of the illustrations, and so deserves special acknowledgement.

DIRECTORY-INDEX

Numbers in **bold** refer to major discussions. Keywords in SMALL CAPITALS refer to articles in the main text.

Abdul Alhazred; 57
ABOMINABLE SNOWMEN; **85**
Absolute Zero: lowest possible temperature ($-273.16°C$); heat is a measure of the movement of molecules; at Absolute Zero molecules are stilled; 194
acceleration; 197
ACQUIRED CHARACTERISTICS; 101, **122–3**
ACTION AT A DISTANCE; **48**, 147
active imagination; 136
ACUPUNCTURE; 39, **123**, 135, 138
Adamenko, Viktor: USSR scientist; 123
Adamski, George; 200
Adonis: in Greek myth, a beautiful youth who spent summer on Earth with Aphrodite & winter in the underworld with Persephone; thus an important fertility personage, symbolizing the cycle of the seasons; 35
Adventure, An (Moberly & Jourdain); 117
Adventures of an Atom (Smollett); 101
Aereda; 44
aeromancy: divination by unusual phenomena in the sky — comets, meteors, atmospheric effects, etc.
aether; 35, 47, 124, 170, 196
African Genesis (Ardrey); 29, 30
afterlife; *see* *life after death
ageing; 213–14
Agen (France); 113
Agobard, St (799–840): Archbishop of Lyon; 86
AI; *see* *artificial intelligence
À la Recherche du Temps Perdu (Proust); 116
Al Azif; 57
albedo (in alchemy); 48
Alchemist's Handbook (Riedel); 48
ALCHEMY; 47, **48–9**, 137, 152, 155
Aldershot Barracks (England); 93
aleuromancy: divination in which predictions are written on slips of paper, put into cakes or cookies, & then distributed among the individuals concerned — for example, Chinese fortune cookies
Al Mamun; 41–2

Almas: race of 'wild men' reported across much of central Asia, thought by some to be surviving Neanderthals; *see* *abominable snowmen
Alpbach (Austria); 122
alpha rhythms; 55, 126
'alphas'; 144
Altai-Himalaya (Roerich); 29
Altamira; 58–9
ALTERNATE UNIVERSES; 115, 116, **161–2**, 163, 166, 194, 214
Amahuaca Indians; 60
Ambrosius Aurelianus; 31
Amherst mystery; 147
ammonoids: widespread class of molluscs, extant c 380–c 65 million years ago; 34
Amon (demon); 51
AMORC; 152
AMULETS; 49
analytical psychology; 136
ANCIENT ASTRONAUTS; 28, **29–30**, 31
ANCIENT MAN; 14, 16–18, 28, **29–31**, 33, 35, 36, 39, 43, 49, 59, 104
Ancient Wisdom, The (Ashe); 37
Andreae, Johann Valentin (1586–1654); 152, 220
Andromeda Galaxy: nearest galaxy to our own (excluding our two satellite galaxies); c2 million light years distant, c150,000 light years across (slightly larger than our Galaxy), & with a spiral structure (like our Galaxy's); 201
angels; 57, 112, 140
angina; 134
animal magnetism; 54
Anthroposophy, Anthroposophical Society; 154
ANTIGRAVITY; **162**
ANTIMATTER; 94, 116, 118, **161–2**, **162–3**, 174, 175, 216
antimatter galaxies; 162
antiparticles; 118, 162–3, 174, 175, 216
antiproton; 174
A-o-re: Yeti civilization, reported 1940 by a Captain d'Auverne, who claimed he was captured by a Yeti who told him of the A-o-re; *see* *abominable snowmen
apantomancy: cluster of beliefs that chance

227

events or encounters (for example, with a black cat) foretell future events
Apollonius of Tyana; 62
Apollo project: US manned lunar-landing project; *Apollo 11* achieved 1st lunar landing 1969; 197
apparitions; see *doppelgängers, *ghosts
Apparitions and Haunted Houses (Bennett); 54
APPEARING PEOPLE; **86**, 98, 194
Aquarian Conspiracy, The (Ferguson); 14
Aquarian Research Foundation; 60
Aquarius: 11th sign of the *Zodiac
Aquinas, St Thomas (c1225–74): Christian philosopher & theologian; 156
Aradia, the Gospel of the Witches (Leland); 35, 81
Arago, Dominique François Jean (1786–1853): French physicist; 175
archetypes (of life); 114–15
Ardrey, Robert (1908–   ); 28, 29, 30
Ariadne; 40
Aries: 1st sign of the *Zodiac; 48, 102
Arion; 40
Aristarchus of Samos (c310–230): Alexandrian astronomer; 18, 168
Aristotle (384–322); premier Greek philosopher, whose views coloured Western thought until the Middle Ages; 34–5, 44
Arjuna; 156
Arnold, Dorothy; 97
Arnold, Kenneth: US businessman; 29, 198–9
Arrhenius, Svante August (1859–1927): Swedish physical chemist; 1903 Nobel chemistry prize; 193, 194
arrow of time; see *time, arrow of
ARTHUR; 28, **31–2**, **36–7**, 37
artificial intelligence; 206, 208–209
artificial selection; 212
asafetida; 61
Ashburner, Dr John; 124
Ashe, Geoffrey: UK archaeologist, historian & writer; 36, 37
Asmodeus; 44
Assyria; 17
Astaroth (demon); 51
asteroids (or planetoids): minor planets (a few yards in diameter upward), probably debris from a planet which never formed; largest is Ceres (c 750km diameter); 220
Astounding Science Fiction: US magazine; 126
astral body; 124
astral level; 125
astral projection; 50, 128–9, 142
Astral Projection (Fox); 128
astro-biology: a development from *astrology; 49, 102, 103

astrobiology: rarely used synonym for *xenobiology
ASTROLOGY; 47, 49, **102–104**
astromancy: precursor of *astrology; since the bodies of the Solar System represented gods, forthcoming actions of the gods could be predicted from the dispositions of the respective celestial bodies (atmospheric effects were also taken into account — see *aeromancy)
astronomy, ancient; 15–16, 17, 38, 39, 42–3, 104 — see also *observatories, ancient
ATLANTIS; **32–3**, 85, 87, 154
Atlantis, the Antediluvian World (Donnelly); 32
Atman; 156, 157
atoms; 34, 101, 162, 174, 176, 194
Attenborough, David (1926–   ): UK naturalist, writer & broadcaster; 92
Attis: Greek nature god who castrated himself after being driven to madness by *Cybele; 35
Aubert, Dr Edward; 124
auditing; 126
auditory hallucination; see *hallucination
Augustine, St (d. c 605); 173
AURA; **123–5**, 137
Australian Aborigines: Caucasoid race; probably came to Australia from Asia, although it has been suggested they are a result of interbreeding between an aboriginal *Homo erectus* population & insurgent *H. sapiens*; 48, 126
AUTOMATIC WRITING; 52, **125–6**, 140, 153, 200
autonomic nervous system; 123, 135, 156
autoscopy; 142
Auvergne: region of S central France; 91
Avalon: in Celtic mythology, an earthly paradise across the sea to the west of Britain, & the burial place of *Arthur; commonly equated with *Glastonbury; 32, 36
Avebury: vast *megalithic monument in Wiltshire, UK; comprised an earth bank over 400 yards in diameter, an outer stone circle, 2 inner stone circles over 110 yards in diameter, & a mile-long avenue of menhirs leading up to this main section; 39
Aymar, Jacques; 126

Baba, Sai see *Sai Baba
Babylon; 17
Bach, Charlotte; 60
background microwave radiation, cosmic; 163, 202
Backster, Cleve; 121, 145, 146
Back to Methuselah (Shaw); 122
Bacon, Francis (Baron Verulam, Viscount St Albans; 1561–1626): English philosopher &

statesman; 220
Badon, Battle of; 32
Baikal, Lake; 94
Bailey, Alice M. (1880–1949): UK mystic; 132
Bailly, Jean Sylvain (1736–93): French astronomer & revolutionary politician; 114
baka; 64
BALL LIGHTNING; 163
Balmacarra (Scotland); 114
Banerjee, Professor Hemendra; 149
baobhan sith; 88
Barbault, Armand: French modern alchemist; 48
Bardo Thodol; see *Book of the Dead
Baring-Gould, Sabine (1834–1924): UK writer & antiquary; 91, 126
Barnard's Star: small, dim nearby star (*c* 6 light years distant), which has the highest known proper motion; 171, 216
Barrett, Sir William F. (1844–1925); UK psychic investigator & physical scientist who helped form the SPR; 106, 126, 139
Barris, George; 55
Barrow, John; 212–13
barrows; 127, 200
baryon number; 174
baryons; 174
Basa, Teresita; 58
Bathurst, Benjamin; 97
Baum, Lyman Frank (1856–1919): US children's writer; 176
BE; see *binding energy
Beard, S.H.; 52
Bear Lake (Utah); 92
Beauchamp, Christine & Sally; 140–41
Beelzebub's Tales to His Grandson (Gurdjieff); 133
Belgrade: capital of Yugoslavia; 95
Bell, Jocelyn (now Dr S.J. Burnell; 1943–); UK radioastronomer; 194
Bellamy, Edward (1850–98): US novelist & journalist; 221
Bellerophon; 40
Bennett, Sir Ernest; 54
Bennett, J.G.; 116, 133
bent pyramid; 41
Berendt, H.C.: Israeli psychic investigator; 110
'Bergères d'Arcadie, Les'; 44
Bergier, Jacques: French investigator of the unusual; 29
Bergson, Henri Louis (1859–1941): French philosopher; 146
Bering landbridge: strip of land thought to have at one time joined Alaska & Siberia, of considerable importance in that it allowed faunal migration from Asia into the Americas; 33
Berlitz, Charles (1913–): US bestselling author; 87
BERMUDA TRIANGLE; **86–8**
Bermuda Triangle, The (Berlitz); 87
Bernal Sphere; 220
Berry, Adrian; 166–7
Berserkirs; 91
Bertrand, Rev. J.L.; 139
beta rhythms; 55
Beyond Biofeedback (Green & Green); 55, 156
Bhagavad Gita; 156
Bhakti yoga; 64, 156
Bible; 47, 51, 81, 199
bibliomancy: seeking guidance for the future by opening a (usually inspirational) book at a random page, reading the 1st paragraph to meet the eye, & interpreting what one reads in the light of circumstances
bicameral mind; see *brain, bicameral
Bierce, Ambrose (1842–?): US writer & journalist; 97
BIG BANG; 105, 161, 162, **163**, 164, 165, 167, 175, 176, 201, 202
Big Crunch; 161, 162, 176, 201
Bigfoot (or Sasquatch): North American equivalent of the Yeti; 85 — see *abominable snowmen
Bimini, submarine ruins off; 33
binding energy (BE); 209–210
biocomps; 206
bio-energy; 149
BIOFEEDBACK; 55, 122, 123, **126**, 135, 145, 151, 152, 156
bion; 148
BIONICS; **206**, 208
Bird, Christopher; 146
birth chart (in astrology); 103
bivalves: class of aquatic molluscs, extant from *c*540 million years ago onward, with a characteristic shell comprising 2 hinged valves; 34
blackbody radiation: emitted electromagnetic radiation from a black body (ideal body which absorbs all radiation that falls on it) characteristic of its temperature; 163
Black Death; 36
BLACK HOLES; 24, 94, 105, 118, 161, **163–7**, 174, 175, 176, 194, 195–6, 202, 212, 214
black magic; 81
Blake, William (1757–1827): UK poet, painter & visionary; 18, 28, 128, 160
BLAVATSKY, HELENA PETROVNA; 32, 33, **49–50**, 132, 153, 154, 160
blessing; 57
BL Lacerta objects: class of energetic galaxies; 195

229

Bloxham, Arnall; 150
Blue Book, Project; 199
Blumrich, Josef F.: US engineer; 199
Blyth, Sergeant Chay; 92
Boas, Antonio; 200
Bodmin; 32
Boehme (Böhme), Jakob (1575-1624): German mystic & philosopher; 48, 154
Bondi, Sir Hermann (1919-   ): Austrian-born UK mathematician & cosmologist; 202
Book of Ceremonial Magic (Waite); 63
Book of Change; see *I Ching
Book of Coming Forth by Day; see *Book of the Dead
Book of the Damned (Fort); 57, 84, 199
BOOK OF THE DEAD; 33-4
Book of the Law, The (Crowley); 50
Book of Time, The (Grant); 117
Book of Werewolves (Baring-Gould); 91
Boötes (the Herdsman): N hemisphere constellation; α Boötis is the bright red star Arcturus; 221
Bothwell, Earl of; 81
Bo tree; 144-5
Boughton, Rutland; 37
Bovis, Monsieur; 60
Boyce, Chris (1943-   ): Scottish science-fiction writer & *CETI theorist; 222
Bracewell, Ronald Newbold (1921-   ): US radioastronomer; 175, 221
Bracewell probes; 221-2
Brahan Seer; see *Mackenzie, Kenneth
Brahman; 156, 157
brain, human; 20, 23, 55, 119, 126, 209 — bicameral; **13-20**, 43, 49, 55, 103, 121, 128, 134, 151, 157 — left; 13, 14, 16, 18-19, 21, 28, 36, 49, 55, 105, 110, 127, 130, 135, 136, 146, 151, 152, 158, 201, 221, 222 — right; 13, 14, 15, 18-19, 21, 47, 49, 53, 55, 58, 105, 106, 110, 115-16, 119, 127, 130, 135, 138, 142, 147, 151, 152, 153, 201, 222 — unicameral; 14, 28
Brasseur, Abbé; 33
Britain, Saxon occupation of; 31-2
British Interplanetary Society; 216
British Medical Journal; 96
Broad, Charlie Dunbar (1887-   ); 146
Brook Farm: utopian community, active 1841-47, at West Roxbury, Mass.; 220
brownies; 89
Browning, Robert (1812-89); UK poet; 153
Brutus: legendary founder of the British race; 37, 89
Buchanan, Joseph Rodes; 56, 117-18, 124
Buchner, Eduard (1860-1917): German chemist; 1907 Nobel chemistry prize; 44

Buddha; 53, 108, 144-5, 158
Buddhism; 156, 157
Buffon, Georges Louis LeClerc, Comte de (1707-88): French naturalist, historical geologist & taxonomist; 122
Bull, Samuel; 54
Burr, Harold Saxton, 123, 125, 138, 149
Bussard, Robert William (1928-   ): US physicist; 216
Butler, Samuel (1835-1902): UK novelist & antiDarwinist; 122

Cabala (or Kabbalah, Qabalah): body of primarily Jewish doctrines concerned with the nature, manifestations & revelations of God; 50, 63
Cabalists; 108
Cabreras, Count de; 95
Cagliostro, Alessandro di, Count (Giuseppe Balsamo; 1743-95): Sicilian alchemist & physician, widely regarded as a charlatan; 114, 152
Calaway Indians; 59
Caledonian Canal (Scotland); 114
calendar; 39, 43
Callan, Sergeant; 96
Calloway, Hugh; 128
Calmet, Dom Augustine: 18th-century French historian & chronicler; 95-6
Camfield, Barney: UK hypnotist; 106
Camlan, Battle of; 32
Campanella, Tommaso (1568-1639): Italian philosopher; 220
Campbell, John Wood, Jr (1910-71): US science-fiction editor & writer, & early supporter of *dianetics; 126, 175
canals, Martian; 175
Cancer: 4th sign of the *Zodiac; 103
cancer, treatment of; 64, 126, 217
cannibalism, acquisition of virtues by; 146
Can You Speak Venusian? (Moore); 169
capnomancy: divination by studying the behaviour of smoke from (originally sacrificial) fires
Capra, Fritjof; 160
Capricorn: 10th sign of the *Zodiac
carbohydrates: aliphatic compounds, most of which have the general formula $(CH_2O)_n$; 170
Carboniferous: period of geological time, $c345-280$ million years ago; in the US often subdivided into Mississippian (345-315my) and Pennsylvanian (315-280my); 30
Carcassonne, Bishop of; 43
CARD PREDICTION; **104**
cargo cults: quasireligious cults found in primitive societies in various parts of the world;

adherents believe that, if they imitate the more socially advanced visitors from the West, a supernatural agency will bring them 'cargoes' of riches; this basic misunderstanding of the nature & reasons for Western behaviour can cause the primitives to perform great feats in expectation of the cargoes' arrival — even building airstrips
Carnac: huge French megalithic monument, probably built as a lunar observatory; 39
Carrington, Hereward (1880–1958): UK-born US psychic investigator; 142
Carrington, Whately: UK psychic investigator; 109
cartomancy; see *card prediction, *Tarot
Casanova di Seingalt, Giacomo (1725–1798): Venetian adventurer & writer; 169
Case of the Midwife Toad, The (Koestler); 101, 122
Cases of the Reincarnation Type (Stevenson); 149
Cassiopeia A; 165
'Casting the Runes' (James); 56
Castle Dor (England); 39
Cathars (in S France, Albigensians): 12th- & 13th-century heretical sect widespread in Europe; 44, 81, 150
Cathars and Reincarnation, The (Guirdham); 150
Catholic Church, Catholicism; 81, 99
catoptromancy: divination by gazing into a 'magic mirror' — see *scrying
CAUSALITY; 104–105, 107, 108, 116, 118, 175, 198, 214
cave paintings; 31
Cawood (England); 114
Cayce, Edgar (1877–1945): US psychic & healer of especial interest in that he could diagnose clairvoyantly; he carried out work also on *Atlantis & *reincarnation; 33, 124
Cazotte, Jacques (1719–92): French writer and occultist; 114
Cellini, Benvenuto (1500–71); Italian Renaissance artist-adventurer; 61
cells; 172, 211
cellulose: a *carbohydrate, main constituent of the cell walls of higher plants, some fungi, & many algae; 193
Celts; 36, 105
Centuries (Nostradamus); 113–14
Cepheid variables; 201
cerebellum; 135
CETI; 175, 206–208, 222
Chakrabarty, Ananda Mohan (1938–   ): Indian-born US microbiologist; 211
chakras; 124

Challenge of Chance, The (Hardy, Harvie & Koestler); 101
chance; 101, 123
changelings: in popular legend, creatures put in the place of babies by the *fairies, who carried the babies off to Fairyland
Charcot, Jean-Martin (1825–1893): French physician, father of neurology; 19, 54, 135, 155
Chariots of the Gods? (von Däniken); 29
Charles Alexander, Duke of Württemberg; 95
charm; 174
charms; see *amulets
Charybdis; 40
Chatham (England); 86
Chautauqua Cooperative Community; 221
cheiromancy; see *palmistry
Chemical Wedding of Christian Rosenkreuz, The (Andreae); 152
Cheops (Khufu): Egyptian pharaoh, early 26th century BC, responsible for the building of the *Great Pyramid; 16, 41–2
chess-playing computers; 208
Chimaera; 39–40, 41
chirology; see *palmistry
Choisnard, Paul; 102
Chrétien de Troyes; 38
Christ; see *Jesus Christ
Christianity, early; 35, 36, 37, 51, 54
Christianopolis (Andreae); 220
Christian Science: founded 1879 by M.B. *Eddy, a sect which believes the Christian faith is a healer of all physical ills; 55
Christos Experiment; 128–9
Churchward, Colonel James; 33
Circe: in Greek myth, enchantress dwelling on the island Aeaea; 40
City of the Sun (Campanella); 220
clairaudience; 105
CLAIRVOYANCE; 105–106, 111, 112, 117, 129–30, 135, 142, 143, 153, 154
Clarke, Arthur Charles (1917–   ): UK science-fiction writer & futurologist; 29, 82
cleidomancy: divination using a key; in simplest form the key is suspended by a thread from the finger & questions asked of it, the behaviour of the key (swinging, rotating) providing the answers; closely related to *dowsing
cloning; 211, 214
cloud-buster; 149
coal, lucky lump of; 49
Cock Lane Ghost; 147, 153
Cocteau, Jean (1889–1963): French poet, playwright, novelist & film director; 44
coelacanth: crossopterygian (tassel-finned) fish,

extant *c*370 million years ago onward; 91, 92, 93
COINCIDENCE; 56, 101, 105, **106–107**, 115, 137
Coliseum (Rome); 61
collective unconscious; 136, 200
Collinson, Admiral; 199
colour (in particle physics); 174
Columbus, Christopher; 87
comets: nebulous bodies orbiting the Sun in usually highly eccentric paths; 170, 193–4 — nuclei of; 94, 95, 193–4
common sense: logical system which depends on everyday observation & simplified deduction; useful only for the broadest descriptions of reality, and even there frequently fails; 24, 121, 167, 198 — *see*, for example, *causality, *pair creation, *quantum mechanics, *Relativity, *Uncertainty Principle
Complete Grimoire (Waite); 63
computers; 173, 208–209
Comte, Auguste (1798–1857): French philosopher, founder of the positivist school; 11, 15
condor, calling of the; 59
Condorcet, Marie Jean Antoine Nicholas de Caritat, Marquis de (1743–94): French mathematician, philosopher & aider of the Revolution; 114
Confessio Fraternitas; 152
Confucius (K'ung Fu-tzu; *c*551–479): Chinese philosopher; 107
conjunctions, planetary; 103
Connemara (Ireland); 88
conscious; 19–20, 57, 112, 116, 123, 131, 132, 135, 136
conservation laws; 161, 175
Constantinople (Istanbul); 33, 81, 128
Conte del Graal (Chrétien de Troyes); 38
continental drift; *see* *plate tectonics
CONTINUOUS CREATION: 167, 202
Conway, David: UK occultist; 51
Copernicus, Nicolaus (Niklas Koppernigk; 1473–1543): Polish cleric & theoretical astronomer who re-presented the heliocentric theory of the *Universe; 11, 168, 169
Corbett, Jim; 105
Cordoba, Manuel; 60
Corineus; 37
Corliss, William F.; 84
Cornwall, Duchy of: English county; 88
corpus callosum; 13
Cosmic Clocks, The (Gauquelin); 102
cosmic egg: the primeval body whose 'explosion' we call the *Big Bang; 165, 202
Cosmic Ice theory; *see* *World Ice theory

cosmic intelligence; 101
cosmic rays: high-velocity electrons & atomic nuclei which bombard the atmosphere; thought to be produced by *supernovae; 101, 219
COSMOLOGIES, UNORTHODOX; 35, **167–70**, 173
Cottingley; 89
Coué, Émile (1857–1926): French pharmacist; 54
Coulomb, Emma; 50
Covington Medical Institute; 117
Cox, Esther; 147
Crab nebula: in Taurus, the expanding cloud of matter marking a *supernova observed by the Chinese in 1054; at its heart lies a *pulsar; 164, 195
Cracknell, Robert; 110, 154
Cretaceous: period of geological time, *c* 135–*c* 65 million years ago; 34
Crete; 32, 40, 41
cricket; 131
Critias (Plato); 32
Croiset, Gerard: Dutch 'psychic detective'; 140
Cro-Magnon Man; **30–31**, 59, 103–104
Crookall, Dr Robert: UK psychic researcher; 143
Cross, Colin; 56
cross correspondences; **125**, 140
CROWLEY, ALEISTER; **50**, 82, 132, 155
cryptesthesia; 126–7
crystal ball, crystal-gazing; 106 — *see* *scrying
Cthulhu Mythos (Lovecraft); 57
Culloden, Battle of (1746); 114
Curious Myths of the Middle Ages (Baring-Gould); 126
curses; 56–7 — *see also* *jinxes and curses
Cybele: Great Mother of the Gods, whose cult spread from Asia Minor into Greece; she has been equated with the Celtic *Earthmother
CYBERNETICS; **208–209**
cyclomancy: divination by a spinning object; for example, a pivoted arrow, a wheel or, as in the party game, a bottle
Cyclopes; 40
Cyclops, Project; 197
Cygnus X-1; 166

dactylomancy: divination using finger-rings, usually much as the key is used in *cleidomancy
Daedalus; 40
Daedalus, Project; 210–211, 216
Daily Mirror: UK newspaper; 110
d'Alembert, Jean le Rond (1717–83); 22
Dalton, John (1766–1844): UK physical chemist whose atomic theory paved the way for

our modern understanding of the structure & nature of matter; 34, 101
Dames, Michael; 39
Darwin, Charles Robert (1809–82): UK naturalist; 122
Darwinism: theory stating that *evolution occurs by *natural selection; that is, as a result of random mutations within a species; most mutations are not advantageous, but individuals possessing characteristics which increase their chances of survival are more likely to breed, thereby perpetuating the mutation; 16, 122
Davenport brothers; 153
David (? — c960 BC): King of Israel; 89–90
David-Neel, Alexandra; 62–3
Davies, Paul: UK cosmologist; 160
Davis, Andrew Jackson (1826–1910): US psychic; 125, 153
Davis, Gordon; 52
Dawn of Astronomy, The (Lockyer); 43
Dean, James (1931–55); 55–6
death-bed experiences, death trance; 121, 139, 146
Dee, John (1527–1608): English astrologer, occultist, philosopher, mathematician & probably spymaster; 57, 106, 112, 140, 152
Deen, Douglass; 58, 138
Dei Gratia; 97
de la Harpe, Jean; 114
de Maillet, Benoit: French diplomat; 122
Demeter; 40
Democritus (c470–c380): Greek philosopher best known for his atomic theory, which envisaged all things as composed of indivisible atoms; 34
demoniacal possession; see *possession
Demonologie (James VI & I); 81
demonomancy: divination by summoning *demons & asking them questions
DEMONS; 33, 49; **50–51**, 61, 63, 81
de Montesquiou, Robert; 117
Dendera, temple at; 16
Denton, William; 56, 118
Descartes, René (Renatus Cartesius; 1596–1650): French mathematician and notable philosopher; contributed also to several fields of physical science; 101, 144
Despoena; 40
destiny, line of; 109
deuterium: 'heavy hydrogen', hydrogen isotope with a neutron in addition to the proton in its nucleus; 210, 216
Devi; 155
Devi, Shanti; 149

DEVIL; 35, **51**, 58, 81, 98, 104, 156
Devils of Loudon, The (Huxley); 57
Devonian: period of geological time, c395–c345 million years ago; 30
dhampir: son born from the intercourse of a *vampire with a woman
Dhyana yoga; 156
Diana: the huntress, Roman goddess of the *Moon, animals, women in childbirth and forests; 35, 36, 81, 82
DIANETICS; 126
dicyanin; 124
Diderot, Denis (1713–84): French philosopher; edited with Jean Le Rond d'Alembert *Encyclopédie* (*Encyclopedia*); 22
Didier, Alexis: French psychometrist; 106
DINOSAURS, EXTINCTION OF THE; 34
disappearances; see *vanishing people
divided brain; see *brain, bicameral
divination; see *prediction
Divine Comedy, The (Dante); 205
Divine King in England, The (Murray); 36
Divining Rod, The (Barrett); 126–7
Dixon, Jeane: prominent US prophetess; 112
Djoser (Pharaoh); see Zoser
DNA recombination; 211–12
Dogon tribe; 30
Donnelly, Ignatius (1831–1901): US writer & politician; 32
Doors of Perception, The (Huxley); 146, 150–51
DOPPELGÄNGERS (phantasms of the living); 12, 47, **51–3**, 98, 124, 142
Doppler Effect: effect whereby the frequency (pitch) of a wave-radiation-producing source is increased, on reception, if the source is moving toward the receiver, decreased if the source is moving away (listen to a passing automobile's engine noise); 201 — *see also* *redshift
Dornbach (Switzerland); 154
Dostoevsky, Fyodor Mikhailovich (1821–81): Russian novelist; 11, 12, 116
Dowding, Air Chief Marshal Lord (1882–1970); 89
Dowie, John Alexander (1847–1907); 173
DOWSING; 14, 17, 28, 36, 38, 53, 102, 106, **126–7**, 129, 147, 153
Doyle, Sir Arthur Conan (1859–1930): UK writer & spiritualist; 89
Dracula (Stoker); 96–7
Draecaena; 145
Dragon and the Disc, The (Holiday); 200
dragons; 41
Drake, Frank Donald (1930–   ): US astronomer and pioneer *CETI theorist; 172, 176
Drake, Raymond; 199

Dramatic Universe, The (Bennett); 116
Drbal, Karel; 60
dreams, prophetic; 110, 112, 128
DREAMS AND VISIONS; 59, 112, **127–9**, 136, 194
Dream Telepathy (Ullman & Krippner); 128
Dreiser, Theodore (1871–1945): US novelist; 52
druids, Celtic: priestly order, banned by the Romans, which flourished in Britain, Ireland & Gaul; it seems certain their learning was extensive & complex, but about it & their ritual comparatively little is known; the building of *Stonehenge has been ascribed to them; 36
Drury, William; 147
Dualism: philosophical or religious system based on the idea of two opposing or complementary principles; 51, 81, 156 — see *Cathars, *Gnosticism, *Manichees, *yin and yang
Du Bois-Reymond, Emil (1818–1896): German physiologist; 44
Duke University; 129, 154
Duncan, Gilly; 81
Duncan, Ronald (1914–   ): UK poet; 55
Dunne, J.W. (1875–1949); 110, 111–12, 115, 117
Dunstan, St; 37
Dyson, Freeman John (1923–   ): UK theoretical physicist; 209
DYSON SPHERE; **209**
Dzu-teh: race of giant manlike creatures said to be found in Tibet and the Himalayas; *see* *abominable snowmen

Earth: age of; 30, 171 — as black hole; 164 — as centre of the Universe; 167–9 — flat; *see* *flat Earth — hollow; *see* *hollow Earth
Earth forces; 36, 38–9, 49, 103, 129, 147, 153
Earth magnetism; *see* *geomagnetism
Earthmother: important Celtic fertility deity, equivalent to *Cybele; 35, 37, 82
earthquakes; 103
Easter Island: most easterly island of Polynesia; controversy has centred on the many stone heads, of height up to 40ft, erected there on burial platforms by a preColumbian culture; 29
ecliptic: the line apparently traced out by the Sun against the backdrop of the stars during the year; 103
ecological niche; 198
Eddy, Mary Baker (1821–1910): US founder of the *Christian Science movement; her ideas generated from her studentship of Phineas Parkhurst Quimby (1802–66), an early psychotherapist whose treatments made much use of *suggestion; 132
Eddy brothers; 153
Eden: according to *Genesis*, the paradisiacal garden created by God for Adam & Eve, & from which they were expelled after eating the forbidden fruit of the Tree of Knowledge; biblical references would suggest that Eden lay in Mesopotamia; recent researchers often equate Eden with the cradle-land of Man
Edinburgh (Scotland); 134
EEG tests; 126
eels; 28, 92
ego; 20–21, 52, 105, 116, 128, 130, 134, 141, 145, 157, 158
Egypt, pyramids of; *see* *pyramids
Egyptians, ancient; 15–16, 30, 41–3, 104, 123, 129
eightfold way; 174
Einstein, Albert (1879–1955): Swiss-US physicist (born in Germany) who proposed the Special (1905) and General (1916) theories of *Relativity; 1921 Nobel physics prize for his work on photoelectric emission; 16, 23, 24, 25, 115, 160, 164, 167, 169, **196–7**
Eisenbud, Jule; 143
ekimmu: in Ancient Assyria & Babylonia, an undead corpse, *vampire-like, condemned to undeath for violation of taboos
Elder Gods; 57
electron: the (negatively) charged particle orbiting the atomic nucleus; 162, 163, 173, 174, 176, 194
ELEMENTALS; 86, **88–9**
ELEMENTS, ARISTOTELIAN; **34–5**, 38
Eliade, Mircea (1907–   ); 59, 60
elixir of life; 47
elves; 89
empathy: ability, akin to *telepathy, whereby emotions can be transmitted from one person to another
enantiopathy; 38
Encyclopedia (ed. Diderot & d'Alembert); 22
Encyclopedia of Witchcraft and Demonology (Robbins); 81
engrams; 126
Enochian; 112
entropy: a measure of the disorganization of the system under consideration; alternatively expressed as a measure of the lack of information obtainable from that system: thus, for example, the works of Shakespeare have a lower entropy than a billiard ball; 24, 212
epicycles; 168, 169
epilepsy; 13, 116, 206
Epsilon Boötis; 221

Epsilon Eridani: nearby star (c10.7 light years distant); 176
escape velocity: velocity a small body has to achieve in order to leave the gravitational field of a large one; 164
Escherichia coli; 211
ESP; 48, 54, 64, 105, 106, 107, 118, 128, **129–31**, 154
ether, luminiferous; *see* *aether
etheric double; 124, 125
Europa; 40
Evans, Sir Arthur John (1851–1941); 41
Eve (Sizemore); 141
event horizon; 164, 175
Everest, Mount, as black hole; 165
Everton (England); 93
EVOLUTION; 29, 30, 43, **45**, **82**, **99**, 101, **119**, **122–3**, **158**, 198, **203**, 213–14, **222**
evolution, further human; 22, 119, 145, 158, 203, 212, **222**
Excalibur; 32
Exeter; 36
exhaust velocity; 215, 216
exobiology; *see* *xenobiology
exorcism: the banishing from places or people, usually by ritual, of evil spirits or *demons; exorcism is found in many religions, both primitive & sophisticated; 58
Exorcist, The (Blatty); 58
Experiment With Time, An (Dunne); 110, 115
extrasensory perception; *see* *ESP
EXTRATERRESTRIAL INTELLIGENCE; **170–173**, 175, 195, **197**, 200, 201, 206, 207–208, 209
extroversion; 136
Eysenck, Hans Jurgen (1916–   ): UK psychologist; 49, 102, 103
Ezekiel; 199

Faculty X; **116**, 151, 152
fairies; 86, 88–9, 98
Fairley, Peter: UK TV journalist & author; 110, 130
Fairy Faith in Celtic Countries, The (Wentz); 88
faith healing; *see* *healing
fakirs; 55, 156
Fama Fraternitas of the Worthy Order of the Rosy Cross; 152
Fascism; 148
Fast, Howard Melvin (1914–   ): US writer; 205
faster-than-light travel; 167, 175, 198, 214 — *see also* *tachyons
'fast' starship; 215
feng-shui; 39
Féré, Dr Charles; 124
Ferguson, Marilyn; 14

fermentation; 44
FERTILITY RELIGION; 17, **35–6**, 37, 39, 40, 81
Feynmann, Richard (1918–   ): US physicist; 1965 Nobel physics prize; 162
Fian, Dr John; 81
fiberoptics; 217, 218–19
Ficus religiosa; 144–5
fifth dimension; 205
Fire From Heaven (Harrison); 84
Fischer, Doris; 140, 141
fish, showers of; 11, 12, 84
Fiske, Virginia (1910–   ); 144
fission power; 209–10
Fitzgerald, George Francis (1851–1901): Irish physicist; 196
Flamel, Nicholas (1330–1418); 48
Flammarion, Nicolas Camille (1842–1925): French astronomer & popularizer of science; 175
Flanagan, G. Pat; 60
FLAT EARTH; 167, 168, **173**
Fleming, Mrs Alice (1868–1948): UK medium; 125
Flight 19; 87
flocculation index; 102
flood; 32
flying saucers, *see* *UFOs
Flying Saucer Vision, The (Michell); 200
folk memory; 89
Forbes, Mrs: UK medium; 125
form; **131–2**
formaldehyde window; 197
Forman, Joan; 117
Fort, Charles Hoy (1874–1932): US writer and student of the unexplained; 11–12, 57, 84, 199
Fortean Society: founded 1931 by *Dreiser, Ben Hecht (1894–1964), *Powys, Alexander Woollcott (1887–1943) & others to further the investigation of Fortean phenomena; 84
Fortean Times, The: UK magazine; 84
Fortune, Dion (Violet Mary Firth; 1891–1946): UK occultist & author of numerous works; 37
fortune-telling; *see* *card prediction, *I Ching, *numerology, *palmistry, *prediction, *scrying, *tealeaf prediction
Forward, R.L.; 216
fossils; 45, 82, 193
Foster, David; 101
Fotheringhay (England), church at; 117
four-card problem; 18–19, 18n, 21
Fourier, François Marie Charles (1772–1837): French socialist; 220
fourth dimension; 115, 197
Four Zoas, The (Blake); 28, 60
Fox, Elizabeth; 155

Fox, John; 153
Fox, Margaret & Kate; 140, 147
Fox, Oliver; *see* *Calloway, Hugh
Fox, Sidney W. (1912–   ): US biochemist & experimental biologist; 172
Francis of Assisi, St (c1181–1226): Italian Christian mystic who founded the Franciscans; 155
Franz Ferdinand (1863–1914): Archduke of Austria; 56
Frazer, Sir James George (1854–1941): UK social anthropologist, author of the influential *The Golden Bough* (published in various forms after 1890); 35, 105
Free Associations (Jones); 11
freedom; 116, 133, 157–8, 221
French Revolution; 22, 111, 114
Freud, Sigmund (1856–1939): Austrian neurologist and psychiatrist, founder of psychoanalysis; 11, 15, 19–20, 54, 125, 128, 135, 136, 137, 148, 157
Freya; 88
Frithelstock Priory; 36
frogs, showers of; 11, 84
Frontiers of Astronomy (Hoyle); 167
Fukurai, Tomokichi; 143
Fuller, John G.; 200
FUNDAMENTAL PARTICLES; 105, 162, 163, **173–5**, 198, 212
Furies; 39
FUSION POWER; **209–11**, 215, 218
fusion rocket; 215, 216
future, nature of the; 104, 109, 110
future shock: term used by Alvin Toffler in his *Future Shock* (1970) to describe the cultural shock which we are beginning to experience as the rate of technological progress accelerates to the extent that most people are unable to keep pace with it, & consequently find themselves lost & bewildered in a world increasingly alien to their understanding; since cultural shock was responsible for, for example, the extinction of the Tasmanian race & the startling decline of the Amerinds, both in a frighteningly short period of time, it is evident that future shock should be taken seriously; no government today appears to be doing anything to ameliorate future shock's adverse affects; 203
futurology: the science of establishing possible and likely future trends by consideration of the complex of all current trends and the interactions between them

Gaddis, Vincent; 84, 87
Gaea; 40

GALACTIC CLUB; 118, **175**
Galanopoulos, A.G.: Greek archaeologist; 32
galaxies; 164–5, 166, 195–6, 202
galaxies, recession of the; 161, 163, 176, 198, 202
Galaxies of Life (Toth); 138
Galaxy (Milky Way); 34, 164–5, 166, 201
Galgani, St Gemma (1878–1903); 155
Galileo Galilei (1564–1642): Italian physicist & astronomer; 175
Gallatin (Tennessee); 12
GAMES THEORY; **131–2**
Gandhi, Mohandas Karamchand 'Mahatma' (1869–1948): Indian civil-rights & nationalist leader; 55
Ganswindt, Hermann: German inventor; 215
Gardner, Gerald Brosseau (1884–1964): UK writer generally regarded as responsible for the witchcraft revival; author of *Witchcraft Today* (1954) & *The Meaning of Witchcraft* (1959); 35, 82
Gardner, Martin: US popularizer of science; 15
garlic; 96
gastropods: class of aquatic molluscs, extant *c* 600 million years ago onward, characterized by a helico-conical shell; 34
Gauquelin, Michel: French statistician & investigator of *astrology; 102–103
Gauric, Luc: Italian seer; 113
Geller, Uri: prominent Israeli-born psychic apparently possessed of paranormal powers; 130, 143, 200
gematria; 108
Gemini: 3rd sign of the *Zodiac; 102
gene replication; 211
genes: the bearers of information in heredity, comprising chain-like nucleic acid molecules (generally DNA, in some organisms RNA); 122, 123, 211–12, 213, 214
GENETIC ENGINEERING; **211–12**, 214
genies; *see* *jinns
geocentric cosmology; 11–12, 167–9
geodetic lines; 39
Geoffrey of Monmouth (Gaufridus Monemutensis; c1100–c1155): Welsh cleric whose *History of the Kings of Britain* was largely responsible for the rise in popularity and spread of the *Arthur legends; 31, 37
geomagnetism: the Earth's magnetism; *also* the study of the Earth's magnetic field (the geomagnetic field) in both the present & the past (palaeomagnetism); palaeomagnetic studies have considerably supported the theory of *plate tectonics; 17, 28, 31, 39, 49, 102–103, 125, 195
geomancy: divination by interpreting randomly created patterns made, for example, by

throwing earth or pebbles on the ground or by randomly stabbing with a pencil at a sheet of paper
George, St; 41
Gervaise of Tilbury (*fl.* 1211); 86
Gesetz der Serie, Das (Kammerer); 106–107
gestalt faculty; 135
Ghost and Divining Rod (Lethbridge); 53, 127
Ghost and Ghoul (Lethbridge); 53
GHOSTS; 12, 47, 51, **53–4**, 56, 98, 105, 140, 146, 147, 148, 153, 200
ghouls; 56
GIANTS; **89–90**
Giant's Causeway: unusual geological structure in Antrim, N Ireland; 90
Gigantes; 89
Gilbert Islands; 59, 129
Gilgamesh; 213
Giza; 41
Glaskin, G.M.; 128–9
GLASTONBURY; 28, 32, **36–7**
Glastonbury Abbey; 36–7
Glastonbury scripts; 52
Glastonbury Tor; 36
Glasyalabolas (demon); 51
Glaucus; 40
glossolalia; 58
Gnosticism: preChristian religious system which maintained material things were evil & spiritual things good; secret knowledge (gnosis) provided the road to salvation; the system had an important influence on some early Christian sects, but this waned after the 2nd century; 81
go; 208
God; 13, 23–4, 38, 42, 51, 81, 122, 128, 156, 157, 202
Goddard, Air Marshal Sir Robert Victor (1897–); 200
Gödel, Kurt (1906–): Austrian-US physicist; 23
Gödel's Theorem: theorem proposed by *Gödel, that *any* mathematical (by extension, logical) system contains statements which can be proved or disproved only by recourse to axioms outwith the system; 23
gods, worship of; 13, 17, 43, 45, 64
Gods and Spacemen in the Ancient East (Drake); 199
Goethe, Johann Wolfgang von (1749–1832): major German writer; 122, 154
Goethe Archives; 154
GOG AND MAGOG; **37**, 89
Gogmagog (Lethbridge); 37
Gold, Thomas (1920–): Austrian-born US cosmologist; 202

Golden Bough, The (Frazer); 35, 105
Golden Dawn, the Hermetic Order of the: English magical society founded *c*1887 by William Wynn Westcott (1848–1925), Macgregor Mathers (1854–1918) & William Woodman (1828–91); its many members included *Crowley, Algernon Blackwood (1869–1951), *Yeats & Arthur Machen (1863–1947); 48, 80
Golding, Evelyn: UK psychologist; 18
Gold of a Thousand Mornings (Barbault); 48
Gold of the Gods (von Däniken); 29
Goliath; 89–90
Gooch, Stan: UK psychologist & writer; 31, 135, 138
Goodfellow, Robin; 89
Gorczynski, Dr R.M.; 123
Gorgons; 40
Gorlois, Duke; 31
Graeae; 40
Graham, Richard; 81
GRAIL; 32, 36, **37–8**
Gramont, Duchesse de; 114
Grandier, Father Urbain; 57
Grant, Joan; 150
Graves, Robert Ranke (1895–): UK novelist & poet, whose many works include *The White Goddess* (1948); 28, 36, 41, 53, 57, 205
gravity; 118, 162, 163–7, **197**, 219
'Great Beast 666'; *see* *Crowley, Aleister
Great Eastern; 56
Great Old Ones; 57
Great Pyramid; 15–16, 17, 29, **41–3**, 60, 85, 200; *see also* *pyramids
Great Work; 48
Great Yarmouth (England); 117
Greaves, John: Oxford scholar; 42
Greeks, ancient; 63, 173
Green, Alyce: US psychologist; 55, 156
Green, Andrew M.: UK ghost-hunter; 53
Green, Celia: UK psychical investigator; 12n, 142
Green, Elmer Ellsworth (1917–): US psychologist; 55, 126, 156
green children; 86
Greene, Graham (1904–): UK novelist; 20
Green Lion; 48
Green Roads of England, The (Hippesley Cox); 38
Greffulhe, Mme; 117
Gribbin, John: UK cosmologist & popular author; 103, 160, 202
Grimble, Sir Arthur; 59, 60, 129
grimoires; 51, 63–4
Groddeck, George; 135
Guide to Modern Thought (Joad); 117

237

Guinevere, Queen: wife of *Arthur & adulterous lover of Sir Lancelot du Lac; 32, 36
Guirdham, Arthur; 56, 150
Gulf Stream; 87
gullibility; 24
GURDJIEFF, GEORGEI IVANOVITCH; 48–9, 85, 106, 128, **132–4**
Gurney, Edmund (1847–1888); 125
gypsies; 104

Hadrian's Wall: 73-mile long wall, begun c AD 122, across the British mainland at the behest of the Roman Emperor Hadrian (76–138); 32
Hahnemann, Christian Friedrich Samuel (1755–1843); German physician; 134
Haldane, John Burdon Sanderson (1892–1964): UK geneticist, futurologist & writer; 84
hallucinated guidance; 17
hallucination; 61, 63, 112, 117, 145 — auditory; 12–13
halo; 123
Hals, Frans (c 1580–1666)
Hammond, Rev. C.; 125
Handbook of Parapsychology (ed. Wolman); 131
Hapgood, Charles; 32–3
Hardy, Sir Alister Clavering (1896–   ): UK biologist; 101, 122–3
Haroun al Raschid; 41–2
Harris, Thomas Lake (1823–1906): US mystic; 132
Harrison, Michael: UK author & scholar; 36, 84
Hatha yoga; 156
Hauffe, Frederica; 153
HAUSER, KASPAR; 11, 86, **90**
Hawking, Stephen (1942–   ): UK physicist; 23–4, 165
Hawkins, Gerald: US astronomer; 39
head, line of the; 109
'head consciousness'; 18, 20, 136
HEALING; 39, 54–5, 64, 81, 126, 132, 134, 145–6
heart, line of the; 109
HEAT DEATH OF THE UNIVERSE; **212–13**
heavenly spheres; 167–9
Heidegger, Martin (1889–1976): German philosopher, precursor of existentialism; 21
Heisenberg, Werner Karl (1901–76): German physicist who in 1927 proposed the *Uncertainty Principle; 23
helium; 163
helium-3; 210, 216
hell; 62
Helvetius, Claude Adrien (1715–71): French *Encyclopédiste* (*see* *Diderot, Denis) whose *The Mind* (1758) caused controversy; 48
Hemingway, Ernest (1899–1961): US novelist; 1954 Nobel literature prize; 20
Henry II; 37
Henry II (of France); 113
Henry III (of France); 113
Henry VIII; 37
herbs, magic and; 63
Herodias; 35
Herodotus (c 485–425): Greek historian & geographer, regarded as the founder of history as a systematic study; 41
Herophilus (c300BC): Alexandrian physician; 144
Herrigel, Eugen; 157
Herschel, Sir William (1738–1822): German-born UK astronomer, who discovered Uranus (1781), showed the Sun moved through space (1783), proved the existence of binary star systems (1803), etc.; 171, 175
Hesse, Hermann (1877–1962): German-born Swiss novelist; 1946 Nobel literature prize; 21, 147, 221
Hewish, Anthony (1924–   ): UK radioastronomer; shared 1974 Nobel physics prize; 194
hexagrams; 107
higher sense perception; 124
Hill, Mr & Mrs Barney; 200
Hill, George; 170
Hilprecht, Professor Herman Volrath (1859–1925); 127–8
Himmler, Heinrich (1900–45); 102, 169
hini xuma; 60
Hippesley Cox, R.; 38
Hiroshima (Japan); 94
History of American Socialism, The (Noyes); 220
History of the Kings of Britain (Geoffrey of Monmouth); 31
Hitler, Adolf (1889–1945); 38, 102, 148, 169
hobgoblin; 89
Hodgson, Dr Richard (1855–1905): UK psychic investigator; 140
Hogmanay; 49
Holiday, F.W.; 93, 200
hollow Earth; 84, **169**
holography; **219**
Holroyd, Stuart; 145–6, 200
Home, Daniel Dunglas (1833–86): prominent Scots-born medium, whose feats were probably the most dramatic & versatile of all time; 49, 138, 140, 153, 154
homing instinct; 17, 28, 38, 102
HOMOEOPATHY; **134**
homoeostatic mechanism; 54, 55
Homo erectus; 30
Homo sapiens; 30 — *see also* *Man
Hood, Robin: legendary medieval English outlaw & rebel against Norman rule; 89

Hörbiger, Hans (1860–1931): Austrian unorthodox cosmologist; 85, 169
horseshoe, lucky; 49
Hotei; 56
houses (in astrology); 103
Howe, Ellic; 102
Hoyle, Sir Fred (1915–   ): UK astronomer, cosmologist, science-fiction writer & popularizer of science; 167, 193–4, 199, 202
HSP see *higher sense perception
Hubbard, Lafayette Ronald (1911–   ): US science-fiction writer and pioneer of *dianetics & scientology; 126, 132
Hubble, Edwin Powell (1889–1953): US astronomer; showed certain *nebulae are in fact external galaxies (1924); 201
Hubble's Constant; 176, 201–202
Hudson, William Henry (1841–1922): UK writer; 55, 115
Huebner (Hübner), Otto; 144
Hugh of Laon (12th century); 32
Human Personality and Its Survival of Bodily Death (Myers); 52, 138
Hume, David (1711–76): UK empirical philosopher & scholar; 20
HUMOURS; 38
Huni (pharaoh); 41
Hunt, Robert; 89
Hurkos, Peter (1911–   ): Dutch-born US 'psychic detective'; 140
Husserl, Edmund (1859–1938): Czech-born German philosopher, founder of the school of phenomenology; 20
Huxley, Aldous (1894–1963): UK novelist; 34, 52, 57, 146, 150–51
Hydesville rappings; 124, 138, 147, 153
Hydra; 122–3
hydrocarbons: organic compounds of carbon & hydrogen atoms only; 170, 211
hydrogen: simplest element (1 proton + 1 electron), usually found as the molecule H_2; comprises 92.7% of the matter in the Universe; 163, 197 — see also *deuterium, *tritium
hydroxyl molecule (or hydroxyl ion): combination of 1 hydrogen atom with 1 oxygen atom to give the negatively charged ion OH^-; 197
Hynek, J. Allen: US astrophysicist and UFOlogist; 199
HYPERSPACE; 175
hypnagogic imagery, hypnagogic state; 112, 128
HYPNOSIS; 19, 50, 54, 55, 57, 81, 106, 125, 134–6, 141, 150, 155, 156, 200, 213
hysteria: psychiatric condition characterized by emotional instability, over-reaction, etc.; 19, 54, 58, 135, 142, 155

I CHING; 107–108, 137
ichthyosaurs: group of marine reptiles, extant c 210–c 65 million years ago; 34
Icosaméron (Casanova); 169
ignis fatuus; see *Will-o'-the-wisp
Immortal Hour, The; 37
IMMORTALITY; 213–14
immunology; 123
implosion (in fusion); 210
imps; 89
Incas: preColumbian people whose empire extended up the West coast of South America from central Chile to Ecuador; their advanced civilization was destroyed by the Spanish under Pizarro in the mid-16th century; 59
incubi: male *demons said to prey sexually on sleeping females; 81 — see also *succubi
individuation; 49, 137
infrared: electromagnetic radiation of frequency lower than that of red light; 196
Inquisition; 81, 152
In Search of the Miraculous (Ouspensky); 134
Institute for the Harmonious Development of Man; 133
insulin; 211
integrated optics; 218–19
intelligence, evolution of; 82, 99, 158, 172, 222
intelligence, nature of; 172–3, 207–208, 208–209, 222
interferon; 211
Interrupted Journey, The (Fuller); 200
interstellar ark; 214–15
interstellar ramjet; 216
INTERSTELLAR TRAVEL; 166, 210–211, 214–16, 222
introversion; 136
intuition; 13, 28, 105
Inverness (Scotland); 114
INVISIBILITY; 217
Invisible College, The (Vallée); 201
Invisible Man, The (Wells); 217
ion rocket; 215
ions: atoms or combinations thereof which have acquired electrical charge through losing (positive ion) or gaining (negative ion) electrons; 215
Iron Age; 36, 127
Isis: dominant Egyptian mother-goddess; 33
Isis Unveiled (Blavatsky); 50
Israeli Parapsychological Society; 110
Ivenes; 58

'Jack and the Beanstalk'; 89

Jack-o'-lantern; 89 — *see* *Will-o'-the-wisp
Jackson, A.A., IV; 216
'Jack the Giant Killer'; 89
Jack the Ripper; 91
Jacobsen, Nils; 138
Jacolliot, Louis; 157
James, Montague Rhodes (1862–1936): UK medievalist & ghost-story writer; 56
James, William (1842–1910): US psychological philosopher who founded the school of pragmatism; 20, 140, 150, 151, 221
James VI of Scotland & (from 1603) I of England & Scotland: Stuart king, investigator of the occult, & scholar; 81
Janet, Pierre Marie Félix (1859–1947): French neurologist & psychologist; 142
Jasbir Lal Jat; 57, 121, 149–50
Jaynes, Dr Julian: US psychologist; 12–13, 15, 17, 28, 36, 39
Jenkins, Stephen; 37, 200
Jerusalem (Blake); 28
Jerusalem, Temple of; 44
Jessup, M.K.; 199
Jesus Christ; 21, 35, 37, 41, 51, 155, 173
jinns (or djinns, genies): invisible & powerful supernatural entities (spirits or demons) frequently encountered in Arab folklore; as jinns may be either good or bad, they seem to correspond to *angels and *demons (fallen angels)
JINXES AND CURSES; 47, 53, **55–7**
Jnana yoga; 156
Joad, Cyril Edwin Mitchinson (1891–1953); 117
Job; 51
jogis; 156
Johnson, Dr Samuel (1709–84): UK writer, wit & lexicographer; 147, 152–3
Johnston, Charles; 153
Jomard, Edmé-François (1777–1862); 42
Jones, Alfred Ernest (1897–1958): UK psychoanalyst, biographer of *Freud; 11, 15
Joseph of Arimathea, St; 36, 37
Joseph of Copertino, St (1603–63); 138
Joshua; 170
Jourdain, Eleanour; 117
Journal of Abnormal Psychology; 57
Jullian, Philippe; 117
JUNG, JUNGIANISM; **136–7**
Jung, Carl Gustav (1875–1961): Swiss psychoanalyst; 48, 49, 56, 57–8, 101, 107–108, 115, **136–7**, 200
Jupiter (planet); 102, 103, 167, 170, 171, 210
Jupiter Effect, The (Gribbin & Plageman); 103

ka; 33

Kabbalah; *see* *Cabala
Kali; 155, 157
Kamiya, Joe; 126
Kammerer, Paul (1880–1926): Austrian biologist & student of *coincidence; 101, 106–107, 122
Kaptar: a race of 'wild men' similar to the *Almas
Karagulla, Dr Shafica; 124
Karma yoga; 156
Kasantsev, Aleksander (1906–   ): USSR science & science-fiction writer; 94
Kaulback, Mrs A.M.; 112–13
Keel, John; 200–201
Keeton, Joe; 150
Kelley, Edward (1555–95): Elizabethan scryer, occultist & associate of *Dee; *Crowley claimed to be a reincarnation of Kelley; 106, 112, 140
kelpie; 88
Kennedy, John Fitzgerald; 112
Kepler, Johannes (1571–1630): German astronomer & mystic; 16
Kerner, Justinus; 153
Keyhoe, Donald; 199
Khufu; *see* *Cheops
Kierkegaard, Sören Aabye (1813–55): Danish philosopher, precursor of existentialism; 11
Kilbracken, Lord; 110
Kilner, Dr Walter J. (1847–1920): UK medical scientist; 124, 149
King, John; 153
King Arthur's Avalon (Ashe); 36
King Kong; 85
Kipling, Joseph Rudyard (1865–1936): UK writer; 1907 Nobel literature prize; 111
Kirlian, Semyon: USSR electrician; 137, 149
Kirlian, Valentina; 137
KIRLIAN PHOTOGRAPHY; 44, 123, 130, **137–8**
Knaresborough (England); 114
Knossos; 40–41
koans; 158, 201
kobolds; German spirits adopting the rôles of either *brownies or subterranean gnomes
Koestler, Arthur (1905–   ): Hungarian-born UK writer; 101, 107, 122
Koresh; *see* *Teed, Cyrus Reed
Krafft, Karl Ernst (1900–45); 102
Krakatoa; 34
Kraken; 91–2
Krishna; 156
Kulagina, Nina; 130
Kulik, Leonid A. (1883–1942): USSR meteorologist; 93–4

ladder of selves; 110–11, 121, **141–2**

Ladram Beach; 56
Lagrangian points; 219, 221
Lake poets: S.T. Coleridge, R. Southey, W. Wordsworth; 160, 220
Lal, Jasbir; *see* Jasbir Lal Jat
lamaism; 62
Lamarck, Jean Baptiste Pierre Antoine de Monet, Chevalier de (1744–1829): French naturalist, taxonomist & evolutionary theorist; 122–3
Lamarckism: theory of *evolution by the inheritance of *acquired characteristics; 122–3
Lamb, F. Bruce; 60
Lambert, C.J.; 56
Lancet: UK medical journal; 85
landbridges; 33
Lang, Andrew (1844–1912): UK folklorist & antiquarian; 35, 105, 106, 126
Lang, Cosmo Gordon (1864–1945): Archbishop of Canterbury; 139
Lang, David; 12, 98
Laplace, Pierre-Simon de (1749–1827): French mathematician & astronomer; 164
larvae: in Ancient Greece, evil spirits which tormented young children
laser (from *l*ight *a*mplification by *s*timulated *e*mission of *r*adiation): device producing an intense beam of light of a single colour; 210, 216, 217–19
laser cladding; 218
laser fusion facility; 210
laser-powered ramjet; 216
laser-sail; 216
LASER SCIENCE; **217–19**
laser surface-alloying; 218
Last Supper; 37
Latrodectus mactans; 134
Lavoisier, Antoine Laurent (1743–94): French chemist; 84
Law of Psychic Phenomena, The (Hudson); 55
Lawrence, David Herbert (1885–1930): UK novelist & poet; 11, 18, 20, 21, 135–6, 220
Lawrence, Thomas Edward ('Lawrence of Arabia'; 1888–1935): UK guerrilla fighter and author of *The Seven Pillars of Wisdom* (1926); 16, 17
laws, scientific; 24–5
Laxaria; 86
Layard, John; 137
LDEs; 221
Lechler, Dr Adolph; 155
Lee, Christopher Frank Carandini (1922–): UK actor; 97
Lee, Henry: UK naturalist; 92
left brain; 13, 14, 16, 18–19, 21, 28, 36, 49, 55, 105, 110, 127, 130, 135, 136, 146, 151, 157, 158, 201, 221, 222
Leftwich, Robert: UK dowser; 127
Legend of the Sons of God (Lethbridge); 30
Leibniz, Gottfried Wilhelm von (1646–1716): German philosopher, mathematician, geologist & historian; 138
Leland, Charles Godfrey (1824–1903): UK folklorist; 35
Lemegoton (Solomon); 51
Lemuria; 33, 154
Leo: 5th sign of the *Zodiac
Leonard, Mrs Gladys Osborne (1882–1968): UK medium; 154
Leopard Men; 91
Le Poer Trench, William Francis Brinsley (8th Earl of Clancarty; 1911–   ); 199
leprechauns; 89
Leshan, Lawrence; 61
Lesser Work; 48, 49
Lethbridge, T.C.: UK archaeologist & antiquarian who made notable contributions in such fields as *dowsing and the study of *ley lines; 30, 36, 37, 39, 47, 53, 56, 106, 110, 113, 116, 127, 129
Leucippus (b. *c* 490 BC): Greek philosopher (whose existence is uncertain) & teacher of *Democritus; 34
Lévi, Eliphas (Alphonse Louis Constant; 1810–1875): prolific French writer on the occult; 62, 63
LEVITATION; 64, **138**, 140, 146, 153
LEY LINES; 28, 36, **38–9**, 93, 127, 200
L-fields; 123
libido; 148
Libra: 7th sign of the *Zodiac
Lichtenburg figure; 137
lie-detector; 98, 145–6
life, origin of; 30, 170, **193–4**
LIFE AFTER DEATH; 58, 125–6, **138–40**, 147, 154
Lifecloud (Hoyle & Wickramasinghe); 193
life field; 44–5, 124, 137
Life Is Only Real Then When 'I Am' (Gurdjieff); 133
life line; 109
light, velocity of (*c* 300,000km/s); 118, 195, 196, 198, 214, 215, 216
Lilith: in Jewish legend, a she-demon or *vampire, the first wife of Adam, dispossessed by Eve; she can be regarded as being to Eve as the (evil) spirit is to the physical body
Lincoln, Henry; 44
Lisbian; 86
lithomancy: divination using stones — either by subjecting unusual stones (for example, gems) to various tests and interpreting the outcome, or by hearing voices, etc., from

extremely unusual stones
Living Stream, The (Hardy); 122–3
Lo! (Fort); 11
Loch Ness monster; **92–3**
Lockyer, Sir Joseph Norman (1836–1920): UK astronomer; detected a 'new' element, helium, in the Sun by spectroscopy; founded *Nature* (1869); 16, 39, 43
Lodge, Sir Oliver Joseph (1851–1940): UK physicist and parapsychologist; pioneering member of the SPR; 53, 56
logic; 25, 105, 134, 157
long-delayed radio echoes; 221
Looking Backward, 2000–1887 (Bellamy); 221
Lord Halifax's Ghost Book; 147
Lorentz, Hendrik Antoon (1853–1928): Dutch physicist; shared 1902 Nobel physics prize; 196
Loudon, nuns of; 147
Louis XVI (1754–1793): King of France 1774–1792; 113, 114
loup-garou; *see* *lycanthropy
Lovecraft, Howard Phillips (1890–1937): influential US writer of occult & supernatural fantasies; 57
Lowell, Percival (1855–1916): US astronomer who pioneered the search for a planet beyond Neptune (Pluto, discovered 1930) & championed the cause of there being a civilization on *Mars; 175, 176
LSD (lysergic acid diethylamide); 145
Luce (France); 84
Lucian of Samosata (*c*125–190): Syrian-Greek satirist; 170
lucid dreams; 128
Lucifer: (a) the name of Satan (see *Devil) before his fall from heaven; (b) the morning star, Venus, in classical mythology; (c) the Sun god; 35, 36
lunacy; 17, 102
Lunan, Duncan A. (1945–   ): UK writer & *CETI theorist; 221
Lundy: small island in Bristol Channel, UK; 89
Luther, Martin (1483–1546): German religious reformer; 51, 173
LYCANTHROPY; 64, 85, **90–91**
Lyell, Sir Charles (1797–1875): UK geologist, champion of the Uniformitarianism of James Hutton (1726–97), the idea that geological & geomorphological change comes about as the result of gradual processes occurring over vast timespans; 16
Lysenko, Trofim Denisovich (1898–1976): politically powerful USSR biologist & agronomist whose rigid adherence to distorted *Lamarckism stifled USSR progress in the biological sciences for a quarter of a century; 122
lysergic acid diethylamide *see* *LSD

McCaffrey, Anne Inez (1926–   ): US popular novelist; 41
M'Clure, Kevin: UK psychic investigator; 110
McCreery, Charles; 12n
McHattan, Joe; 98
machine intelligence; 208–209
Mackenzie, Kenneth (?–?1670): UK seer, the 'Brahan Seer'; 114
Mackenzies of Lochalsh; 114
magic; 47, 48, 49, 105, 108, 152 — *see* *primitive magic, *ritual magic
Magic, An Occult Primer (Conway); 51
Magic and Mystery in Tibet (David-Neel); 62–3
magnetic bottles; 215
Magog; *see* *Gog and Magog
Magonia; 86
Mahabharata; 156
Mahayana Buddhism; 157
Mahesh Yogi, Maharishi; 155
malaria; 134
Malory, Sir Thomas (d. 1471): English writer & adventurer; 32, 38
mammals, origin of; 30
Man; 34 — ancestors of; 30, 36, 49, 59, 82, 103 — origins of; 30 — *see also* *ancient Man
Man and Time (Priestley); 115–16
mandrake: *Mandragora officinarum*; in North America the mayapple, *Podophyllum peltatum*, although quite unrelated, is often called mandrake; **63**
Manichees: religious sect, an extension of Christianity, founded 3rd century by a Persian wise man, Mani; 81, 156
Man, Myth and Magic: UK partwork encyclopedia of the occult; 57
manna; 170
Manning, Matthew: UK clairvoyant; 130
Mansfield, Katherine (Kathleen Mansfield Beauchamp; 1888–1923): New Zealand writer; 133
Man's Latent Powers (Payne); 123–4
Mantell, Captain Thomas; 199
mantra; 155
Manual of General Science (Wilson); 16
Maps of the Ancient Sea Kings (Hapgood); 33
Marie Antoinette (1755–93): wife to Louis XVI; Queen of France 1774–92; 113, 114, 117
Mariner 2; 170
Mariner 9; 175
MARS; 84, 94, 102, 103, 167, 171, **175–6**, 205
Marshack, Alexander; 31

Marshall, Mrs; 111
Martians; see *Mars
'Martian Shop, The' (Fast); 205
Martinique; 110
Mary Celeste; 97
Mary, Queen of Scots (1542–87): Queen of Scotland 1542–67; mother of *James VI & I; 114
Masks of Time, The (Forman); 117
Maslow, Abraham (1908–70): US psychologist; 126, 143–4
mass ratio; 215
mastabas: rectangular stone tombs of the Ancient Egyptians, generally with three chambers, from one of which led a shaft to the burial chamber below; 41
Masters, Anthony: UK writer; 96
matter-antimatter drive; 216
Matthew; 51
Maugham, William Somerset (1874–1965): UK writer; 160
Maxwell, James Clerk (1831–79): prominent UK physicist, best known for Maxwell's equations which describe how, in a particular space, magnetic & electric fields behave & interrelate; 196
Maya: preColumbian central American civilization, at its height c300–900; 33
May Lectures (1974); 145–6
maypole; 35, 36
Medici, Alessandro de (1510–37); 125
Medici, Lorenzo de (1449–92); 125
medicine; 38, 123, 134 — see also *healing
MEDIUMS 49–50, 109–110, 125, 138, **140**, 141, 143, **154**
Medun (Egypt); 41
Medusa; 40
Meetings with Remarkable Men (Gurdjieff); 106, 132, 133
Megalithic Lunar Observatories (Thom); 39
MEGALITHIC MONUMENTS; 16–17, 30, 31, 38, **39**, 41–3, 90, 104
Meh-teh: another name for Yeti — see *abominable snowmen
melatonin; 144, 145
Melwas, King of Somerset; 36
Memories, Dreams, Reflections (Jung); 136
Mendel, Gregor Johann (1822–84): Austrian monk whose experiments with pea plants elucidated the mechanism of heredity; 122
Mendelssohn, Kurt; 41
men in black; 201
Men Like Gods (Wells); 221
Menlung Glacier; 85
Mercier, Louis-Sébastien (1740–1814): French writer; 115

Mercury (planet); 103, 167, 171
Merlin; 31
mermaids; 41
mescalin; 145, 151
Mesmer, Franz (or Friedrich) Anton (1734–1815): German/Austrian physician; 54, 106, 134–5, 149, 153
'mesmeric fluid'; 134
mesmerism; see *hypnosis
meson; 174
Messier, Charles (1730–1817): French astronomer; 201
meteorites; 34, 84, 93–4, 172, 193, 219
metoposcopy: character-reading using the lines of the forehead; divination therefrom, analagous to *palmistry, is metopomancy
Michael, St; 36
Michel, Aimé; 199
Michelangelo; 125
Michell, John; 28, 36, 39, 84, 200
Michelson, Albert Abraham (1852–1931): US physicist; 1908 Nobel physics prize; 196
Microstomum; 122–3
microwave radiation: electromagnetic radiation of wavelength between c 1mm and c 30cm (about 0.04–12in); 165, 220
microwave radiation, cosmic background; 163, 202
Middleton, J. Connor; 111
Midnapore (India); 91
Midsummer Night's Dream, A (Shakespeare); 89
Mightiest Machine, The (Campbell); 175
'migma' fusion cell; 210
Mikhailova, Nelya; 125
Miller, Henry (1891–1980): US novelist; 136
Miller, Howard: US psychologist; 20, 116
Miller, Neal E.; 126
mind; see *brain
mini black holes; 165
Minkowski, Hermann (1864–1909): Russian-German mathematical physicist; 115
Minos; 40
Minotaur; 40
miracles; 21
'missing link'; 30
mistletoe; 35–6
Moberly, Charlotte; 117
Modern Utopia, A (Wells); 221
Moldavia; 96
Mompesson, Mr; 147
Moody, Raymond Avery (1944–   ): US physician; 139
Moon; 39, 167, 169, 175, 219 — and magic; 63 — effect on Man; 17, 31, 102–104, 123 — inhabitants of; 175 — rock from; 219 — worship of; 35, 36

Moon Goddess; 35
Moore, Patrick Alfred (1923–   ): UK astronomer, writer & broadcaster; 169
Moray Firth (Scotland); 92
More, Sir Thomas (1478–1535): English diplomat & writer; 220, 221
Morgan, Ted; 160
Morley, Edward Williams (1838–1923): US physicist & chemist; 196
Morning of the Magicians, The (Pauwels and Bergier); 29
Morris, Robert (1942–   ): US psychic investigator; 53
Morris, William (1834–96): UK designer, artist, poet & novelist; 221
Morte Darthur, Le (Malory); 32, 38
Moss, Dr Thelma; 137–8, 149
Mother Earth; 82 — *see also* *Cybele, *Earthmother
mounds; *see* megalithic monuments
Mu; 33
Muldoon, Sylvan; 142
Mulhattan, Joe; 98
MULTIPLE PERSONALITY; 52, 57–8, 110–11, 121, 136, 137, 138, **140–42**, 150
multiverse; 163, 166
Mumler, William; 143
munguni; 48
muon; 174
Murray, Margaret (1863–1963): UK anthropologist; 35, 36, 39, 81, 82
music of the spheres; 169
Myers, F.W.H. (1843–1901): UK psychic investigator; 52, 125, 138
Myiciura, Demetrious; 96
Mysteries (Wilson); 28, 93, 110, 117, 121, 141
Mysterious Fires and Lights (Gaddis); 84
MYTHICAL MONSTERS; **39–41**

Nagasaki (Japan); 94
Naitaka; 92
'Nameless City, The' (Lovecraft); 57
Napier, John; 85
Napoleon Bonaparte (1769–1821): Corsican-born French militarist, Emperor of France 1804–14; 42, 97
Narlikar, J.V.: Indian cosmologist; 202
National Radio Observatory, Green Bank; 176
Natural History of the Vampire, The (Masters); 96
natural selection; 122–3, 222
Nature's Divine Revelations (Davis); 125
Nausea (Sartre); 151
Nazca lines (Peru); 29–30
Nazism; 57, 169
Neanderthal Man; **30–31**

nebulae, gaseous; 171, 193, 201
necromancy: (a) technique of divination which employs raising and communicating with the souls of the dead; (b) more loosely, demonology or black *magic
NECRONOMICON; **57**
negative gravity; 162
Nemi; 35
Neptune (planet); 101, 103, 167, 171
Ness, Loch (Scotland); 92–3, 114
'Nessie'; *see* *Loch Ness monster
Nessiteras rhombopteryx; 92
Neuilly-sur-Seine (France); 139
neurosis; 21, 126, 136
neutrino; 105, 174, 175, 176, 216
neutron: the uncharged particle in the atomic nucleus; 162, 163, 174, 176, 209, 210
NEUTRON SOUP; **176**, 194
neutron stars; *see* pulsars
New Atlantis (Bacon); 220
New Lanark (Scotland); 220
New Model of the Universe, A (Ouspensky); 85, 128
News From Nowhere (Morris); 221
News of the World; 93
Newton, Sir Isaac (1642–1726): English scientist responsible for developing the integral calculus, the theory of universal gravitation, the Binomial Theorem, the corpuscular theory of light &, perhaps most important, his 3 Laws of Motion: (1) a body continues in a state of uniform motion unless a force acts upon it; (2) acceleration is proportional to the magnitude of this force and occurs in the same direction as the force; (3) every action is opposed by an equal & opposite reaction; his 2 greatest works were *Philosophiae Naturalis Principia Mathematica* (1687) & *Opticks* (1704); towards the end of his life he carried out researches into *alchemy; 25, 44, 57, 152, 160, 164
Nicolson, Iain; 166
Nietzsche, Friedrich (1844–1900): German philosopher who in *Also Spracht Zarathustra* (1883–92) introduced the idea of the 'Superman'; 11, 16, 17, 151
nigredo; 48
Nile; 42, 43
Nirvana; 156
North Berwick witch trial; 81
Nostradamus (Michel de Notredame; 1503–66); 111, **113–14**
Noyes, John Humphrey (1811–86): US religious socialist; 220–21
nuckelavee; 88
nuclear-electric ion rocket; 215, 216

nuclear fusion; *see* *fusion power
nuclear pulse rocket; 210–11, 215–16
NUMEROLOGY; **108**, 114
Nuremberg (Germany); 90

Oberon; 89
objective mind; 55, 61
observatories, ancient 39, 42–3; *see also* *astronomy, ancient, *megalithic monuments
OCCAM'S RAZOR: philosophical principle that, should several rival theories fit the facts, the simplest corresponds to reality; 167, 198
Occult, The (Wilson); 47, 85, 101, 116, 151
Occult Science in India (Jacolliot); 157
Ockendon, Ann; 150
odic force; 124
Odysseus; 40
Odyssey; 40, 63
Ogopogo; 92
Ohio Snake mound; 39
Olcott, Colonel Henry Steel (1832–1907); 49, 50
old religion; *see* *fertility religion
Old Straight Track, The (Watkins); 38
Old Testament; 30
omega particle; 174
omphalomancy: divination by studying one's own navel
Once and Future King, The (White); 38
Onegan, Lake; 92
Oneida Community: utopian community, active 1848–c 1880, near Oneida, NY; 220–21
O'Neill, Gerard Kitchen (1927–   ): US physicist; 219, 220
O'Neill, Jane; 117, 118
oneiromancy: divination by interpretation of dreams — *see* *dreams and visions
Ontario Cancer Institute; 123
'On the Psychology and Pathology of So-called Occult Phenomena' (Jung); 136
onyomancy: division of *palmistry concerned with the fingernails
OOBEs; *see* *out-of-the-body experiences
oppositions, planetary; 103
Orage, A.R.; 133
orgasm; 63, 148, 155
orgone box; 148, 149
orgone energy; 134, 149
orgonomy; **148–9** — *see also* *Reich, Wilhelm
Original Theory and New Hypothesis of the Universe, An (Wright); 171
Origin of Consciousness in the Breakdown of the Bicameral Mind, The (Jaynes); 13
Origin of Species..., On the (Darwin); 122
Orion, Project; 215

ornithischians: group of *dinosaurs
OSCILLATING UNIVERSE; 161–2, 162–3, **176**, 198, 202
Osiris: Egyptian god, ruler of the underworld, a creative life-force; 33, 35
Osis, Karlis: US parapsychologist; 139
Ostrander, Sheila; 137
Osty, Eugène (1874–1938): French physician & psychic investigator; 109–110, 129
ouija board; 58, 110, 125
Ouspensky, Peter Demianovitch (1878–1947); 85, 128, 133, 134
OUT-OF-THE-BODY EXPERIENCES; 34, 58, 124, 128, 139, **142–3**, 153
Ovid (Publius Ovidius Naso; 43 BC–AD 18): Roman poet; 90
Owen, Dr & Mrs George; 147–8
Owen, Robert (1771–1858): UK utopian socialist & industrialist; 220
Oxford University Society for Psychical Research; 110
OZMA, PROJECT; **176**

pair creation; 167, 174
Palladino, Eusapia (1854–1918): Italian medium; 154
PALMISTRY; **108–109**
Pan: Greek fertility god, often equated with the Christian *Devil; 35
PANSPERMIA; 30, 122, **193–4**
Parade; 112
paragnosts; 140
PARALLEL WORLDS; 98, 115, **194**, 200
Paranormal, The (Gooch); 138
paranormal phenomena: those phenomena whose mechanisms cannot be explained in terms of currently acceptable science; 21, 22, 47, 86, 110–11, 126, 127, 129, 130, 135, 136, 141, 142, 148
PARANORMAL PHOTOGRAPHY; **143**
parapsychology; *see* *dowsing, *dreams and visions, *ESP, *levitation, *life after death, *mediums, *out-of-the-body experiences, *paranormal photography, *poltergeists, etc.
Parapsychology Foundation (New York); 139
Parise, Felicia; 130
Parsons, Elizabeth; 147
Parzival (von Eschenbach); 38
Pascal's Triangle: the triangular table of numbers produced by writing the coefficients in the terms of the expansions of $(a+b)^0$, $(a+b)^1$, $(a+b)^2$, $(a+b)^3 \ldots (a+b)^n$; 207
Pasiphae; 40
Pattern of Islands (Grimble); 59
Pattern of the Past (Underwood); 38–9
pattern, pattern recognition; 24, 25, 115, 135,

208–209
Patterns of Prophecy (Vaughan); 58, 110, 112, 114–15
Pauwels, Louis: French investigator of the unexplained; 29
Payette, Lake; 92
Payne, Phoebe; 123–4
PEAK EXPERIENCE; 20, 126, **143–4**
Pearce, Ian; 54–5
Pelée, Mont; 110
pendulum; 106, 113, 126, **127**, 129
Penfield, Wilder: US experimental neurologist; 20
pentacle; *see* pentagram
pentagram: regular 5-pointed star, a geometrical figure believed to have magical properties, in particular to protect against spirits or *demons; 61
Penzias, Arno: US electronics expert; 202
Percival; 38
perfect numbers; 108
Perlberg (Germany); 97
Perseus; 40
personality; 121, 138, 150
Personal Knowledge (Polanyi); 160
Petronius Arbiter, Caius (d. AD 66); 90–91, 129
phantasms of the living; *see* *doppelgängers
phantom pregnancy; 19, 135
Phenomena (Michell & Rickard); 84
'Philip'; 147–8
Philistines; 89
Philosophers' Stone; 48
photochemistry, laser-activated; 217
photodynamic therapy; 217
photography; 101 — *see* *Kirlian photography, *paranormal photography, *psychic photography
photon; 163, 195, 216
photon rocket; 216
photosynthesis; 217
Piccardi, Professor Giorgio; 102
Pilgrimage of Thomas Paine, The (Hammond); 125
Pillars of Hercules; 32
pineal door; 128
PINEAL EYE (or pineal gland); 101, **144–5**
pion; 174
Pioneer 10: US Jupiter flyby probe, launched 1972; 195
Piper, Leonora E. (1857–1950): prominent US medium subjected to intensive investigation by both the American Society for Psychical Research and the SPR; 125, 138, 140, 154
Piri Re'is map; 33
Pisces: 12th sign of the *Zodiac
pisgies; 88

piskys; 88
pixies; 88, 89
PK; *see* *psychokinesis
Plageman, Stephen; 103
planchette; 125
planets — effects on Man; 17, 102–103, 104 — motions of; 11, 12, 15 — of other stars; 171–2, 209
PLANT COMMUNICATION; **145–6**
plants, magic and; 63
plasma: virtually completely ionized gas; 210, 215
plasma confinement; 210
plasmid transfer; 211
plate tectonics, theory of: fundamental theory that the Earth's surface is made up of plates in relative motion, thereby accounting for continental drift & earthquake & volcanic activity (both generated at plate boundaries); new plate material emerges at midocean ridges, on either side of which it is carried away by the process known as seafloor spreading; where plates 'collide' one is forced beneath the other, which gives rise to ocean trenches, arcs of volcanic islands, & deep seismic & volcanic activity; at continental margins, mountain ranges may be thrust up in such 'collisions'; the theory is now accepted by almost all Earth scientists
Plato (*c* 427–347): Greek philosopher & founder of the Academy (*c* 385 BC); his best known work, the *Republic*, presents a *utopia ruled by philosophers, who symbolize the rational part of the soul; 16, 32, 33, 220, 221
plesiosaur: aquatic reptile, extant *c* 200–*c* 65 million years ago; 92–3
Pliny the Elder (*c* 23–79): Roman writer & natural historian; 63
Pluto (planet); 103, 167
podomancy: practice akin to *palmistry, but using the soles of the feet
Pogossian; 132
Poincaré, Jules Henri (1854–1912): French mathematician, philosopher & cosmologist; 196
Polanyi, Michael; 160
Polaris: α Ursa Minoris, variable star at present close to the Earth's N celestial pole; 42
pole star; 42
POLTERGEISTS; 11, 12, 14–15, 21, 47, 49, 53, 57, 58, 125, 130, 135, 136, 137, 138, 140, **146–8**, 153, 201
polysaccharides: *carbohydrates, polymers of simple sugars (monosaccharides); 193
Pope, Alexander (1688–1744): UK poet; 160
Popper, Sir Karl Raimund (1902–   ):

Austrian-born UK philosopher of science; 160
porpoises, calling of the; 59, 129
Poseidon; 32, 40
Positive Philosophy (Comte); 11
positivism; 22
positron; 162, 174
POSSESSION; 47, **57–8**, 64, 110, 141, 147, 150
Poussin, Nicolas (1594–1665): French Baroque painter; 44
Powell, Arthur E.; 124
Power of the Pendulum, The (Lethbridge); 37, 110, 129
Powys, John Cowper (1872–1963): UK novelist; 52
prana; 123, 124, 156
precession of the equinoxes: the cyclical change (period *c* 26,000 years) of the orientation in space of the Earth's rotational axis; 43
PRECOGNITION 58, 104, 106, **109–111**, 112, 113, 114, 115, 118, 128, 129, 130, 132
PREDICTION; 104, 108, 109–110, **111–12**
Prelude to a Landing on Planet Earth (Holroyd); 145–6, 200
premature burial; 96
Price, James; 48
Priestley, John Boynton (1894–   ): UK novelist essayist & playwright, many of whose works are connected with *time, scientific developments & matters strange; 115–16
prima materia; 48
prime numbers: those integers which are not multiples of other integers (except themselves & 1); for example, 7 is a prime number but 8 is not (2 × 4 = 8) 207–208
PRIMITIVE MAGIC; 31, 35, **58–60**, 81
Prince, Professor Morton; 140, 141
Prince, Dr Walter Franklin; 140, 141
Principles of Geology (Lyell); 16
Principles of Nature, The (Davis); 153
Principles of Psychology (James); 140
Probability of the Impossible, The (Moss); 138
Proceedings of the Society for Psychical Research; 139
Proctor, Richard Anthony (1837–88); 42–3
Projection of the Astral Body, The (Muldoon & Carrington); 142
proteinoid microspheres; 172
protolife globules; 172
proton: the (positively) charged particle in the atomic nucleus; 162, 163, 165, 173–4, 176, 194, 209
Proust, Marcel (1871–1922): French novelist; *A la Recherche du Temps Perdu* published 1907–19; 116, 151, 157
Proxima Centauri; 214, 215

psi; *see* *ESP
PSR 1913 +16; 195
psychedelic drugs; 145
psychic archaeology; 118
Psychical Research Foundation (North Carolina); 53
Psychic Discoveries Behind the Iron Curtain (Ostrander & Schroeder); 137
psychic photography; 138
psychic projection; *see* *doppelgängers
psychoanalysis; 54, 136, 148
Psychoanalysis of Ghost Stories (Richardson); 96–7
Psychoanalytic Society; 148
psychokinesis; 48, 64, **129–30**
Psychological Types (Jung); 136
psychometry; **117–18**
psychosomatic illness; 126
pterosaurs: group of flying reptiles, extant *c* 200–*c* 65 million years ago; 34
Ptolemy (Claudius Ptolemaeus; 2nd century AD): Alexandrian cosmologist, geographer & mathematician; his geocentric ideas, presented in his *Almagest*, dominated cosmological thought until the Middle Ages; 11
Puck; 89
Puharich, Andrija; 200
PULSARS; 165, 166, 176, **194–5**
Pup; *see* *Sirius
Puthoff, Harold; 142–3
Puységur, Marquis de (1751–1825); 54, 106, 134
Pygmy Theory; 89
PYRAMID POWER; **60**
Pyramid Power (Flanagan); 60
PYRAMIDS; 16, 29, 33, **41–3**, 90
pyromancy: divination involving the use of fire
Pythagorean school: school of Greek philosophy centred on the ideas of Pythagoras, who probably lived *c* 570–*c* 500; 108, 168–9

Qabalah; *see* *Cabala
QSOs; *see* *quasars
quantum field; 174
quantum mechanics: one of the most important theories in 20th-century physics, applicable as it is (essentially) only to the small-scale; impossible to explain without the use of higher mathematics, it can be viewed as the mathematical/statistical expression of *quantum theory; 23
quantum numbers; 174, 175
quantum theory: theory originated by the German physicist Max Planck (1858–1947) based upon the (now seemingly proved) idea that neither energy nor matter are infinitely

247

subdivisible; Planck christened the smallest unit of energy the 'quantum'; the 'size' of the quantum depends upon the frequency of the radiation concerned — thus an ultraviolet quantum (say) contains more energy than a red quantum (say), since ultraviolet light is of higher frequency (shorter wavelength) than red light; the product of the frequency and the 'size' of the corresponding quantum ($h =$ Planck's constant) appears to be a universal constant; more recently the idea has been extended to describe *time; 61

quantum tunnelling; 165

quarks; 174

QUASARS; 166, **195–6**, 202

quasi-stellar objects; see *quasars

Quin, Frederick Foster Harvey: UK physician; 134

Rabelais, François (c 1494–1553): French monk, doctor and satirist; 50

rabies; 90

rabbit's paw, lucky; 49

Race, Victor; 134

Radiant Universe, The (Hill); 170

radiesthesia; 127

radio: electromagnetic radiation of wavelength between c1mm and c100km (about 0.04in–60mi); 195, 196

radioactive decay: process in which the unstable nuclei of certain (radioactive) elements spontaneously disintegrate, emitting alpha, beta & gamma particles, & being transformed into nuclei of elements of lower atomic number; 161, 209

radiocarbon; 94, 161

Rafinesque, Constantine Samuel (1773–1840); 171

Raifuku Maru; 88

raising the dead; 64

Raja yoga; 156

rakshas; 85

Ramakrishna Paramahansa (1836–86); Indian saint whose teachings are that all religions are as one; 128, 157

Ramapithecus; 30

ram-augmented interstellar rocket; 216

ramjet, interstellar; 166

Randi, James: US conjurer; 15

Rank, Otto (1884–1939): Austrian-born US psychoanalyst; 54

Rasmussen, Knud Johan Victor (1879–1933): Danish explorer of Arctic regions; 59

ray of creation; 133

reality, nature of; 61–2

redcaps; 88

Reddae; 43

Red Sea, dividing of; 170

redshift: increased wavelength in the radiation received from receding objects owing to the *Doppler effect; 195, 201

Rees, Martin John (1942–   ): UK astronomer; 166

Reese, Bert: US clairvoyant; 105

REICH, WILHELM; 134, **148–9**

Reiche, Maria; 30

Reichenbach, Karl von; see *von Reichenbach, Karl

REINCARNATION; 34, 57, 121, **149–50**, 213

Reines, forest of; 113

Reiter's Syndrome; 211–12, 214

'relativistic' starship; 215

RELATIVITY; 25, 61, 112, 118, 162, 164, 167, 169, 195, **196–7**, 198, 202, 214, 215 — Special Theory; 175, **196–7** — General Theory; **197**

Remembrance of Things Past (Proust); 116

Rennes-le-Château (France); 43–4

RENNES-LE-CHÂTEAU, MYSTERY OF; **43–4**

Renouvier, Charles Bernard (1815–1903); 20

Republic (Plato); 220

Researches in Magnetism (von Reichenbach); 124

Revelation; 50, 116

REVELATIONS, MYSTICAL; **150–52**

Rexroth, Kenneth (1905–   ); 155

Reynolds, Charles; 143

Reynolds, Mary; 140

Rhine, Joseph Banks (1895–   ) & Louisa E.: distinguished US parapsychologists whose work has done more than that of any other to give respectability to the subject; the Rhines have applied both statistics and the scientific method to their research; 53–4, **129–30**, 154

Richardson, Maurice: UK writer and journalist; 96–7

Richet, Charles Robert (1850–1935): French physiologist & psychic investigator; 1913 Nobel physiology or medicine prize; 126–7

Rickard, R.J.M.; 84

Ridgway, Captain John; 92

Riedel, Albert: US modern alchemist; 48

right brain; 13, 14, 15, 18–19, 21, 47, 49, 53, 55, 58, 105, 106, 110, 115–16, 119, 127, 130, 135, 138, 142, 147, 151, 153, 157, 201, 222

rigor mortis: muscular stiffening after death; 96

Rines, Dr Robert (1922–   ); 92

rising sign; 102

RITUAL MAGIC; 51, **61–4**

Robbins, Russell Hope; 81

Robinson, Marie; 58

Rocard, Professor Y.; 102

rocket, principle of; 215

Roerich, Nicholas Konstantin (1874–1947): USSR painter and early *UFO sighter; 29
Roff, Mary; 57
Romania; 96
Romeo Error, The (Watson); 121, 125, 146
Roots of Civilization, The (Marshack); 31
Roots of Coincidence, The (Koestler); 107
Roots of Witchcraft, The (Harrison); 36
Rosenblum, Art; 60
Rosenkreuz, Christian; 152
Rosicrucian Anthology, A; 152
ROSICRUCIANS; 44, **152**
Rosy Cross, Brotherhood of the; *see* *Rosicrucians
Round Table: table said to have been made at the behest of or for *Arthur; 150 knights could sit around it &, since there were thus no favoured positions, arguments as to precedence were avoided; 38
Rousseau, Jean Jacques (1717–78): Swiss-born French writer & philosopher, a contributor to *Diderot's *Encyclopedia*; 95
Rubner, Max (1854–1932): German physiologist; 44
Russell, Bertrand Arthur William, 3rd Earl Russell (1872–1970): UK philosopher, mathematician, educationalist & writer; 160
Russian Revolution; 93, 133
Ryall, Edward; 150

Sabbats; *see* *witches' Sabbaths
sadism, origin of; 17
Sagan, Carl (1934–   ): US planetary scientist & proponent & popularizer of ideas on extraterrestrial life and intelligence; 15, 207
Sagée, Emilie; 52, 53
Sagittarius: 9th sign of the *Zodiac
SAI BABA; **64**
Sai Baba of Shirdi; 64
'St Antony the Hermit'; 44
St Elmo's fire; 138
St Rémy (France); 113
St Sulpice (France); 43
Sakria; 86
Salmon, Ross; 59
Salon (France); 113
samadhi; 156, 157
Sampson, Agnes; 81
Sanderson, Ivan T.: US Fortean; 84
Santorini (Thēra): Aegean island on which have been found the remains of a Minoan settlement destroyed in a volcanic eruption *c*2500BC; 32, 96
Saqqura (Egypt); 41
Sarajevo (Yugoslavia); 56
Sargant, William Walters (1907–   ): UK psychiatrist and writer; 57, 58
Sargasso Sea; 28
Sarmoung Brotherhood; 132
Sartre, Jean Paul (1905–1980): French novelist, playwright and existentialist philosopher; 133, 151
Sasquatch; *see* *Bigfoot
Satan; 51 — *see also* *Devil
satellites, artificial; 218
satellite solar power stations; 218, 220
satori; 158, 221
Saturn (planet); 102, 103, 167, 171
Satyricon (Petronius); 129
Sauniére, Bèrenger; 43–4
Sautuola, Don Marcelino de; 58–9
scepticism; 24
Scharnhorst; 56
Schiaparelli, Giovanni Virginio (1835–1910): Italian astronomer; 175
schizophrenia; 144
Schmeidler, Dr Gertrude; 130, 131
Schneider, Rudi (1908–57) & Willi: Austrian mediums; 154
Schopenhauer, Arthur (1788–1860): German philosopher; 160
Schreiber, Flora Rheta; 141
Schroeder, Lynn; 137
Schultz, Johannes; 54
Schwartz, Jack; 156
Schwartzschild, Karl (1873–1916): German astronomer; 164
Schwartzschild radius; 164
Science and the Supernatural (Taylor); 130–31
scientology; 126
sciomancy: divination by looking at people's shadows
Scorpio: 8th sign of the *Zodiac
Scott, Sir Peter (1909–   ): UK naturalist; 92
Scott, Sir Walter (1771–1832): UK writer, poet & antiquary; 89
SCRYING; 106, **112**, 140, 152
Scully, Frank; 200
Scylla; 40
Seaborn, Captain Adam; 169
Seabrook, William; 99
sea cow; 41
Seaforth family; 114
SEA MONSTERS; **91–3**
Sea Monsters Unmasked (Lee); 92
séances; 52, 138, 140, 153
'Sea Peoples'; 17
sea serpents; 91–2
second sight; 35, 105
Secret Doctrine, The (Blavatsky); 50
secret fire; 48, 49
Secret Life of Plants, The (Tompkins & Bird); 146

Secret of the Golden Flower, The; 49
Secret Places of the Lion, The (Williamson); 29, 200
Seeress of Prevorst, The (Kerner); 153
SEERS AND PROPHETS; 106, 110, 111, **112–15**
'Self-Actualizing People, A Study of Psychological Health' (Maslow); 143–4
self-consciousness; 13
self-hypnosis; 106
Selma (Alabama); 98
Selye, Hans (1907–   ): Austrian-born Canadian physician & physiologist; 54, 55
Semon, Felix; 126
sensitives; *see* *mediums
serial time; 111–12
Serios, Ted; 143
serotonin; 144–5
SETI; 172, 176, **197**, 206, **221–2**
Seton, Alexander (1555–1622); 48
Severn River (Wales); 90
sextiles; 103
sexual magic; 36, 50, **63**, 155
Seyfert galaxies: class of energetic galaxies; 195, 202
Shackleton, Basil; 109
Shakespeare, William (1564–1616); 89
Shakti; 155
shamanism; 17, 31, 59–60, 129, 140
Shamanism (Eliade); 59
Shambala; 37
Shape of Minds to Come, The (Taylor); 150
Shaw, George Bernard (1856–1950): Irish man of letters; 1925 Nobel literature prize; 85, 122
Shax (demon); 51
'sheep & goats' experiment; 130
Sheila-na-gigs: fertility (*Earthmother) symbols in the form of statuettes of a crouching naked woman with exaggerated genitalia; 35, 39
Shipton, Eric; 85
Shipton, Mother (*c* 1488–?   ): English seer; **114**
Shiva; 155
Shiva Nova laser fusion facility; 210
Shklovskii, Ioseph: USSR astrophysicist & xenobiologist; 165–6
Showery, Allen; 58
Shrewsbury (England); 90
Shuttlewood, Sir Arthur: UK UFOlogist; 200
siddhis; 64
Sidgwick, Henry (1838–1900); 125
Silbury Hill (Wiltshire, England); 39
Silbury Treasure: The Great Goddess Rediscovered (Dames); 39
silicon chips; 205, 219

Singh, Rev.; 91
singularity, spacetime; 163, 164, 166
Sion, Priory of; 44
sirens; 41
Sirius: α Canis Minoris, brightest star in the night sky; a binary, its minor component (the Pup) was the first *white dwarf to be identified (1862 & 1914) — of volume just over three times that of Earth, it masses almost as much as the Sun; Sirius was of major religious importance to the Ancient Egyptians; 30, 43
Sirius Mystery, The (Temple); 30
Sizemore, Christine; 141
Skinner, Burrhus Frederic (1904–   ): US psychologist & author; 221
Slimey Sim; 92
Slipher, Vesto Melvin (1875–1969): US astronomer; 201
'Smith, Mrs'; 150
Smollett, Tobias (1721–71); 101
Smyth, Charles Piazzi; 42
Snefru (pharaoh); 41
Soal, S.G.: UK mathematician & psychic investigator; 52, 109
Sobha Ram; 149, 150
Society for Psychical Research (SPR; London): world's foremost organization to investigate matters relating to the afterlife, mediumship and the paranormal; 50, 54, 125, 128, 129, 138, 139, 149, 153–4
solar energy; 218, 219–20 — *see also* *satellite solar power stations
Solar System: gravitationally bonded system comprising the Sun, at least nine major planets, their satellites, myriad asteroids & comets, & associated gas, dust & debris; 18, 34, 170, 171, 194
solar systems, formation of; 171
Solomon: King of Israel *c* 970–933; **44**, 51
Solomon, Seal of; 62
Solon (*c* 639–559): *archon* of Athens from 594, one of the great statesmen & lawgivers of Ancient Greece; 32
somatic system; 125, 135
Sourcebook Project; 84
Southend (England); 52
SPACE COLONIES; 215, 218, **219–20**
space-men; *see* *ancient astronauts, *extraterrestrial intelligence
spacetime: the fabric of the Universe, of dimensions both spatial & temporal; 47, 112, 115, 116, 163, 197, 198, 202, 205, 213 — *see* *Relativity
Space Vampires, The (Wilson); 97
spectacles, invention of; 101

Spence, Lewis: UK occultist; 51, 53
Sperry, Roger Wolcott (1913–   ): US pioneer of split-brain research; 13, 14, 18, 147
spin: property of *fundamental particles, analogous to angular momentum; 162
spirits; 60, 61, 110, 138, 140, 153, 154
SPIRITUALISM; 49–50, 54, 118, **138**, **139–40**, 147, **152–4**
Spiritualist movement; 49–50
split-brain research; 13, 14–15, 18, 19, 47, 115–16, 147
spontaneous combustion; phenomenon whereby human beings spontaneously burst into flames for reasons not understood; cases are not particularly frequent, but a number have been well documented; at one point a connection was made between it and consumption of alcohol, but this connection seems tenuous at best; characteristics are localized burning (in some cases, the chairs of victims have been virtually unscathed) and, apparently, extremely high tempratures; it seems likely that the phenomenon is caused by an electrical discharge of some kind, but its nature, if so, is unknown; 84, 163
SPR; *see* Society for Psychical Research
SPRING-HEELED JACK; 86, **93**
squares (in astrology); 103
squid; 92
Squirrel, Mr; 117
stage fright; 18
Stalin, Joseph (1879–1953): USSR dictator (from 1929) & military leader; 122
Stanford Research Institute (Cal.); 142
Starseekers (Wilson); 18n
starships; *see* *interstellar travel
Star Trek; 216
Steady State Theory; **167**, **202**
Steele, Dr E.J.; 123
STEINER, RUDOLPH; 33, 132, 152, **154**
Steppenwolf (Hesse); 21, 147, 221
Stevenson, Dr Ian; 111, 149, 150
Stewart, Gloria; 109
STIGMATA; **154–5**
Stoke-on-Trent (England); 96
Stoker, Abraham ('Bram'; 1847–1912): UK theatrical manager & novelist, author of *Dracula* (1897) and others; 96–7
Stoker, Charlotte; 96
Stone Age; 31, 59
Stonehenge: Stone Age & early Bronze Age megalithic observatory on Salisbury Plain (Wiltshire, England); 17, 33, 38, 39, 42
Stony Tunguska River (Siberia); 93
Straight Track Postal Club; 38
strangeness; 174

stress; 54, 126
striges: in Ancient Greece, *vampire-like creatures; in some accounts, particularly partial to cradle-snatching
Study of History, A (Toynbee); 116
subatomic particles; *see* *fundamental particles
subjective mind; 55, 61
succubi: the female equivalent of *incubi; according to the early Christians, *Lilith was the Queen of the Succubi
suggestion; 64, 135
'Suggestion About Mysticism, A' (James); 150
Summers, Montague (1880–1948): UK writer & antiquary; 96
Sun; 12, 18, 39, 102–103, 167, 168, 173 — as black hole; 164 — inhabitants of; 171, 175 — as neutron star; 194 — worship of; 30, 36
Sun sign; 102, 103
sunspots; 102, 123
super black holes; 164–5, 166
superfluidity; 194
Superminds (Taylor); 130–31
Supernature (Watson); 60
supernova: cataclysmic explosion of certain stars at the ends of their lifetimes; during the explosion they may outshine the rest of their galaxy; 164, 165–6, 194, 195
superstition; 106
survival; *see* *life after death
survivalism; 140
'S.W.'; 58
Swann, Ingo: prominent US psychic; 143
Swann's Way (Proust); 116
Swedenborg, Emanuel (1688–1772): Swedish natural scientist & religious mystic; 153, 154
'Sybil'; 141
Sylvania, utopian community in North Ohio; 220
Symmes, John Cleves (1742–1814): US unorthodox cosmologist; 169
Symzonia ('Seaborn'); 169
synchronicity; 56, 101, 107–108, 115, 137

taboos (or kapus, tabus, tapus): things forbidden; two types can be distinguished — positive, which arise out of awe or respect, such as touching holy remains — & negative, arising from fear of the consequences, such as incest; some taboos, such as cannibalism, are less easy to classify
table-turning, table-rapping; 132, 153
TACHYONS; 116, 174–5, **198**, 214
Takata, Maki; 102
talismans; see *amulets
Talmud: important Jewish compilation, begun 5th century, of lore & teachings; there are

two versions, Babylonian & Palestinian; 51
Tantra; 155
TANTRISM; 50, **155**
Taoism; 50, 157
Targ, Russell; 142–3
Tarot; 104
tasseomancy; *see* tealeaf prediction
Tate, Genette; 98
Tau Ceti: nearby Sun-like star, *c*12 light years away; 176
Taured; 86
Taurus: second sign of the *Zodiac; 102
Taylor, Catherine & Michael; 58
Taylor, John 19th-century UK mathematician; 42
Taylor, Professor John Gerald (1931–   ): UK mathematician; 121, 130–131, 138, 150
tealeaf prediction (or tasseomancy): divination based upon the interpretation of patterns formed by tealeaves (or coffee grounds, etc.) left at the bottom of the cup after someone has finished drinking
Tedworth, phantom drummer of; 147
Teed, Cyrus Reed (1839–1908): US unorthodox cosmologist & occultist; 169
Teed, Mr & Mrs Daniel; 147
telepathy; 21, 52, 53, 106, 112–13, **129–30**, 138, 140
telescope, invention of; 101
Telliamed (de Maillet); 122
Templar, Knights; 44
Temple, Robert K.G.; 30
Teniers, David (1610–1690): Flemish painter; 44
Territorial Imperative, The (Ardrey); 28
Tesla, Nikola (1856–1943): Croatian-born US inventor; 128
Testament of Solomon; 51
thaumaturgy: the performance of the miraculous — *see* *miracles, *healing
Thayer, Tiffany; 84
Thelema; 50
Theosophical Society; 49, 50, 154
Thēra; *see* *Santorini
thermodynamics: important branch of physics concerned with interchanges between different forms of energy; 212
Theseus; 40
Thessaly, women of; 63
theta rhythms; 55
Things (Sanderson); 84
third eye; *see* *pineal eye
Thom, Alexander (1894–   ): UK professor of engineering science who almost single-handedly established the case that many *megalithic monuments were designed to be

astronomical observatories; 39
Thuban: α Draconis; 42
Thule Group; 57
Tibet; 50, 62–3
Tiller, William; 125
Timaeus (Plato); 32
TIME; 47, 99, **101–19**, 151 — arrow of; 116, 162–3, 198 — as 4th dimension; 115, 197 — nature of; 104, 110, 111, **115–16**, 162, 196–7, 213
time dilation; 118, 215
Time Machine, The (Wells); 115
Time Must Have a Stop (Huxley); 34
TIME REVERSAL; **116**
TIME SLIP; 115, **116–18**
Times, The: UK newspaper; 123
TIME-SYMMETRIC UNIVERSE; 116, **198**
TIME TRAVEL; 104, 115, **118**
Tintagel Castle (Cornwall, England); 31
Tipler, Frank; 212–13
Titanic; 111
Titans; 89
Titicaca, Lake: world's highest navigable lake, in the Andes on the Bolivia-Peru border; 59
Titurel; 38
TM; see *transcendental meditation
toboscope; 123
Together We Wandered (Lambert); 56
Tompkins, Peter; 146
Topkapi Palace (Constantinople); 33
Toth, Max; 137–8
Toulouse; 81
Toynbee, Arnold Joseph (1889–1975): UK historian; 116, 151
trance state; 114, 125, 128, 134, 135, 140, 200
Tranent (Scotland); 81
transcendental ego; 116
TRANSCENDENTAL MEDITATION; 55, **155–6**
transvestism; 60
Transylvania; 96
Treatise on Astro-Biology (Krafft); 102
trines; 103
tritium: heavy isotope of hydrogen, with 1 proton & 2 neutrons in its nucleus; 210
trooping fairies; 88
Troy; 37
True: US magazine; 200
True and Faithful Relation of What Passed for Many Years Between Dr John Dee and Some Spirits, A (Dee?); 140
True History, The (Lucian); 170
Tsiolkovskii, Konstantin Eduardovich (1857–1935): USSR pioneer of rocketry & spaceflight ideas; 219
Tuatara; 144
Tukulti-Ninurti (13th century BC): King of

Assyria; 17
tulpa; 62–3
TUNGUSKA EVENT; 22, 34, **93–5**, 175, 194
Twenty Cases Suggestive of Reincarnation (Stevenson); 149
2001: A Space Odyssey (Clarke); 29

UFO Experience, The (Hynek); 199
UFOS; 29, 39, 84, 87, 93, 98, 101, 136, 149, 153, 163, 169, 194, **198–201**
ultraviolet: electromagnetic radiation of frequency higher than that of violet light; 145, 196, 217, 219
Ulysses; 63
Uncertainty Principle: idea put forward by Werner *Heisenberg, that the position & velocity of a particle cannot be simultaneously determined (since the determination of one property alters the value of the other — for example, if you determine its position by looking at the particle your eye is responding to photons 'bouncing off' the particle, and this 'bouncing off' affects the particle's velocity); this principle, extended to other cases, marked the end of Newtonian (that is, deterministic) scientific thought so far as the study of the true nature of reality is concerned; 23
unconscious; 14, 15, 19–20, 47, 53, 57, 111, 112, 126, 128, 135, 136, 140, 147, 153, 157, 201
undead; *see* *Zombies
Underwood, Guy; 28, 38–9, 127
Undiscovered Country, The (Jenkins); 37, 200
unicorns; 41
'unit of pure thought'; 20, 116
UNIVERSE; 11, 24, 25, 50, 84, 107, 161–2, 163, 165, 167–70, 175, 176, 196–7, 198, 201–202, 212–13
Universe, expanding; 116, 161, 163, 176, 198, 201
Universe, Laws of; 24–5, 161, 175
Universe, oscillating; *see* *oscillating Universe
universes, alternate; *see* *alternate universes
uranium: radioactive metal whose isotope U^{235} (halflife 710 million years) is used as a nuclear fuel and in the atomic bomb; 209, 217
Uranus (planet); 103, 167, 171
urea (CO(NH$_2$)$_2$); 44
Uri (Puharich); 200
Uther Pendragon; 31
UTOPIA; **220–21**
Utopia (More); 220
utopias; 169, 220–21

Vala, or the Four Zoas (Blake); 160
Valdes, Armando; 98

Vallée, Jacques: French writer and investigator of the mysterious; 101, 199, 201
VAMPIRES; 88, 91, **95–7**
Van de Kamp, Peter (1901–   ): Dutch-US astronomer, best known for his work on possible planets of *Barnard's Star; 171
van Eeden, Frederik; 128
van Helmont, Jan Baptista (1577–1644): Flemish alchemist & physician, who first showed that there is more than one air-like substance — calling such substances (approximately) 'gases'; 48
VANISHING PEOPLE; 12, 22, 86–8, **97–8**
vardøgers; 52
Varennes (France); 113
Vaughan, Alan: Editor of *Psychic*; 58, 110, 111, 112–13, 114–15
Vaughan, Thomas (?–1666): English alchemist & mystic; 155
Vela Nebula; 195
Velikovsky, Immanuel (1895–1979): influential USSR-born US unorthodox cosmologist; 170
Vennum, Lurancy; 57, 150
Venus (planet); 103, 167, 170, 171, 200
Venus figurines; 35
Verity, L.S.; 52
Vernon Advertiser: US newspaper; 92
Verrall, Mrs A.W. (1859–1916): UK medium; 125
Versailles, Palace of; 117
videodisks, laser-read; 218
videophones; 218
View Over Atlantis, The (Michell); 36, 39
Viking probes; 175–6
virginity; 41
Virgo: 6th sign of the *Zodiac; 103
virtual particles; 174
visions; *see* *dreams and visions
VITALISM; **44–5**, 122
Vogel, Dr Marcel; 145–6
'voices'; *see* *hallucination, auditory
Voliva, Wilbur Glenn (1870–1942); 173
Voltaire (François-Marie Arouet; 1694–1778): French philosopher, satirist & writer; 22, 38
von Däniken, Erich (1935–   ): popular proponent of the *ancient-astronaut theory; 29, 31, 199
von Eschenbach, Wolfram; 38
von Hahn, Helena; *see* *Blavatsky, Helena Petrovna
von Neumann, John (1903–57): Hungarian-born US mathematician, noted especially for his contributions to game theory; 222
VON NEUMANN PROBES; 173, **221–2**
von Reichenbach, Baron Karl (1788–1869):

124, 149
VOODOO; **64**, 99
Vorin, Joseph; 86
Vortigern; 31

Wadkins, Tommy; 145–6
Waite, Arthur Edward (1857–c1940): prominent US-born UK historian of the occult & the *Cabala; 63
Walden Two (Skinner); 221
Wallachia; 96
Walpurgisnacht: pagan festival, the night of 30 April/1 May, on which witches are said to congregate to consort with the *Devil
Walton, Travis; 98
Wandlebury (England); 37
Warlock of the Glen; *see* *Mackenzie, Kenneth
Warminster (England); 200
War of the Worlds, The (Wells); 176
wart charming; 35, 47, 64, 81, 135
water-divining; *see* *dowsing
Waterford, Henry, Marquis of; 93
'waterhole'; 197
water kelpie; 88
Watkins, Alfred (d. 1935); 38
Watson, Lyall: South African-born bestselling writer; 60, 121, 125, 130, 146, 154
Webb, Geoffrey; 36
Webb, James; 132
Welles, Orson (1915–   ): US broadcaster & actor; 176
Wells, Herbert George (1866–1946): UK novelist & speculative writer; 115, 176, 217, 221
Wentz, Evans; 88, 89
werewolves; *see* *lycanthropy
'What Makes a Life Significant?' (James); 221
Wheatley, Dennis (1897–1977): UK popular novelist; 96
White, Terence Hanbury (1906–64): UK novelist; 38
white dwarf stars: one of the possible final states of stars — a superdense, extremely hot object slowly burning away to form a dead black dwarf; 30, 166
White Goddess, The (Graves); 28, 36
Whitehead, Alfred North (1861–1947): UK philosopher & mathematician; 146
WHITE HOLES; 161, 162, 166, 167, **202**
White Holes (Gribbin); 202
White Horse at Uffington; 39
white magic; 63
Whitman, Walter ('Walt'; 1819–1892): US poet; 21
Whitmire, Daniel P.; 216
Wickramasinghe, Chandra: Indian astronomer; 193–4

'wild men'; 86
Wild Talents (Fort); 11
William of Newburgh (1136–98); 86
Williamson, George Hunt; 29, 200
Williamson, Orion; 98
Will-o'-the-wisp: or *ignis fatuus* (foolish fire) or Jack-o'-lantern, in legend a damned spirit bearing its own hell-fire, light from which at night over marshes lured travellers, thinking that the flickering light was from a distant window, to their deaths; in fact, the Will-o'-the-wisp is caused by the spontaneous combustion of marsh gas from decaying organic material; 89
Wilson, Mount, 100in telescope on; 201
Wilson, Colin (1931–   ); 16, 21, 23, 24, 47, 84–5, 93, 95, 97, 101, 110–11, 116, 205
Wilson, Robert: US electronics expert; 202
Windows on the Mind: The Christos Experiment (Glaskin); 128–9
Winkle, Rip Van: character created by US author Washington Irving (1783–1859); 115
WITCHCRAFT; 35–6, 47, **64**, 81–2
Witchcraft Act, repeal of (1951); 82
Witchcraft Today (Gardner); 35, 82
Witch Cult in Western Europe, The (Murray); 35
Witches (Lethbridge); 37
witches' Sabbaths; 81
Wizard of the Upper Amazon (Lamb); 60
Wöhler, Friedrich (1800–82): German chemist; 44
wolf-children; 11, 91
Wolsey, Thomas (c1475–1530); 114
World Ice Theory; 85, 169
World of Light, The (Huxley); 52
World of Ted Serios, The (Eisenbud); 143
Worlds in Collision (Velikovsky); 170
Worlds in the Making (Arrhenius); 193
Worlds Within (Glaskin); 129
World War I; 111, 133, 136, 148, 154
World War II; 38, 94, 122, 127, 133, 169
wormholes; 166, 202
Worth, Patience; 125, 150
Wrekin, the; 90
Wright, Jackson & Martha; 98
Wright, Thomas (1711–86): UK philosophical cosmologist; 171
writing, invention of; 15, 31

X (Fort); 84
X, Faculty; *see* *Faculty X
xenobiology (or exobiology): branch of biology concerned with the possible nature & functionings of lifeforms other than those from Earth — *see* *CETI, *extraterrestrial intelligence, *SETI

X-rays: electromagnetic radiation of extremely short wavelength (c 0.1pm–1nm) and high energy; 166, 195, 196, 219

Y (Fort); 84
yang; see *yin and yang
Yeats, William Butler (1865–1939): Irish poet and 'occasional occultist'; 1923 Nobel literature prize; 51–2, 88
Yeti; see *abominable snowmen
yin and yang; 23, 107
Ymir; 89
YOGA; 124, 128, 155, **156–7**
yogism; 50, 64, 121
York (England); 114

ZEN; **157–8**, 201, 221
Zener cards; 109, 129, 130
Zen in the Art of Archery (Herrigel); 157
Zeus: supreme Olympian god; 40
Zion (Illinois); 173
Zodiac: the band of the heavens on either side of the *ecliptic, & the 12 major constellations in this area, each equivalent to 30° of the sky; in *astrology these constellations determine the 'signs' of the Zodiac: Aries, Taurus, Gemini, Cancer, Leo, Virgo, Libra, Scorpio, Sagittarius, Capricorn, Aquarius, Pisces; 16, 103
ZOMBIES; 64, **98–9**
Zoroastrianism; 51
Zoser (pharaoh); 41

'Z-pinch' pulsed fusion system; 210
Zukav, Gary; 160
'zyme'; 115

Contributors

Begg, Paul G.; 86–8, 90, 93, 97–8
Farson, Daniel; 39–41, 85, 88–90, 90–93, 95–7, 98–9
Grant, John; 23–6, 34–5, 37–8, 44–5, 48, 49, 82, 93–5, 99, 104–105, 106–107, 116, 118–19, 158, 161–3, 163–73, 175–6, 193–5, 197–8, 201–203, 206–208, 209, 212–13, 217, 221–2
Holdstock, Robert; 211–12, 213–14
Holroyd, Stuart; 50–51, 61–4, 64, 104, 107–109, 111–12, 142–3
Langford, David; 173–5, 206, 208–209, 209–211
Lawton, A.T.; 163–7
Marriner, Brian; 49–50, 64
Nicolson, Iain; 163, 195–6, 214–16, 219–20
Pick, J.B.; 131–2
Turner, Robert; 57
Wenyon, Michael; 217–19
Wilson, Colin; 11–22, 28–34, 35–7, 38–9, 41–4, 47, 48–9, 51–7, 57–60, 64, 81–2, 84–5, 101–104, 105–106, 109–111, 112–16, 116–18, 121–31, 132–42, 143–58, 160, 173, 196–7, 198–201, 205, 220–21